the book of the afghan hound

by joan mcdonald brearley

Cover:
The sensational Khyanti's Moon Bandit, Field Champion, illustrates the perfect form of the coursing Afghan Hound which made him #1 in the country in 1975! This outstanding coursing dog is owned by Kate Relick, Team Sunarise, San Jose, California.

Frontispiece:
Dorothy and Brandt Houtsma's Ch. Sandhihi Joh-Cyn Taija Baba, the eighth top-winning Afghan Hound in the history of the breed in America, is captured here overlooking Los Angeles from a Trousdale hilltop in California. This magnificent photograph represents the camera artistry of Joan Ludwig.

Designed by Kerry Donnelly

ISBN 0-87666-665-9

Distributed in the U.S.A. by T.F.H. Publications, Inc., 211 West Sylvania Avenue, P.O. Box 27, Neptune City, N.J. 07753; in England by T.F.H. (Gt. Britain) Ltd., 13 Nutley Lane, Reigate, Surrey; in Canada to the book store and library trade by Clarke, Irwin & Company, Clarwin House, 791 St. Clair Avenue West, Toronto 10, Ontario; in Canada to the pet trade by Rolf C. Hagen Ltd., 3225 Sartelon Street, Montreal 382, Quebec; in Southeast Asia by Y.W. Ong, 9 Lorong 36 Geylang, Singapore 14; in Australia and the south Pacific by Pet Imports Pty. Ltd., P.O. Box 149, Brookvale 2100, N.S.W., Australia. Published by T.F.H. Publications Inc. Ltd., The British Crown Colony of Hong Kong. Printed in Hong Kong.

Contents

Kay Finch, photographed in 1976 by Mughabghab.

DEDICATION
This book is dedicated with deep affection to

KATHERINE SEAMON FINCH

my dear friend and mentor, who, in her infinite wisdom and knowledge of our breed, knew that her beloved Crown Crest Khalifah was destined for me, and to

CHAMPION CROWN CREST KHALIFAH

one of the top-producing bitches in the breed, foundation of my Sahadi Kennels, understanding friend and my constant companion throughout her lifetime, and to

ALL MY SAHADI AFGHAN HOUNDS

who gave their affection and devotion to me, where it was appreciated the most, thereby endearing this breed to me forever. . .

ACKNOWLEDGEMENTS

A book on the Afghan Hound, with its ancient and romantic heritage, could not be undertaken without the cooperation of many, many fanciers willing to share their knowledge, reflections from the past and the benefits of their years of experience.

First and foremost, it is with sincere gratitude that I acknowledge the support of Kay Finch. Whatever my accomplishments in the dog fancy may be I owe all to her inspiration, guidance and enthusiasm. Thanks are due Diane LaGreca, President of the Afghan Hound Club of America, whose cooperation and encouragement were offered so generously; Robert R. Shomer, V.M.D., for his expert counsel; Ernest H. Hart for his anatomical drawings for this book; and special thanks go to my parents for specific, required research on what is also their favorite breed, and for instilling in me my great love for animals, which has been the joy of my life.

I am also indebted to the staffs of the American Kennel Club library, the 42nd Street Library in New York City and the Museum of Natural History. I owe thanks to the hundreds of Afghan Hound fanciers all over the world who took the time to fill out the questionaires for this book which revealed so many fascinating insights on numerous aspects of our breed, including the detailed information supplied by my "foreign correspondents". . . Elise Abraham for her contribution to the chapter on Israel; Myles and the late Greta Phillips; and especially Inger James for background and statistical material on the breed in Canada; and to Robin Hernandez, my liason in Mexico. An extra special thank you goes to Betsy Treharne for material and photos from several countries around the world. I am especially thankful to all the breeders, owners, exhibitors and admirers of our magnificent breed for sharing photographs of their dogs for this book devoted to the glorification of the Afghan Hound!

THE AUTHOR

Ch. Crown Crest Khalifah, one of the top producing bitches in the history of the breed, was the foundation bitch behind the author's Sahadi Kennels. Bred by Kay Finch, Khalifah had ten champions to her credit, with others pointed.

ABOUT THE AUTHOR

Joan Brearley is the first to admit that animals in general—and dogs in particular—are a most important part of her life. Since childhood there has been a steady stream of dogs, cats, birds, fish, rabbits, snakes, alligators, etc., for her own personal menagerie. Over the years she has owned over thirty breeds of pure-bred dogs as well as countless mixtures, since the door was never closed to a needy or homeless animal.

A graduate of the American Academy of Dramatic Arts where she studied acting and directing, Joan started her career as a writer for movie magazines, actress and dancer. She studied ballet at the Agnes DeMille Studios in Carnegie Hall and was with an oriental dance company which performed at the Carnegie Recital Hall. She studied journalism at Columbia University and has written for radio, television and magazines, and was a copywriter for some of the major New York City advertising agencies working on the Metro-Goldwyn-Mayer Studios, Burlington Mills, *Cosmopolitan* magazine, White Owl Cigar, and Manischewitz Wine accounts.

While a television producer-director for a major network she worked on Nick Carter, Master Detective; Did Justice Triumph; and news and special feature programs. Joan has written, cast, directed, produced and, on occasion, starred in television commercials. She has written special material for such personalities as Dick Van Dyke, Amy Vanderbilt, William B. Williams, Gene Rayburn, Bill Stern, Herman Hickman and many other prominent people in the entertainment world. She has appeared as a guest on several of the nation's most popular talk shows, including Mike Douglas, Joe Franklin, Cleveland Amory, David Susskind and the Today Show, to name just a few. Joan was selected for inclusion in the *Directory of the Foremost Women in Communications* in 1969, and the book *Two Thousand Women Of Achievement* in 1971.

Her accomplishments in the dog fancy include breeding and exhibiting top show dogs, being a writer and columnist on various magazines and author of over twenty books on dogs and cats, including *This Is the Irish Setter, This Is the Siberian Husky, The Book of the Doberman Pinscher,* etc. For five years she was Executive Vice-President of the Popular Dogs Publishing Company and editor of *Popular Dogs* magazine, the national prestige publication for the fancy at that time. Her editorials on the status and welfare of animals have been reproduced as educational pamphlets

by dog clubs and organizations in many countries of the world.

Joan is just as active in the cat fancy and in almost as many capacities. The same year her Afghan Hound Ch. Sahadi Shikari won the Ken-L Ration Award as Top Hound of the Year, one of her Siamese cats won the comparable honor in the cat fancy. She has owned and/or bred almost all breeds of cats. Many of her cats and dogs are Best In Show winners and have appeared in magazines and on television. For several years she was editor of the Cat Fanciers Association Annual Yearbook, and her book, *All About Himalayan Cats,* was published in 1976.

In addition to breeding and showing dogs since 1955, Joan has been active as a member and on the Board of Directors of the Kennel Club of Northern New Jersey, The Afghan Hound Club of America, the Stewards Club of America and the Dog Fanciers Club. She has been an American Kennel Club judge of several breeds since 1961. As a guest speaker at many dog clubs and humane organizations she has crusaded for humane legislation for animals and won several awards

15

and citations for her work in this field. She is one of the best known and most knowledgeable people in the animal world. Joan is proud of the fact that her Ch. Sahadi Shikari was top-producing Afghan Hound in the history of the breed for several years, and still remains in the No.2 position today. No other breeder can claim to have bred a Westminster Group winner in their first home-bred litter, an honor also won by Shikari.

Joan looks forward to the near future when she will once again breed dogs at her Sahadi Kennels and Cattery to continue her line of dogs which excel in the breed rings, obedience trials, in the field and on the race tracks. Meantime, Joan continues to write dog books (a novel about the dog fancy is also in the works), does free lance publicity and public relations work, exhibits her needlepoint (for which she has also won awards), haunts the art and auction galleries and maintains her reputation as a movie buff.

This impressive list does not include all of her accomplishments, since Joan Brearley has never been content to have just one interest at a time, but has always managed to dove-tail several occupations at the same time to make for a fascinating career.

PREFACE

To know an Afghan Hound is to love one. . . and you are to be considered fortunate to be able to enjoy the pleasure of their company. If you are about to purchase your first Afghan Hound, you are to be congratulated! You have selected a breed rich in history, high in intelligence and possessed of the ultimate in beauty and grace of motion. The Afghan Hound is all this, and more.

You will find that your Afghan Hound is as happy draped languorously on a sofa or chair as it is on the track of a hare in the brush or a lion or gazelle in the mountains. Afghan Hounds are affectionate, yet at times outrageously aloof. They are completely clownish one moment, somber as the Sphinx the next.

Not only is the Afghan Hound of today in more beautiful coat than ever before in its romatic history, but it also does not shed, does not bark any more than he deems absolutely necessary and does not have the doggy odor associated with dogs in general, and hounds in particular.

Even though today's Afghan Hound is not called upon to hunt for his own or his master's food, to zealously defend the entrances to ancient walled cities or to patrol the outskirts of nomadic desert caravans, you will discover he still retains the innate desire to guard his home and family proudly, as he has done in centuries past. He is an excellent hunter and a worthy companion, and he has established a place for himself as a top show and obedience contender in the dog world.

It is a source of supreme satisfaction to me that due to the continued success of my book *This Is The Afghan Hound*, published in the 1960's, the publishers requested this second volume to bring the history of the breed up to its present status in the 1970's.

Needless to say, during the intervening years in my never-ending quest for additional facts I have unearthed new material and have continued to gather many more treasured old photographs from prominent Afghanites. These are included in *The Book Of The Afghan Hound*, along with dozens of photos from my personal collection of the great dogs of yesteryear.

Literally hundreds of questionaires and requests for photographs were sent out seeking information on the progress of the Afghan Hound for this concise, yet comprehensive, new volume. I hope both books will be enjoyed by all who love the breed and that they will be considered my tribute to the dogs whose unique beauty has earned them the title of King of Dogs.

Will there be a third book on the Afghan Hound in the 1980's? Of course! As more and more dog fanciers become aware of the joys of owning an Afghan Hound, with their great majesty, marvelous personalities and royal heritage, there will always be more to reveal as they continue to distinguish themselves in the show rings all over the world.

Joan McDonald Brearley
January, 1978

Chapter I

Ancient History of the Breed

Some three thousand years before Christ, when the warring northern and southern kingdoms of Egypt were uniting to form the First Dynasty of Egypt, the acknowledgment of the existence of a slender hound of the Afghan-type was first being recorded on papyrus and portrayed in hieroglyphics on the walls of the pyramids in Egypt's Valley of the Kings.

Archeological histories estimate that the breed has existed as long as seven thousand years, with its origin seeming to center around the Mountain of Moses on the Sinai Peninsula. There are also historical theories of simultaneous appearances of the same type of dog all over the Asian continent as well.

In Afghanistan, the country from which the dog derives its name, it is regarded, though unofficially, as the "national dog," and native Afghans claim and believe this monkey-faced or baboon dog, as it was often referred to, was the chosen dog to accompany Noah on his ark in the year of the great flood. They also uphold the belief that the Afghan is the dog portrayed in the rock carvings on the cave walls in the northern province of Balkh. This is why the Afghan has also been called the Balkh Hound.

The correct interpretation of these ancient and obscure carvings, and the conjecture regarding the Afghan Hound's being the only dog mentioned in the New Testament of the Bible, will always be open to argument or personal opinion. This topic is sure to be the basis of heated discussions when Afghan fanciers get together, even more so when Saluki and Greyhound people get together with Afghan people because fanciers of all *three* breeds like to believe that it was their breed that was really the first, with the other two coming later!

We do know this: the general Afghan-type dog goes back so far that historian Jackson Sanford states in a scientific paper that the Afghan Hound represents a form of animal structure found on earth over one hundred thousand years ago. Based on bone structure comparisons, the Afghan is a contemporary of the very earliest Asian dog-like animals which are believed to have inhabited even the North American continent two million years ago.

In the earliest written records of those early dogs there is almost a constant "mixing and matching" of the Afghan Hound with the Greyhound and Saluki, with the points of variance being mainly the outward appearances of each, namely, coat and feathering. There is much reference to what might easily be a composite of all three throughout these histories. It is only when man began to analyze the work each species was expected to perform in the different countries and climates that we see the Afghan breed begin to emerge and develop as the superior hunter because of their coat, long-range eyesight and their reputed "pivotal hipjoints."

Arnold Fletcher, one-time Deputy Director of Habibia College in Kabul, Afghanistan, claims that a Greyhound's legs would have snapped on the quick turns necessary when doubling back on prey, but the almost pivotal hipjoints of the Afghan Hound enable it to turn almost within length of itself. Also, the smooth-coated Greyhound fell subject to respiratory diseases in extremely cold temperatures of the upper snow regions, whereas the Afghan Hound prospered under the protection of its heavy coat.

While this profusion of coat guarded it against the cold, it also shielded this fleet-footed mountain hunter from the merciless sun while it coursed the desert. With its huge, thickly-padded paws and powerful hindquarters, the Afghan Hound was also the perfect "desert dog," with equal ability to skim across the hot desert sands or to scale rocky tops in the mountainous territory. And so, the Asians and Middle Easterners came to develop and further employ this "dog of all seasons" as an important part of their livelihood and very existence on earth.

This exotic headstudy of Can. Ch. Oranje Anisette typifies the Afghan Hound gaze into the distance as if in memory of ages past. . . Anisette is co-owned by Jan Priddy and Gary Anderson, the Volant Hounds, Seattle, Washington. Photo by Art Priddy.

In order to trace the origin and uses of this dog through the centuries, we must remember that the Afghan Hound of the past did not present the same picture it does today. The beautifully-coated, well-fed Afghan Hounds that give rise to the choruses of "Ohs" and "Ahs" in today's showring certainly are not representative of the breed in ancient times. The appearance has changed, and so has the purpose to which the dog is put. We must recall the differences in the borderlines of the countries during past centuries. Constantly moving native tribes and traders kept national borders irregular and indistinct. But each "country," even as it was then, found its own use and purpose for this hound in its ultimate scheme of life.

In Egypt, for instance, where only a select few animals such as the Brahman bull and the cat were revered, the Afghan-type dog won sovereignty for itself by becoming a companion to kings. Afghans also played a significant part in the national religion. Legend has it that a dog guided Isis, goddess of motherhood and fertility, when she searched for her brother and husband, Osiris, a wise king of Egypt who was brutally murdered and tossed into the Nile by his brother. The dog's role in aiding his most triumphant return and elevation to the status of a great god also immortalized the dog in the land of the Pharoahs.

Even beyond this royal role as companion to kings, these Egyptian dogs were used as

20

guards, walking sentry duty each night with an eye for raiding tribes creeping in from the desert to steal. Sleeping by day and walking guard in pairs at night around the oases and cities, the Afghan Hounds were also taught to steal from neighboring encampments for the good and profit of their masters. This is a trait that has remained with the Afghan Hound through the centuries. Present day Afghan Hound owners readily admit that their dogs are expert at thievery, and that every pure-bred Afghan Hound still harbors a bit of larceny in its soul!

In the Middle Ages, dog teams were used to pull carts of cloth, tea, furs, incense and other commodities between Persia, India, Arabia, Russia and China. They seem to have penetrated as far north as Scandinavia and as far east as China. Woodcuts after Olaus Manus depicting Scandinavian hunters on skis armed with crossbows in the 16th century show dogs bearing a strong resemblance to the Afghan Hound running alongside them.

Examples of Asian art bear out the appearance of this type of dog in Chinese sculpture and carved jade. The Cairo Museum is reported to have on display a piece of pottery which was unearthed from King Tutankhamen's tomb on which Afghan-like creatures are pictured in chase.

El Qahira's Egyptian Pharoah, photographed near an Egyptian Sphinx statue by her owners, Steve and Linda Smith of San Jose, California.

THE AFGHAN HOUND IN AFGHANISTAN

In Afghanistan, the dog excelled as a hunter. Hunting is, and always has been, the most popular pastime in Afghanistan. Wealthy Afghans, aboard their excellent horses, equipped with guns and hounds, hunted expressly for sport. At times they also employed falcons which rode on their gauntlets until released to swoop down and distract the prey as it was chased and surrounded by the dogs.

Afghan Hounds are sighthounds, rather than hunters by scent. Their exceptional vision has always meant that they can spot prey far off. Once sighted, they bring into play their fantastic running speed, which has been estimated to reach as much as twenty-five miles an hour at full speed. Afghans generally hunt in pairs, a male and a female, with the female usually choosing to circle the prey, bounding and barking wildly to distract it while the male awaits the opportunity to leap at the prey's throat, where he hangs on until the neck is snapped and broken. Their great speed and power enables them to hunt gazelles, snow leopards, wolves, hyenas, jack-rabbits and any other animals of similar size. Their powerful, twisting jaws make a kill almost certain.

The poorer people of Afghanistan, however, hunt for the most basic reasons. . .for food and for skins to wear and sell. With the tribesmen, however, the Afghan Hound is taught to hunt without devouring or killing the catch, but merely to keep it at bay, allowing the master to deliver the death blow so that the game may be eaten without sacrilege. According to the Mohammedan religion, only slaughtered game may be consumed.

In Afghanistan ordinary or "mongrel" dogs are regarded as unclean and are often clubbed and stoned in the streets. The Afghan Hound, however, is admired and respected by all. To the rich he is a skilled and swift hunter; to the poor he is an invaluable guard and provider of food and clothing.

Whatever the Afghan Hound's use or purpose has been down through the centuries, it has withstood the changing sand of time and has remained a dog of great intelligence and beauty. While written records might be inadequate, incomplete or even question-

Ch. Xanadu's Sweet Xephyr, owned by Johanna Tanner of Friendswood, Texas.

able, it is generally agreed that the exotic Afghan Hound is of the pre-Christian era.

One of my favorite readings on the Afghan Hound, which so clearly defines their abilities as guard dogs, appeared in Hutchinson's Encyclopedia and has been reprinted elsewhere over the years. It is an accounting by an observer named Mali who wrote about a visit he made to the North-West Frontier in India. I quote a portion of it here:

"Chaman, you must know, is one of our principal posts on the North-West Frontier. A former Commander-in-Chief decreed that a post should be established at Chaman to be fed by a light railway from Quetta. Two mud forts guard the railway station, one on each side; each fort is manned by one company of Indian infantry and one squadron of native recruits and *by dogs*.

"What strikes the newcomer entering either of the forts at any hour of the day is the large, extraordinary-looking creatures sprawling all over the place, fast asleep. In size and shape they somewhat resemble a large Grey-

hound, but such slight resemblance is dispelled by the tufts with which all are adorned: some having tufted ears, others tufted feet, and others, again, possessing tufted tails.

"They are known as Baluchi Hounds, and they get their daily food ration from the commissariat babu; he is the only permanent resident of the fort. They will have no truck with any stranger, white or black.

"When 'Retreat' sounds, the pack awakes, yawns, pulls itself together, and solemnly marches out to take up positions close to the newly arrived night guard. *They appear to be under no leadership*, yet as the patrols are told off a couple of dogs attach themselves to each patrol, and they remain with their respective patrols till 'reveille' next morning. Between a deep ditch and wall of the fort is a narrow path. Throughout the night, this path is patrolled by successive couples of dogs. Immediately after one couple has completed the circuit of the walls and arrives back at the main gate, another couple starts out.

A miniature which is found at the Victoria and Albert Museum in London, England, depicts a wild boar hunt in the Sikh tradition when hunting was done with dogs as well as swords and spears. The title is *Maharan Jawar of Mewar Hunts a Boar* and is catalogued as "about 1835." ⟶

Some of the stamps featuring Afghan Hounds issued by foreign countries over the years.

"When it is remembered that these extraordinary hounds have never had any training whatsoever, that their duties are absolutely self-imposed—for no human being has the slightest control over them—the perfection of their organization and the smoothness with which they carry out their tasks make mere man gasp!"

THE AFGHAN HOUND IN AFRICA

As time evolved and borders expanded, it was also inevitable that the remarkable hunting dog would find its way further south on the African continent. The natives of Africa have used the Afghan Hound for hunting for almost as long as the other peoples of that area. The Africans used them primarily to hunt the East African leopards. They also hunted them in pairs, but preferred to use two males together, instead of a male and a female. More strength was needed to bring down the leopards, and two males were found to have more of the necessary strength.

In Africa the dogs required little training to arouse their instincts to hunt. Since the country was so rustic, they were hunted off lead, responding to hand signals given by their masters, who followed behind them on foot. Because the African brush was dense, the dogs did not get too far ahead, enabling the hunters to keep within sight and scent of the prey along with the dogs.

The African leopards usually took to the trees while the dogs kept them at bay. When the noise of the barking got them to a panic stage, they usually tried to jump for freedom. The dogs eventually ran them down. Once they had chased the leopard into a clearing, the same circling of the dogs came into play, with one jumping for the neck to break it or to sever the jugular vein. Frequently both dogs grabbed for the neck in a particularly active chase.

Through the ages, hunting was destined to remain the Afghan's lot in the countries of its early beginnings, but once the first dogs found their way to Europe and America, the devotees of the breed had an entirely different mode of life for it. In the days ahead the Afghan Hound was destined to become a companion and show dog!

Chapter II

The Afghan Hound in Great Britain

Following World War I the Afghan Hound became increasingly popular in Great Britain. The war was responsible for British military men being sent to all corners of the British empire and many other countries of the world. In some of those countries, especially along the northwestern border of India, the people were already utilizing the services of this unusual breed. It was during a tour of duty that these dogs came to the attention of Captain John Barff. It was Captain Barff who imported the famous Zardin to England from the Seistan province after the dog had been exhibited briefly in India in 1906.

Zardin was a sensation in Britain. He caused so much talk that he was soon referred to as the "finest oriental greyhound ever seen in England" and was requested to make a personal appearance before Queen Alexandra at Buckingham Palace. Once out of quarantine, he succeeded in winning the foreign dog class at Britain's Crystal Palace show in 1907, being shown by Mrs. Barff. He was then undefeated in fifty-two consecutive shows.

References and illustrations in old English dog chronicles refer to Zardin and the other early imports as Persian Greyhounds, Afghan Greyhounds, Oriental Greyhounds, Tazi, Thasis, Kurrum Valley dogs, Baluchi Hounds, Balkh Greyhounds, Kabul Greyhounds, Barakzai and Barukhzy Hounds. The latter name derived from the name of the royal family of Afghanistan and the name used by the early hunters said to have first bred them for killing lions in that country. Unlike other imports, Zardin carried the full coat, topknot and ringed tail that is so distinctive of the breed. He stood as the specimen that established the Afghan Hound as a separate and "new" breed. New to Britain, that is.

Captain Barff later sold Zardin to a London animal dealer named Shackleton, who bred him to other bitches imported by Captain Barff. Just prior to World War I, however, unexplained and unconfirmed circumstances—more than likely a siege of distemper—wiped out all of Shackleton's stock, and nothing further was ever heard of Zardin's progeny.

It has been said that Zardin's remains are at rest in the British Museum, but this is not so. A friend of mine, a researcher on the staff of the zoology department, reports that there is no indication of this. Only a photograph of Zardin had been received, and even that photograph was not recovered after the devastating bombings of London during the war. She was able to locate mounted skins, formerly on exhibition but now in storage, of two Afghan Hounds named Shahzada and Mooroo, presented by Mrs. J.A. Whitbread to the museum in 1901 and 1903 respectively. But, alas, no

Ch. Rifka's Moti of Carloway, beautiful bitch bred by the late Mrs. C. Race, whose Rifka Kennels were in England.

The legendary Zardin was the first Afghan Hound brought to England. He was imported to the British Isles in the late nineteenth century by his owner, Captain John Barff. During his career Zardin was undefeated in 52 consecutive shows and caused a sensation in the show world that can still be felt in the breed today.

signs of the remains of the legendary Zardin! His major claim to fame must be that he was the Afghan they had in mind while writing the very first Standard for the breed in 1912.

All through the early history of the breed in England, years before Zardin's appearance, the names of military men keep popping up in the annals of the early importations. Time and again we see not only the name of Captain Barff, but the names of Captain F. Martin, Captain Cary Barnard, Colonel Marriott and Major T. Mackenzie; all were entering their strange looking dogs in the foreign dog class at the shows in the late 1800's.

Major Mackenzie had a winner at the Bristol show, a dog named Mukmul that later took second place at the Barn Elms show in 1887 where Mackenzie showed his bitch Mooroo. More than likely, bearing in mind this date, it is Mooroo II whose remains are in the British Museum. Major Mackenzie also had a dog named Koosh, the grandsire of his bitch, Khulm. He was considered an authority on the breed during this period just before the turn of the century and did much winning and importing.

An Afghan Hound named Gazelle, and later called Shahzada (and which was shown under both names), was owned by the J.A. Whitbreads. Shahzada was the winner of second prize in the foreign dog class at the 1895 Crufts Dog Show, and in 1897 he competed against another Afghan Hound named Dilkoosh. Dilkoosh appeared in the stud book as an Afghan Bamkhzy Hound! Shahzada ended up in the British Museum!

Another outstanding import at the time was a dog named Mustapha, owned originally by the Shah of Persia.

It seemed only natural that a breed of dog reported to have killed leopards in its native land, having a running speed of twenty-five miles an hour or more, was destined to be appraised in racing circles. In England up to that time, the Greyhounds had the edge on speed. Clifford Hubbard in his British book, *The Afghan Hound*, relates that a red bitch named Baz, imported for a Mr. N. Dunn by an Indian Army officer who purchased her from a desert caravan, was bred to a Greyhound named Explosion with the explicit purpose of giving additonal stamina to the Greyhound.

What is perhaps even more incredible, Baz was eventually registered in the Greyhound stud book in 1911, by special resolution of the National Coursing Club! It is also interesting to know that the get of this crossbreeding all carried the Afghan Hound ringed tail! For all intents and purposes it can be said that it was a satisfactory combination which did add stamina without sacrificing speed, and they were willing to go on record with it!

Another early breeder, Mr. W.K. Taunton, began to see the advantages offered by this new breed. Not only did he see them in a new light when they began to defeat the other breeds of dogs he was showing at the time, but he saw possibilities in crossing them with sheepdogs. Subsequently, some of his Afghan Sheepdogs were winning at the shows. A bitch from one of his "legitimate" litters named Motee won a first prize in the foreign dog class at Bristol in 1886, defeating her kennel mate, a Chow Chow, listed in the catalogue as a Chinese Edible Dog. Motee and a dog named Roostam were later sold by Mr. Taunton to Mr. R.R. Tufnell. Mr. Tufnell did quite a bit of exhibiting and from a litter he bred and whelped in 1883 came Rajah II.

Afghan Bob, owned by Captain Cary Barnard, was the next dog to create new interest in the breed. Brought from Peshawar in 1902, his success was enhanced by his being illustrated in Robert Leighton's book, *The New Book of the Dog*, published in 1907. The book also featured an illustration of a bitch named Fatima, said to be a Zardin daughter owned by Captain F. Martin. He was well-known in Afghan Hound circles in those early days, and was assigned to the 25th Punjabi at Rawalpindi.

Not only did these representations show the dogs as being very unkempt looking, they hardly resembled today's Afghan Hound at all! They are quite improved when depicted in the oil paintings of some of the artists of that time. In 1909 the famous F.T. Daws painted Zardin and a bitch named Afghan Lass. R.H. Moore did many drawings of the breed as well.

A 1925 issue of the *Kennel Gazette* of the United Kingdom reveals that it was 1907 when the first registration was made with the Kennel Club. It included a statement that the Afghan Hound had now earned a position on the register as a recognized breed.

WORLD WAR I

Breeding and importing Afghan Hounds came to a virtual halt during the hostilities of World War I. It wasn't long after the treaty was signed that the far-sighted Miss Jean Manson and Major and Mrs. G. Bell-Murray brought several Afghan Hounds from the Far East as a foundation for their kennels in Great Britain. Arriving by way of Miss Manson's The Cove Kennels in Scotland, these first few imports were to become the dominating force behind the British breeding program for many years to come.

In 1921 Miss Manson and the Bell-Murrays started breeding in earnest with their white bitch, Begum, which they obtained in 1913 in Quetta, Afghanistan. Four years later they obtained a dog named Rajah. They also brought with them Afghan Hounds named Straker, Ooty, and the first brindle seen in Britain, a bitch named Pushum. Two daughters from a breeding of Rajah to Begum were entered at the 1924 Crufts Show. One was named Kanee and the other became Ch. Ranee. Miss Manson's dog, Buckmal, whelped in March, 1923, was England's first male champion, earning his title in 1927. His sire was Ooty and his dam was Pushum. Mrs. A.B. Willans Shadi was the first bitch champion in England, a title she earned in 1927 also.

Her sire was Baluch out of Oolu and she was also bred by Jean Manson.

MRS. AMPS AND THE GREAT GHAZNIS

In 1925 Mrs. Mary Amps brought several Afghan Hounds to England to continue her Ghazni Kennels in Britain. Her husband, Major Amps, remained in the Far East. One of the dogs she brought with her was Khan of Ghazni, renowned for having killed three leopards in his native land. It was also Mrs. Amps who imported the first blacks to England. The most famous of her imports, however, was her Ch. Sirdar of Ghazni, whelped in June, 1923, and referred to as the "father" of the breed because of prominence as a show dog and his potency as a sire.

Sirdar was born in the royal kennels of King Amanullah of Afghanistan and his breeder, as entered on his registration papers by Mrs. Amps, was listed as Afghan Shikari Paghman, sire and dam unknown. His brother and sister were registered along with Sirdar in July, 1926. Mrs. Amps had purchased the dogs from the British legation in Kabul. Sirdar was the first Afghan Hound in England to win a Challenge Certificate, which he earned in 1926. He became a champion in 1927, the same year he was immortalized on canvas by the famous artist, F.T. Daws, who was captivated by his unusual appearance.

It did not require an artist's eye to see the two distinctly different types of Afghan Hounds represented by the Bell-Murray and the Ghazni dogs. The Bell-Murray strain was larger and from the hot desert climates, while the Ghazni dogs were smaller and had the coat for warmth for the mountain climates. It was almost inevitable that a strong controversy would arise between the two factions. The issue of size was hotly disputed since England's first champion, Miss Manson's Buckmal, stood 32 inches at the shoulder while Mrs. Amps' Sirdar measured just 24 inches, which Mrs. Amps admitted was a little on the small side.

This conflict came to public attention, and was further revealed in Charles Harrisson's book, *The Afghan Hound*, wherein he reported that Mrs. Amps and Sirdar made an appearance at a particular show not for competition but to prove Sirdar was still alive. It was further stated by a columnist writing on the incident that Sirdar had never looked better and was guarded by a plain clothes policeman all that day as a precaution against threats received by Mrs. Amps in an anonymous letter. Fortunately, the breeders recognized that each type had something to offer the other lines and breedings eventually produced well.

Hutchinson's Encyclopedia states that Mrs. Amps must be regarded as the pioneer in the breed, since Sirdar was said to be, the finest Afghan Hound seen since Zardin. Sirdar later became the sire of six champions, three males and three bitches.

The third breeder of prominence in England was Miss Evelyn Denyer. She was active in the early 1920's along with Jean Manson and the Bell-Murrays, and used the "of Kaf" suffix on her dogs. She was largely responsible for putting together a Standard for the breed after the formation of the Afghan Hound Club in 1925. Miss Clara Bowring was the club's first Treasurer and also a devoted advocate of the breed. Her brother, stationed in India, sent her Afghan Hounds since there seemed to be some difficulty in getting the dogs out of Afghanistan.

This club and its active members were instrumental in getting the breed recognized by the kennel club in 1925 and the first

Another of the all-time Afghan Hound "greats," Ch. Garrymhor Zarbardast Arken, owned by the Arken Kennels.

Int. Ch. Sirdar of Ghazni is pictured in this reproduction of the famous oil painting done in 1927 by artist F. T. Daws. Sirdar has been referred to on occasion as the "father" of the breed, winning fame in England as a sire as well as a show dog.

Challenge Certificates were offered at Crufts in 1926. Mr. A. Croxton Smith judged an entry of 41 and awarded the dog certificate to Evelyn Denyer's (now Mrs. J. Barton) Taj Mahip of Kaf and the bitch certificate to Jean Manson's Ranee.

It was also at this time that Mrs. Olive M. Couper established her Garrymhor line and it was she who contributed the article on the breed which appeared in *Hutchinson's Encyclopedia*. Will Hally was another writer that helped to popularize the Afghan Hound, and Norman Hadden, whose Moti was known as far back as 1912, was still contributing to its welfare.

1929 was the year Ch. Asri-Havid of Ghazni came upon the scene. This black and tan son of Ch. Sirdar of Ghazni became the property of Mrs. Phyllis Robson, and was the first black and tan champion in England as well as the first Best In Show winner in the breed. He was also winner of obedience certificates. This remarkable dog and Mrs. Robson were almost inseperable during the dog's lifetime and he was her only dog until his death from ulcers in June, 1937. Mrs. Robson, an ardent advocate of pure-bred dogs and dog shows, became an editor of the internationally acclaimed *English Dog World* and was Chairman of the Afghan Hound Association founded in 1933. With Mrs. Amps as its first President, the group set about writing a new Standard for the breed (and another in 1946!). Mrs. Robson died in 1959.

Pictured is one of the winning Afghan Hounds owned by Betsy Porter of Cheshire, England, photographed in 1937.

Dr. Betsy Porter was another of the early members of the club and used el Kabul as a kennel name. Dr. Porter was active in the breed throughout her lifetime and was a frequent visitor to the United States. She was invited to judge at the 1960 Potomac Afghan Hound Club Specialty Show in this country.

In 1930 International Champion Badshah of Ainsdart was whelped. Bred by Mrs. J. Morris-Hones at her Ainsdart Kennels, the sire was Ch. Sirdar of Ghazni and the dam was a bitch named Ku Mari of Kaf. In 1932 Q.A. Shaw McKeen imported Badshah for Prides Hill Kennels in the United States where the dog was an important stud force and greatly responsible for the breed's popularity

in this country. Another Sirdar son, Omar of Geufron, bred to Sabana of Kaf, produced Ch. Shah Shuja of Geufron. It was this dog that brought Mrs. E. Eileen Drinkwater into prominence in the breed. Omar was to sire three champions in a litter of five puppies and was destined to become the first Best in Show Afghan Hound in the United States after his arrival in the States.

Captain T.S. Waterlow Fox, first President of the Afghan Hound Club, used the "of Wyke" suffix on his dogs. It was Captain Fox who eventually took over Evelyn Denyer's stock when she left the country with her husband, J. Barton. Mrs. L. Prude's Ch. Baber of Baberbagh became a Sieger (champ-

Ch. Badshah of Ainsdart, owned by Q.A. Shaw McKean of Prides Crossing, Massachusetts. One of the early greats, Badshah was on the 1935 championship list and was photographed here in 1944.

ion) in Germany when exported in 1932 to Mrs. G.E.W. Jungeling. Perhaps the best known of her Baberbagh line was Marika of Baberbagh, an important bitch during this period. Mrs. Couper's Ch. Garrymhor Souriya was another, and attained her championship before reaching 14 months of age.

Other important kennels during these early times were Isabel Bradshaw's Wahsdarb, Mrs. B. Rothwell-Fieldings' Kuranda, Miss H. Semple's Pushtikuh, Howard Gibson's Acklam, Mrs. Sydney Rhodes' Tuclo, Mrs. M. Wood's Westmill, Eileen Drinkwaters' Geufron and the kennels of Mrs. J. Chesterfield-Cooke and Mrs. M.E. Till.

THE CHAMAN KENNELS

In 1937 Mrs. Molly Sharpe brought out her string of Afghan Hounds to race. Perhaps the most famous of all the dogs at her Chaman Kennels was her International Champion Garrymor Faiz-Bu-Hassid, who was often captured on film in an almost completely horizontal line, so far straight out ahead and to the rear were his legs while racing. Bred by Olive Couper, he was also Mrs. Sharpe's first

Afghan Hound. His sire was an import from India, Ardmore Anthony, and was out of Mrs. Couper's Ch. Garrymor Sourija.

Hassid sired several champions for Mrs. Sharpe. One son went to Canada and became Canadian Champion Pic of Chaman; another became Italian Champion Sabue of Chaman. Perhaps the most famous of the show dog contenders was Mrs. Sharpe's International Champion Taj of Chaman, who, along with his predecessor, Zardin, were the only two Afghan Hounds undefeated in the breed during their show ring careers.

Even though Mrs. Sharpe didn't get into racing until 1937, Afghan Hounds had been racing in England since 1933. They were started on hare, and when they proved to be more than just holding their own with the Greyhounds, an Afghan Hound Coursing Club was formed. Racing the Afghan Hound has been a popular sport in that country ever since.

THE SECOND WORLD WAR

Just as with the first World War, World War II also caused havoc in the dog fancy. Not only in Great Britain, but all over Europe. Dogs were put to sleep because of injuries after bombings or because food was scarce. In many cases, especially in Europe, they were frequently being devoured by starving

Ch. Bondor Azaim Khan, magnificent dog bred at the Bondor Kennels in England.

Frederick T. Daws, the prominent English artist, painted this oil of four Afghans. Left to right are Ch. West Mil Omar of Prides Hill, Ch. Badshah of Ainsdart, Int. Ch. Sirdar of Ghazni and, in the foreground, Ch. Azri Havid of Ghazni. Marion Foster Florsheim brought this painting to the United States from England. It now is proudly displayed in a place of honor in Kay Finch's livingroom.

people. Breeding and importing almost ceased, and many devoted breeders began to look toward exporting their most valuable dogs to America to preserve their bloodlines. Fortunately for U.S. breeders, many Afghan Hounds that would have normally enjoyed a grand career in their own country were sent off to America to help establish the breed here.

Within a few years after the end of the war, some of the better established kennels from the pre-war period were flourishing once again. Somehow they had managed to keep some of their best bloodlines and were back at breeding by the second half of the 1940's.

The Afghan Hound Association held its first post-war championship show in June, 1946, with Molly Sharpe's dog, Taj of Chaman, winning the dog Challenge Certificate and her bitch Tajavia of Chaman winning the distaff side. The first post-war Crufts show took place in October, 1948. With the increased new interest in the breed it was plain to see that additional clubs would be necessary to serve and educate the newcomers. In

1946 the first of the regional Afghan Hound Clubs was formed. This was the Southern Afghan Hound Club. A month later, in November of 1946, a Northern Afghan Hound Association came into being. These two regional groups along with the well-established Afghan Hound Association were to monitor the breed in Great Britain for many years to come.

THE BLETCHINGLEY KENNEL

The most prominent new kennel during the post-war period was Mrs. F.C. Riley's Bletchingley Kennels, which were to claim an enviable number of champions and show winners. Her bitch, Ch. Bletchingley Zara, a daughter of Ch. Bletchingley Tajomeer, was the first important champion for her. Tajomeer's son, Ch. Bletchingley Tribesman, was another who earned his championship title in 1951.

Mrs. Riley bred English Cocker Spaniels before becoming enamoured of Afghan Hounds. Her first exposure to the breed was when she agreed to take care of an Afghan

Hound for a friend. That was Ch. Rana of Chaman. She was so taken with the breed that she purchased Rana's litter sister, Shiba of Chaman. Shiba became the foundation bitch at her Bletchingley Kennels.

In 1942 the first litter was whelped at Bletchingley. Mrs. Riley bred Shiba to Taj Ameer of Chaman. This breeding produced the famous Ch. Bletchingley Tajomeer, the ancestor behind all of the top-winning Bletchingley dogs. A total of 11 champions were bred at Bletchingley, plus several champions for kennels overseas. The sensational Ch. Bletchingley Zelda was Reserve Best in Show at the Ladies Kennel Association at the biggest one-day all-breed Championship show in the British Isles up to that time. Few bitches in those days achieved Best in Show wins, so this award was particularly treasured.

Mr. Riley judged the Afghan Hound entry at the 1967 Crufts show and both Mr. and Mrs. Riley have officiated at many C.C. shows. Mrs. Riley also judges Cockers. Both active in club work, Mrs. Riley is a former President of the Southern Afghan Club and Mr. Riley was Chairman of the Afghan Hound Association in the past.

Their Ch. Bletchingley Houndsman was exported to Sweden in the 1960's after earning his English title. He was successful in the rings in that country and was a significant influence in the breed as a stud. Some of their other prominent dogs are Ch. Bletchingley

Talookdar, sire of the Wallace Pede's American Ch. Bletchingley Ragman of Scheherezade, as well as the English Ch. Saluna and Bletchingley Masterman.

HORNINGSEA KENNELS

Soon after World War II another major kennel force was in evidence. Mrs. Marna Dod was to establish her famous Horningsea Kennels in Herts. Over the next three decades and until her death in 1976, Marna Dods was to breed numerous champions and to maintain her keen interest in the breed. Her Ch. Horningsea Khanabad Suvaraj, while bred by Miss M. Niblock, became Dog of the Year in Britain for 1967. It was also through Mrs. Dod's Ch. Horningsea Tiger's Eye that brindle Afghan Hounds were again popular in England.

The lovely Ch. Horningsea Mahrousse, owned by the Hebels.

Many Horningsea Afghan Hounds were exported to countries around the world where they did impressive winning and enhanced the status of the breed by their stud force. Horningsea Solari, owned by Madam Bernard of Lyon, France, was Best Dog at the Paris Internationale dog show for two years in a row during the mid-sixties. He also won at dog shows in Spain, Italy and Monte Carlo. Solari's sister, Samarina, went to the Swedish kennels of Madam Tolle and whelped a litter sired by Ch. Horninsea Tiger's Eye. Two other Horningsea Khanabad Suvaraj sons went to Germany, another to Trinidad and one to the United States. A Tiger's Eye son was Best In Show in Australia and Horningsea Tzaama and Horningsea Taducheepa, Tiger's Eye's sister, distinguished themselves at the

Actress Helen Hayes with Champion Bella-Mu Ivory Tower, owned by John and Madelyn Lacarrubba. This Specialty Best of Breed winner was bred by Dr. and Mrs. Robert Sergio.

Kophi Kennels of Myles and the late Greta Phillips in Canada. Others have been exported to Italy, and of late to Israel.

The complete list of champions and show winners is long, but in addition to the great Ch. Horningsea Khanabad Suvaraj, some outstanding specimens were Aramis, Mustagh, Silver Fox and Mrs. Dod's famous bitch, Ch. Horningsea Kayacci. Her Mustagh Ata and Malghun won the Afghan Hound Brace Class at the Crufts show one year.

Mrs. Edgar Abson's Netheroyd Kennels produced the first black champion bitch, Netheroyd's Turkuman Camelthorn. She was the dam of the famous Turkuman Nissim's Laurel, the black dog with white socks which won the Afghan Hound Club of America Specialty Show in 1950 and the Hound Group at the Westminster Kennel Club Show the same year. Bred by Juliette de Bairacli-Levy and bearing her Turkuman kennel name, he was sent to the United States in the mid-forties where he was co-owned by Sol Malkin and Sunny Shay and attained his championship there in 1947. Laurel was sired by Chota Nissim of Ringbank and represented the fifth generation of successful "natural foods" feeding advocated by his breeder.

Miss Eileen Snelling's Khorrassan Kennel was based on some of the Turkuman line, with the bitch Natara of Westover and Turkuman Pomegranite. Her first champion was Ch. Moonbeam of Khorrassan, who earned his title in 1951. Her Portrait, Ivory, Marabout and other cream dogs helped to establish this strikingly beautiful color in England.

Also during the 1950's American servicemen who had been stationed in Britain or had passed through that country during their tours of duty also got caught up in the excitement of the post-war dog fancy. Most prominent of these was Major (later Lt. Col. Rtd.) Wallace Pede and his wife, Kay, who enjoyed much success during their soujourn in England. Their Bletchingley Ragman of Scheherezade won the Hound Group at Crufts in 1961 over 1,414 hound dogs and was Third Best in Show over a total entry of 7,892 dogs, winning his second Challenge Certificate.

Unfortunately, the Pedes were obligated to sail for America before Ragman could win his third C.C. and his English championship title. The dog was a popular favorite in England and it was agreed that he could have attained the title had he been shown at the Manchester Show the following month.

Ch. Horningsea Tiger's Eye, bred by Marna Dods and an important dog in the breed in Scandinavia as well. Tiger's Eye was largely responsible for brindles becoming popular in England.

Kay and Wally Pede were photographed with three of their English dogs in 1959. The Pedes came to America in 1961, where they continued their breeding under their kennel name of Scheherezade.

33

Ragman's son, the black and tan Alibaba of Scheherezade, was a Best In Show winner and was that country's top-winning Best In Show Afghan Hound for 1960. Ragman was second only to Alibaba in total Best In Show wins for 1960. Both dogs distinguished themselves as studs before sailing for America aboard the Queen Mary in March, 1961, and helped to establish the Pede's Scheherezade Kennels in both England and the United States upon their arrival in this country. Wally Pede is a judge as well as breeder and has served on the Board of Directors of the Afghan Hound Club of America.

SHEILA DEVITT AND CARLOWAY

Sheila Devitt acquired her first Afghan Hound in 1945. Starting "at the top" in the show ring, the dog won Reserve Best In Show all-breeds and Best Bitch. Sheila had always been interested in the breed but after this auspicious beginning she was hooked on showing as well. Actually, it was her mother who founded Carloway with Lakeland Terriers; Carloway being the name of the family estate in Scotland.

After her initial success, Sheila bought three more Afghan Hounds, two dogs and a bitch all by Turkuman Dammer Pine Tree. Unfortunately, she lost both dogs before maturity. This meant looking for suitable mates for the two bitches.

In 1946 Sheila got Jalalabad Barwala from Dr. Byron Unkauf and it was Barwala who became the foundation of the Carloway Kennels. However, tragedy was to strike again. Barwala was crippled in an accident and could no longer be shown, and his son Dil Khan of Carloway, who with two C.C.'s undoubtedly would have been Carloway's first champion, died in 1949.

In 1952 Barwala's daughter Sharmain became the first champion, followed by Zog and then Yussef, who sired nine champions and nineteen grandchildren.

In 1964 Sheila married Michael Gilleney, a BBC television producer, and gave up showing and began concentrating on judging. The majority of the Carloway hounds were dispersed. When the Gilleneys moved to Malta in 1967 she brought a Waliwog ex Ch. Manodari puppy with them. In 1970 and 1974 she bred litters and kept one from each.

Sheila has judged in many foreign countries and judged Crufts again in 1976.

During the 1950-1960 years, Sheila Devitt was most active in showing her famous Carloway dogs. By the end of the 1950's she had finished Ch. Pasha of Carloway, Ch. Tarquin of Carloway had earned his title for owner Mrs. C. Race, and her bitch Ch. Muphytt of Carloway gained her title at the Afghan Hound Association championship show under the Belgian breed authority Madame Dechess.

Mrs. Race and Sheila Devitt imported Wazir of Desertaire from Kay Finch; he was later owned by the Les Bridges. This Ch. Crown Crest Mr. Universe ex Ch. Zar-Kari of Shamalan son became an English champion in 1968. Mrs. Race had established her Rifka Kennels in 1950. Unfortunately, Mrs. Race died before fulfilling a judging assignment at the 1971 Crufts show, which had been a long-time wish. However, there is now a memorial trophy in her honor for Best of Breed.

Miss M. Niblock's Khanabad dogs were still winning nicely at this time. Her two top bitches, Khanabad Azrar and Astrajid, were producing well for her. Miss Niblock was a pioneer breeder of blue Afghan Hounds through the bloodlines obtained from Cynthia Madigan's Branwen Kennels in Spain.

Ravelly Patrols Ali Bey, owned by Reg Lloyd, was the first male champion who earned the title after the war. Mrs. S. Rhodes' bitch, Ajawaan Chita Mia, was the first postwar champion bitch.

Many other kennels were making their mark during this time. Mrs. I.B. Kershaw and Mr. L. Kershaw and their Fartonia Afghan Hounds were winning, taking Best of Breed at the 1960 Open Show. Their stud was Rabiouw Wahad Khalil. The J.C. Scotts owned the Bhagti Kennels in Yorkshire and Mr. Scott also served as a breed columnist for *Dog World*. Mr. and Mrs. Charles Harrisson were also active in the breed. Their Vishnu Kennels were based on Miss Niblock's stock. The first English champion out of her kennel was the Harrisson's Khanabad Asravi of Vishnu. Asravi's litter sister Astrajid was the second champion for Miss Niblock. Both were sired by Ch. Horningsea Majid ex Khanabad Azrar. Azrar, bred by the Harrissons, was the dam of Ch. Khanabad Horningsea Suvaraj, a Dog of the Year (mentioned earlier in this book.) The Harrison's Jali of Vishnu also had several top awards to his credit.

The Patrol Kennels of Mrs. Ruth Y. Har-

Above: Ch. Xzari of Carloway, beautiful bitch representing the quality bred from Sheila Devitt's Carloway line.

Above, right: Ch. Zara of Khorrassan, self-masked cream bitch bred by Miss Eileen Snelling of England.

Right: English Champion Bondor of Tiazabad, a winner at the British shows in the early 1970's.

rison is not to be confused with the above mentioned Charles Harrisson's Vishnu Kennels. Mrs. Betty Clarke and her Shanshu Kennels should not be confused with Mrs. C.C. Clarke's of Kandahar which should not be confused with Dorothy Clarke's Valdoren Kennels!

Other breeders of note during the years after World War II were Miss Doris Venn's Conygar Kennels, Miss F.G. Ide's Jalalabad line, Mrs. Cooper's De Flandre and the following list all of which have been worthy of mention in any book written so far on our breed:

Miss Burchett's Palitana, Baroness Westenholz's Closmidi, Mrs. D. Hall's Barbille, Mrs. J.V. Polson's Khassar, Miss Joanne Chambers' Otontala, Mrs. C.A. Jenkin's Folkestone, Mrs. F.W. Cockings' Murgar, Miss J.L. Edwards' Satania, Mrs. J.H. Parker's Three Streams, Mrs. Kara Tziros' Tzaharane, Ali Hupka's Barakzai, Mrs. Margaret Masters' Brabourne, Mrs. Violet Gilligan's Shemsuki, Messrs. Wilson and Walker's Khonistan and Miss Patricia Kean's Ajman.

Later still, the Rev. Ford and Miss H. Barnes had the Davlin Kennels and Mr. and Mrs. Pollock showed under the Tarril kennel name. Their chief winner was a dog sired by the American import, Ch. Wazir of Desertaire; this dog won the Hound Group at Crufts in 1966.

Mrs. Daphne Gie's Jagai Kennel produced the 1969 Crufts Hound Group winner. His name was Ch. Rangitsinghi of Jagai, owned by Mrs. J. Holden. Mr. W. Kelley was known in the breed, but only started breeding in the 1960's under his Sherdil kennel name.

THE SOARING SIXTIES

By the end of the 1960's breed registrations and show entries had climbed to such great numbers that the Afghan Hound Association started appointing two judges to officiate in the rings at the shows. Registrations for 1969 were over 2,900. This was partly due to established breeders producing better and better dogs and from the numerous newcomers and young people attracted to this glamorous breed. Sadly, part of the increase came from people who thought they could make a lot of money selling exotic dogs.

Fortunately, additional breed clubs were formed which helped somewhat in regulating the breed. In August of 1964 the Midland Afghan Hound Club started; in April, 1968

Ch. Wazir of Desertaire was imported to England and became the property of the Les Bridges. The breeders were the John Buchanans of California. The sire was Am. and Mex. Ch. Crown Crest Mr. Universe and the dam was Am. Ch. Zar-Kari of Shamalan.

the Western Afghan Hound Club formed; and in February, 1970 the Afghan Hound Society of Scotland was able to oversee the breed in that country.

Along with the increase in numbers, additional shows were being held. In April of 1969 the Northern Afghan Hound Club held their first championship show and in February of 1971 the Southern Afghan Hound Club held their first championship show.

BRITISH KENNELS OF THE SEVENTIES

By 1970 the Afghan Hound in England was still climbing in popularity—and registrations! In 1971 it showed the largest increase in registrations of any breed, with 853 more Afghan Hounds registered with the Kennel Club than in 1970. Considering the size of the British Isles and their general preference for smaller and sporting dogs, this figure represents an amazing increase.

In 1973 in Great Britain the Afghan Hound was ranked #11 in popularity of all breeds with 4,820 registrations for that year.

In the United States it was ranked #28 with 10,549 individual registrations.

There is little wonder, with registrations numbering in the thousands, that the Afghan Hound Association is an active group. Some of the most active kennels in the 1970's include Mr. and Mrs. P. Harris' Ghaziris Afghans in London, the Kent kennels of Mrs. L.I.M. Busby (the Clearways line) and Marilyn Willis (Springett Kennels) as well as the kennels of Mrs. Ruth Bumstead (Whitelands), Mrs. Ivy Atkins (Kohinoor) and Mrs. J. Bowden (Pinecroft) all in Sussex.

In Lancastershire there are the Accadistran Kennels of Mr. Barry and Mrs. Pauline Sidebottom. Mrs. J. Wonnacott is still active with Afghan Hounds at her Phillips Farm in Cornwall, and in Herts Miss J. Dove has the Saringa Afghan Hounds. Herts is also the area where, until her recent death, Mrs. Marna Dods had her famous Horningsea Afghan Hound Kennels.

There are two kennels in Essex: Norman and Miriam Butcher offer stud service and have puppies for sale occasionally at their Tinoth Lodge and Mrs. Yvonne Morel also has stud service at her Zaramah Afghan Hound facilities. Angela Draper is in Hants, Miss L.H. S. Smith owns the Begaville Afghan Hounds, and in Oxon it is Miss Margaret Niblock that has established her Khanabad Kennel in 1946. She is a specialist in exotic colors as well as type and temperament.

In South Humberside there are also two Afghan Hound enthusiasts; Mrs. C.K. Mumber has her Carmichan Afghan Hound Kennels and Mr. and Mrs. H.A. Richards also have Afghan Hounds. In Northumberland Mrs. Hilary Harcourt-Brown breeds puppies and offers dogs at stud under her Kharisar kennel name. In Cheshire Jill R. Morris operates the Studholme Kennels and, just as the kennel name implies has dogs at stud.

The Whodeanie Kennels of Mr. D.J. McCann are located in Worchestershire; in West Yorkshire the Karakuli Afghan Hound Kennels are owned by Mr. and Mrs. N. Crowther. In Dumfries Mr. Robert A. Greenshields is active in the breed, and in Bucks there is the Bondor Kennel.

The beautiful Shahmoon of Grandeur, owned by Sue Garland of New York City and photographed by A.M. Tomko III.

Chapter III

The Afghan Hound in the United States

The Afghan Hound's beginning in the United States was an excellent one. Its heritage in this country sprung from worthy importations of Jean Manson and the Bell-Murray lines, and from Mary Amps' famous Ch. Sirdar of Ghanzi. It has been estimated that from 15% to 25% of the breeding in the United States was founded on these two lines.

FIRST REGISTRATIONS

Miss Manson's breeding was behind the very first litter of three brindle Afghan Hound puppies registered with the American Kennel Club in the October 1926 *Stud Book*. Owned by the Dunwalke Kennels, the bitch was named Tezin and the two brothers were Bolan and Bokhara. The records show they were whelped in August, 1925. Bred in Scotland, the sire was Bhaloo and the dam was Oolu. Their ancestry traced back to the dogs originally imported from the Middle East.

This does not mean, of course, that no other Afghan Hound had touched our shores before these three. Another male was registered that same year. Named Kandahar, he was purchased as a champion by Mr. Joseph P. Widener from Jean Manson at the Philadelphia Sesquicentennial Exposition. Kandahar led a good life, coursing with all the Greyhounds on the Widener estate. There had been other imported Afghan Hounds residing in various sections of the East which are said to have arrived in the years following World War I, but obviously they were never registered with the AKC.

Three of the early all-time great dogs in the breed! Allah Baba, Taejon of Crown Crest and Jubilee Julian, all owned and shown by Kay Finch. This classic photograph was taken at one of the Morris and Essex Kennel Club shows.

FIRST AMERICAN-BRED REGISTRATION

In 1928 Faida O'Valley Farm was registered by Joseph B. Thomas of Stamford, Connecticut. Known for years as a Borzoi fancier, Mr. Thomas imported two Afghan Hounds from the Bell-Murrays. Their names were Shiek and Zun and from their mating came Faida, whelped in October 16, 1927.

FIRST AFGHAN HOUND SHOW DOG

Mrs. Sarah Waller of Chicago, Illinois, claims the honor of having the first show winner in the breed. Her golden brindle bitch Rettet's Fuzzi of Elenor was winning the breed at the northeastern shows and the catalogues listed the breeder as Mrs. Clifford, England. Mrs. Clifford's breeding was founded on Bell-Murray stock. Entries ran around half a dozen during the late twenties when Fuzzi was being shown.

It was during these Wall Street crash years that Mrs. Waller was showing Fuzzi and Edward E. Abrams was showing his Abdoul in the Philadelphia area.

THE POST DEPRESSION ERA

In spite of the crash and the ensuing economic and financial depression, Zeppo Marx, one of the famous Marx Brothers, imported two Afghan Hounds to appear in one of their movies in May, 1931. Aside from their debut in motion pictures, Westmill Omar and Asra of Ghazni were also to achieve fame in the dog world. Shortly after the movie was completed, they were sold to George S. Thomas, an internationally known English judge, who in turn sold them to Q.A. Shaw McKean for his Prides Hill Kennels.

Q.A. SHAW MCKEAN AND PRIDES HILL

Asra of Ghazni was to become a most prolific producer and the dam of seven champions. Her first litter of five was whelped on April 1, 1932, with G.S. Thomas listed as breeder. Before her death at the age of fourteen, Asra had whelped some seventy-odd puppies to help establish the breed in this country.

AMERICA'S FIRST BEST IN SHOW AFGHAN HOUND

On the advice of Mr. Thomas, Shaw McKean also purchased the smoke-colored brindle dog Badshah of Ainsdart, born on May 28, 1930. Badshah was imported by McKean in 1932 and became an international

40

The first Afghan Hound bitch to win a Best In Show! Mrs. James M. Austin and Ch. Lakshmi of Genfron Catawba are pictured receiving another Best In Show cup for their win at the 27th Annual Maryland Kennel Club Show on February 4, 1940. Presenting the award is Mr. John M. Hurst, president of the Maryland Kennel Club at that time. Percy Jones photograph.

champion. He also distinguished himself by becoming the first Afghan Hound to win a Best In Show award in the United States at the Ladies Kennel Club Show in 1934. His breeder was Mrs. J. Morris-Jones, England. The first Best In Show bitch in America was the self-masked cream, Lakshmi of Geufron-Catawba, in 1939.

FIRST AMERICAN CHAMPION

The first Afghan Hound to earn an American championship title was Kabul of Prides Hill in October, 1934. The first champion bitch was Barberry Hill Dolly in 1935.

Badshah of Ainsdart was largely responsible for Shaw McKean and his neighbor Bayard Warren becoming interested in the Afghan Hound as a racing dog. Mr. Warren had purchased some of the early Omar-Asra

Winner of the Hound Group at a California dog show many years ago was Barberryhill Dolly, owned by Venita Varden, (Mrs. Jack Oakie). Dolly was the first bitch Champion in the U.S. and was handled by Phyllis Rainer, who became manager of Mrs. Oakie's Oak-Varden Kennels. The wife of one of the show officials is presenting the trophy.

puppies and the two men began to entertain thoughts about the possibility of racing them on the nearby Wonderland dog track using mechanical hares. That is, they ran them at Wonderland until the Greyhound owners learned about it and prevailed upon the track management to put a stop to it. Nevertheless, it was Shaw McKean who initiated Afghan Hound racing in America. He was also influential in founding the Afghan Hound Club of America and served as its first President from 1938 through 1941.

VENITA VARDON AND OAKVARDON

From one of the breedings between Omar and Asra came Barberryhill Illusion, dam of the famous Ch. Barberryhill Dolly, Venita Varden's famous brood and show bitch. Movie comedian Charles Ruggles had first shown Dolly in 1931. When he died in 1937, Venita inherited his breeding. It was Venita Varden, married to another famous comedian, Jack Oakie, who was responsible for Dolly's sparkling career.

In 1938 she imported a dog from India

Mrs. Jack Oakie's English and American Ch. Westmill Natanz pictured winning the Hound Group in 1941 at the San Bernardino show under judge Beatrice Hopkins Godsol. Handling for Mrs. Oakie was Phyllis Rainer.

named Umberto, a dog from Ireland named Hanuman of Enriallic, and two from England, Ch. Westmill Natanz and Westmill Razuran. Natanz won two Bests In Show. Using Oakvarden as her kennel name, many show dogs were bred at her kennels before her untimely death in a plane crash in 1948. She was also a popular show judge (including Westminster, 1942) and served as President of the Afghan Hound Club of America in 1944.

Ch. Barberryhill Charlie, Dolly's litter brother owned by Athos Nilson, was not only the third Afghan Hound to win Best In Show in this country but was Canada's first Best In Show Afghan Hound. The year was 1937 and his great win did much to bring the Canadian dog fanciers' attention to the breed. Ch. Oakvarden's Ranee was the second Afghan Hound to win a Best In Show in Canada.

Westmill Omar and Asra of Ghazni were also known for producing two top Afghan Hounds that were to leave their mark on the breed. Mr. McKean's Zahera of Pride's Hill became the dam of seven champions. The other, Kundah of Pride's Hill, was the mater-

nal grandsire of Ch. Rudiki of Pride's Hill. Rudiki, Badshah and Zahera are prominent names in pedigrees in this country and are as respected for their greatness today as they were in their heyday.

AMELIA WHITE AND KANDAHAR

When talking about the early pioneers in the breed, the name of Amelia E. White inevitably comes into the conversation. Amelia owned the famous Kandahar Kennels in Santa Fe, New Mexico, which were managed for her by Alex Scott. The fame of this impressive kennel spread far and wide from their southwest location.

Her original stock came from the Prides Hill bloodlines, as early as 1933. Amelia also acquired from George Thomas the imported Ch. Tufan of Ainsdart, registered in America in September, 1934. Tufan was the litter brother to the famous Int. Ch. Badshah of Ainsdart and became the same valuable stud force in that part of the country that Badshah was in the East.

In 1937 Tufan was bred to a bitch named Ch. Shabra. The breeding produced another early "great" in Ch. Yusseff, C.D. It was Yusseff that was behind the Taejon of Crown Crest lines, as was Flo Flo of Ghazni, dam of nine champions, making her one of the all-time top-producing bitches in the breed. Yusseff sired a total of ten champions, making him one of the top sires in the breed.

Amelia White also owned Ch. Amanullah of Kandahar, the first multiple Best In Show winner in this country. He amassed a total of nine Bests during his ring career. He was sired by Int. Ch. Badshah of Ainsdart out of Zahera of Prides Hill. Amelia was a charter member of the Afghan Hound Club of America (which was experiencing birth pains during these mid-thirties) and was highly respected for her early contribution to the breed.

EARLY WEST COAST SHOW DOGS

Jamshepur Fatima and her litter sister Jamshepur Souriya were whelped in India on January 23, 1928. They were imported to this country by Laurence Peters and were among the first Afghans to appear in the show ring in California. They were entered at the August 10, 1929 Long Beach Kennel Club Show under judge Ralph White.

Little else was heard about Souriya after this initial appearance, but Fatima was exhibited until 1938. In 1936 she was bred to

Best In Show at the Riviera Kennel Club Show in California many years ago was Ch. Umberto, owned by Venita Varden, wife of movie star Jack Oakie. The judge was Anton Korbel, and the grand dam of the dog fancy, Mrs. M. Hartley Dodge, presented the trophy. A.R. Hill handled for Mrs. Oakie. Joan Ludwig photo.

Ch. Ophaal of Crown Crest, a world-famous Afghan Hound, was a champion in many countries, including Germany, Belgium and Holland. Imported as a stud force by Kay Finch for her Crown Crest Kennels in California, Ophaal has left a legacy to the breed. His name, and his memory, live on and are revered whenever Afghan Hound "greats" are recalled. . . .

Ch. Abba of Cy Ann, bred in 1941 by Mr. and Mrs. Cyrus Rickel of the Cy Ann Kennels and owned by Dr. Gertrude F. Kinsey of New York City. The sire was Ch. Omar of Fort Worth *ex* Ch. Tanyah of Cy Ann.

Tufan and they were credited with starting the breed on that coast. They produced several champions. Fatima was owned by a Mrs. Richmond who showed her around the same time Mrs. M. West was showing Shahjehan of Larkbeare at the Golden Gate Kennel Club Show.

During the mid-thirties, Laurence Peters imported a dog, Tazi of Beg Tute, and a bitch, Saki of Pagham. Saki was a grey and was very influential in the early U.S. blue Afghan Hounds, including those behind Joseph Felts' dogs, which included Felts Thief of Bagdad.

A Badshah son, Ch. Sahib of Prides Hill, whelped in 1938, was being shown by the well-known breeder-judge, Dr. Frank Porter Miller, who showed him to his championship.

THE CYRUS RICKELS AND CY-ANN

Mr. and Mrs. Cyrus Rickel were the owners of the Cy-Ann Kennels in Fort Worth, Texas. Their breeds had included many terriers before 1937 when they fell in love with the strange "new" breed, the Afghan Hound.

The Rickels produced several top-winning Afghan Hounds over the years. Mr. Rickel also enjoyed a long career as a judge and as a charter member of the parent club. It was a career that would cover a span of more than three decades before his death in 1972.

Rickel's Ch. Tanya Sahib of Cy-Ann has the great distinction of being the winner of the very first Afghan Hound Club of America Specialty Show in 1940 under judge Dr. Eugene Beck. Mr. Rickel judged at the parent club himself in 1951 and put up Lee and Howard Iverson's Ch. Blu Arabis of Kuvera as Best of Breed. He officiated again in 1959 when Sunny Shay's Ch. Shirkhan of Grandeur was the victor. On a third occasion, in 1968, he placed Ch. Dahnwood Gabriel, owned by the Herman Felltons, in the top spot. No other judge in the history of the club had been invited to judge the parent Specialty three times!

Cy Rickel also served the club as Vice-President for many years and was a member of the committee for the Afghan Breed Standard, revised and accepted by the American Kennel Club in 1948. He was also a director of the American Kennel Club at one time. Cy Rickel was loved and respected by all who knew him and for the contribution he and Mrs. Rickel made to the breed. Though he judged other breeds as well, Afghan Hounds were among the favorite interests in his life and owners all looked forward to his presence at ringside.

THE CHARLES WERNSMANS AND ARKEN

Charles and Lillian Wernsman came early to the breed and owned one of the all-time Afghan Hound "greats," the imported Ch. Garrymhor Zabardast of Arken. He was Best of Winners at the first Afghan Hound Club of America Specialty Show in 1940 and sire of the Wernsman's famous Ch. Rajah of Arken. Rajah was Best of Breed winner at three consecutive parent club Specialties. . . in 1942, 1943 and 1944. This set a record for club winners, which still holds in the 1970's.

In the early days, it was also a familiar sight to see the Wernsmans arrive at a dog show with practically every dog in their kennel in tow. It was their explicit intention to give the breed a large entry to help the Afghan Hound gain recognition with the American Kennel Club!

Ch. Crown Crest Kabul, pictured here at 3½ years of age. Kabul, bred by Kay Finch and owned by Mary Nelson Stephenson was a Specialty and Best In Show winner. A black-masked apricot, Kabul was sired by Ch. Ophaal of Crown Crest *ex* Ch. Crown Crest Tae-joan.

THE ROBERT BOGERS

Robert and Muriel Boger were staunch advocates of the breed from those earliest days, also. Muriel served the Afghan Hound Club of America as both Secretary and Treasurer from its beginning in 1938 until 1946 when Charlotte Coffey took over the reins and she moved up to the Presidency! She held this position for three terms. During the years Muriel was President, Bob served as its Delegate to the American Kennel Club. Muriel also wrote the *American Kennel Gazette* breed column during the 1940's.

Muriel and Bob were both Afghan Hound judges and Muriel judged the parent club Specialty in 1942 and gave Ch. Rajah of Arken the Best of Breed award. Bob judged the show in 1946 and put up Leah McConaha's Ch. Karach of Khanhasset. When he judged the show again in 1960 his winner was Kay Finch and Charles Costabile's Ch. Crown Crest Mr. Universe.

MRS. LAUER FROLICH AND ELCOZA

During the decade of the thirties, Mrs. Lauer Frolich became enamoured of the breed. She imported two top brindle dogs from the El Kabul Kennels of Dr. Betsy Porter in England. The two dogs came over on the ship Somaria, which was torpedoed and sunk on its return voyage during World War II hostilities. The two were brother and sister, Sardar Khan el Kabul and Rani el Kabul, and they formed the foundation of her Elcoza Kennels. Sardar became a champion and from his mating to Flo Flo of Ghazni many champions were produced.

While Rani was not campaigned to a championship, she produced five champion offspring as her contribution to the breed. Mrs. Froelich also bred Poodles and is still a very active and popular judge at the shows today. She was judge at the parent club Specialty show in 1957 when the author's Ch. Crown Crest Jesi Jhaimz was Best of Winners and Kay Finch's Ch. Crown Crest Zardonx won Best of Breed.

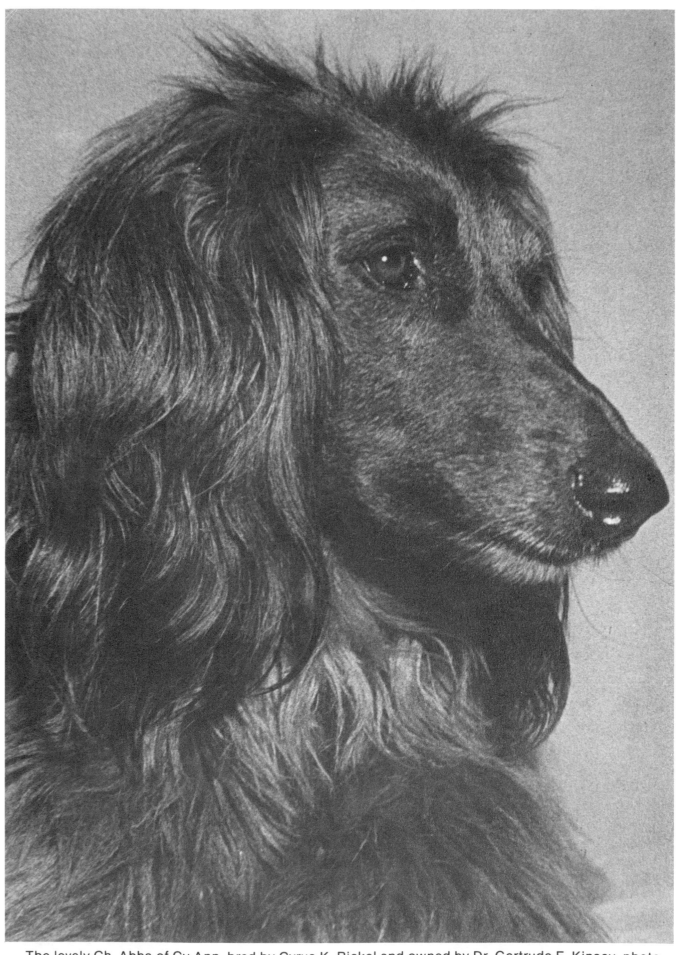

The lovely Ch. Abba of Cy Ann, bred by Cyrus K. Rickel and owned by Dr. Gertrude F. Kinsey, photographed by Angela several years ago.

The first direct import to the U.S.A. from Afghanistan. . . Ch. Egypt's Echo of Crown Crest. This exquisite gray bitch was a sister to Ch. Egypt's Eudora; both produced finest quality offspring. Known as the "Peter's strain," these two bitches stemmed from the rare Fatima bloodline imported from India, as well as the Tazi-Saki line from Afghanistan. Owned by Kay Finch.

Mrs. Bamberger, wife of the Governor of Utah, poses for a picture with Int. Ch. Rudika of Blakeen and Int. Ch. Rana of Chaman of Royal Irish in Salt Lake City many years ago. The dogs were owned by Marion Florsheim.

Clean sweep for the Patrician Afghan Hounds. . . Winners Bitch to Patrician's Victoria (handled by Joe Emmert), Winners Dog to Geoffrey of Patrician and Best of Opposite Sex to the dam of both of them, Ch. Crown Crest Taejhanne, under judge Leo Murphy at a Beverly Riviera Kennel Club Show several years ago. Ludwig photo.

DR. EUGENE BECK

Dr. Eugene Beck owned the red bitch, Cleopatra, which, when bred to Shaitan Bedar, produced Far Away Loo, dam of Ch. Majara Mahabat and Khanhasset Ginger of Grandeur. Cleopatra was whelped in 1935 and was sired by Int. Ch. Badsha of Ainsdart out of Lulu Catron's Westmill Taree. Taree was one of the earliest registered Afghan Hounds in America. The year was 1932.

Dr. Beck was the judge invited to adjudicate at the first Afghan Hound Club of America Specialty Show in 1940. Dr. Beck chose the Rickel's Ch. Tanyah Sahib of Cy-Ann as his Best of Breed.

DR. ARTHUR W. COMBS AND ARTHEA

Dr. Combs was the judge at the second parent club Specialty and put up Dr. G. Kinsey's Ch. Hazar as the winner. Dr. Combs' wife was also active in the fancy showing her Shetland Sheepdogs during the 1940's. The Combs owned three generations of Arthea dogs—son, mother and grandmother, named Kusra Khylie, Ch. Zudiki and Ch. Tahida.

LEAH MCCONAHA

Mrs. S. Ferguson McConaha, or Leah Posar McConaha as she was also known, bred and owned the famous Ch. Ali Khyber, truly one of the immortals of the breed. Whelped in February 1941, this black-masked red dog had over 70 Bests of Breeds, invariably placed in the Groups, and over half of his placements were Firsts! Harry Hill handled him to nine Bests In Show before he was retired for a year during the wartime travel restrictions. After the war, in his first six shows he took all six Bests of Breed, placed in the Group each time and won three more Bests In Show!

Ali Khyber remains the second ranking top-producing stud in the history of the breed with 34 champions to his credit. His most prominent son was Karach of Khanhasset, also owned by Leah McConaha and winner of the parent club Specialty show in 1946 and 1947 under judges Bob Boger and Charles Wernsman. Karach sired only one litter before his early death in April, 1947, this by Far Away Loo. The entire litter was kept by breeder Marjorie Lathrop of Majara fame and produced six champions. The immortal Majara Mahabat was one; Mihri and Mustapha were two others that achieved recognition.

Best In Show at a Lake Mohawk Kennel Club Show several years ago was Mr. and Mrs. Frederick A. Jagger's Ch. Majara Mahabat. Mrs. Saunders L. Meade was the judge, George M. Moen presented the trophy and Mrs. Jagger is shown handling Mahabat.

One of the greatest! Ch. Ali Khyber of Khanhasset is shown after taking Best In Show and Best American Bred In Show at the March 26, 1944 Elm City Kennel Club Show. The judge is Mrs. A.M. Lewis and Harry Hill handles for owner Mrs. L.P. McConaha. James Dwyer, club president, is shown at right.

Mrs. Leah P. McConaha, owner-handler of the old-time great Ch. Ali Khyber, accepts the award for Best Hound from judge Louis Murr at the March, 1942 Providence Country Kennel Club Show in Rhode Island. Percy Jones photo.

Leah also bred Ch. Karan of Khanhasset, winner of the 1948 parent club Specialty under judge E.E. Ferguson.

Another of Ali Khyber's famous sons was Ch. Khyber Kim, C.D., the first Afghan Hound owned by Dorothy and Waldron Macdonald. Dorothy has always been a staunch supporter of the breed and became very active in the parent club many years ago. She first served as the Club's Secretary from 1961 until 1967, when she moved up to the Presidency where she served through 1970.

LOUISE SNYDER AND WINDTRYST

Louise Carwithen French owned some of the Arthea bloodlines through her Ch. Agha Kaimaaken of Arthea. She was the breeder of Ch. Windtryst's Afire, as well as a line of Afghan Hounds that kept her busy in the show rings for many years.

The stately Mrs. French (now Mrs. George Snyder of Malvern, Pennsylvania) has been dedicated to both Afghan Hounds and Pekingese for many years and is very active in humane work as well. Louise for many years has run The Crop Shop in Pennsylvania, a store that specializes in English saddlery.

While Louise has not bred or owned Afghan Hounds for some years now, she has kept a few excellent Pekes and still enjoys her Afghan Hound judging assignments.

A glimpse of a past "great!" Am. and Can. Ch. Khyber Kim, C.D., in a never-before published photograph, courtesy of Mr. and Mrs. Waldron S. Macdonald of Concord, Massachusetts.

Best In Show for Ch. Karach of Khanhasset in 1947 at the Elm City Kennel Club Show in New Haven, Connecticut. Handler was Harry Hill, the judge Mrs. L.W. Bonney. Mr. Victor Sausville, president of the club, presented the trophy. Karach was owned by Leah P. McConaha of Great Neck, Long Island, New York.

During these same years, many other names that are still recognizable in the breed were coming into the show scene. Mrs. Madelaine Austin, Mrs. D.A. Holmes, Mrs. A.B. DeWitt, Gretchen Williams and her Prides Hill dogs in the mid-thirties, Dr. Marxmiller with his Dellire line, Mr. and Mrs. Herbert Brothers of Ohio, Mrs. D.A. Porter and her Kingsway Kennels in Denver, Mr. and Mrs. Lemuel Ayers and the Balmor line, Mrs. Thomas Richard Cowell of Washington, D.C., the John E. Morses who maintain their Jac-a-leen Kennels in Gillette, New Jersey, and, of course, there were others.

There were many interested and dedicated fanciers in the 1930's that were to "blaze a trail" for the breed in the "fabulous forties!"

The American entry in World War II brought many difficulties to the fancy. Importing was difficult, if not impossible, and the rationing of food and gasoline curtailed many show careers. However, the United States did benefit from the hostilities in some ways. Many Europeans sent their dogs to this country, virtually to save their lives. Feeding dogs, especially large breeds, was difficult and, rather than have them starve to death, they sold them to Americans who were better off and could preserve their foreign lines by bringing them into their own kennels. Many great dogs that might not otherwise have found their way to this country arrived to enhance our bloodlines. Rather than a show career in Europe, the owners had to settle on seeing them in back of the winning American lines. It was our good fortune, to be sure.

When these facts are taken into consideration along with the realization that the already established kennels had been doing some very good breeding since the end of World War I, you get a very healthy outlook for the breed. Not that things didn't slow down during the war years, they did. But just as in Europe and Britain, there were a few who put the continuation of the bloodlines above all else and continued their breeding programs in order to carry on. Marion Foster Florsheim was one of those who carried on.

This photograph, showing Mrs. Louise French Snyder with two of her Afghan Hounds, was taken in 1948 and is one of her and the author's favorite photos! The dogs are Ch. Windtryst's Afire and Ch. Agha Kaimaakan of Arthea.

MARION FOSTER FLORSHEIM
AND RUDIKI

The glamorous Marion Foster Florsheim and her fabulous International Champion Rudiki of Pride's Hill brought true fame to the breed all during the decade of the forties. Whelped in 1937 and sired by the equally fabulous International Champion Badshah of Ainsdart out of Shireen of Prides Hill, Rudiki was acquired and campaigned by Marion to what was probably the most famous show ring career ever enjoyed by an Afghan Hound up to that time. Marion and Rudiki were almost inseparable and he traveled with her everywhere, by plane or car, to dog shows or to social functions.

During his show career he won 15 Bests In Show, 27 Best American-bred In Show, 40 Best Hound wins and 73 additional Group Placements out of 77 Bests of Breed. This was a truly glorious and remarkable show record at the time. Reported to be an almost carbon copy of his illustrious grandsire, Ch. Sirdar of Ghazni, Rudiki sired over two hundred puppies in his lifetime, with 31 of them finishing for their championships. This grand total qualified Rudiki as one of the top-producing sires in the history of the breed. Even today, he is fourth-ranking sire in the breed.

Mrs. Florsheim also imported Ch. Rana of Chaman (of Royal Irish) from the Chaman Kennels of Molly Sharpe in Ireland. These two sires, Rana and Rudiki, were to form the basis of Marion's Five Mile Kennels and

The late Marion Foster Florsheim, one of the avant-garde in the breed in this country, with her famous International Champion Rudiki of Pride's Hill, photographed many years ago.

Marion Foster Florsheim and Int. Ch. Rudika of Blakeen visit the editor of *The Saturday Evening Post* to discuss the magazine story and cover displayed in the background, which featured three of Mrs. Florsheim's dogs. The March 18, 1944 cover marked the first color cover on the *Post*, and the first time a dog was on the cover. Rutherford Boyd of New Jersey rendered the painting from which the cover was reproduced.

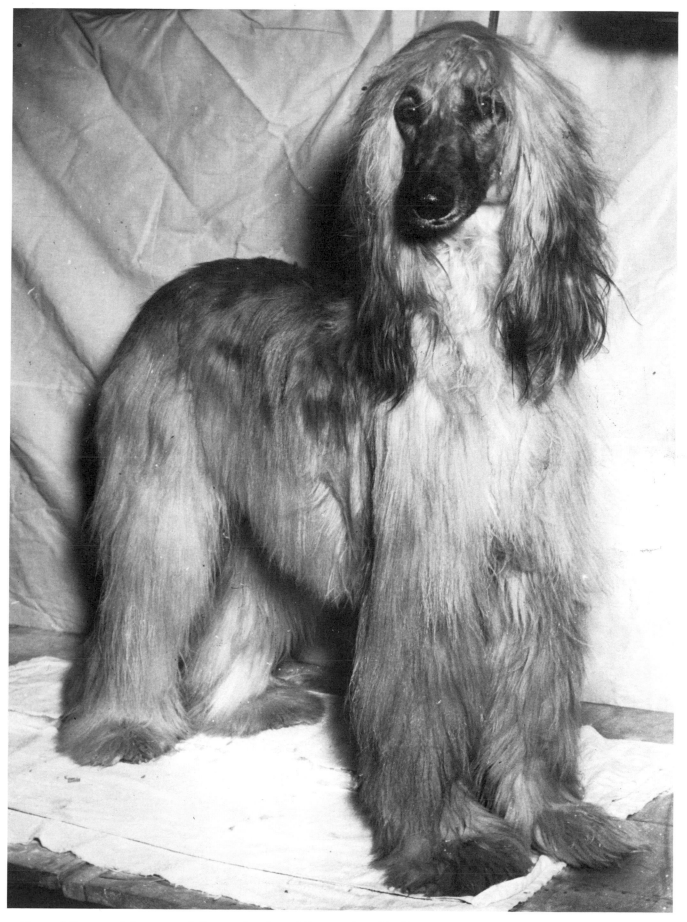

One of the most famous of the early show bitches, Int. Ch. Rudika of Blakeen, owned by the late Marion Foster Florsheim of Connecticut.

Two of the breed's "famous firsts". . . Ch. Yenghiz Khan of Five Mile (a home-bred son of Int. Ch. Rana of Chaman) and Int. Ch. Rudiki of Prides Hill, his grandsire. Owned by the late Marion Foster Florsheim.

One of the best-known photographs of Int. Ch. Rudiki of Prides Hill, owned by the late Marion Foster Florsheim.

would produce some of the greatest show winners in the breed over the next decade. Rana sired 11 champions in his time and also had a remarkable record for the show ring. He was later owned by Margaret Hawkins, and had to put down in July, 1949, a victim of cancer.

Rudiki's best-known son, perhaps, was the top-winning Ch. Ali Khyber. He was to top his sire and become the second-ranking stud dog in the history of the breed by producing 34 champion get. His sister, Ch. Rudika of Blakeen, (later co-owned with Charles Costabile) was a Best In Show winner and a top-producing bitch with six champions to her credit. Rudika, a multiple Best In Show winner, was never defeated by another bitch of any breed. She had 21 Bests of Breed, 19 Group Firsts, 21 Group Placements, three Best American-bred wins and a Best In Show to her credit.

Rana produced two excellent sons, Ch. Yenghiz Khan of Five Mile, owned by the Wilfred Kennedys of Detroit, and Ch. Azri-Havid of Five Mile, owned by Eve Gudgeon of Canada. A daughter, Zumurrud, was owned by Mrs. John Bamberger of Salt Lake City, who later acquired Rana himself.

Old time great Int. Ch. Rana of Chaman of Royal Irish, imported from Scotland by the late Marion Foster Florsheim. During his show ring career in the United States Rana won 3 Bests In Show, 11 Hound Group Firsts, 32 Seconds and 38 Bests of Breed. This photograph was taken in 1942.

Harry and Marion Florsheim are pictured arriving at Roosevelt Airport in the 1930's with one of their Afghan Hounds. Mrs. Florsheim, a well-known pilot, and her husband were a familiar sight at airports all over the world.

Another Best In Show for Int. Ch. Rudiki of Prides Hill. . . this win was at a Lackawanna Kennel Club Show many years ago. The late Mrs. Marion Foster Florsheim handles her famous imports.

Airborne Afghans! Marion Foster Florsheim's famed Int. Ch. Rudiki of Prides Hill sees his two sons Trolie and Jerry off to Los Angeles for their first dog show! Accompanying them on their flight from LaGuardia airport was Miss Helene Arlington, a dog writer and Afghan enthusiast.

Best In Show for Ch. Yenghiz Khan of Five Mile, owned by Mrs. Marion Foster Florsheim and handled for her by Bill Adair. Mr. G.V. Glebe was the judge at this Steel City Kennel Club show in Evanston, Illinois, many years ago.

The late Marion Foster Florsheim's famous trio of Afghan Hound show winners in the 1930's. . . Ch. Rana of Chaman of Royal Irish, imported from Scotland, Ch. Rudiki of Prides Hill, and Champion Rudika of Blakeen. These three Afghans did much to popularize the breed in this country.

Marion was to breed many, many champions at Five Mile Kennels in Darien, Connecticut , and helped many other people in the breed by getting them started with the best possible breeding stock. During World War II, when she was a pilot for the Air Force Ferry Command, between assignments Marion would take the dogs on special flights to visit kennels all over the country and Canada, which did much to popularize the breed. Marion was also one of the first to have an Afghan Hound brace: Rudiki and his daughter, Ch. Maharanee Kohibaba, C.D., one of the first obedience titled Afghan Hounds in the breed.

It was three of the Five Mile dogs that graced the first color cover of the *Saturday Evening Post,* complete with a story about Marion and the breed. The March 18, 1944 issue of the Post featured an oil painting by Rutherford Boyd of Rudiki and two of his

sons. Rudiki also appeared on the cover of the November 26, 1945 issue of *Life Magazine.* These are perfect examples of how Marion managed to keep the Afghan Hound in the public eye! She also wrote the breed column for *Kennel Review* magazine during the forties.

In 1947 when her beloved Rudiki died on Christmas Eve, Marion closed down her Five Mile Kennel. Her concentration turned to judging, some writing and enjoying her art collection. She owned a famous F.T. Daws oil painting of four Afghan Hounds on a mountain ledge, which she later gave to Kay Finch as a gift. It still hangs along with Mrs. Finch's other Daws art. Kay sculpted a magnificent bronze figure of Rudiki as a gift for Marion in 1948, the year after his death. Marion wrote Kay after receiving it, "It is so magnificent it did not even make me sad."

On July 20, 1976, Marion herself succumbed to cancer in San Francisco. As I personally marked her passing, I recalled my friendship with her over the years and repeated again how grateful I was that several years ago Marion turned over to me her vast collection of photographs of the old time dogs which comprise a major portion of my own personal collection of the old "greats"—most of which are included here. Her collection included the original cover of the *Saturday Evening Post*, which I keep framed on my Sahadi Kennel wall and is reproduced in this book, also.

I also recall how touched and pleased I was the day Marion took me aside at a party and told me how delighted she was with my book and how grateful she was for the things I had to say about her dogs. She then asked me to autograph her copy for her! As Reigh Abrams said so well after learning of her death, it was truly the end of an era in Afghan Hounds. And Reigh would know, since the Abrams were two of the people Marion helped when they first got into the breed.

KAY FINCH AND CROWN CREST

Kay Finch saw her first Afghan Hound in the garden of the Coronado Hotel in San Diego in 1940. She was determined to have one of what she says "looked like a cream-colored, long-haired goat!" After two years of searching ads in the newspaper, one told of a litter for sale in a Laguna pet shop. Kay brought home "Omar." Unfortunately he was a fence jumper and on one of his freedom jaunts got hit by a car.

Kay's second Afghan Hound was Abu, from Mildred Stein. Kay was anxious to show Afghan Hounds and began searching for another dog. As a gift from her husband Braden, Kay acquired Felts' Thief of Bagdad, her first champion and Best In Show winner, "Thumper" was soon joined by a black bitch, Ch. Five Miles Banu, and a rich red bitch, Big Carmelita. After a breeding of Carmelita and Thief, Crown Crest Kennel was on its way to breaking breed records!

Kay finished Thief of Bagdad and her next champion was his son, Felts' Allah Baba. He died, however, when only five. Taejon was next and chosen from a snapshot of a litter sent to Kay. Kay and Braden motored to Illinois and came back with Taejon and his brother Bascha. Taejon was to hold the show record for five years and sired 34 champions. His total show record was 19 Bests In Show

The great lady herself. . . Kay Finch, owner of Crown Crest Kennels, with more than 100 Afghan Hound champions to their credit. Now past 70 years of age, Kay is still active in the show ring and producing great quality dogs worthy of the name Crown Crest!

all-breeds, four Specialty wins, 49 Hound Groups and 72 Bests of Breed out of 77 times shown. This includes two Hound Groups at the prestigious Westminster Kennel Club Show.

After their son Cabell saw the famous Ophaal in Germany, Kay waited two years before finally importing the dog in 1954. Ophaal was to prove a sensation in this country. Already a champion in Germany, Belgium and Holland, he made his American championship in no time. He became the sire of 28 champions, five of which were Best In Show winners.

The "queens" at Crown Crest were equally prominent in those early days. Ch. Tae-Joan became the dam of 16 champions. Ch. Hope, another Taejon daughter, was the dam of 10 champions and dam of the fabulous Ch. Crown Crest Mr. Universe.

Kay considered Mr. U "the ultimate!" A champion in Canada also, he became the sire of forty champions and had a show record of

Kay and Braden Finch photographed in California in the mid-1950's with Ch. Felt's Thief of Bagdad.

35 all-breed Bests In Show, 100 Hound Groups and four National Specialty shows, and like all the Crown Crest dogs, always owner-handled! He won the parent club Specialty show in 1960 under judge Robert Boger.

Another of Kay's favorites and big winners was American, Canadian and Mexican Ch. Crown Crest Zardonx. He sired 15 champions, won 98 Bests of Breed, 57 Hound Groups, 12 all-breed Bests In Show and three Specialty Shows before retiring from the show ring. Ch. Crown Crest Dhi-Mond was another of the Gem litter that sired 13 champions, including two Best In Show winners. Dhi-Mond didn't like the shows, so was not campaigned after achieving his championship title, but he certainly made his contribution to the breed through his get.

By the middle seventies, Crown Crest had bred well over one hundred champions in all. A truly enviable record, and the contribution that Crown Crest and especially Kay

have made to the breed may never be equalled.

On Kay's 70th birthday recently, many of her friends got together and planned a party for her, complete with a 4½ foot long cake with candy Afghan Hounds, Mexican Dancers, memorial chairs for the Afghan Hound greats she had at Crown Crest and a song written especially for the occasion and played and sung by Don Ide. There was also an enormous scrapbook with a fur Afghan Hound representing Taejon on the cover which contained hundreds of birthday cards from all over the world paying tribute to the lady that helped so many of them in the fancy. There was a scroll with the names of the guests and those who had contributed money to be presented to a humane society. Orchid leis were flown in from Hawaii by Dr. Rudy Maffei, her good friend, and two club members were stopped at the Mexican border when they tried to bring in 250 Mexican flowers! Joan Ludwig was there to photograph it

Kay Finch with three puppies from her Crown Crest Kennels in Corona del Mar, California. These three are from the litter which produced the famous Int. Ch. Crown Crest Mr. Universe.

Ch. Felt's Allah Baba, Best In Show at the 1951 Afghan Specialty Show held in conjunction with the Harbor Cities Kennel Club event. Owned by Kay Finch of Crown Crest Kennels; Athos Nilsen handled under judge Leo Murphy. Presenting the Rudiki Memorial Trophy Is Sujata Asoka. Joan Ludwig photo.

Ch. Felt's Thief of Bagdad wins Best In Show at the October 1, 1948 Pasadena Kennel Club Show under judge E.E. Ferguson. Athos Nilsen handled this glorious silver-blue male for owner Kay Finch.

Kay Finch's Ch. Taejon of Crown Crest takes his third consecutive Best of Breed win at the Westminster Kennel Club Show. The year was 1954, and Taejon went on to capture his second consecutive Hound Group win.

A family portrait of breeder Kay Finch and one of the "winningest" litters ever bred. The famous "Gem Litter" was sired by the famous import American, Dutch, Belgian and German Ch. Ophaal of Crown Crest. The dam is Ch. Crown Crest Tae-joan. This litter included Int. Ch. Zardonx, Rubi, Topaz and Dhi-mond, all bearing the famous Crown Crest kennel name prefix.

all for posterity and several of the breed magazines turned over entire issues of their magazines to personal advertising tributes to Kay. Kay in turn took a full page ad to thank everyone for the marvelous tribute and to publish the Ludwig photos!

In January, 1962, Braden Finch died. Braden was an exemplary person in every way. A dedicated civic leader since their marriage in 1923, he was part of the strength behind the "Crown." I was particularly pleased when Kay revealed that she had had copies made of my memorial tribute to Braden which was published in my breed column in *Popular Dogs.*

Needless to say, Kay carried on all the traditions of Crown Crest with her usual enthusiasm and flair, and today Crown Crest has branched out into Salukis and Whippets which Kay manages to show when she is not judging most all breeds of dogs at shows all over the world.

SUNNY SHAY AND GRANDEUR

It is difficult to know where to begin with the saga of Sunny Shay and her world-famous Grandeur Kennels. Carol Reisman once said "The total Sunny Shay is too much to cover with one interview." I am inclined to agree, but since she has always been so much a part of the Afghan Hound scene, every conceivable effort must be made to try to acknowledge the remarkable line of dogs for which she is responsible.

Sunny's first Afghan Hounds were purchased off the bench at Westminster when she spied two of Q.A. Shaw McKean's dogs. It was a case of love at first sight and a love Sunny never got over. While only ten years old at the time, Sunny already had an eye for good dogs and became deeply involved immediately. She purchased Far Away Loo as her foundation bitch from Marjorie Walker of the Far Away Kennels, and a breeding of Loo and Ch. Ali Khyber produced Sunny's famous

Ch. Khanhasset Ginger of Grandeur. Ginger in turn produced Ch. Blue Boy of Grandeur and there by hangs the tale of Shirkhan and a multitude of other Grandeur greats for Sunny's kennel.

However, it was Blue Boy's sire, Ch. Taj Akbarou of Grandeur, that Sunny to this day believes was the greatest Afghan Hound ever. He lived to be 22 years old, and Sunny claims that "Scootchie," as she called him, was born obedience trained. He was sired by Nehru of Ku and his dam was Doreborn's Karya. When bred to Mahdi of Grandeur the litter produced the legendary Shirkhan and the author's Ch. Kalli of Grandeur. There was another male in the litter, but it did not survive.

At the same time that Sunny was winning with Blue Boy, another milestone was about to be recorded in Afghan Hound history. Sunny imported the great Ch. Turkuman Nissim's Laurel. Bred by Juliette de Baircli Levy, this stylish black dog was destined to break records in this country. Co-owned with writer Sol Malkin, "Kaftan" earned his championship title in 1947. In 1950 he won Best of Breed at the Afghan Hound Club of America Specialty Show and then went on to win the Hound Group at the Westminster Kennel Club Show under judge Alva Rosenberg. Over a quarter of a century later Afghanites are still talking about the magnificent picture Sunny and Kaftan made as they glided up and down the ring in perfect synchronization, with Sunny wearing a black riding outfit with white gloves and stock and the black dog with white socks! Kaftan died in 1958.

Ch. Khanhasset Kush and Sunny Shay of the Grandeur Kennels, photographed back in the 1930's.

But the supreme win was to come in 1957 when Sunny and Shirkhan put on an equally breath-taking performance and went all the way to Best In Show at Westminster under judge Beatrice Godsol. It was the dream come true for Sunny who had vowed to win the "Garden" at nine years of age when she won a blue ribbon there in the 1920's with her Wire Fox Terrier, Sniggy Wig of Grandeur.

Sunny and Ch. Shirkhan of Grandeur went on from their Garden win to achieve many more successes. 26 Bests in Show had been won by the time he was retired and he is the top-producing sire in the history of the breed with 42 champion sons and daughters to his credit. This is a truly remarkable ach-

Some Grandeur "greats" with their owner, Sunny Shay. Left to right, Far Away Bakhar, Ch. Hakim of Grandeur, Ch. Turkuman Nissim's Laurel and Koriki of Grandeur, a daughter of Barberryhill Dolly. This photograph was taken several decades ago.

One of the greatest Afghan Hounds in the history of the breed! Ch. Turkuman Nissim's Laurel, co-owned by Sunny Shay and Sol Malkin of New Canaan, Connecticut, is pictured winning Best in Show at the June, 1950 Cincinnati Kennel Club Show. Jerry Rigden handled for owners under judge Robert G. Wills. Mr. H.W. Nichols, Jr., president of the club, and Mr. R.R. Deupree complete the picture.

Another of the old-time greats, and one of the foundation studs at Sunny Shay's kennel was Ch. Taj Akbarou of Grandeur. He is pictured here winning the Hound Group at the 1947 Albany-Troy show, handled by Sunny Shay.

Ch. Shirkhan of Grandeur (and friend) pose proudly in front of a display of some of the trophies amassed during his show career. Shirkhan is the only Afghan Hound to win a Best In Show at Westminster and ranks today as the fourth most-winning Afghan Hound in the history of the breed in America! Besides having won 26 Bests In Show, he is also one of the top-producing sires of all time and received the Quaker Oats Award for Top Hound of 1957. Shirkhan was bred by Sunny Shay, who co-owned him with Dorothy Chenade. He was sired by Ch. Blue Boy of Grandeur *ex* Mahdi of Grandeur.

ievement. In 1954 Shirkhan became the third Afghan Hound to win the Quaker Oats Award for the most Hound Group wins during that year.

Other Grandeur "greats" are too numerous to mention, and even though Sunny Shay could sit back and rest on her laurels, we love to think of her recent statement which gave us all an indication of her future. . . she said, ". . . for all the Afghan lovers of the world, Sunny Shay is alive and well at Grandeur, where the best is yet to come!" Sunny has had her detractors over the years. Anyone as dynamic, and outspoken and successful as she is would naturally cause comment. But no one can deny her knowledge of the breed or the long line of great Afghan Hounds that have carried the Grandeur name. During the Westminster Kennel Club festivities in New York City in February, 1977 at a party given for Sunny by Roger Reckler to commemorate the twenty years that have passed since Shirkhan's Best In Show win at the Garden, a lot of glasses were raised and a lot of complimentary toasts were made to Sunny Shay for a contribution to the breed that will be everlasting!

Best of Breed at the 1956 Brooklyn Kennel Club Show was Ch. Hajji Baba of Grandeur, bred, owned and handled by Sunny Shay. Hajji won the breed from the classes over specials.

MARJORIE LATHROP AND MAJARA

Marjorie Jagger's famous Majara Kennels were lauded for producing an unbroken line of six generations of Best In Show Afghan Hounds. Perhaps the greatest, and certainly one of the most memorable, was the great Ch. Majara Mahabat. Early in his show career Mahabat won two consecutive Bests of Breed at the Afghan Hound Club of America Specialty Show under judge Leah McConaha in both 1948 and 1949. Mrs. McConaha judged two years in a row; and so, no reason not to give the top award to Mahabat the second year as well.

Mahabat—Marjorie called him "Junior Bug" for some strange reason—died in 1958, but not before producing many outstanding offspring. Perhaps his best known son was Marjorie's Ch. Majara Mihrab. In 1953 Dr. Arthur W. Combs awarded the Afghan Hound Club of America Specialty Show Best of Breed win to Mihrab. Mihrab died in December, 1959. Both he and Mahabat were descendants of the famous Badshah.

Ch. Majara Mihrab, pictured winning Best In Show at the 1954 Marion Ohio Kennel Club Show. Handled by Charley Meyer for owners Mr. and Mrs. Frederick Jagger of Somerville, New Jersey. Frasie photo.

Another Majara "great" was the lovely bitch Ch. Majara Mirza. Mirza, whose show record was the greatest of all Afghan Hound bitches up to that time, was the 1951 winner of the Quaker Oats award for having won nineteen Hound Group firsts during that year. In her one and only litter sired by Mihrab, she produced five champions, including Ch. Majara Machiche, a Best In Show winner in Spain. Mirza was eleven years old when she died in December of 1959.

The list of Majara champions and show winners is too long to include here, but it was impressive, as was the list of Majara dogs that formed the foundation of other successful kennels in succeeding years. We can only hope they are grateful for what Marjorie and the Majara hounds passed along to them. . .

Some time after the death of her husband, Frederick Jagger, Marjorie married Dixon Lathrop and between hospital bouts, carried on her breeding and exhibiting in the fabulous new kennel Dixon designed and built for her in Chester Springs, Pennsylvania. After only a few years of marriage, Dixon was killed when struck down by a car on the Pennsylvania Turnpike.

Ch. Majara Mirza, owner-handled by the late Marjorie Jagger of the Majara Kennels in New Jersey, accepts Best In Show awards from judge Mrs. Richard Quigley at the 1951 Back Mountain Kennel Club Show. Austin K. Howard, club president, completes the picture. Shafer photograph.

Ch. Majara Metaab, owned by Ralph E. Murphy of Kansas City, Kansas, is pictured winning a Hound Group. Handler was James B. Stewart.

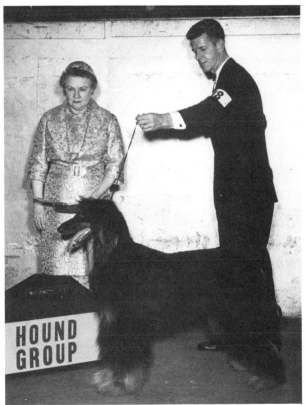

During the 1960's Marjorie began a judging career and, just two months before her death on December 19, 1966, judged the Afghan Hound Club of Southwestern Ohio Specialty Show. The Majara Dynasty, or the "Royal Family of Afghan Hounds" as Marjorie herself called her kennel, will long be remembered for their many champions and the valuable bloodlines that are behind so many other important kennels of today.

It should be noted that another great Majara dog was Ch. Majara Mardan-I-Ghayb, owned by Virginia and Edwin Paige.

The foundation of Marjorie's Majara kennels was also drawn to a degree from the Dunrobin bloodlines of Rudolph and Harriet Engle. The Engles were deeply involved with their Afghan Hounds in the early days, and their Zombie of Dunrobin was a mascot of the U.S. Coast Guard during the war. Harriet Engle was also a judge of the breed until her death in 1958.

RUTH TONGREN AND BEN GHAZI

Ruth H. Thom, later Mrs. Robert Tongren, made her first appearance in the breed with her Ch. Five Miles Punjab ben ghaZi in the 1940's. Punjab was a gift from a friend

Lovely windblown headstudy of Ch. Majara Marfu, owned by Mrs. Donald Patterson of Mission, Kansas.

Ch. Khalife of Grandeur, owned by John Collette and bred by Sunny Shay. This Best In Show winner was sired by Jui Pathan *ex* Zari of Grandeur.

Ch. Kaftan Khan of Grandeur is the sire of Ch. Kai of Grandeur, Ch. Kaftan Korrigan and the Best In Show-winning Am. and Ber. Ch. Kai's Turkhan of Grandeur. He is owned by Carol Esterkin, Kaftan Kennels, Tarzana, California.

Ch. Shirkhan of Grandeur is shown here winning another Best In Show, this time at the important Beverly Riviera show in May, 1957 under judge Leo Murphy. Shirkhan was always owner-breeder-handled by Sunny Shay, and at this time was co-owned with Dorothy Chenade of Hicksville, Long Island, New York.

One of the great bitches in the breed. . . Ch. ben-ghaZi's Apryl, bred and owned by Ruth "Babbi" Tongren of Bloomfield, Connecticut.

Khabira Omar, photographed in 1971 by his owner, Jennifer Sheldon of Massapequa, New York. The sire was Ch. Sarkhan of Kharysthan.

named George, he had just inherited a fortune and took her to see a litter of puppies in Darien, Connecticut. It turned out to be the Five Mile Kennels and a litter sired by Rudiki, bred by Marion Florsheim!

Babbi, as she was called, was given her choice and Punjab went with her and her daughter to California to live. It was while living in California that Babbi got hooked on dog shows and has been at it ever since.

As a complete novice at her first show, Babbi took Punjab in the ring on a piece of clothesline, made every mistake in the book, but still came home with the Breed! The judge that recognized the quality of the dog was Dr. William Ivens, owner of the Holiday House Kennels where he bred Poodles and Afghan Hounds over the years. "Punk," as Babbi called him, finished his championship in 1951.

Next came Kurki and Karli ben ghaZi, sired by Punjab. He was featured in a photograph with Babbi in a 1950's issue of *National Geographic* about dogs and dog shows. Karli finished his championship in 1952 and was co-owned by her with her mother, Josephine Baird. He was the only Afghan Hound to win the parent club specialty from the classes.

Ch. Kurki ben ghaZi, owned by Ruth Tongren.

The famous Ch. Karli ben ghaZi, owned by Ruth Tongren of Connecticut. Karli was a top-winning show dog in the 1950's.

This he did in 1952 under judge Alex Scott. In 1955 he won the show again under judge Dr. Eugene Beck and went on to win the Potomac Afghan Hound Club Specialty show the same year under Mrs. M.C. Gibson. Karli is also one of the top-producing sires in the history of the breed with fourteen champions to his credit.

During the second half of the 1950's Babbi was to find additional success in the show ring with her Ch. Crown Crest Rubi. Rubi became a champion in 1956. He was a gorgeous red dog, bred by Kay Finch, sired by her imported Ch. Ophaal of Crown Crest ex Ch. Crown Crest Tae-Joan. Rubi was Best of Winners under judge Teddy Hays at the 1956 Afghan Hound Club of America Show to start his ring career, and won the Tara Afghan Hound Club Specialty that same year under judge Percy Roberts.

The Robert Tongrens have bred many champions and winners over the years, including the magnificent ben ghaZi Apryl. Apryl was featured in full-color in *Life Magazine* in an article on dog racing, draped around Guy Tongren's neck. She was always one of Babbi's favorites, and, fortunately, was saved when their house caught on fire in March, 1975.

Babbie Tongren and Ch. Kurki ben-ghaZi photographed many years ago for an article about dogs by *National Geographic* magazine.

Now, the Tongrens concentrate on their judging assignments, with Babbi doing some writing again for the leading dog magazines.

THE DEWEY ABRAMS AND DUREIGH

While shopping around for a Boxer, Reigh Abram saw her first Afghan Hound and was sold on the breed. After much inquiry, she was advised to consult with Marion Foster Florsheim. It was during the Rudiki heyday and Reigh and Dewey Abram purchased a five-months old brindle daughter of that famous sire. Her name was Tachi.

They next purchased an older bitch and bred her when it became clear Tachi would not be a show dog. The five puppies from this litter were not what they had hoped for either, but, by a strange quirk of fate two years later, Marion Florsheim offered them a 2¼ year old daughter of Rudiki. The bitch was out of his sister, Int. Ch. Shireen of Ainsdart, and a little on the small side, but with a gorgeous head of the exotic type that Mrs. Florsheim believed would produce well for them. Her name was Ch. Bey Bombey of Five Mile. She was the real start of Dureigh.

Their breeding program began in earnest. Ch. Dureigh Bey Abrama was bred to Turkuman Tar of Grandeur and gave them Ch. Dureigh Dark Victory. Ch. Dureigh Bey Bombey was bred to Ch. Keya Khan, whose

Ch. Dureigh's Dragon Shadow, owned by the Ron Kohls of Sykesville, Maryland. Shadow is sired by ben-ghaZi's Maracaibo *ex* Dragon Lady of Dureigh. Breeders were Dewey and Reigh Abram, Wellington, Ohio.

Ch. Dureigh's Song of the Dragon pictured winning Best of Breed at 10 years of age at the South Western Ohio Afghan Hound Club Specialty Show under judge Mary Nelson Stephenson. George Bruning presents the trophy to handler-owner Dewey Abram, Dureigh Afghans, Wellington, Ohio.

71

Ch. Kheiba of Tajmir, owned by the Soroya Kennels of Mr. and Mrs. E.F. Winter. Kheiba was bred by Patricia Sinden and sired by Ch. Karli ben ghaZi *ex* Ch. Crown Crest Khittiku, C.D. She is the dam of several champion get.

Hound Group winner at the 1944 Seneca Kennel Club show was Ch. Zabardasta of Arthea, owned and handled by Mrs. H.A. Brothers of Ohio.

A Best In Show win for Charles Costabile's Ch. Khanhasset's Kanda under judge Lewis G. Spence at the 1946 Brazos Valley Kennel Club Show. Emory Wolfe, handler, is shown with Judge Spence and Dean Charles N. Shepardson, who is presenting the trophy.

ben ghaZi's Invicta, owned by Douglas W. Troll of Wilmington, Delaware. Shafer photograph.

Ch. Winston's Windsong of Dureigh, owned by Dewey and Reigh Abram, Dureigh Afghans, Wellington, Ohio. His sire was Dureigh's Swan Son and dam was Dragon Lady of Dureigh. This photograph was taken in June of 1968.

Stud Dog Class winner at a recent South Western Ohio Afghan Hound Club Specialty Show was Ch. Dureigh's Song of the Dragon with his get Ch. Dureigh's Rajah-ett of Ebonwood, Ch. Kush of the East, Ch. Dureigh's Lady Lisa and Bad Penny of Dureigh. Owners Dewey and Reigh Abram are pictured on either side of judge Mary Nelson Stephenson.

background went back to Asri-Havid of Five Mile. It was these two lines that the Abrams tried to carry on.

The Abrams' top-winning dogs have included Dureigh Swan Song, Dureigh Dragon Lady, Dureigh Golden Harvest, to name just a few, as well as Ch. Hill Banks Hazizi of Dureigh and Ch. Haru and High and Mighty. Dewey and Reigh have made their mark in the breed over the decades and continue their keen interest in breed activities and get great pleasure out of watching the steady progression of quality that bears the kennel name of Dureigh.

PAT IDE AND HUZZAH

Pat Ide was lucky enough to own a Ch. Rajah of Arken daughter as her first Afghan Hound. Purchased out of a newspaper, sight unseen, Pat bought Lazy T's Shomi el Merrylane, a black-masked red. Afghans were still rare in those days and at her first show she won Best of Breed over another entry. Pat wanted company for Shomi and bought Kashmir Kahn of Crown Crest, an oyster-color brindle sired by Ch. Felt's Allah Baba out of Ch. Egypt's Echo of Crown Crest.

At this time, Pat had a modeling career and was a serious student of the piano, so had little time for showing and kennel club work, though she was a member of the Del Monte club. Even so, Kahsi managed to garner some group placings and Bests of Breed on the show trail. When Pat went to Japan, she took Kashi with her. Though she has been told she earned her Japanese championship, it was never confirmed—though time and again a Japanese man would place garlands of flowers around Kashi's neck which Pat believes must have counted for something!

After Japan, Pat enrolled in college and there met and married Don Ide. When Shomi died of old age, they got Crown Crest Bhotar, sired by Ophaal out of Kashi's dam. Bhotar was a racing dog, however, and was defeated only once in a year and a half on the track. He was later killed by a car while chasing a cat.

The Ide's also owned Ch. Crown Crest Valentino, a son of Bongo Bongo and Crown Crest Taejamaya. He had a career of Bests of Breed and Group Placements from the classes. Tino lived to a ripe old age. The Ides purchased Red Rock Duhst, C.D., as a brood bitch. She was a result of Ophaal, Taejon, Zardonx, Rreks and vdOM bloodlines and had elegance and type which she passed on to

Ch. Demon-ben-Hajji of Grandeur, owned by the Farleys of Kearney, Nebraska.

Gary Anderson with Can. Ch. Oranje Anisette and Nightwatch v Onika, and Jan Priddy with the cats Kanga and Rabbit. Jan and Gary are co-owners of the Volant Hounds, Seattle, Washington.

Best In Show for Ch. Rajah of Arken, owned by Mr. Charles Wernsman, at the 1942 North Westchester Kennel Club Show held at Katonah, New York. The judge was Dr. Howard W. Church; the handler was Mrs. Margaret C. Holmes. Percy Jones photograph.

her progeny. She was a daughter of Crown Crest Red Rock Luv, C.D.X., owned by Barbara Keeler.

Pat makes no bones about her gratitude for the help and friendship of Kay Finch. For more than twenty years she has been a shining example to Pat in her kennel pursuits.

THE JOHN BUCHANANS AND DESERTAIRE

The John Buchanans were in other breeds when they got into Afghan Hounds in the 1940's. John and Ruby owned the Desertaire Kennels nestled in the foothills of the San Bernadino Mountains of California. During the forties, their English Champion Wazir of Desertaire was well known but their association with Kay Finch was what led them to their first Afghan Hound. It was 1947 when they acquired a cream bitch, Crown Crest Zazu. In 1948 they got Ch. Egypts Eudora of Crown Crest.

During the years they were involved in the breed, only three litters were whelped at their kennel, using studs such as Taejon and Mr. Universe, who produced well for them. Their 1959 litter by "Mr. U" produced four black-masked silver puppies which at nine months of age won Best In Show Team at the

Three generations of champion breeding from the Stormhill Kennels of Virginia and Sandy Withington, Pasadena, California. Pictured are Ch. Stormhill Silver Dream (Ch. Taejon of Crown Crest *ex* Ch. Kandorissa of Aldachar), Ch. Stormhill San-Dahl (Ch. Stormhill Silver Dream *ex* Ahshu of Aldachar), and Ch. Pandora of Stormhill (Ch. Shirkhan of Grandeur *ex* Ch. Stormhill San-Dhal).

Harbor Cities Kennel Club Show. This litter also produced the aforementioned Wazir that was owned by the Les Bridges in England. Out of Ch. Zar-Kari of Shamalan, Wazir was the top sire in Britain for 1964 and was sire of English Ch. Bondors Serenade, top-winning Afghan Hound in England, 1964-65.

The Buchanans were both members of the Afghan Hound Club of California for many years and John served as its president for four years during the sixties. Ruby was a V.P. for one year and also served on the Board. Ch. Bascha also appeared in the movie *"It's A Dog's Life"* and on programs with Frank Sinatra and Art Linkletter.

MURIEL STONE

Muriel Stone acquired her first Afghan Hound in 1942. It was the start of her Timbala Kennels in Massachusetts, and, from that day forward, it seemed as if few things in the world mattered more than her pursuit of happiness within the breed. Pert Muriel could always be counted on for pleasant conversation about dogs, because there wasn't a mean bone in her body. She was soft spoken and could always find a good word to say about other people's dogs as well as her own.

Muriel was a founding member of the Colonial Afghan Hound Club and was active in it and on the Board of Directors over the years preceding her death in 1973. Perhaps her most famous dog was Ch. Amir Kazan of Timbala, but she played no favorites at home. Timbala's Dracula of Shahan, Caliph of Timbala, Turkomen of Timbala and Timbalas Jambala of Grandeur were equally loved and admired by her.

A Britisher by birth, Muriel married a Canadian and after travels with him through several countries of the world they settled in Massachusetts and saw the eventual beginning of her small kennel, where the number of dogs, or litters bred, were not allowed to exceed their ability to give each and every one of them her individual love and attention. Muriel didn't show her own dogs but could always be found at ringside with a cluster of friends enjoying the show—whether she had one of her own dogs there or was merely rooting for another!

ELIZABETH HARVEY TREHARNE AND ROBECLI

Elizabeth Harvey Treharne has owned Afghan Hounds since 1943. Her first Afghan

Famous show-winning trio representing the Summerwine Kennels of Sharon and Monroe Jackson of Dallas, Texas. Left to right, Ch. Summerwine's Lela of Kashmiri, Ch. Summerwine's Cuba Libra, and Ch. Summerwine's Pisco Punch. Cuba Libra and Pisco Punch are both Specialty Best of Breed winners and Pisco is a multiple Group winner as well.

"A precious gem in a tiny package. . ." Ch. Baroda of Milapat was the first of a long line of Afghan Hounds owned by artist Elizabeth Harvey Treharne of New Jersey. Baroda was bred by Mildred Paterson. Brown photograph.

Bakali Black Label, bred and owned by G. Cumberland, is a foundation bitch at the Bakali Kennels in Owings Mills, Maryland.

Hound was Ch. Baroda Gem of Milapat, bred by Mildred Patterson of the Milapet Kennels in Maryland. She was a linebred grand-daughter of the famous Ch. Rudiki of Prides Hill. The sire was Ch. Far Away Kub-i-Bes-man, out of a rich red bitch named Marion.

Gem was 17 years of age when she died. She finished for her championship in June, 1945. The well-known breeder-judge who put Gem up at the show the day she finished her championship said, "Too bad such a precious jewel comes in such a small package." Gem was only 24 inches at the shoulder. She was a silver with smoke boots.

Betty is written about in our chapter on the Afghan Hound in Art, since she has been painting the Afghan Hound down through the years. She also produces a complete line of dog stationery and paintings on glass. By the middle of the 1970's Betty and her entire family are still devoted to the breed, and daughter Betsy especially excels as a handler with the dogs from their kennel.

VIRGINIA BURCH AND EL KEVIR

Virginia Burch got her first Afghan Hound right after she was married. Her hus-band wanted a Boxer and she wanted a Dal-mation, but they were offered an Afghan Hound free and they took it! Other Afghan Hounds followed, and in 1954 she bred her first litter from their bitch, Bathsheba. The Burch's most prominent dog, however, was Ch. Caliph el Kevir, whelped in September of 1949. He won a major at his first show under Cy Rickel at the July, 1951 Santa Barbara show when he was 22 months old. He finished in November, 1952. He was descended from two of the fastest racing dogs in England, Ch. Taj Akbar of Chaman and Ch. Garrymhor Faiz-Bu Hassid; he sired three champions.

THE TOWNSENDS AND JANDA

Dan and Jean Townsend got their first Afghan Hound in 1945. The dog was Ala Ba-ba of Dellire, and they got him from Tilly Beyer. Their second was Maharani Maarjim, from Jean Zimmerman. A total of four litters were bred at Janda, and the Townsends have been active in the California clubs. Dan was President for two years and has been a Vice-President and Treasurer also, since his interest was mostly with the club's activities.

No longer active in the breed, the Town-sends have just one Afghan Hound at home, a

Ch. Jui of Grandeur, lovely blue bitch, was whelped in 1957 and was the first offspring of the renowned Ch. Shirkhan of Grandeur to finish to the championship title (in April, 1959). Jui was purchased by the Dale Henrys of Oklahoma.

twelve-year-old bitch named Suzy and a Shih Tzu. It was their friends, Bob and Tillie Bey-er, who got them interested in Afghan Hounds and club work and showed their Ch. Rudok el Encino during the years the Town-sends were active.

The forties also produced Betty Richard's Camri Kennels. Her Ch. Javelin of Camri, a lovely brindle, did his share of winning, and his son, Garlands Talisman of Camri, was ex-ported to England for the kennels of Miss Stephanie Hunt-Crowley.

Fanciers heard the names of Betsy Prior, who later became a judge of the breed, and of the late Esther Pinney, who passed on in Jan-uary, 1973.

It was also during the "fabulous forties" that Mr. and Mrs. Donald A. Smith acquired their first Afghan Hound. They got their bitch in 1947. In 1951 Don became Secretary-Trea-surer of the Afghan Hound Club of America and has been an active member ever since. From Secretary-Treasurer he moved up to the Presidency in 1955 and became President once again after a brief period of service by Alys Carlsen in 1960. Don then remained in the top position until Dorothy Macdonald was elected in 1967. Don has served on the Board and is currently a member of the Committee on Biological Defects.

THE FIFTIES

In 1950 Virginia Thomas' husband bought her her first Afghan Hound, Kandor-issa of Aldachar, from Mrs. Alice Bracher. Gini Withington finished Kandy for Virginia as Best of Opposite Sex to Taejon at an Orange County show in California in 1953.

Ch. Sashay el Sayyad, bred, owned and shown by Grace Beyer, Chatsworth, California. Daughter of the glorious Ch. Crown Crest Kabul, Sashay is shown here taking Winners Bitch honors under judge Kay Finch on the way to her championship.

Shortly thereafter she was bred to "Johnny" and from this litter of eight Gini Withington got her famous Ch. Stormhill Silver Dream. Also in this litter was Faith, owned by the Ted Mikas, Hope, which became one of Kay Finch's top bitches, and Candace, owned by Mr. and Mrs. Lou Blix. All produced show-winning offspring. "Kandy" produced another litter by Ch. Delhi Downs Duirke el Sayyad, but, unfortunately, the puppies did not go to show homes. Kandy died at the age of fourteen.

THE BEYERS AND EL SAYYAD

In 1950 Bob and Tillie Beyer gave Grace Beyer an Afghan Hound as a gift. The 3½ month old puppy grew up to be Ch. Melek el Sayyad and was the first of several champions at Grace and Glenn Beyer's el Sayyad Kennels.

Grace joined the Afghan Hound Club of America in 1952 and in 1953 Grace and Glenn joined the Afghan Hound Club of California, having moved to that state from Detroit. Both the Beyers were very active in the club and only an illness a little later on

curtailed their breeding plans a few years. In the 1960's Grace became active once again, and in 1964 was elected the first woman president of the Afghan Hound Club of California.

Grace's best known Afghan Hound bitch was Ch. Sashay el Sayyad. Sired by Ch. Crown Crest Kabul ex Tangye el Sayyad, she rules the kennel. She was the top-winning bitch on the West Coast for 1961. Other el Sayyad Afghan Hounds were Carousel, Mexican and American Ch. Sarder el Sayyad, Ch. DelhiDowns Duirke el Sayyad, Ch. Donna-Shmain (sired by Ch. Akaba's Top Brass), Solo and a bitch named Charade, bred by Virginia Thomas who brought to el Sayyad the bloodlines of Duirke, Kandorissa and Shirkhan of Grandeur.

Outside the dog fancy, Grace has also served twice as President and Parlimentarian of the Chatsworth Woman's Club. Glenn is an engineer at Lockheed Aircraft and they live in Hidden Hills in the Calabasas area of California. Grace is also a judge of Afghan Hounds and owns and operates The Poodle Palace, a grooming shop for Poodles which

Grace Beyer and her beautiful bitch, Ch. Sashay el Sayyad, a top-winning bitch on the West Coast in 1961. She is pictured winning under breeder-judge Gini Withington at a California show.

she opened in 1958 after buying their first Poodle as a playmate for Melek.

THE WITHINGTONS AND STORMHILL

One of the most active and "winningest" kennels in the breed today is Stormhill, owned by Gini Withington in Pasadena, California. Started in 1952, Gini owned and trained the first Afghan Hound to obtain a Utility Dog degree in the U.S.A. Koh-I-Baba was his name and he was a "famous first" for all those who really believed that a dog with a mind of its own could really be trained to a degree!

Other honors won by Stormhill were their three all-breed Best In Show winners, five Specialty Show winners, and the 1964 Top Afghan Hound in the U.S.A. This was their brindle bitch, American and Mexican Ch. Pandora of Stormhill, sired by the great Ch. Shirkhan of Grandeur. Whelped December 29, 1960, she was a mahogany brindle out of Ch. Stormhill San-Dhal and produced thirteen champions before her death in October, 1972.

Gini and William Withington were in-

The Group and Specialty-winning Ch. Majestic Knight of Stormhill, bred and owned by Virginia and Sandy Withington, Stormhill Kennels, Pasadena, California. The sire was Ch. Mecca's Zeus *ex* Ch. Pandora's Xotica of Stormhill. Photo by Joan Ludwig.

A classic photo of "die-hard dog show enthusiasts!" Even the torrential rain didn't prevent owner Gini Withington from racking up another win for her top bitch, Ch. Pandora of Stormhill, at the 1964 Glendale, California, show! Even the camera lens of famous dog photographer Joan Ludwig got spotted! This photo is one of her favorites, also.

Ch. Smoke Dream of Stormhill, the beautiful brindle owned by Joe and Rosemarie Crandahl, Aryan Afghan Hounds, Livonia, Michigan. Mrs. Crandahl handles Smoke Dream to this 1965 Genesee Valley Kennel Club Best In Show win.

strumental in the formation of the first racing and coursing clubs in California; recently their daughter Sandy has gained much attention as the co-owner of Stormhill and as its handler. Trained in Junior Showmanship, she has shown many winners to their championships and is a distinct asset to the breed and the fancy. She also has judged many Match Shows and Sweepstakes all over the country.

Gini is still breeding Afghan Hounds of great quality, has exported them to foreign countries and has judged all over the world since 1959. Like many of the other kennels of long standing, the list of Stormhill champions

Ch. Kubar of Stormhill, owned and shown by Gini Withington in California.

and show winners is too long to be included, but it was Ch. Stormhill Silver Dream that launched their fame in the fifties, the great Pandora climbing the ladder of success in the sixties and Ch. Majestic Knight of Stormhill carrying on in the seventies!

Gini trained and showed a friend's Afghan Hound in 1947. This bitch was Shelgrove Drissa, who, when bred to Ch. Kandika's Kanda, produced Ch. Koh-I-Baba, U.D. When she married Bill, she joined the Stormhill Kennels, also, which had been active in German Shepherds during the 1940's.

THE GUTHRIES AND CHARIKAR

Richard and Georgiana Guthrie have been in Afghan Hounds for many years and have always had a keen interest in both exhibiting and racing their dogs. Members of the earliest West Coast racing clubs and responsible for their success and advances, the Guthries have been known for their fine dogs and have bred them as well. Most outstanding was their blue domino male, American, Canadian and Mexican Ch. Charikar Dominator Joh-Cyn, whelped in January, 1961. The sire of two champions, he traced his ancestry back to the von de Oranje Manege line on his dam's side. Unfortunately, he died in November, 1964.

Georgiana is an Afghan Hound judge and, when not fulfilling judging assignments, still exhibits Afghan Hounds, including a lovely domino she was campaigning in the 1970's, Charikar Rou-Dom Warrior. Her association with the Afghan Hound goes back many years, back to her school days when she was friendly with a girl named Jenny McKean, who told her stories about the strange dogs her father was raising in Massachusetts. Her father was the famous Q.A. Shaw McKean! Georgiana looked up the Afghan Hounds at the dog shows and was fascinated.

In later years, Georgiana became "spellbound" by Ch. Taejon of Crown Crest, and determined to have a puppy of his. In 1954 they bought a red daughter of his and named her Tamerlane of Charikar. Their second was El Kevir's Pheasant, and she became their first champion. This Ch. Crown Crest Taejallah daughter was bred to Tamerlane and produced a litter, one puppy of which Dick finished to a C.D. title and another puppy became American and Mexican Ch. Charikar Pavane. Still staying with the Taejon line, their next purchase was to become their Group-winning American and Mexican Ch. Stormhill Szum Czarny—the principal stud at their Charikar Kennels.

When Roland Muller brought the black and tan Swedika Joh-Cyn to California, it changed their thinking and their breeding. She was a daughter of the two top-winning Afghan Hounds in Europe, Int. Ch. Tanjores Domino and Int. Ch. Tajamahal Kenya, who have eleven championship titles between them. In March of 1961 the Guthries obtained a silver blue puppy which they named Charikar Dominator Joh-Cyn. He was a domino, having a dark widow's peak, and

Ch. Cammar's Pa'Yunga of Grandeur in an unretouched photograph taken by owner Bobbie Caminez, Cammar Kennels, Sherman Oaks, California.

finished in less than five months with major wins and Bests of Breed along the way. He earned championships in Mexico and Canada as well.

Tragedy struck as he was reaching the peak of his career, and he, along with his kennel mates Czarny and another bitch, died at the hands of a poisoner. Fortunately, they saved a young son, Charikar Wazir, and two daughters, Lebwa and Yasmin.

BARBARA MARCUS AND CAMMAR

Barbara Caminez Marcus became interested in Afghan Hounds when she saw Sunny Shay's Kaftan competing in a 1950 Harbor Cities California dog show. In 1956 Sunny brought Shirkhan to California to show at a specialty and Barbara's interests once again soared. Sunny sent her Ch. Cammar's Pa-'Yunga of Grandeur, who did a lot of winning with Frank Sabella during the six years before he was killed by a car. He arrived in 1959.

In July, 1965 her husband Frank saw to it that Bobbi got another Afghan Hound. It was Ch. High Ho's Moon Majesty O'Bahara, which she co-owned with Bettye Kirksey Scott. "Sully" was a Shirkhan grandson and a son of Bud Stephenson's Ch. Patrician's Sherwood.

Barbara's kennel name is Cammar, the same signature she uses when taking professional photographs at the dog shows—many of which are included in this book.

PAT SINDEN WALLIS AND TAJMIR

Pat Sinden Wallis has been active in the breed since the 1950's and has come up with several top-winners over the years. Basing her Tajmir Kennels on a foundation bitch from Kay Finch, her Ch. Crown Crest Jasmine, Can. and Am. C.D, was bred to Ch. Hassen-Ben of Moornistan and produced one of the Top Ten Afghan Hounds in the country. His name was Ch. Tajmir's Redstone Rocket.

Ch. Tajmir Bhi-Jhupiter, black-masked apricot son of the famous Ch. Karli ben ghaZi *ex* Ch. Crown Crest Khittiku, C.D. Jupiter is shown here before his championship winning the local Hound Group at 16 months with handler Bill Irwin. He was bred and owned by Patricia Sinden, Tajmir Kennels, Chicago, Illinois. This win was under famous Irish Setter man Jack Spear.

Rocket won the parent club Specialty show in 1964 under judge Mrs. Hayes Hoyt. In 1963 he was not only top Group-winning Afghan Hound but ranked among the Top Five of all Hound Group winners. He was co-owned by Pat and Joan Fantl.

Some of Pat's other top winners were Best In Show American and Canadian Ch. Tajmir Bhi-Jhupiter, C.D., Best In Show Ch. Tajmir Khachmi and Ch. Tajmir Titan.

WILLIAM MOORE III
AND MOORNISTAN

Bill Moore got his first Afghan Hound in Europe. When he was in Berlin, Germany, in 1948 he attended dog shows there and got to know some Afghan Hound fanciers. In 1950 he purchased Djadji von Faulkenwald and brought her back to the United States with him.

Bill got to know Marjorie Lathrop and went to the shows with her back in the early fifties, even though his German bitch was ineligible. Bill bred the bitch to Majara Mahabat and when it didn't take tried Mihrab. From this mating he got the litter that produced his Ch. Maymun of Moornistan. She became the dam of the #1 winning bitch, the Kauffman's Ch. Samaris of Moornistan, when bred to Ch. Zaamarakuri of Ghazni.

Bill also bred Maymun to Shirkhan and got Ch. Mirasia of Moornistan and Ch. Moonshyn of Moornistan, which his brother finished. Other Moornistan dogs from Bill's kennel were Ch. Hassan-Ben, Ch. Amos, Ch. Monterey and Tangerine, to name just a few winners.

Bill Moore, a member of the Board of Directors of the Afghan Hound Club of America, is a dentist and resides in Pennsylvania. He looks forward to judging the breed at some time in the future.

Ch. Amos of Moornistan winning Best of Breed at the 1965 Bucks County Kennel Club Show under the late and famous breeder-judge Marjorie Lathrop. Owned, bred and handled by Dr. William Moore III of Pennsylvania. Shafer photograph.

Ch. Moonshine of Moornistan, bred by Dr. William Moore of Pennsylvania. Moonshine was sired by the famous Ch. Shirkhan of Grandeur and is the sire of a Best In Show dog, Ch. Holly Hill Draco, bred by Sue and Ned Kauffman.

THE WAINERS AND SHAMALAN

Richard and Shirley Wainer started their Shamalan Kennels in California in 1953 when they purchased their first brindle bitch, Khediviah of Shamalan. Although she was never finished to championship, many of her children and grandchildren made her proud of their ring careers.

"Shammy" was bred only once to Ch. Rudok el Encino, owned by Tillie Beyer, and whelped a litter of eight. Their home-bred Ch. Cha Cha Cha of Shamalan was their most famous dog, winning many Groups, a Specialty and an all-breed Best In Show. He won Stud Dog Class at the California specialties twice under the handling of Shirley Wainer and is the sire of several champions and show winners.

KAREN ARMISTEAD AND KAJA

In 1953 an East Coast Afghan Hound fancier became entranced with the breed. Karen and her husband Julian Armistead of Brooklyn, New York, fell in love with their first Afghan Hound, Ch. Modessegh of Karikal.

Few people in the breed can surpass Karen's great love and devotion to the breed and her concentration on the black Afghan Hounds. Her Ch. Kora produced Ch. Kora's King David, which in turn produced Ch. Kaja's Silky Boy, which in turn produced Caroline of Kalizma. This was a strong line of

Ch. Kaja's King Tut, photographed on the day he finished his championship. This lovely black was handled by Karen Armistead and is co-owned by her with Selma Tenenbaum of Brooklyn, New York. Tut is one of the champion sons of Ch. Kora's King David.

The judge's top choice! Best In Show honors went to Richard and Shirley Wainer's Ch. Cha Cha Cha of Shamalan at the 1965 Toledo Kennel Club Show under judge Charles Krebs. Mrs. Wainer handled Cha Cha Cha to the win. Ritter photo.

A beautiful body shot of Ch. Pandora of Stormhill, the lovely brindle bitch bred and owned by Gini Withington of Calfornia. Pan, as she was called, is one of the top-winning bitches in the history of the breed, and was sired by the great Ch. Shirkhan of Grandeur.

Ch. Modessegh of Karikal.

quality black Afghan Hounds—all champions and all bearing a strong resemblance, the hallmark of good breeding! David also sired Ch. Kaja's King Tut and, by a different dam, Ch. Kaftan of Taejalong, owned by Martha

Ryan and bred by Fred Fauler, Jr. This dog captured Best Puppy at the 1966 Afghan Hound Club of America Specialty Show. David's daughter Naja of Taejalon was first in puppy bitch class.

Karen is very active in the parent club and is one of the authors of the club's pamphlet entitled *Introduction to the Afghan Hound.*

THE JENSENS AND PAMIR

In 1953 Donald and Georgjean Jensen started their Pamir Afghan Hound Kennels in Bonita, California. In the ensuing years Pamir produced over thirty champions, including three generations of Best In Show winning males. In 1970 their Ch. Pamir Ho Chester was top winning owner-breeder-handled Afghan Hound in the U.S.

Some of their best known dogs were Ch. Pamir Storm Ho, Ch. Pamir Marco, American, Canadian and Mexican Ch. Pamir Ho

Ch. Kaja's Caroline of Kalizma, co-owned by Karen Armistead and Elise Abraham, was Best of Winners at the 1973 Afghan Hound Club of America Show and is pictured here winning under Anna Katherine Nicholas at the 1973 Long Island Kennel Club Show.

Ch. Jamica's Rani Fafnir, a black and tan owned by Mrs. Cheever Porter of New York City, is pictured winning the Hound Group at the 1977 Hartford Kennel Club Show under judge William Kendrick. Jane Forsyth handled.

Moornistan's Monterrey and friend relax on the greens of the Pebble Beach Golf Course in California. Monterrey was bred by Dr. William Moore, III, of Elverson, Pennsylvania and later sold and shown in California in the early 1960's. Photo by Julian P. Graham.

Akaba's Gi Gi in White was photographed at 14 months of age at owner Lois Boardman's kennels in Woodland Hills, California. Gi Gi, when bred to the famous Ch. Shirkhan of Grandeur produced many champions which bore the best qualities of both of them!

Chester, and more recently, American, Canadian and Mexican Ch. Pamir Sweet William. To produce dogs of this quality it was necessary to have top brood bitches, as well. These were Ch. Patrician Victoria, dam of eight champions (six in one litter), Ch. Pamir Sali, dam of six champions, and Ch. Kabul's Carol of Patrician, dam of five champions.

ROBERT C. COTES

During the mid-1950's when Bob Cotes was just 17 years old he became the winner of the nation-wide Gaines Research Center's Youth Award. He was named "Boy Show Dog Fancier of the Year." A one hundred dollar cash award was given along with a citation which read: "Robert C. Cotes, 17, of Salinas, California, received the title 'Boy Show Dog Fancier of the Year' for his all-round interest in breeding, showing and kennel management. He showed his Afghan Hound to her championship, raised a litter and has five points on a young male. To gain experience he worked as a kennel boy at a cocker and a Poodle kennel, grooming, conditioning and showing dogs for other owners. As Secretary of the Monterey County Dog Breeder's Association, he is active in an official capacity at shows, is establishing his own kennel and works as kennel manager and assistant in surgery at a veterinary hospital."

Bob was also a member of the Northern California Afghan Hound Club. The bitch he finished to championship was Ch. Crown Crest Khayti, and the litter he raised which was mentioned in the citation was sired by Ch. Taejon of Crown Crest. Another victory for Bob was when he entered his dog, Crown Crest Bhoti, at an Oakland, California, show shortly after his Gaines award and won Best Junior Showman in Show.

THE KAUFFMANS AND HOLLY HILL

Sue Kauffman saw her first Afghan Hound shortly after she married Ned. She thought the dog was the weirdest thing she ever saw. She says she decided she was going to get one and did!

The first was purchased from Eunice Clark's Hughcliffe Kennels in 1953 or 1954, they aren't sure which. The dog was not a winner. When they got tired of making points for everyone else they bought another Afghan Hound. This time they bought from William Moore a bitch named Samaris, who turned out to be the top-producing bitch in the history of the breed to date with nineteen champions to her credit. They were always pleased that they took the judgement of Louise Snyder and Bill Moore and took Samaris instead of the black-masked cream, Laloome, which was also for sale. With the help of Samaris, Holly Hill produced over fifty champions in the next years. In 1958 she was the top-winning bitch in the country. She won five Group Firsts with handler Tom Crowe and both of the Kauffmans. One of her daughters, Indus, produced fifteen champions.

An important Best In Show win for Ch. Pamir Storm Ho, owned by Mary Evelyn James of Jefferson City, Tennessee. This win was under judge Dr. Frank Porter Miller at the 1961 Meridian Kennel Club Show. Handled for owner by Frank Richmond.

The Kauffmans think their success was based on the fact that Sue bred the dogs as a hobby to get what she wanted, and not as an ego trip. Ned liked the dogs and the game as a sport. Sue did the training, and Ned did the showing.

In 1963 the Kauffmans turned to judging, not just Afghan Hounds but many breeds. They have since sold Holly Hill and "retired" to Florida in 1968. For the record, Samaris was born February 14, 1957 and died in December, 1971. Her sire was Ch. Zaamarakuro of Ghazni and her dam Ch. Maymun of Moornistan. She was purchased from her breeder, Dr. William Moore III, at five months of age for two hundred and fifty dollars. She was not only top producing

Ch. Khabiri of Grandeur is pictured winning Best In Show at the 1962 Lackawanna Kennel Club Show. Owned by Jennifer and Werner Sheldon and handled by Jennifer Sheldon, this magnificent show dog was the foundation of their Khabira Kennels.

Ch. Mandith Salute was photographed after winning Best In Show at the 1970 Augusta Kennel Club Show under judge J.J. Duncan. Presenting the trophy is Mrs. Ruth Jaquer. Salute is owned by the Mandith Kennels and handled by Michele Leathers. Earl Graham photo.

Afghan Hound, but also a top record holder of all-hound breeds. Her best known son, Ch. Holly Hill Desert Wind, holds the record as the top-winning Afghan Hound in the history of the breed.

THE SHELDONS AND KHABIRA

Mary and Werner Sheldon began showing Afghan Hounds in 1955. There first great dog was Ch. Khabiri of Grandeur, one of the greatest showmen in the breed and a Best In Show winner, handled by their young daughter Jennifer. It was with this shiny black dog that Jennifer won Junior Showmanship honors at Westminster. She was their handler from 1960 until the time of her marriage.

The Sheldons have bred several litters over the years and have finished several champions, among them, Ch. Shahti Ben Kajar, their first champion, followed by Khabiri, from whom they adapted their kennel name to Khabira, and Ch. Khabira Khan, Shady Lady, Laurel Ridge Khalib, Ch. Khabira Blue, Ch. Sharkhan of Kharysthan and Khabira Midhi.

Werner is also a judge and has officiated at shows all over the country.

It must also be noted that it was the Sheldon's Ch. Khabiri of Grandeur that sired Ch. Holly Hill Desert Wind, the #1 winning dog in the history of the breed.

PAT LEARY AND LALA ROOKH

It was also during the mid-fifties when there was another outstanding Junior Handler in the breed. Pat Leary won the competition at the Westminster Show with her Ch. Lala Rookh of Estioc, and also won the parent club Specialty in 1956 with Lala under judge Teddy Hays. The Thomas O'Connors were the breeders of the black and tan bitch, and they bred several other champions at their Estioc Kennels in New Jersey during this period.

CHARAJ KENNELS

Robert Stein of Dayton, Ohio, established his Charaj Kennels in 1955 with Ch. Estioc El Noumahal as his foundation bitch. Sired by the famous Ch. Karli ben ghaZi out of a Ch. Majara Mahabat daughter, the subsequent breeding of Noumahal to Ch. Majara Menelek started Charaj on its way to fame in the Afghan Hound fancy.

Noumahal's first and only litter of seven

produced four champions including the Group-winning bitch, Ch. Charaj El Sheba. Many other successful champions were to follow from both Dureigh and Grandeur breedings; they were shown during the 1950 and 1960's. The Stein's Charaj Prince Charles was bred from a mating of Akaba's Blackjack out of their obedience title-holding bitch, Ch. Charaj El Jasmine, C.D.

During the 1970's Robert Stein increased his participation in the breed with several judging assignments.

THE FELLTONS AND MANDITH

While the Felltons had been interested in the dog fancy since the 1930's, it was 1956 when they acquired their first Afghan Hound. Even though Longlesson Bard was given to them as a pet, he finished his championship and won the 1959 Tara Afghan Hound Club Specialty Show.

Ch. Longlesson Jason, Ch. Longlesson Ophelia, Ch. ben ghaZi Mandith Bagheera and Ch. Mandith Gladmore Paprika followed and formed the nucleus of their Mandith Kennels in Marietta, Georgia.

Breedings from this early stock produced many champions and show winners for the

This charming photograph of a girl and her dog was taken several years ago.

Hullabaloo's Gloryland is photographed in this impressive windblown pose at 18 months of age. Glory was Winners Bitch at the 1973 Tara Afghan Hound Club Specialty Show and was sired by Continental Maajah Mazara *ex* Ch. Hullabaloo Jalal Dixieland. She was bred and owned by Mrs. Earl M. Stites, Arlington, Texas.

Coastwind Yacova is pictured winning a major at the 1976 Sun Maid Kennel Club Show under judge Joan Brearley. Yacova, whelped in July, 1974, was sired by Coastwind Chinquapin *ex* Coastwind Escapade and is co-owned by Dr. and Mrs. Philip Haims and the Coastwind Kennels. Yacova has also captured major wins at the Northern California Afghan Hound Specialty and the Afghan Hound Club of Greater Denver shows.

Ch. Bakali As You Like It, bred and owned by G. Cumberland of Bakali Afghans. She is pictured going Winners Bitch at the 1974 Tara Afghan Hound Specialty Show under judge Ed Gilbert.

Ch. Charaj Shahbandar, bred and owned by Robert Stein, Charaj Kennels in Dayton, Ohio. The sire was Ch. Dureigh's Golden Harvest *ex* Ch. Charaj El Sheba. Whelped in 1961, he is the sire of one champion.

Another of the early Afghan Hounds, this one owned by D. and M. Ross Taylor of Wynnwood, Pennsylvania.

Two beautiful black and tan Afghan Hound puppies from Robert Stein's Charaj Kennels.

A beautiful photograph of Ch. Hullabaloo's Mardi Gras owned by Trill and Dotti Torrilhon. Mardi Gras is a Breed, Group and Specialty Show winner and is pictured here at 18 months of age. Bred by Betty and Earl Stites, he was Best of Breed at the 1974 Afghan Hound Club of Greater Chicago Specialty Show.

Felltons, including Ch. Mandith Salute and Ch. Dahnwood Gabriel—both Group and Best In Show winners. Gabriel ended his career with the honor of being the sixth ranking winner in the history of the breed to date. Sire of 11 champions, he had fourteen Bests In Show, forty-six Group Firsts, and three Specialty Bests. It was 1968 when he won the Afghan Hound Club of America Specialty under judge Cy Rickel. His sire was Ch. Crown Crest Zardonx ex El Amron Tarquin.

The Felltons are both judges of several breeds and active in parent and local club work. Judith has served as President of the parent club and Herman as President of the Doberman Pinscher Club of America. He also wrote the breed column for the *American Kennel Gazette* for several years.

THE EARL STITES AND HULLABALOO

Betty and Earl M. Stites have lived in Arlington, Texas, since 1972, but they resided in California in the days when they first became interested in the breed. This was in 1956 when they co-owned the black dog Ch. Crown Crest Bongo Bongo with Kay Finch. Earl became instrumental in getting racing and coursing started in northern California, and later in southern California by way of the Withingtons, in the early 1960's.

Never breeders on a large scale, the Stites were content to breed only when they were ready to exhibit another dog. While they were especially pleased with Bongo's two Group wins, being their first champion, during the 1970's they were particularly proud of their Ch. Hullabaloo's Mardi Gras, owned by Trill and Dotti Torrilhon, because he is a Group and Specialty Best In Show winner. Their Ch. Hullabaloo Jalal Dixieland, dam of Mardi Gras, is their outstanding brood bitch. More recently, their Ch. Hullabaloo Bourbon Street started her career as Winners Bitch at the 1970 Northern California Afghan Hound

Ch. Dahnwood Gabriel is pictured winning Best In Show at the 1969 Memphis Kennel Club Show under judge Dr. Rex Foster. The trophy is being presented by club president C.W. Flowers. Handling is Michele Leathers for owners Mr. and Mrs. Herman Fellton, Mandith Kennels, Atlanta, Georgia.

Club Specialty Show. She was also a winner of the Brood Bitch clas at the Dallas Specialty in 1972 and 1974.

It was in 1953 when, with the help of Wendell Howell of Whippet fame, the Stites introduced racing to the San Francisco Bay area. The Stites were in charge of the first annual sighthound races in 1963, held in conjunction with the Santa Barbara Kennel Club Show.

Earl has served as President of both the Afghan Hound Clubs in California and Chairman for the AHCC. Betty has been Secretary of both clubs and is currently Corresponding Secretary of the Afghan Hound Club of America.

Joan Brearley with Ch. Crown Crest Jesi Jhaimz, her first Afghan Hound. He was the first champion at her Sahadi Kennels and a sire of champions. His sire was Ch. Taejon of Crown Crest *ex* Ch. Breezealong of Kandabar.

JOAN BREARLEY AND SAHADI

I was sitting in the balcony of Madison Square Garden in 1955 when Ch. Taejon of Crown Crest won the Group at the Westminster Kennel Club show. I made a promise to myself that one day I would have a son of his that looked just like him. A letter and a deposit went off to Kay Finch immediately.

100

On July 20, 1955 a telegram from Kay announced the arrival of the Wild West litter —and Jesi Jhaimz! Jaimie, truly a small silver replica of Johnny, arrived along with Devi Kharrokit, who was going to the Curnyns in Massachusetts. I was breeding Poodles at the time and every last one of them adored Jaimie, also.

I also love black Afghan Hounds, and my next was a black purchased from Kay that was the only litter mate of Ch. Shirkhan of Grandeur. Her name was Kalli of Grandeur and she finished her championship almost simultaneously with Jaimie. Jaimie was never campaigned, however, since the day he finished his championship at the Garden, Shirkhan won Best In Show!

Around this same time Kay telephoned and said she had a bitch she believed would be the perfect foundation for my Sahadi Kennels. It was Crown Crest Khalifah, sired by the great Ophaal out of Tae-joan. I could not refuse this great opportunity and Khalifah was mine! Kay kept her until she was in whelp to Taejon and put half her championship points on her while we were waiting. On May 22, 1957 Khalifah arrived at Sahadi! We were inseperable from that moment on! Khalifah was one of the greatest things that ever happened to me.

Her seven Taejon puppies arrived on June 18th and Kay and I as co-breeders split the litter. Three carried the Crown Crest name and three carried my Sahadi name. The

The author's favorite head study of her beloved Ch. Crown Crest Khalifah, sired by Kay Finch's Int. Ch. Ophaal of Crown Crest ex Ch. Crown Crest Tae-joan. Whelped September 19, 1955, Khalifah died April 15, 1966. The constant companion of the author throughout her lifetime, the author dedicated her first book on the breed to Khalifah in tribute to her contribution to the breed as one of its top-producing bitches. Bred to Ch. Shirkhan of Grandeur, she is the dam of Ch. Sahadi Shikari, the #2 winning Afghan Hound in the history of the breed.

Ch. Sahadi Scaramouche, bred and owned by Joan Brearley, is pictured winning a 5-point major at the 1962 Afghan Hound Club of America Show by going Best of Winners. He came up from the Best Bred by Exhibitor class. Sire was Ch. Shirkhan of Grandeur ex Ch. Crown Crest Khalifah.

Opposite:
Sahadi Apache Geronimo wins Group First from the classes under judge Anna Katherine Nicholas at the 1965 Willimantic Kennel Club Show. Bred and owned by Joan Brearley, Sahadi Kennels, formerly in Englewood, New Jersey and now in Lakewood, New Jersey. The sire was Ch. Crown Crest Jesi Jhaimz ex Ch. Crown Crest Khalifah.

Ch. Crown Crest Khalifah (fourth from left) is pictured winning the Brood Bitch class with five of her ten champion get at the Afghan Hound Club of America Specialty Show in 1963 under judge Kay Finch. The incomparable Khalifah was also Best of Opposite Sex to her Best of Breed son, Ch. Sahadi Shikari (fifth from left) at this same show and was also winner of the Veteran Bitch class. Khalifah was the top-producing bitch in the breed in 1961 and one of the top fifteen in all breeds according to *Popular Dogs* magazine. Left to right are Ch. Sahadi Sessu, Ch. Sahadi Sinbad, Ch. Sahadi Scaramouche, the great lady herself, and Ch. Sahadi Shikari—all sired by Ch. Shirkhan of Grandeur. Far right is Ch. Sahadi Comanche Brave Eagle, a son sired by Ch. Crown Crest Jesi Jhaimz. This family portrait is a tribute to one of the top-producing bitches in the history of the breed.

seventh was Crown Crest Taejakbar Khan. Khan and the three I kept all became champions. These were Ch. Sahadi Sabrina, Ch. Sahadi Saan and Ch. Sahadi Sadruddin. Once back in condition after the puppies, I finished Khalifah to her championship and looked forward to her second litter sired by Ch. Shirkhan of Grandeur, the litter that was to make breed history. Nine puppies, three brindles and six blacks, were born on January 21, 1959. It produced the famous Ch. Sahadi Shikari, the #2 ranking Afghan Hound in the history of the breed. His show record is featured in our Chapter on the Top Ten Afghan Hounds, and I am truly proud of it, and grateful that he went to people like Dr. and Mrs. Earl Winter who loved him and campaigned him so well!

I am also proud to say that I know of no other breeder—in any breed—who has bred a Garden Group winner in their first home-bred litter!

I kept Ch. Sahadi Sinbad (Pirate was a Group dog also), Ch. Sahadi Scaramouche, and Ch. Sahadi Sequin, the only bitch in the litter, who was sold later to Nancy McCarthy. She already had Ch. Sahadi Sessu, and these two, which she finished to championship, were to be the foundation of her Kharontule Kennels. Ch. Sahadi Sessu was later to become a top-producing sire with ten champions to his credit.

The rest of the litter was sold to families who did not show, though Satan had half his points. I tried to buy them all back, but could not.

Ch. Sahadi Shikari is pictured winning another Best In Show under judge Marie Meyer, with Frank Sabella handling for owners Dr. and Mrs. Earl Winter of Oshkosh, Wisconsin. Actress June Lockhart presented the trophy.

Utopia's Samarian Masquerade was whelped in 1971 and had 9 points toward championship before her untimely death in November, 1976. This glorious Ch. Sahadi Sessu granddaughter was owned and loved by Mr. and Mrs. Mark Rosen of Boxford, Massachusetts.

A lovely headstudy of Ch. Sahadi Sadruddin, beautiful black-masked son of the famous Ch. Taejon of Crown Crest *ex* Ch. Crown Crest Khalifah. Owned and shown by Joan Brearley, Sahadi Kennels, and co-bred by her and Kay Finch. This photograph was taken in 1959 by Edmond Vianney.

Ch. Crown Crest Khalifah and her favorite Himalayan cat are shown in the library of the Sahadi Kennels with owner Joan Brearley. This informal photograph was taken in 1965.

Khalifah's third litter was by Ch. Jaimie, and her fourth by her Shirkhan son, Sinbad, and both litters produced champions, Group, Best In Show and Specialty winners.

Khalifah died in April, 1966. Around the same time I sold my home and kennel and moved to New York City briefly before going to Philadelphia for five years to be editor of *Popular Dogs* and to compile the Phillips System. In 1972 Sahadi moved to a rooftop apartment in New York City where I am once again concentrating on toy breeds, writing books about dogs, judging and accepting free lance assignments in all fields.

Pirate, my constant companion throughout life, died on April 6, 1973 at 14 years of age. I look forward to the day when Sahadi will own and breed Afghan Hounds once again.

HOUSE OF ORANJE

While Lila Stafford bred her first litter of Afghan Hounds in 1956, it wasn't until 1967 that she established her House of Oranje kennel in Scottsdale, Arizona to breed Afghan Hounds.

As the name implies, Lila Stafford's kennel was founded on breeding stock from Eta Pauptit's v d Oranje Manege Kennels in Holland. Lila imported four excellent v d O M bitches and also imported Dutch and International Ch. Xingu v d Oranje Manege to use as a sire for the bitches.

She owns International and Canadian Ch. Velica v d Oranje Manege, Canadian Champion Janine v d Oranje Manege, Int. Ch. Icarie v d Oranje Manege, Catrinka v d Oranje Manege, Oranje Vuurig Kasul and Oranje Meisje Miju.

Lila Stafford is seen at the shows on the West Coast and in her "native" Arizona, and was active in the publication of a Newsletter written by and for the disciples of Eva Pauptit's breeding and entitled *vdOMers*.

Like so many of us, Lila Stafford, when asked about her feelings for the breed, tells us that she cannot conceive of anything more beautiful—and awesome—than an Afghan Hound moving with the elegant grace and power that reveal its true purpose and heritage.

LOIS BOARDMAN AND AKABA

It was in 1957 that Lois Boardman got her first Afghan Hound. Mrs. Virginia Thomas gave Lois a bitch named Aijalon's Hearts

Ch. Sahadi Saan was another of the champions finished at Sahadi Kennels. The sire was Ch. Taejon of Crown Crest *ex* Ch. Crown Crest Khalifah. Co-breeders were Kay Finch and Joan Brearley, his owner-handler. This photograph was taken in 1959.

Ch. Sahadi Sinbad, one of the stud dogs at the author's Sahadi Kennels, is pictured here winning the Hound Group.

Canadian Champion Janine v d Oranje Manege, imported and owned by Lila Stafford, House of Oranje, Scottsdale, Arizona.

Ch. Akaba's Top Brass, owned, bred and shown by Lois Boardman of Calabassas, California. Brassy was winner of the Hound Group at the Westminster Kennel Club Show in 1962 and was the top-winning Afghan Hound in the nation that same year according to the Phillips System.

Ch. Akaba's Sterling Silver, one of the main stud forces at Richard Souza's Coastwind Kennels in Salinas, California.

Ch. Akaba's Faust of La Scala, bred by Lois Boardman from her famous Ch. Shirkhan of Grandeur ex Ch. Akaba's Gi Gi in White litter. This lovely cream and grey brindle finished for championship with three majors and a Group Second from the classes. Owner-handled by the William Rollin Peschkas of Shawnee Mission, Kansas.

A'Flame. Cee Cee was sired by Ch. Delhi Downs Duirke el Sayyad out of Ch. Kandorissa of Aldachar. Cee Cee did not care for shows, so Lois bred her to a dog named Abez, sired by Taejon ex Kandorissa, and got a gorgeous all-white bitch Akaba's Gigi in White.

It was also around this time that Lois leased and bred Genii Al Peraa to Ch. Shirkhan of Grandeur, while he was on the West Coast in January 1958. From this breeding three champions were finished: Ch. Akaba's Shara of Grandeur, owned by Sunny Shay; Ch. Akaba's Know It All; and her great show dog and sire, Ch. Akaba's Top Brass. "Brassy," always owner-handled, became one of the breed's top-winning show dogs. He had many Bests in Show to his credit, including the parent club Specialty in 1962 under judge Dr. William Waskow and the Breed and Hound Group at Westminster Kennel Club show the same year. At the end of his show career in 1963, Brassy had the honor of being top Afghan Hound dog in the nation for 1962 and West Coast winner for 1961, 1962 and 1963. He was also the sire of 24 champions.

The list of Akaba's winners goes on and on, as does the list of breeders who had the good sense to breed to the Akaba studs or to acquire puppies from Lois's breeding program. Fortunately, Lois had advanced far enough along in this program so that when a terrible fire claimed the lives of 26 of her dogs in February of 1969, she had enough stock around to pick up the pieces along with what was saved from the kennel.

Lois is now an Afghan judge and has curtailed her breeding for what she says is an indefinite period, but this does not mean that she has no plans for the future nor that she will not always be found in the company of Akaba Afghan Hounds.

Ch. Akaba's Kobalt Khan of Sara, a silver-gray brindle, is pictured winning at a show on the 1965 Texas circuit, where he won both majors and 11 points toward championship. He is handled here by Evonne Chashoudian for owners Dr. and Mrs. Robert Curtis. His sire was Ch. Shirkhan of Grandeur *ex* Gigi in White. The breeder was Lois Boardman.

Ch. Akaba's Kobalt Kommander is pictured winning Best of Breed over specials from the classes at the 1965 Pontiac Kennel Club Show. Kommander was bred by Lois Boardman and he is handled here by Carole Newkirk for his owners, the J. Dormans.

Ch. Akaba's Stone Flower of Karima, Hound Group winning Afghan Hound owned by Dr. and Mrs. S. Mughabghab of Sayville, New York.

Dorothy and Brandt Houtsma's Ch. Sandhihi Joh-Cyn Taija Baba is pictured winning a California Specialty Show under judge Colonel Wallace Pede. Mr. Houtsma handled.

MIKAI

Virginia Mika had her Mikai Kennels in West Covina, California. During the 1950's her Ch. Desert Chieftan of Mikai, C.D., was riding high in both the show ring and obedience circles.

A Best In Show winner, Chief won his C.D. title in short order, and went on to work for his C.D.X. In addition to his show and obedience work, Chief was a potent sire. One of his get, Ch. Shah Zada of Mikai, owned by William Walsh, out of Ch. Faith, C.D., was a Hound Group winner at 16 months of age. Many others were show winners as well, including Caprack's Cochise of Mikai and Dezi Fury of Mikai.

When he wasn't competing at the shows, Chief pursued a motion picture career and appeared in the movie *Kismet* and *It's a Dog's Life*.

110

THE HOUTSMAS AND SANDHIHI

Brandt and Dorothy Houtsma saw their first Afghan Hound at the 1957 Golden Gate Show and bought their first, Stormhill San-Dhi, from the Withingtons after seeing Silver Dream!

San-Dhi was shown and had a Best of Breed from the classes. In 1958 she was bred to Ch. Crown Crest Kabul. Out of this litter were several champions and San-Dhi's Kuza Nama of San-Dhihi, C.D.X., won in three consecutive shows. Hatim Tai and Taman made up the Houtsma's record-holding brace.

Perhaps their best-known dog was Ch. Sandhihi Joh-Cyn Taija Baba, one of the Top Ten Afghan Hounds in 1965. Another of their dogs is Ch. Sandhihi Dominja Joh-Cyn, also closely bred from the Domino-Kenya breeding they admired so much. Taija Baba, a multiple Group and Specialty show winner, is owner-handled by Brandt Houtsma.

EL KHANI

Connie Hendricks of Riverside, California, owned the el Khani Kennels and referred to her dogs as the "aristocrats from Afghanistan." Connie was interested in racing her Afghans and wrote some very informative articles on the subject which appeared in a magazine called *Afghan Parade*. Connie was both editor and publisher of this excellent magazine which declared itself as being dedicated to the intelligent advancement of the Afghan Hound.

Starting in 1957, *Afghan Parade* was published every two months and was consistently a quality publication. Many regretted that it stopped being published so soon after its initial appearance.

THE END OF THE FIFTIES

Of course, many other fanciers of our breed were an active part of the show scene. Names like Ellie and Doug Venn, Dorothy Rambo and her Hound Bey Kennels were heard. Jinx Junkin had her Gai Day Kennels in Santa Fe where she bred a litter by Shirkhan which produced the lovely black, Uday Shankar of Grandeur. William Walsh had his kennels in New Jersey and was showing Shah Zada of Mikai on the East Coast. Carl Scott from Delaware was also exhibiting a Mikai dog, his showy black-masked silver Mikai's Whirling Dervish. Doris Culver was showing her Lucver dogs and would be active in the parent club in the years to come. Leo Murphy was judging the breed.

Actor Maurice Evans, extreme left, was on hand at the Astor Hotel in February, 1959 to present the Ken-L-Ration awards to the owners of the dogs in each of the 6 Groups that won the most Group Firsts for the previous year. Hound Group winner was Sunny Shay, accepting for Ch. Shirkhan of Grandeur.

Like father, like son. . . In 1965 Ch. Sahadi Shikari, son of the 1959 winner, won the Ken-L-Ration Award for having won the most Hound Groups for that year. Bill Veeck made the presentation to the winners at a banquet at the Hotel Delmonico in New York City. Bred by Joan Brearley; owner Dr. Earl Winter accepted the award.

Ch. Khabira's Laurel Ridge Khalib, pictured winning at the 1967 Wilmington Kennel Club Show. This half-brother to Ch. Khabiri of Grandeur was a breed winner from the classes and is handled here by owner Jennifer Sheldon, Massapequa, New York.

Opposite:
Ch. Sahadi Sabrina, exquisite black-masked silver daughter of Ch. Taejon of Crown Crest ex Ch. Crown Crest Khalifah. Sabrina was a foundation bitch at the author's Sahadi Kennels during the late 1950's.

Ch. Kai of Grandeur is pictured after winning at a 1971 show on the way to her championship. She was bred and is owned by Carol Reisman, Afghans of Kai, Woodmere, New York.

Ch. Sahadi Sadruddin and author Joan Brearley enjoy a friendly embrace. This photograph appeared as a full-page picture in the *American Kennel Club Gazette* magazine entitled "Pals." "Pedro" was sired by Ch. Taejon of Crown Crest *ex* Ch. Crown Crest Khalifah. Photograph by Edmond Vianney.

Karamoor's Oenone of Gralior is pictured taking Best of Winners decision at the 1976 Nashville Kennel Club Show. The sire was Ch. Wildenau's Bonvivant *ex* Canadian Ch. Karamoor's Isis of Gwalior. This lovely brindle is owned by Vikki Highfield and is shown here by Miss Scarlett Highfield, both of Birmingham, Alabama.

Shahruba of Grandeur, pictured at 15 months of age. He was winner of the Best of Winners award for a 3-point major at the 1954 Lake Mohawk Kennel Club Show. He was owned, bred and handled by Alice E. Schmidt of Somers, New York.

A show winner in the 1950's owned by Kathleen Morochko of Long Island, New York.

Best HOUND

Ch. Windtrysts's Ba-Feeldi is pictured winning the Hound Group under Maxwell Riddle at the 1952 Sewickley Valley Kennel Club Show. Ba-Feeldi was owner-handled by Louise French (now Snyder) of Malvern, Pennsylvania.

Dam of 3 champions, Ch. Turkafa of Grandeur was sired by Ch. Turkaman Nissims Laurel *ex* Ch. Khanhasset Ginger of Grandeur. This photograph of Turkafa was taken in November, 1959.

Dale and Beverly Henry moved to Oklahoma where they resumed their JU-I Kennels with the black and tan Nissim Laurel son, Ali Baba of Grandeur. Howard and Lee Iverson had a Specialty winner in 1951. Emory Jarrot from Savannah, Georgia, was showing his Estioc Ebn Khaken and seeing Doris and Gordon Wheeler and their Kandullah dogs at the shows. The Baroness Hilda de Rothschild reared a litter sired by Rubi, Doris Hillen was upholding the breed in Portland, Oregon, and we heard about Mrs. Jantos and her son Gene and their Best In Show Champion Artemus of Province.

The William Waskows were as active as ever and members of the parent club. Dr. Waskow was to become Delegate to the American Kennel Club for the Afghan Hound Club of America from 1955 on. A popular judge, he also officiated at the 1962 parent club Specialty show where Ch. Akaba's Top Brass was the winner and another Shirkhan son, Ch. Sahadi Scaramouche, was Best of Winners and Best bred by Exhibitor!

To say the breed was becoming more and more popular would be putting it mildly. Every indication pointed to the entries and registrations increasing and we all knew the only way the breed was going was UP!

PETER BELMONT AND ELMO

Peter Belmont II lives an active and varied life, but a life that centers around the breed he loves best. . . the Afghan Hound. His Elmo Kennels are in Wichita, Kansas, where Peter is an Associate Professor of Art at the University of Kansas. This follows a distinguished academic career including a doctorate from the Department of Art and Education at Teacher's College, Columbia University. Whenever possible Peter has traveled and checked out the Afghan Hound population in such countries as Egypt, Greece, England, Puerto Rico, Mexico and Canada.

Peter's interest in the breed began in 1966 when he acquired Ouijah of Al-Yram from Joan Brearley. Ouija, a Ch. Sahadi Sinbad daughter was bred to Ch. Ruhah's Windman of Grandeur and produced Ch. Elmo's Ahdana who finished with five 3-point majors, owner-handled by Glorvina Schwartz. Ahdana was then bred a second and a third time to Ch. Coastwind Gazebo. The breedings to Gazebo produced Ch. Sandina Sorceress of Elmo, Ch. Sandina Snapdragon and Ch. Sandina Satan.

Ch. Samaris of Moornistan is shown here with handler Tom Crowe. Sammi had a remarkable show career, with 5 Group Firsts and many Group placings to her credit. Retired to motherhood in 1960, Sammi produced many champion offspring, including Best In Show and Group winners.

Mex. and Can. Ch. Coastwind Graffiti wins the impressive Stud Dog class at the 1974 Afghan Hound Club of Dallas Specialty Show under judge Georgianna Guthrie. Peter Belmont and Graffiti are seen next to the judge, and from left to right are Elmo's Black Jazz with James Civitano, Elmo's Bokhara's Barrage with Gary Whitson, Elmo's Portiananka with Carole Alford, Elmo's Blue Graffiti with Fred von Ahrens, and Elmo's High Priestess with Jane Whitson. This win was a true tribute to one of the breed's outstanding top sires.

Ch. Khabiri Midhi is pictured in a touching embrace with Claudia Sheldon, daughter of Werner and Mary Sheldon of the Khabira Kennels, Massapequa, New York. Midhi was sired by Ch. Arkhan of Kharysthan *ex* Khabira Angora and was photographed here in 1972.

A typical Elmo puppy seeking the approval of his master. . . This one grew up to be Elmo's Blue Graffiti, bred, owned and shown by Peter Belmont, Kansas City, Missouri.

Ch. Majara Mudarris was sired by the great Ch. Ali Khyber and owned until his death at the age of 14 by Dr. and Mrs. Frederick Clarke of Pennsylvania.

Ch. Ammon Hall Judas is pictured winning Best In Show at the 1965 Mahoning Shenango Kennel Club Show. The judge was Walter Schneider. Judas is owned by Dr. Joseph Pois of Pittsburgh, Pennsylvania.

Ch. Horningsea Salim Dor, owned by Florence R. Ewald, wins Best In Show at the 1958 Forsyth Kennel Club Show in Winston-Salem, North Carolina. Dr. Arthur W. Combs was the judge and Gordon Barton handled for the owner. Robert Bland, Jr., president of the club, presents the trophy.

While Peter doesn't believe in keeping more than three dogs at a time so that they can each get their deserved attention, he did acquire a co-ownership on American and Canadian Ch. Coastwind Graffiti. Under Peter's handling, he finished in the United States in 10 shows, in Canada in three shows and is on his way to his Mexican title, which includes an all-breed Best In Show in that country at his first show.

Surprisingly, Peter will tell you he hates dog shows, hates exhibiting, but is now judging our breed to make a further contribution to the breed he admires.

JAY AMMON AND AMMON HALL

Jay Ammon's first Afghan Hound was Holly Hill Lorna Doone, whelped in 1960. Sired by Dureigh's Golden Harvest out of top-producing Ch. Samaris of Moornistan, she finished her title with four majors, including one at a Specialty show under Dr. William Waskow. She then was bred, in accordance with an inbreeding plan Jay had, to her uncle, Ch. Hassan Ben of Moornistan. This mating was to produce Jay's first home-bred champion, Ammon Hall Dealer's Choice. A second breeding to Ch. Holly Hill Draco represented the second generation of inbreeding which produced Ammon Hall Judas, multiple Best In Show and Specialty winner.

A litter sister to Judas, named Jezebel, was bred to Ch. Holly Hill Black Magic. This litter produced Ch. Ammon Hall's Hundred Proof that became the top-winning bitch in the country for 1967. Jay's third litter was sired by Ch. Holly Hill Desert Wind, which produced· Ch. Ammon Hall's Nomad, who enjoyed a remarkable show career. Jay then leased Ch. Holly Hill Hex, a Samaris daughter by Ch. Sahadi Sessu, and bred her to Ch. Holly Hill Sultan. The litter produced several champions and two Best In Show winners, Ch. Ammon Hall Ter-Caj of Tajmir and American and Canadian Ch. Ammon Hall Guru.

THE LA GRECAS AND GRAN SALAAM

The LaGrecas, Frank and Diana, are devoted to our breed. Ever since 1960 when they purchased their first Afghan Hound, a black-masked brindle, they have been active in the fancy. La Gran Salaam de Grandeur finished with major wins and has a Group to his credit. Ch. Khabira Zabrula was next and when bred to Abba Dabba produced Ch. Gran Salaam Kabriz, who finished his cham-

Ch. Gran Salaam D'Artagnon, photographed at 3 years of age winning a 4-point major under breeder-judge Cyrus K. Rickel at the 1969 Westbury Kennel Association Show. Handler was Jane Kamp Forsyth for owner Frank LaGreca of West Hempstead, New York.

Ch. Gandhi of Lakoya, photographed winning Best of Breed in 1962 at the Redwood Empire Kennel Club Show with handler Frank Sabella. This win was under the late George Beckett, and Gandhi went on that day to win Group Second under judge Heywood Hartley.

Ch. Gran Salaam Kabriz is pictured winning at a 1969 show under judge Mary Nelson Stephenson. Owned by the Frank LeGrecas of West Hempstead, New York, his sire was Ch. Le Gran Salaam de Grandeur ex Ch. Khabira Zabrula. He was handled to his championship by Jane Forsyth. Breeder was Diana LeGreca.

Ch. Le Gran Salaam de Grandeur is pictured winning at a January, 1962 show on the way to his championship. Owned by Frank and Diane LaGreca, this Shirkhan son was handled for them by Sunny Shay.

Ch. Gran Salaam Echo of Holly Hill, photographed at 12 years of age with her breeder-owner Diane LaGreca. This lovely, magnificently coated bitch was sired by Ch. Le Gran Salaam de Grandeur ex Ch. Samaris of Moornistan.

119

pionship in just two months. Kabriz sired their Ch. Gran Salaam D'Artagnan.

In 1964 the LaGrecas leased the well-known Ch. Samaris of Moornistan from the Kauffmans and bred her to Abba Dabba. This breeding produced Ch. Gran Salaan Echo of Holly Hill, who won a Best Puppy ribbon at the parent club Specialty. In 1970 they purchased El Sayyad's Tauras who also finished his title. Ch. Ninth Turn Argus was their next Afghan and was specialed until Diana took over as President of the Afghan Hound Club of America.

HELENE JEFFREY

Mrs. John Jeffrey came to showing dogs from the sport of horses. A regular at ringside for the horse shows, Helen Jeffrey was told that she "must" show her first Afghan Hound, the striking gold and cream male, Ch. Gandhi of Lakoya. His breeder, Mrs. E.C. Ragle, was the one who insisted that the dog be shown. Sired by Ch. Kujur ben ghaZi (a grandson of Int. Ch. Asri-Havid of Five Mile) out of the exotically-colored Zorah of Lakoya (she was black, silver and blue), they were an impressive combination of the important old

Shangrila Pharahna Domin'x, owned by Johanna Tanner of Friendswood, Texas. The sire was Shangrila Pharoah Domino ex Ch. Akaba's Royal Gold. Domin'x had 10 points, including a major, toward championship at the time this photograph was taken.

Elmo's Lion in Winter was sired by Ch. Coastwind Graffiti ex Khamelot's Portia Panache and owned by Connie Nibarger, Kon Robbi Afghans, Wichita, Kansas. Bred by Peter Belmont, this photo was taken when the little Lion was 4 months old.

Arken, Prides Hill, Chaman and Blakeen bloodlines.

Mrs. Jeffrey used Frank Sabella as the handler for Gandhi during his show ring career in the 1960's. One of his early triumphs was a five-point major win under judge Louis Murr at a Northern California Afghan Hound Specialty Show. From there began a sparkling career including many Specialty and all-breed wins during which this elegant hound defeated an amazing number of competitors, much to the satisfaction of those who loved him best, Mr. and Mrs. John Jeffrey of Orinda, California.

DR. KENNEDY AND SHANGRILA

Dr. Gerda Maria Kennedy of Broken Arrow, Oklahoma maintains a kennel of approximately 85 dogs, three Lipizzaner horses, two cats and a flock of ducks and geese on her 13 acre spread. When she acquired her first Afghan Hound in the early 1960's she started a breeding program that was to produce American and Canadian Ch. Shangrila Pharahna Phaedra, who tied for 8th place among the top-winning Afghan Hounds in the history of the breed. Whelped December 10, 1967, Phaedra's sire was Ch. Sandhihi Joh-Cyn Taija Baba, who, it is interesting to note, is the dog with whom Phaedra tied for the #8 position! Her dam was Ch. Shangrila Pharahna Cleopatra.

When she was retired in December, 1972 she had 13 all-breed Bests In Show, four Specialty wins, 49 Group Firsts with 21 Group placements and 80 Bests of Breed. In 1972 she was the country's top Afghan Hound. Herman Fellton judged the parent club Specialty in 1970 and gave Phaedra the top win. Formerly a surgeon in Vienna, Dr. Kennedy retired from medicine when she married William Kennedy and has now retired from the show ring as of December, 1973 to concentrate on judging and breeding.

SANDINA AND THE SCHWARTZES

In the mid-sixties Glorvina Schwartz took up the torch to bring Afghan Hounds further glory. Formerly in Pugs, she was cap-

Lovely headstudy of the shiny black Ch. Sandina Satan, owned by Andrew Dragwa of Clifton, New Jersey. The sire was Ch. Coastwind Gazebo ex Ch. Elmo's Ahdana. Mr. Dragwa is the president of the Afghan Hound Club of Northern New Jersey.

Sandina Scorpio is shown winning at the 1974 Westchester Kennel Club Show under judge Joan Brearley. Scorpio is owned by Andrew and Julie Dragwa of Clifton, New Jersey, and is handled by their daughter.

FIRST

121

Am. and Can. Ch. Sandina Starstream, #1 Afghan Hound and #1 Sighthound all-breeds for 1975, is pictured here winning one of his 14 Bests In Show. This win was under judge Ruth Turner at the 1974 Lackawanna Kennel Club Show. Bred, owned and handled by Glorvina Schwartz, Sandina Kennels, Tuxedo Park, New York.

tivated by the beauty of the silky-coated hounds and combined her own and her husband Sandy's nick-names to establish the Sandina Kennels at their home in Tuxedo Park, New York.

In the decade or more that Glorvina has been breeding and exhibiting, it has become a recognized fact that there are few others in our breed that can groom or handle an Afghan Hound more adroitly or with more zeal and attract more attention to their place in the fancy than she can. The talent combined with a carefully planned and executed breeding program have brought Sandina ultimate success.

I am pleased to say that the Schwartzes tell me that it was my original book, *This is the Afghan Hound*, that peaked their interest in the breed. Peter Belmont's breeding, based on my Sahadi stock (by way of Ch. Sahadi Sinbad), was responsible for their early winners and the enthusiasm that was to carry them to their success in so many subsequent years.

It seems only natural that Glorvina would come up with a top winner. Her American and Canadian Ch. Sandina Starstream was the Nation's Number One Sighthound for 1975. His sire, the multiple Best In Show winner Ch. Coastwind Gazebo, won the parent

#1 hound in the nation in 1975, Ch. Sandina Starstream, is shown with his daughter, the #1 Afghan Hound bitch for 1975, Ch. Sandina Susquehanna. Both Afghans were bred by Glorvina Schwartz, Sandina Kennels, Tuxedo Park, New York.

Am. and Can. Ch. Caravan's Blue Passion is the dam of many champions and is a multiple Best In Show winner. She is pictured winning a Hound Group under judge Romona Jones at a 1972 dog show. Passion is owned and handled by Glorvina Schwartz, Sandina Kennels, Tuxedo, New York.

club Specialty in 1969. His dam, a multiple group winner and also an American and Canadian champion, was Ch. Akaba's Blue Bonnet of Sandina. Her important Group wins included a Group One at the 1970 Boardwalk Kennel Club and Group Fourths at Chicago International and at Westminster in 1971. His #1 Afghan Hound position represented a total of 12 Bests In Show, 31 Group Firsts and 55 Bests of Breed. The accumulated Phillips System points added up to more than any other Afghan Hound in breed history had scored for the title.

Bonnie Boy, as he was called at home, was retired from the show ring just before his fourth birthday, content to pass on his greatness to his progeny through stud service and to make way for American and Canadian Ch. Sandina Sparkling Champagne, who by the mid-seventies was amassing a show record which is sure to equal and probably surpass his own. "Pinky" is co-owned by Glorvina and Vikki Highfield of Birmingham, Alabama and shown to perfection by Glorvina. As his name implies, this champagne colored Afghan Hound was whelped in April, 1974, and sired by Ch. Dynasty's Wild Goose Chase out of Ch. Caravan's Blue Passion. In 1976 Pinky was #3 Afghan Hound and #5 in the Top Ten Sighthounds for that year.

Alexander Schwartz is active in club work as well and is a guiding force behind such important kennel clubs as Westchester, Ramapo and Tuxedo Park. He is also one of Glorvina's staunchest supporters!

Ch. Akaba's Blue Bonnet of Sandina, a multiple Group-winning brindle bitch, is pictured finishing her championship. Blue Bonnet is the dam of Ch. Sandina Starstream, #1 Afghan Hound in the nation for 1975. Owned by Glorvina Schwartz of Tuxedo Park, New York, Blue Bonnet was also Best of Breed winner at the 1971 Westminster Kennel Club Show.

Ch. Sandina Sorceress of Elmo is pictured finishing her championship at the 1971 Westbury Kennel Club Show under Mexican breeder-judge Rod Quevedo. Sorceress is handled here by her breeder, Glorvina Schwartz, and was owned by Peter Belmont.

Ch. Sandina's Sparkling Champagne went Best of Breed at the 1976 Kennel Club of Northern New Jersey Show under judge Joan Brearley. "Pinky" went on to win his first Best In Show this day, a win he repeated the following—and many times since! He is handled by his breeder, Glorvina Schwartz, who co-owns Pinky with Vikki Highfield.

Ch. Dynasty's Marked Card is pictured winning the Hound Group at the 1972 Indianhead Kennel Club Show. This black-masked grey brindle dog is a multiple Group winner and was bred, owned and shown by Fredric M. Alderman, Afghans of Dynasty, Mundelein, Illinois.

Ch. Dynasty's Midnight Cowboy, pictured winning with breeder, owner-handler Fredric Alderman, Afghans of Dynasty, Mundelein, Illinois. The sire was Ch. Akaba's Royal Flush *ex* Belden Blue Angel.

Dynasty's Kristol Pistol, owned by Nora Dodson of Tucson, Arizona.

Ch. Dynasty's Angel Dust, captured on film during a quiet moment at the home of her owner, Diane Austin, Creekside Afghans, Frankfort, Kentucky. Angel was owner-handled to her championship and has a Group placement to her credit. The sire was Best In Show-winner Ch. Coastwind Abraxas *ex* Ch. Dynasty's Devilish Angel.

FREDERIC ALDERMAN AND DYNASTY

A major force in the show ring during the last several years has been the dogs bearing the Dynasty name.

In the earliest days of this kennel, the first Afghan Hound was purchased from Leo Goodman's Belden Kennels. A mixture of Crown Crest and Dureigh bloodlines, when bred to the Akaba line produced a succession of champions that were to establish the Dynasty name in the show rings. Akaba's Blue Angel was to bring to Dynasty their Ch. Dynasty's Wildcard. Wildcard whelped a litter by the great Ch. Coastwind Gazebo and contained two champions, Superstar and Supercharger.

Another important stud for Dynasty, which helped to boost the list of champions to 28 to date, was the Group-winning Ch. Akaba's Brass Cinder-Fella, the dog that received the Afghan Hound Club of Greater Chicago Stud Dog of the Year award three times in a row.

One of their most important bitches was Ch. Akaba's Unsinkable Molly Blue, who was named the nation's top-winning bitch during her ring career.

When Wildcard was bred to Ch. Coastwind Abraxas, the litter of ten produced seven champions and Wildcard was named the Top Producing Bitch for 1975. From this litter Dynasty kept two stud dogs, Ch. Dynasty's Wild Streak and Ch. Dynasty's Wild Goose Chase, a Group and a Specialty Show winner.

Dynasty has also received three Breeder of the Year awards given by their club, the Afghan Hound Club of Greater Chicago.

COASTWIND

Starting with linebred stock from Akaba Kennels in the 1960's, Richard Souza and Michael Dunham founded the Coastwind Kennels in California. Their first sensational winner was the glorious black-masked red, Ch. Coastwind Gazebo. His top-producing sister, Ch. Coastwind Serendipity, was equal-

Ch. Akaba's Brass Cinder-Fella is a multiple Group winner and sire of several champions to date. The sire was Ch. Akaba's Top Brass *ex* Ch. Akaba's Glacier Blue. He is owned and handled by Fredric M. Alderman, Mundelein, Illinois.

A lovely headstudy of Dynasty's Good Golly Miss Molly, bred and owned by Fredric Alderman, Dynasty Afghans. "Goodie" deserves a prize for a most unusual name, for one thing!

Dynasty's Shooting Star, pictured at 13 months of age, was bred by Fredric Alderman and owned by Diane Austin, Creekside Afghans, Frankfort, Kentucky.

Ch. Dynasty's Wild Goose Face, whelped in January, 1974, is a multiple Group winner that finished his championship with 4 major wins. He won three Hound Group Firsts from the classes with his owner-handler, Annette S. Constantine of Longwood, Florida. He is pictured here winning at the 1976 Tampa Bay Kennel Club Show.

Ch. Akaba's Unsinkable Molly Blue, owned by Fredric Alderman. This lovely silver-blue bitch is a multiple Group and Specialty winner and was bred by Lois Boardman. The sire was Ch. Akaba's Sterling Silver ex Ch. Akaba's Glacier Blue.

Ch. Coastwind Obsidian was the winner of two Specialty Shows in one weekend: the Afghan Hound Club of Omaha, under Werner Sheldon, and the Afghan Hound Club of Greater Detroit, under Joan Brearley. Both wins were under the handling of Richard Souza. Obsidian is co-owned by Walda Kolbo and the Coastwind Kennels.

Coastwind Iron Butterfly, litter sister to Ch. Coastwind Phobos, is co-owned by Val Little and the Coastwind Kennels.

Ch. Coastwind Renoun Sherry is pictured winning at a 1972 show. This beautiful bitch's sire was Akaba's Geronimo Blue *ex* Ch. Coastwind Serendipity. Sherry is owned by the Coastwind Kennels, Salinas, California. She is handled here by her co-owner Richard Souza.

Ch. Coastwind Calliope is co-owned by Donna Towey and the Coastwind Kennels. She was handled by Richard Souza to this 4-point major win on the way to championship.

Ch. Coastwind Abraxas wins Best of Breed from the classes at the Afghan Hound Club of California Specialty Show under judge Dr. Gerda Kennedy. He is co-owned by Michael Dunham and Richard Souza.

131

Ch. Coastwind Peony and handler Richard Souza. This beauty was bred and is owned by the Coastwind Kennels, Salinas, California.

18 months, he defeated more than 30,000 dogs in ring competition, more than any other Afghan Hound in breed history!

When speaking of breed history, it must also be noted that Gazebo ranks #7 in the Top Winning Afghans in the history of the breed. He was sired by Akaba's Allah Kazam ex Ch. Shaadar's Flajnhe of Karlyle. As a sire he is equally successful; by the mid-seventies over thirty of his offspring have completed their championships. His son, Ch. Sandina Starstream, was the #1 Afghan Hound in the nation for 1975.

The first breeding of Serendipity to Akaba's Geronimo Blue produced Ch. Coastwind Nepenthe, which was to become another important sire at Coastwind. In each of his first three litters he produced a Specialty winner: Abraxas, Jacoranda and Obsidian. Nepenthe's litter brother, Coastwind Holy Man, is in Australia with David Roche and is a top-producing sire in that country.

Working on the premise that linebreeding is best, Mike and Dick have produced a line of top dogs that would impress anyone who is interested in the breed. There seems to be no end to the list of champions and show winners coming up from their breeding com-

ly as great and from these two stalwarts all subsequent successful breeding at Coastwind can be traced.

Gazebo's first impact in the show ring came in 1969 when he was #1 Afghan Hound in the country. He amassed a total of 13 all-breed Bests In Show, three Specialty show wins (including the Afghan Hound Club of America in 1969 under breeder-judge Louise Snyder), 52 Hound Group Firsts and 100 Bests of Breed. Although only campaigned for

Ch. Coastwind Passionella was sired by Akaba's Geronimo Blue ex Ch. Coastwind Serendipity. This Coastwind Kennel brood bitch is handled here by Richard Souza, who co-owns her with Michael Dunham.

Coastwind Michele, sister to Obsidian and Calliope, is owned by Sandi Rolfe and the Coastwind Kennels. She is pictured here winning under judge and breeder Beverly Cadbury. The sire was Ch. Coastwind Nepenthe *ex* Zardin's Zybele of Infashia.

binations. To name just a few more, there was Ch. Coastwind Jubilan Tiger Paw, Ch. Coastwind Abraxas, Ch. Coastwind Phobos, American, Canadian and Mexican Ch. Coastwind Graffiti, Ch. Coastwind Ouija and Ch. Coastwind Peony.

These and others of equal quality are responsible for the assured success for Coastwind Kennels in the future history of the breed.

SUMMARY

As mentioned in the introduction to this book, almost 80,000 Afghan Hounds have been registered with the American Kennel Club in the past twelve years since my first book on the breed was published. It is plain to

see that all of these dogs and their owners, whether they were shown successfully or not, cannot be written about within this new book. . .

I have made mention of any that were truly outstanding, set or broke records for the breed, and I have tried to cover the leading contenders according to the various rating "systems" and Top Ten listings. Those, and most of the others, are covered in the text, or in photograph, or both.

My next book on the Afghan Hound is already being compiled and will concentrate on the breed from the end of this book forward, because I can see more wonderful things happening in the breed in years to come!

Ch. Kophi's Princess Zokara Khy, whelped in 1973, completed her championship in 1974. Bred by Greta Phillips and owned by Mrs. Penny Williamson of Willowdale, Ontario, Canada, her breeding goes back to a great Ch. Shirkhan of Grandeur ex Ch. Crown Crest Khalifah litter. Her wins, from the classes, were 1 Canadian-Bred Best In Show, a Group First and several Group placements.

Chapter IV

History of the Afghan Hound Around the World

AFGHAN HOUNDS IN CANADA

In 1928 the Afghan Hound was introduced to Canadian dog-lovers. Three Afghans, two males and a female, were seen at the Coliseum in Montreal. They belonged to the Elenor Kennels, which were also exhibiting Samoyeds at the same show. Canadian Kennel Club records show, however, that it was on May 14, 1935 that the first Afghan Hound was registered in that country. Ramy was his name, a fawn male bred by Shaw McKean in the United States and owned by Mrs. Constance Corbet. During the years he was shown, he won three Hound Groups in the Maritimes.

In 1937 Barberryhill Dolly and Barberryhill Charlie were exhibited on the West Coast of Canada where Dolly won a Hound Group. But it was Barberryhill Charlie, owned by Athos Nilson, that made breed history by winning two Bests In Show and the honor of being the first Afghan Hound in that country to do so. He was entered in the 1937 studbook as a Canadian champion, as well.

In Vancouver, B.C., that same year three other Afghan Hounds made their appearance in the show ring. Tazi of Beg Tute was a direct import from Afghanistan. A foreign news correspondent, Laurance Peters, purchased him in the village of Beg Tute while on assignment in Afghanistan. Tazi was a fawn-colored male.

It was in the fall of 1938 that one of the pillars of the breed in Canada became active in Afghans. Mrs. Mary Matchett imported Pic of Chaman, a lovely red, in whelp by Ch. Taj Akbar of Chaman, from Molly Sharpe of Scotland. Pic was to be the first at Mrs. Matchett's world-famous El Myia Kennels in Highland Creek, Ontario. Pic, whose sire was Ch. Garrymhor Faiz Bu Hassid ex Manda of

A handsome father and son team of Canadian champions owned by Mary Matchett of Canada's famous El Myia Kennels. On the left is Ch. Kurram El Myia and on the right Ch. Hindukist El Myia.

Chaman, whelped her litter on November 5, 1938 on Canadian soil. This litter produced Group-winning offspring and established the El Myia name in the breed, a name that stood for quality right on up through the time of Mrs. Matchett's death in 1966. In 1939 eight Afghan Hounds were registered in Canada and four of the eight were Pic's offspring.

The late Int. Ch. Kurram El Myia was the winner of four Canadian Best In Show awards and 16 Hound Group First. He was owned by Mary Matchett of the El Myia Kennels in Canada.

While Pic herself was the only Afghan Hound registered in 1938, three other Afghan imports followed her to El Myia. There were two bitches, Mando of Chaman (Pic's dam) and Taj Marie of Chaman. The dog was named Taj Asra of Chaman. Later, when Rosa Wilkenson arrived in Canada from England with two dogs and a bitch from her Televee breedings, a single litter was bred from her Damascus out of Repentance. Mary Matchett purchased the dog named Tangar that proved to be a big winner. When Mrs. Wilkinson later left the fancy, all her dogs went to El Myia—which accounts for so many Televee names being found in the old El Myia pedigrees.

Pic won her championship in 1940 and was a Best In Show winner at the 1941 Toronto Kennel Club Show in August of that year. Other Best In Show winners and top studs from Mary Matchett's kennel were Ch. Kurram El Myia, Ch. Tukh Tuffenuff El Myia, Ch. Kurramson El Myia and Can. and Am. Ch. Khubsurat Khan. Also her Ch. Khyber El Myia and Atashi Nagina El Myia were truly outstanding dams.

THE FORTIES IN CANADA

By the end of the 1930's two Afghan Hounds had won Bests In Show in that country. The first was Barberryhill Charlie; the second was V.W. William's bitch, Ch. Oakvardon's Ranee, a Barberryhill Dolly daughter bred by Mrs. Jack Oakie. Ch. Pic was the second bitch and the first Canadian dog to win a Best In Show. In 1942 Marion Foster Florsheim took her famous Ch. Rudiki of Prideshill to Canada to obtain his championship there, which he did—along with capturing four Best In Show wins from the classes! In fact, Mrs. Florsheim cleared the boards when her Ch. Rana of Chaman of Royal Irish won the Best In Show awards at the other two shows and her Canadian championship at the same time!

1942 was a good year for Afghan Hounds. Elsewhere in Canada the cream dog, Burma Kush El Myia, a Ramy son owned by Patrick J. Brennan, won a Group from the classes and Mrs. Matchett's Kurram El Myia, owned by Mr. and Mrs. Wiethoff, won the Hound Group from the classes at the Guelph Kennel Club Show. Kurram earned his championship during 1943 and by the end of that year, out of six times shown, he had won six Group Firsts and three Bests In Show. Mary

Best In Show in Canada! Marion Foster Florsheim's Int. Ch. Rudiki of Pride's Hill took top honors at a Hamilton show in the 1930's, marking his 8th Best In Show, 31 Best Hound awards, 56 Placements and 58 Bests of Breed.

Matchett had reason to be proud. Three of the top five winning dogs in Canada in 1943 were El Myia dogs.

Over the years Mary Matchett showed extensively in both Canada and the United States. The author had the privilege of knowing her. She was a dedicated dog lover and her dogs could be recognized anywhere because of the beautiful, profuse coats they carried. We talked at great length on the benches of the Westminster Kennel Club shows during my early days in the breed and I liked her very much. The Canadians can be proud and grateful for both her introduction and contribution to the breed in their country.

In 1944 four Bests In Show were won by Afghan Hounds. Three of these went to Marion Florsheim's Ch. Rudiki of Pride's Hill. The honors that year had to be shared, however, with Ch. Asri-Havid of Five Mile who captured a Best In Show and five Group Firsts. Asri-Havid was sired by Ch. Rana of

Ch. Rana of Chaman of Royal Irish, imported from Scotland by Marion Foster Florsheim in the 1930's, is shown winning one of two Canadian Bests In Show. She is one of the all-time Afghan Hound greats and recorded this win while in Canada to earn her championship title.

Can. and Am. Ch. Khubsurat Khan was a Best In Show winner in Canada and was owned by Mary Matchett of the El Myia Kennels of Ontario.

Chaman of Royal Irish *ex* Ch. Rudika of Blakeen. He was owned by Mrs. Eva Gudgeon, a newcomer to the breed at that time and owner of the Birchwood Kennels in Ontario. Mrs. Gudgeon produced many top-winning Afghan Hounds in the years that followed.

In 1945 the Canadian registrations were starting to climb as the breed began to gain in popularity. There were 37 registrations during 1945, but it turned out to be a "peak" when shortly afterwards registration dropped noticeably and didn't show another rise until 1957. However, the wins for 1945 went deservedly to Canadian Afghans. One Best In Show was awarded to Mary Matchett's Ch. Kurram El Myia and two to her cream dog, Ch. Tanger El Myia, owned by Clyde Ritchie.

In the mid-forties the E. Holloways of Brampton, Ontario, established their Queensway Kennels. Their line was based on their imported stock starting with Patrols Alybay and Patrols Ghenkude. A litter from these two produced Ch. Queensway Yama Bahama, the first Afghan to carry their kennel prefix and a show winner for them. Their Ch. Queensway Boom-Boom was a Best In Show winner during the 1940's, and while their active participation in the show ring ended before the 1950's, they still continued to breed on a limited scale for a while after.

137

THE FIFTIES IN CANADA

At the start of this new decade there were eight Best In Show awards for Afghan Hounds from 1949 through 1951. Five Reserve Bests In Show were won and ten Canadian-Bred Bests In Show won by five of Eva Gudgeon's Birchwood Kennel dogs. In fact, through 1954 Eva Gudgeon and Mary Matchett accounted for all of the Canadian Afghan Hound wins with their Ch. Tukh Tuffenuff El Myia, Ch. Birchwood Astara, Ch. Birchwood Riffie El Myia and Ch. Birchwood Salomi El Myia. The single exception to their winning streak was Clyde Ritchie's Ch. Maharajah of Whynhaven.

The 1955 Best In Show winner was Ch. Crown Crest Taejmahal, owned by Mrs. Inez Stewart, who imported Taejmahal from Kay Finch in California.

By the mid-fifties in Quebec, the famous Zarada Kennels of Miss Vera Hampton were beginning to make their mark. Ch. Zarada's Kumala Khandari, a son of Mary Matchett's famous Canadian and American Ch. Khubsurat Khan, brought the Zarada prefix into prominence. Later when Vera Hampton was no longer active in the fancy, her stock could be found behind the Douglas' Maimana Kennels.

Starting in 1957, there was once again a surge in popularity of the breed. There were

The late Greta Phillips romps with Am. and Can. Ch. Kophis Apollo, on her left and Am., Can. and Eng. Ch. Aryana Shalym, on her right.

Ch. Zarada's Kumala Khandari was the Top-winning Canadian Afghan for 1962, #2 for 1963, #5 for 1965 and #1 for 1965. In his show career he won 7 Group Firsts and many Group placements. He was bred and owned by Mrs. Vera Hampton, Zarada Kennels, in Quebec.

37 registrations with the Canadian Kennel Club and in addition to the 17 Bests In Show won during the latter part of the 1950's, several American dogs were coming to Canada to earn their championships and to win their share of Bests In Show. Canadians were seeing Ch. Crown Crest Mr. Universe, Ch. Crown Crest Zardonx, Ch. Shirkhan of Grandeur, Ch. Crown Crest Mr. California and Ch. Smokedream of Stromhill, to name a few. There were many, many more to follow in the years to come, whose owners wanted to add that additional title to their credits.

THE SIXTIES IN CANADA

The 1960's got off to a slow start. Mary Matchett had stopped showing in the ring, though Ch. Tangar Televee El Myia was still being shown by Robert Lane of Montreal. A total of 216 Afghan Hounds were in competition during 1960, mostly in the Ontario area. In 1961 Ch. Zaradas Kumula Khandari was being campaigned and he became Canada's #1 Afghan Hound for 1962 and #2 Af-

Best In Show for Am., Can. and Bermudian Ch. Horningsea Tzaama, owned and shown by Greta and Myles Phillips, Kophi Kennels, Ontario, Canada. Tzaama was #3 Dog all-breeds in Canada for 1968.

ghan Hound for 1963. In 1965 he was #1 Afghan Hound once again and #5 of all the Hounds in that country.

In 1963 Greta and Myles Phillips began their Kophi Kennels in Ontario. Ch. Kophi Sultana Mystique, sired by Ch. Murina Televee El Myia (a Tangar brother) out of a Queensway dam, was their brood bitch, and she gave them their start by producing many champion offspring that found their way into the show rings in Canada and the U.S. She was also the Phillips' first Canadian champion and finished her title in September, 1964. She whelped her first litter in 1966.

Greta Phillips was another of those completely dedicated fanciers who always seemed determined to breed the "perfect" dog and somehow her enthusiasm made you think that someday she would! The Phillips and their Kophi Afghan Hounds lived in King's Castle, an enormous castle built in 1854 and com-

plete with a resident ghost! I remember very clearly the conversation Greta and I had about their experiences with this ghost, when Greta discovered that I had done a college term paper on phenomena dealing with the occult sciences.

The Phillips loved their castle and their dogs, and a magnificent oil painting of Greta and two of the dogs occupied a prominent place at the castle. It was painted by Paul Buchanan, one of Canada's leading portrait artists, before her untimely death on August 6, 1973. The Phillips' Kophi breeding was based on a combination of American, British and Canadian bloodlines, and their Ch. Kophi Apollo and Ch. Kophis Mystic Sir Arctic were Canadian Best In Show winners. Sir Arctic was later owned by Mrs. Parker Harris of Skaneateles, New York. Another import, Ch. Horningsea Tzaama, also won a Best In Show.

139

The late Greta Phillips and two of her Kophi Hounds were captured realistically by famous Canadian artist Paul Buchanan.

The Best In Show winning Am. and Can. Ch. Kophi Sir Artic was photographed with Myles Phillips, Kophi Kennels, Ontario, Canada. Sir Arctic has left his mark on the breed in both the U.S. and Canada.

In 1965 the Phillips went to England and brought back a 10-week-old male that later became Canadian, American and Bermudian Ch. Horningsea Tzaama. In 1966 Tzaama, sired by Ch. Horningsea Tiger's Eye ex Horningsea Sundownah, became #1 Afghan and #8 Hound in Canada. In 1967 he was #2 Afghan and #6 Hound, in 1968 #1 Afghan Hound and #3 in all breeds.

In 1966 the Phillips imported England's top-winning Afghan Hound, English Ch. Aryana Shalym, who later earned his Canadian championship as well. A top stud and show winner, he sired many U.S. and Canadian dogs before his death in 1971.

One of the Phillips' very first champions was Mystic Maple Sugar, who won his title in 1967. In the following years Greta showed Kophi's Princess Shahndrea and Kophis Duke of Tirik. Kophis Prince Ronzha and Kophis Prince Randidi were Canadian champions, also.

Very outgoing and very, very determined to make a contribution to the breed, we can now, unfortunately, only speculate on what Greta and Myles' full contribution to the breed would have been. Myles still maintains his interest in the breed they both loved so much.

By the middle of 1964 The Afghan Hound Club of Canada was organized. Founding members included Mary Matchett, Greta and Myles Phillips and Mrs. Betty Thompson. Mary Matchett was Honorary President as well as on the Board of Directors. Their first activity was a Booster Show held in conjunction with the Scarborough Kennel Club championship all-breed event in September, 1964. The champions present were Ch. Televee Tangar El Myia and Ch. Televee Muringa El Myia, shown by Mary Matchett herself. This was to be her last appearance in the show ring. Also present were Ch. Zarada's Kumala Khandari, Ch. Kophi Sultana Mystique and the Best In Show dog from the U.S., Can. and Am. Ch. Smokedream of Stormhill.

By 1966 awards were given by the club for the top winning Afghans in Canada and for Canadian-Bred Best In Show winners. In 1971 a top-winning bitch award was also offered.

Can. and Am. Ch. Kophi's Duke of Tirik, one of Canada's top-winning Afghans, was photographed with part of his collection of trophies that were gathered during his show ring career! Tirik is owned by the Rikaabah Afghans, the registered kennel of Jack and Elaine White, Ontario, Canada. Tirik had four Bests In Show to his credit, plus 1 Specialty Best Canadian-Bred In Show and 6 Best Canadian-Bred In Show all-breeds. Tirik was whelped in November, 1966; his sire was Can., Am. and Eng. Ch. Aryana Shalym *ex* Kophi's Mystic Sharma.

Can. Ch. Elmo's High Priestess is pictured winning under breeder-judge Kay Finch at the 1974 Afghan Hound Club of Greater Houston Specialty Show. Priestess finished her Canadian title in four straight shows. She has two crosses back to Ch. Crown Crest Khalifah in her background through Ch. Sahadi Sinbad. Pictured with her is breeder-owner Peter Belmont, Elmo Afghans, Kansas City, Missouri.

141

Alijons Deimos is pictured after winning his class at the 1976 Afghan Hound Club of Canada Specialty Show under Kay Finch. Twilya Ortheck is the owner.

Myles Phillips of Canada sent us this photo of two famous breeders, Kay Finch and Lois Boardman, exclaiming over what is near and dear to their hearts. . . an Afghan Hound puppy!!!

Can. Ch. Wiky van de Oranje Manege, owned by Mrs. Sally Wille of Vancouver, Washington. The breeder was Eta Pauptit. Born in Holland, Wiky is a grandson of Eta's great Int. Ch. Xingu von de Oranje Manege.

The mid-sixties saw yet another Afghan Hound kennel make its impact on the show scene. Mr. and Mrs. David Marsh arrived in Canada from England with some of their Marchionique Afghan Hounds. They became the center of an active group of Afghanites in the Winnipeg, Manitoba, area. Later their bloodlines blended with the Kophi and Rokeish breeding.

The Western Gazehound Club held its first specialty show in 1967 for all seven of the sighthound breeds, in Vancouver, B.C. Best of Breed at that first Specialty went to Ch. Aladin's Torch of Ahab's Tent, an Afghan owned by a visitor from Seattle, Washington. His name was Forest Hansen, who is also an Afghan Hound judge in the United States.

In the late 1960's Susan Ball established her Rokeish Kennels in Gormley, Ontario. With the DiMarco's Amberhall Kennels in Fonthill started, the Telharesha Kennels in Hillsburg came into the show scene with owners Louise Judge and Ruth Chambers. On the West Coast William Green from the United States started his Khyber Khan Kennels in Aldergrove, B.C.

In 1969 the Afghan Hound Club of Canada held its first annual specialty in Toronto. Marna Dods from England was the judge. Best of Breed went to Ch. Aryan Don Juan, owned by Mr. P.C. Pavlic of Livonia, Michigan. Best Canadian-bred dog was Ch. Kophis Duke of Tirik. This specialty show has become more and more popular each year with entries coming from all over Canada and the U.S.

The #1 Afghan Hound for 1969 was also Canada's #1 Hound. It was Ch. Kophis Mystic Sir Arctic. Mystic, a lovely white dog, was bred and owned originally by Greta Phillips. The sire was Ch. Djandja Radja of Stormhill ex Ch. Kophis Sultana Mystique. The #3 Afghan Hound that same year was the Phillips' Ch. Kophis Duke of Tirik, owned by Mr. J.A. White and sired by Ch. Aryana Shalim ex Kophis Mystic Sharma.

143

Top, left:
The renowned Canadian artist Rene H. Folmer poses with one of his beloved Afghan Hounds. Born and educated in the Netherlands, Rene Folmer started painting as a hobby in 1967, but by 1972 it was a full-time profession. He now has a studio in Alberta where he works in oils and pastels, with an emphasis on animals.

Top, right:
Bostone Karmhin, whelped in 1975, is co-owned by Rene Folmer and Jocelyn de Jong of Alberta, Canada. Sired by Am. and Can. Ch. Cadbury hill Vida Blue *ex* Ch. Cadburyhill Asrana Alarikan, she was the winner of the Senior Puppy Sweepstakes in April, 1976. She will be campaigned.

Left:
Ch. Mirabad's Caiphas of Spectrum, whelped in 1971. By 1975 he had 44 Bests of Breed, 1 Canadian-Bred Best In Show, 1 Canadian Bred Best In Specialty, 10 Group Firsts and many placements. In 1973 he was in the top 15 Afghans, in 1974 he was #5, and in 1975 #2 Afghan Hound in Canada. He is owned by Inger James of Vancouver.

The Best In Show-winning Am. and Can. Ch. Dic Mar's Blue Note is owned by Helen and Patrick Ferrara of Centerreach, New York. Blue Note is a multi-Best In Show winner in Canada, and is pictured here winning a Group First under judge Nutbeem at the Thousand Islands Kennel Club Show in Canada.

Ch. Kophi's Duke of Mylgaven, owned by Jane Sparling and bred by Greta Phillips, was Canada's #4 Afghan Hound and #8 Hound for 1972. He has 1 Best in Show, 1 Canadian Best in Show, 4 Group Firsts and several Group placings to his credit.

Can. Ch. Badshahi's Tarnished Angel is owned by Sonny Pires, Vancouver, B.C., and co-bred with Fred Alderman. Her show record includes 1 Best In Show, 1 Canadian-Bred Best In Show, and she was #8 Afghan Hound in 1973 and #9 in the top ten bitches for 1975.

Can. Ch. Wildenau Streaker of Rakala was sired by Am. and Can. Ch. Rokeish Sorroco *ex* Cadburyhill Via Wildenau. His owners are Gord and Pat Rose, Rakala Kennels, Ontario.

Am., Mex. and Can. Ch. Coastwind Graffiti and his daughter, Am. and Can. Ch. Daturrah Belshazzar, are shown winning at the Barrie Kennel Club Show in Ontario, Canada. Bel was bred and is owned by John and Marilyn Charlesworth of the Daturrah Kennels in Ontario. Bel is handled here by Archie Nagel; Graffiti, on the left, is handled by owner Dr. Peter Belmont. The judge was Mrs. Yan Paul.

Ch. Sinorama of Hindamir was #10 Afghan in Canada for 1971 and is a multiple Group winner as well. He has a Specialty Best In Show from the classes and is the sire of 7 champions. Hindamir's sire was Am. Ch. Sahadi Sinbad ex Am. Ch. Panorama of Stormhill. He was bred by the E. Nelsons and owned by Susan Ball, Rokeish Kennels.

Spectrums Dreamspeaker is pictured at 11 months of age. This Canadian show dog is owned by Art and Inger James.

146

THE SEVENTIES IN CANADA

By the beginning of the 1970's Canada was suffering from what the United States had been suffering for a long time. . . over breeding! Popularity had produced much indiscriminate breeding. Highways and airplanes had shortened the distances between kennels and show sites and the dog fancy was really expanding, which made attending shows in both countries a lot easier and breeding more and more a possibility. It took a toll in some areas, yet the quality of the breeding did show obvious improvement where new bloodlines were needed.

The 1970 winner of the Afghan Hound Specialty in Toronto was Ch. Zaradas Siyah Punjab, owned by Peter and Kathleen Douglas of Quebec. The Alberta Specialty that year was won by a beautiful brindle dog from the classes, Sinorama of Hindamir, owned by Susan Ball of the Rokeish Kennels. The sire was Ch. Sahadi Sinbad ex Ch. Panorama of Stormhill.

In 1971 there were three Canadian bred dogs in the Top Ten Afghan Hound listings. Ch. Lophis Apollo was #3 Afghan and #6 Hound, Ch. Kophis Duke of Tirik was #5 Afghan and #9 Hound and Ch. Chinook of Rokeish, bred by Susan Ball and owned by Dr. D. Marsh, was also among the winners.

By 1972 five Afghans bred in Canada made the Top Ten. #2 Afghan and #3 Hound was Ch. Kophis Mystic Sir Arctic; #4 Afghan and #8 Hound was Ch. Kophis Duke of Mylgraven, owned by J. Sparling of Toronto; #6 Afghan was Ch. Amberhall Scorpio, owned by R. Dingman, Telakko Kennels; #7 Afghan was Ch. Kophis Apollo; and #10 Afghan was Ch. Amberhall Aquarius, bred and owned by B. and G. DiMarco, owners of the Amberhall Kennels.

In 1973 Ch. Amberhall Aquarius moved up to #1 Afghan Hound in Canada and #4 Hound. Ch. Rokeish Sorroco, bred by Susan Ball and owned by Pat Rose of the Rakala Kennels in Ontario, was #3 Afghan and #10 Hound.

There were nine Best In Show wins for Afghans in 1974, plus 15 Canadian-Bred Best In Show awards. Ch. Amberhall Aquarius held his top spot as #1 Afghan, #1 Hound and was #3 all-breeds. Ch. Sir Arie of Bahala, owned by K. White of Calgary, was #2 Afghan and #6 Hound.

In 1975 three Amberhall Kennel dogs were in the top four Afghans represented on

Am. and Can. Ch. Rokeish Sorroco, owned by Mrs. Pat Rose, Rakala Kennels, Ontario, Canada. Bred by Susan Ball, Sorroco is a Canadian-Bred Best In Show winner in Canada.

Ch. Amberhall Serpents Tooth was bred by B. and G. Di Marca and is owned by B. and H. Whitney. Whelped in 1971, Serpents Tooth's sire was Can., Am. and Mex. Ch. Rìptide Vodka of Holly Hill ex Ch. Holly Hill Delta of Ninth Turn.

Can. Ch. Amberhall Scorpio, whelped in 1970, is pictured here winning one of his two Bests in Show. He has also won a Specialty Best of Breed, 1 Canadian-Bred Best In Show, 4 Group Firsts and several Group placements. Scorpio was #6 Afghan Hound in Canada in 1972 and #4 in 1975. His first owner was J. Dingman; he is now owned by Bryce and Pauline Anderson of Ontario.

the list. Aquarius remained #1 in the breed and Hound Group and was #4 all-breeds. Ch. Mirabad's Caiphas of Spectrum was #2, bred by the Mirabad Kennels of Inger James in Vancouver. The #3 Afghan award went to Ch. Amberhall Serpents Tooth, owned by R. Whitney, Cabaret Afghans in Ontario, and #4 Afghan Hound was Ch. Amberhall Scorpio, owned by B. and P. Anderson, Boequa Afghans in Niagara Falls, Ontario.

And so it went as the second half of the 1970's continued to see the breed maintain its position in the Canadian dog world. We can see additional kennels springing up and entering the fancy, and more and even better quality Afghan Hounds coming up in the Canadian show rings, Afghan Hounds that can well hold their own against the Afghans being shown in other countries around the world.

Am. and Can. Ch. Daturrah Belshazzar is an excellent combination of British and American bloodlines. The sire was Coastwind Graffiti and the dam was Korinda of Shirina, who was brought to Canada from Britain in 1967 when Marilyn and John Charlesworth migrated to Ontario and established their Daturrah Kennels.

Ch. Rujha's Karezak Karhime is shown after winning a Group Second at the 1976 Prince Albert show. Karezak is owned by Mrs. Margaret Mercer of Alberta, Canada.

AFGHAN HOUND BEST IN SHOW WINNERS
IN CANADA FROM 1937 THROUGH 1975

Dogs	Owners
Ch. Barberryhill Charlie	Athos Nilson
Ch. Oakvardons Ranee (F)	V.W. Williams
Ch. Pic of Chaman (F)	Mary Matchett
Ch. Rana of Chaman of Royal Irish	Marion Florsheim
Ch. Rudiki of Prideshill	Marion Florsheim
Ch. Kurram El Myia	Mary Matchett
Ch. Asri-Havid of Five Mile	Eva Gudgeon
Ch. Tangar El Myia	Clyde Ritchie
Ch. Tukh Tuffenuff El Myia	Mary Matchett
Ch. Maharajah of Wyndhaven	Clyde Ritchie
Ch. Birchwood Astara (F)	Eva Gudgeon
Ch. Birchwood Riffie El Myia	Eva Gudgeon
Ch. Jubilee Julian of Crown Crest	Kay Finch
Ch. Birchwood Salomi El Myia (F)	Eva Gudgeon
Ch. Kurramson El Myia	Mary Matchett
Ch. Crown Crest Taejmahal	Inez Stewart
Ch. Crown Crest Zardonx	Kay Finch
Ch. Kubsurat Khan	Mary Matchett
Ch. Shamask Jhamil	Shamask Kennels
Ch. Shirkhan of Grandeur	S. Shay/Chenade
Ch. Queensway Boom-Boom	E. Holloway
Ch. Crown Crest Mr. Universe	Kay Finch
Ch. Horningsea Shah Sahban	J. Wass
Ch. Crown Crest Mr. California	F. Hansen/McIlvaine
Ch. Smokedream of Stormhill	R. Crandahl
Ch. Kopperwoods Hells Gatekeeper	M. Goodrich
Ch. Aryan Boomerang	D.T. Sansone
Ch. Aryan Shamaar	R. and P. Pfaff
Ch. Duchess Royal Grey Mystic	K. Titen
Ch. Aladins Torch of Ahabs Tent	F. Hansen/McIlvain
Ch. Horningsea Tzaama	G. and M. Phillips
Ch. Holly Hill Desert Wind	Mrs. Cheever Porter
Ch. Jan's Goldfinger v Zervlistan	J. and R. Zervoulis
Ch. Kophis Mystic Sir Arctic	G. and M. Phillips
Ch. Aryan Don Juan	P.C. Pavlic
Ch. Karistains Tajik Sherif	M. Hahn
Ch. Sebastian of Carnaby	H. and A. Mercer
Ch. Moornistan Moonraker	L. Martel
Ch. Ben ghaZi's Golden Ikon	S. and A. Seefeld
Ch. Wind Star Pythias	R.O. Willard
Ch. Rujha's Blessed of Allah	Ruiz/Taylor
Ch. Kophis Apollo	Greta Phillips
Ch. Rujha's Mohammed of Khyber Khan	Green/Ruiz
Ch. Kophis Tirik	J. White
Ch. Tajmas Lluva Bhoi of Zardonx	M. Winston
Ch. Chinook of Rokeish	Dr. D. Marsh
Ch. Pamir Ho Chester	D. Jensen
Ch. Ammon Hall Nomad	Playfair/Grey
Ch. Tully's Big John	Betsey and Allen Tully
Ch. Patrician Funny Money	H. Lovett
Ch. Kophis Duke of Mulgraven	J. Sparling
Ch. Kismets Jaccala	S. Cook/P. McNeill
Ch. Tinker-Belle of Stormhill (F)	V. and P. Mazzaglia
Ch. Caravan's Blue Passion (F)	Glorvina Schwartz
Ch. Amberhall Scorpio	Dingman
Ch. Amberhall Aquarius	B. and G. DiMarco
Ch. Shangrila Pharana Phaedra (F)	Dr. Gerda Kennedy
Ch. Badshahi's Tarnished Angel (F)	S. Pires
Ch. Dic-Mars Blue Note	H. and P. Ferrara
Ch. Dynasty The Devil With You	G. Bossick
Ch. Sir Arie Bahala	K. White
Ch. Cadburyhill A Clockwork Blue	N. and C. Tyrell
Ch. Dhon-Dhis Fakhr Phipps	D. Cerino
Ch. Pandoras Sheik of Stormhill	Virginia Withington
Ch. Ben Haasin Czar Illya	H. Haas
Ch. Pla-Vog's Go Get Em Tiger	J. Tomasi/T. Planck
Ch. Khayyam's Apollo	Betsey and Allen Tully
Ch. Akaba's Phantom	G. Johns
Ch. Pamir Sweet William	Jensen
Ch. Sandina Starstream	Glorvina Schwartz
Ch. Benvikki's Jeetson Neerhuc	H. and D. Hutchings
Ch. Gini's E. Magnus Rex of Foxrun	C. Molinari/V. Stees

CANADIAN SPECIALTY SHOW WINNERS
or
CANADIAN-BRED SPECIALTY BEST IN SHOW WINNERS

The Afghan Hound Club of Canada held its first annual Specialty Show in 1967. The following list of names and owners represent the winners of those Specialty Shows from 1967 through 1975.

Dogs	Owners
Ch. Aladin's Torch of Ahabs Tent	F. Hansen/McIlvain
Ch. Torrent of Rokeish	Susan Ball
Ch. Aryan Don Juan	P.C. Pavlic
Ch. Kophis Mystic Sir Arctic	Greta and Myles Phillips
Ch. Kophis Duke of Tirik	J. White
Ch. Sinorama of Hindamir	Susan Ball
Ch. Zaradas Siyah Punjab	P. and K. Douglas
Ch. Mecca's Fallstaff	G. Guidebeck
Ch. Kabik's Rodan	P. and M. Raysbrook
Ch. Rujha's Mohammed of Khyber Khan	J. Ruiz/Green
Ch. Badshahi's Tarnished Angel (F)	S. Pires
Ch. Amberhall's Serpents Tooth	B. and H. Whitney
Ch. Amberhall's Bees Knees (F)	J. DiMarco
Ch. Jenfield's Soodi	J. Beard
Ch. Khayyams Apollo	A. and B. Tully
Ch. Mirabad's Caiphas of Spectrum	Inge James
Ch. Cadburyhill A Clockwork Blue	N. and C. Tyrell
Ch. Amberhall Scorpio	B. and P. Anderson
Ch. Wildenau's Bon Vivant	Ingrid Stewart
Ch. Dynasty The Devil With You	G. Bossick

AFGHAN HOUND CANADIAN-BRED
BEST IN SHOW WINNERS 1937 THROUGH 1975

Dogs	Owners
Ch. Tukh Tuffenuff El Myia	Mary Matchett
Ch. Birchwood Riffie El Myia	Eva Gudgeon
Ch. Maharajah of Wyndhaven	Clyde Ritchie
Ch. Birchwood Astara (F)	Eva Gudgeon
Ch. Birchwood Salomi El Myia (F)	Eva Gudgeon
Ch. Birchwood Shireen (F)	Eva Gudgeon
Ch. Kurramson El Myia	Mary Matchett
Ch. Birchwood Asri Havid	Eva Gudgeon
Ch. Kuhbsuat Khan	Mary Matchett
Ch. Yogi El Myia	Mary Matchett
Ch. Queensway Yama Bahama	Ernest Holloway
Ch. Televee Tangar El Myia	Mary Matchett
Ch. Queensway Boom-Boom	Ernest Holloway
Ch. Kophis Duke of Tirik	J.H. White
Ch. Kophis Mystic Sir Arctic	Greta and Myles Phillips
Ch. Kophis Apollo	Greta Phillips
Ch. Chinook of Rokeish	Dr. D. Marsh
Ch. Kophis Duke of Mulgraven	J. Sparling
Ch. Rokeish Sorocco	Pat Rose
Ch. Taj Malis Karim of Zardonx	K. and L. LeBlanc
Ch. Gyhbala of Inshallah	G. Lange
Ch. Amberhall Scorpio	Dingman
Ch. Badshahi's Tarnished Angel (F)	S. Pires
Ch. Amberhalls' Bees Knees (F)	J. Di Marco
Ch. Shah Maharaja	H. and K. Reilly
Ch. Mirabad's Caiphas of Spectrum	Inge James
Ch. Sir Arie Bahala	K. White
Ch. Rujah's Elisha of Mardoane	W. and S. Doane
Ch. Kophis Princess Zokhara Khy (F)	O. Williamson

Netherlands and International Champion Xingu v d Oranje Manege, imported and owned by Lila Stafford, House of Oranje, Scottsdale, Arizona.

International Champion Xenos von de Oranje Manege, bred by Eta Pauptit at her famous von de Oranje Manege Kennels in Holland.

THE AFGHAN HOUND IN HOLLAND

A Dutch kennel that figured prominently in the history of the breed is the Oranje Manege Kennels of Miss Eta Pauptit. Miss Pauptit acquired her first Afghan Hound from Hans Jungeling in 1936. The dog, a gift from her father, became Int. Ch. Barukhzy's Khan, a gold, whelped October 5, 1930. A double grandson of the early English Ch. Sirdar of Ghanzi, his sire was Int. Ch. Baber of Baberbagh out of Int. Ch. Shahibe of Wahsdarb.

Over the years there have been many litters whelped at her kennels, many of them top show and racing dogs that have done a lot of winning all over the world. It was from Miss Pauptit that Kay Finch imported her great Int. Ch. Ophaal of Crown Crest, the sire of many American champions and an all-time top sire for the breed. He is perhaps Miss Pauptit's most famous dog. Before Ophaal came to this country in the 1950's, he sired some of the outstanding racing dogs in England. One of these was Arabdur, the record-holding winner of over fifty First Prizes, including a racing derby and a world show race.

Miss Pauptit's interest in racing dogs and horses was well known. In fact, her kennel name was derived from the name of her father's riding academy. The Oranje refers to the royal family of the Netherlands since they boarded their horses there. Over the years over one hundred champions were produced at her kennels and six racing champions.

Pictured is the beautiful Dutch and International Champion Xinga von de Oranje Manege, bred by Eta Pauptit of the Netherlands.

The all-time world record title-holding Afghan Hound bitch in the breed is Ch. Tajmahal Kenya, a champion in Norway, Sweden, Finland and the Northern International Federation. She is owned by Mr. and Mrs. John J. Guzevich of Las Cruces New Mexico.

In 1972 Eta Pauptit made her second visit to the United States. She visited with many American friends and expounded some of her theories on the raising and handling of Afghans. Fortunately, Miss Pauptit survived the rigors of the German occupation of Holland during World War II and in subsequent years she has, in addition to Afghans, acquired and bred world-famous Shih Tzus. The list of her outstanding dogs—in both breeds—is impressive and is found in important pedigrees all over the world.

By the 1970's Eta Pauptit had reduced her Afghan Hound stock to a single Afghan (his name was Drambuie) and a few Shih Tzu which she still showed occasionally. Drambuie was sent to her by Lila Stafford of Arizona who has concentrated on her bloodlines and uses the House of Oranje as her kennel prefix.

Frau Erika Rodde in Germany and Mrs. Skilton in Australia are carrying on her breeding in other parts of the world, along with Anne Van Der Vlis in the Netherlands Antilles, while Mr. and Mrs. E. Grevelt have picked up the torch in Holland.

While Eta Pauptit was one of the earliest advocates of Afghan racing, often campaigning an Afghan as a racing dog before ever entering it in the show ring, by the 1970's racing was a firmly established part of an Afghan Hound's career.

RACING IN HOLLAND

The International Union of Sighthound Clubs awards a double championship that is a highly respected title all over Europe. Dogs must win a placing in the European Renkamp race and placings in three other international open races in three different countries, as well as two International Championship certificates, to earn their titles.

This organization is referred to in Holland as the Union Internationale des Clubs de Levriers and is located in Amsterdam, though it was founded by a Belgian in 1922. Most European countries, including Sweden, Finland and Czechoslovakia, belong to it, with each country having three representatives in the organization: one for overseeing the racing, another for the showing of dogs and a secretary. Two major racing events take place in September of each year either in Holland, Germany, Austria or Switzerland.

There are the UICL European Championships for dogs with the highest record for the preceding year from each country, and then the UICL Titelrennen Championships which are open to all, including show dogs.

151

AFGHAN HOUNDS IN DENMARK

When Denmark began to take an active interest in the breed in the early 1960's, the El Kamas Kennel came into prominence with their Ch. Horningsea Jamussah. From a breeding with this import they finished Int. Ch. El Kamas Wladimir. They were so pleased with the results that they imported other Horningsea dogs, including a Ch. Horningsea Tiger Eye's daughter.

It did not take long before Denmark was breeding Afghan Hounds of great quality that could stand up against the best of Sweden and Finland, and these three countries were soon sharing the wins at the shows.

One of the most important breeders in Denmark today is Karin Fonsholm. Originally in Great Danes, 1961 was the year that an Afghan Hound puppy arrived for her from the kennels of Marna Dods in England. The puppy grew up to become Danish, Norwegian and Swedish Ch. Horningsea Jamussah.

Coats on the Danish dogs are heavy and the dogs generally bear a strong resemblance to the English stock. In that country, two first prize wins with two different dogs are required before a kennel prefix is granted to breeders by the Danish Kennel Club. Entries for the breed at the shows run to around 80 at each show and racing follows the judging of the regular championship classes.

The Afghanclubben is the name of the breed club in Denmark and it is one of the only two clubs for sighthound fanciers in that country. The club's president in the mid-seventies was Ulf Jorgenson who, with his wife Lotte, is very active in the breed. The other club, the Myndeklubben, encompasses the activities of all the other breeds of dogs.

The Danish shows are all benched and Denmark has no professional handlers, so showing dogs is less hectic and political than in some other countries, as Karin Fonsholm told us on a visit to this country. The Danish "prestige" show is held in June each year in Copenhagen and is called the Copenhagen International. Judges of international reputation are invited to officiate.

A Danish breeder of note is Mrs. Elisabeth Gjerloff. She is the owner of the Kennel El Shahnameh. A long-time fancier in that country, she is known for her El Shahnameh Aughori, Ali-Basimh and Amulette. Amulette was one of her top brood bitches.

In June of 1976 Kay Finch imported a magnificent black-masked golden bitch, now

The beautiful Boxadan El Achika Crown Crest was imported from Denmark in June, 1976 by Kay Finch. Her sire was Df., Nord., Int. Ch. Tuohi-Tikan Kekale ex El Khyrias Sakhanja. She was bred by Hanne Lasse and was whelped October 25, 1972. Although never shown in Europe, she attained her American championship.

Int. Ch. Kahala's Nightfall, winner of the 1976 National Afghan Hound Specialty Show in Sweden under judge Kay Finch. Nightfall is a son of the #1 ranking Afghan Hound in the U.S. for 1975, Ch. Sandina Starstream. His breeder was Glorvina Schwartz, Tuxedo Park, New York.

Am. Ch. Boxadan El Achika Crown Crest, from Hanne Lasse of Denmark, her breeder. Whelped in October, 1972, this beautiful bitch was never shown in Europe. Her sire was Danish, Norwegian and Int. Ch. Tuohi-Tikan Kekale and her dam was El Khyrias Sakhanja. Under Mrs. Finch's guidance, her contribution to the breed in the United States, when bred to top studs here, will be impressive.

THE AFGHAN HOUND IN SWEDEN

The first Afghan Hounds were seen in Sweden during the 1930's, but it wasn't until late in the 1940's that the first serious breeders began to import dogs from England and the other European countries. Madam Ingrid Trolle imported Int. Ch. Baghdad R'Akela from Belgium. Akela and a few later importations bred in England formed the basis of her kennel. Int. Ch. Taj Arad of Chaman was imported for the Indra Kennels and produced many champions.

In 1953 Int. Ch. Xenos von de Oranje Manege arrived and sired Int. Ch. Tanjores Domino and Int. Ch. Tajmahals Kenya. Domino was brought to the United States and was shown to his championship here by Mrs. Cynthia Guzevich.

After World War II, Mrs. F.C. Riley exported Ch. Bletchingley Houndsman to Sweden. An excellent example of the Bletchingley lines, he was an instant success in the show ring and did much to further the breed there. During the mid-fifties, Kay Finch's Crown

Silverdens Azo-Arry-Jazzo, sired by Swedish Champion Azor *ex* Olivehill's Maharsis Amrita.

Crest Kaejorg arrived. Crown Crest Kaejorg was the first American Afghan Hound to be imported and produced Int. Ch. Tajmahal Nefertiti. Rueben of Carloway was imported by the Sultan Kennels, and sired Int. Ch. Saphir before getting killed. Rueben was Best Sighthound twice at the Gothenburg shows.

In the 1960's the Silverlidens Kennel of Inga-Britt Andersson began winning at the shows with her dogs. Her cream dog, Silverlidens Bewita-Xenia also won two Challenge Certificates. Darjeelings Akela won championship titles in both Norway and Sweden and earned C.C.'s in both countries. Astrid Finne owned the Kennel Tanjore, and imported Int. Ch. Nabob von de Oranje Manege. She also imported from America Lakoya's Ali Farouk a black-masked brindle and showed in during the sixties.

Miss Agneta Lonnqvist owned the Jawahar Kennel in Hagersten. Her black and tan bitch, International and Scandinavian Ch. Tajmahal Kenya II, amassed a notable

Scandinavian Ch. Tazi Blue Devil, Afghan Hound of the Year in Sweden for 1972. Bred by Joan Rowe in the U.S.A., he was sired by Am. Ch. Akabas Royal Flush *ex* Venezuelan Ch. Dasha of Scheherezade.

show record for the breed. Out of 21 times shown, she won 21 presentation prizes, 12 Best Afghan Hound in show, seven Best Afghan Hound Bitch in show, and 11 Best in Group wins. She also had eight CACIB wins. Her daughter, Jawahars Tiffany, at the age of two years had won three CACIB C.C.'s, one Best Afghan Hound in show, two Best Bitch in show and a Group First. She has also been an outstanding brood bitch for Miss Lonnqvist's kennel.

Swedish Ch. Ashima, sired by Jawahars Mahmoud *ex* Silverlidens Bahljezea.

International and Scandanavian Champion Jawahars Cirman, Gazehound of the Year in 1969 in Sweden. The sire was Int. and Scand. Ch. Panameric of Stormhill *ex* Int. and Scand. Ch. Taj Mahal Kenya II.

Scandanavian Champion El Khyrias Diablo, sired by American import Int. and Scand. Ch. Panameric of Stormhill *ex* Int. and Scand. Ch. El Kamas Nahrimah.

Swedish and Finnish Ch. Kirman Kuppari, bred in Finland and sired by Int. and Scand. Ch. Tuohi-Tikan *ex* Takabbor Kandy.

THE AFGHAN HOUND IN FINLAND

The Afghan Hound is a popular breed in Finland. It averages around 100 registrations each year and many champions are finished each season at the shows. Relatively scarce during the 1950's, the breed increased during the 1960's and several prominent kennels were established. Today the leading kennel is Kennel Tuohi-Tikan owned by Anna-Leena and Pirkko Konttinen in Helsinki. It was the Konttinens that imported Panameric of Stormhill from Gini Withington in California during the second half of the 1960's. The dog made a definite impact on the breed in his new country and has produced many show winners and champions.

One of the Konttinen's best known international champions was Tuohi-Tikan Opaali, a winner in Sweden, Italy, Finland, Norway and Germany. They also export many of their top dogs: Tuohi-Tikan Naskal went to Sweden and Tuohi-Tikan Nalja went to Denmark. These Panameric puppies were important additions to the bloodlines in their new kennels.

Several other kennels in Finland are based on Tuohi-Tikan bloodlines. Mrs. Satu Karlsson owns Int. Ch. Tuohi-Tikan Tuuli-hattu; he is a sire of CACIB and CC winners. Mrs. Karlsson was also the owner of Chandhara's Wild Willow, a black English import later sold to Mrs. Marja Rantala for her Ran-Har Kennels.

Mrs. Tuula Stenman owns the multiple Best In Show winner, Fin., Swed., Nord. and Scan. Ch. Tuohi-Tikan Kekale. Erkki Keinanen owns the black and silver Fin. and Nord. Ch. Tuohi-Tikan Kaappari. Veronica Witikka owns Fin. and Swed. Ch. Tuohi-Tikan Hurmuri; Mrs. Marja Laiinen owns Ch. Tuohi-Tikan Puhui and Mrs. Ulla Toivonen owns Tuohi-Tikan Humupekka. This impressive list, representing the Afghan Hound in all colors, is an indication of the influence the Tuohi-Tikan Kennels had on the breed.

The imported Int. Ch. Cleopatra of Scherehzade and the great stud, Int. Ch. Tajmahal Abd-ul Djari, were strong influences as were the Mazar-I-Sharif and el Miharaja Kennels.

Mrs. A. Tuominen based her breeding on a combination of the Tuohi-Tikan breeding with the Silverlidens'. She produced a litter sired by Tuohi-Tikan Keikari, a silver and blue domino out of her Silver-lidens Bexona-Zardi.

This delightful 5 month old Swedish Afghan Hound puppy is Fargil's el Shahnawaz.

Pictured on the left is Int. and Scand. Ch. Eduardo del Flamante and right is Swedish Champion Ashima. Eduardo's sire was Int. and Scand. Ch. Panameric of Stormhill and the dam was Int. and Scand. Ch. Tiara del Flamante.

155

In Finland the Kennel Immerwach is owned by Mrs. Inger Westerlund. In the 1960's she produced a litter of black and tans sired by the Int. Ch. Tajmahal Abd-Ul Djari out of Isania Chira.

The Kennel El Ashabad is owned by Lilja and Pekka Pelkonen, and the Kennel Kirman of Hilkka Nousianinen were both located in Helsinki. Hilkka Nousianinen owned the Finnish and Swedish Ch. Sadruk Del Flamante. Mrs. Raija Outinen, owner of Finnish and Swedish Ch. Koh-Gard Zam, was also active in the breed during the 1960's. Susanne and Charlotte Hogstron owned Afghan Hounds during the decade of the 1960's, with their bloodlines tracing back to the Horningsea and Tuohi-Tikan lines.

Another large kennel was the Kennel El Miharaja owned by Miss Carita Lindelof. With champions finishing in several countries, Miss Lindelof was proud of her 1966 Hungary Sieger Alimann Khan El Miharaja. She imported Am. Ch. Seria of Scheherezade and other international champions at her kennel include Safarina Begum El Miharaja, Aniara Begum El Miharaja and Amanullah Khan El Miharaja. She has Afghans exported to Sweden, Denmark, Norway and the United States.

Kay Finch gets in some early show training with Crown Crest Kaejorg, a two-month-old son of the great Taejon that was sent to Stockholm, Sweden, for a show career. This was the first Afghan Hound to be exported to Sweden.

Int. Ch. Tanjores Domino, imported by Mr. and Mrs. John Guzevich of Las Cruces, New Mexico, earned his championship in Norway, Sweden, Finland, Austria and then in America. This tally makes Domino the all-time championship holder in our breed to date.

One of the author's favorite photographs. . . Gloria Gustavson photographed several years ago with her horse and Afghan Hound from the El Coza bloodlines.

THE AFGHAN HOUND IN IRELAND AND SCOTLAND

While Afghan Hounds found their way to Scotland by way of the Cove Kennels (which accepted imports directly from Afghanistan in the 1920's with the arrival of the Manson/Bell-Murray dogs), Captain Hamilton was the first to bring the Afghan Hound to Ireland. It was in 1927 when the first one was registered with the Irish Kennel Club, owned by another military man, Lt. Col W. Adye-Curran of Blackrock, County Dublin.

The name of the dog was Kibi of Cove and it was bred by Jean Manson; the sire was Potentate out of Aru.

Ireland produced the first international champion in the breed. Daniel I. Cronin of Kilarney bred Zandi of Enriallic,who was to attain this honor. Her sire was Rupee out of Souriya of Enthriallic. She was whelped in December, 1932.

In 1936 in Scotland Mrs. A. Bhanubandh's Afghan Hound, Int. Ch. Chota Sahib, won his championship at the Scottish

157

Kennel Club Show and went on to become an Irish champion as well. Early in the history of the breed, Mrs. A.B. Willan's Shadi also won Challenge Certificates at the Scottish Kennel Club Show in 1927.

After World War II it was Mrs. M. O'Toole's Kohistan line that helped further the breed in Ireland. Mrs. O'Toole's Int. Ch. Vendas Tash-Down won the dog Challenge Certificate at Crufts in 1948 when he was twelve years of age and went on to win the Hound Group!

Mrs. Bowdler Townsend owns the Moonswift Kennels in Ireland. Her home-bred Moonraker of Moonswift became an international champion. He was sired by Ch. Horningsea Sheer Kahn ex Indira of Carloway. Her first champion, however, was Conygar Janze of Carloway.

In the 1970's Mrs. H. E. Clark in the North of Ireland, who owns the Ballymarcrea Kennels, is producing show dogs for the breed in that country.

Int. Ch. Moonraker of Moonswift. This red dog was very influential in the breed in Ireland and earned his Irish Championship in 1969. Bred and owned by Mrs. Diana Bowdler-Townsend, the sire was Ch. Horningsea Sheer Khan ex Indira of Carloway.

Madame Michele Demarne, one of the oldest breeders of Afghan Hounds in France with her French Ch. Ben Xahar des Ailes. Madame Demarne is president of the Club Francais des Amateurs de Levriers D'Asie, a club for Salukis and Afghan Hound fanciers which is affiliated with the Central Canine Society in France.

French Ch. Nhorah des Ailes, owned by Madame Michele Demarne of Le Bourget, France. This photograph was taken in 1967. She is a French and International champion and C.A.C.I.B. winner.

AFGHAN HOUNDS IN FRANCE

Madame Michele Demarne is the oldest breeder of Afghan Hounds in France, using the des Ailes kennel identification. She is also President of the Club Francais des Amateurs de Levriers D'Asie, a club devoted especially to Afghan Hounds and Salukis and affiliated with Societe Centrale Canine.

Madame Demarne's most prominent dog is the French Ch. Nhorah des Ailes, or as

An Afghan Hound owned by Madame Jacqueline Fourniols at her Elevage de la Goutte d'Or in the south of France. This dog is descended from a 1958 American import from Sunny Shay's Grandeur Kennels.

Madame Jacqueline P. Fourniols' Afghan Hound, descended from a Grandeur dog with Shirkhan lines, that she imported from Sunny Shay, is Quartz de la Gouette d'Or.

French show winner Guamlaken de la Goutte d'Or, owned by Madame Jacqueline P. Fourniols from the South of France. Madame Fourniols has been breeding Afghan Hounds for many years. This was one of her top dogs in 1969.

Pictured is the residence in La Bourget, France, where Madame Michele Demarne lives. One of the oldest breeders of the Afghan Hound in that country, Madame Demarne has put an "X" over the kennel, or "la maison des chiens," though it is plain to see that two of them prefer to be on guard on the front lawn!

written in French, Championne de France de Beaute Afghan. Nhorah has appeared in motion pictures and on television in France and is frequently used for press fashion photographs.

Some of her other show winners are Tanit Zerda des Ailes, a champion in 1972; Tamar des Ailes; a daughter of Nhorah, Kalinda des Ailes; and Sheir Khan des Ailes, owned by Madame Courgeaud and a C.C.C. and C.A.C.I.B. winner. All are winners at the L'Esposition de Paris de Versailles, the most prestigous show in France.

In the South of France in Bayonne there is another old-time Afghan Hound breeder of note. Madame Jacqueline P. Fourniols operates her Elevage de la Goutte d'Or Kennel and has introduced Grandeur breeding into her lines since 1958 through descendents she imported from Sunny Shay.

In 1962 Madame Galiber finished her Int. Ch. Ibn Sina du Loiret. More recently, Madame Etanchau has been showing Kirghiz des Ailes, Madame Sarguier her El Khadour des Ailes, Madame Smaegge her Jimmingo des Ailes and Madame Coupaye her Kali des Ailes.

A multiple Best In Show winner, Int., Chilean, Spanish and Portugese Champion Huilaco's Black Shaliman is the winner of 9 C.A.C.I.B. certificates and is owned by the Huilaco Kennels in Madrid, Spain. The sire was Int. Ch. Stumpy Acres Show Spell and the dam was Int., Chilean and Portugese Champion Hilaco's Akaba's Diddi, the dam of 11 champions.

Vaz's Silver Girl is owned by Madame Michele Demarne of France. This bitch's background stems from Grandeur stock sent to Madame Demarne in Le Bourget.

THE AFGHAN HOUND IN SPAIN

The most important Afghan Hound kennel in Spain and Portugal during the 1970's was the Huilaco Kennels of Norman Huiolobro in Madrid. The Huilaco Kennels have bred over 35 champions to date, based on breeding stock from the United States. These lines include top dogs and bitches from the Crown Crest, Grandeur and Akaba Kennels.

Senor Norman Huidobro is a Chilean who has been living in Spain for several years and, during his travels, has managed to finish champions in Italy, France, Portugal, Monaco, Chile, Argentina, Mexico, Uraguay, Colombia, Venezuela and most recently Spain.

The first dog imported for the Huilaco Kennels (while they were still located in Chile) was a dog bred by Sunny Shay named Kutsadrab of Grandeur. The sire was Kakashah Larch Tree and the dam was Sheba of Grandeur. Next to arrive was Huilaco's Akabas Diddi. Diddi's sire was Ch. Khalife of Grandeur ex Ch. Akaba's Raven of Sanallah. This bitch, after first finishing her championship in Chile, next finished in Portugal and made international championship in 1974. By the mid-seventies she had produced, in just three litters, 11 champion get and four others which have all but completed their titles.

For her first breeding Diddi was sent to Uraguay to be mated to Stumpy Acres Show Spell, a black-masked silver dog. Percy, as he is known in South America, was the Winners Dog at the Chicago Afghan Hound Specialty Show the year Sheila Devitt of the famous Carloway Kennel in England came to the United States to judge it. Percy became an international champion soon after his arrival in South America. Six out of nine puppies from this first litter of Diddi's and Percy's became champions. Unfortunately, a dog named Huilaco's Akabas Wallace, imported along with Diddi, died shortly after arrival.

160

Columbian, Mexican, Portugese, Venezuelan and International Champion Ch. Antar Tizoc of Crown Crest was the top-winning Afghan Hound in Spain for 1976. He is pictured here winning a Group at the 1973 Asociacion Canofila Mexicana show. Bred by Rodrigo Quevedo, Jr., this dog has been Best In Show at all-breed shows and specialties. Whelped in Mexico City, the sire was Crown Crest Citation of Devi-Baba *ex* Mexican Ch. Antar Af-Zar Xochiquetzal.

In 1970 Huilaco's Antar Rakashi, bred by Carol Esterkin and Rodrigo Quevedo, was also imported for the Huilaco Kennels. Sired by Ch. Taj Arru of Grandeur ex Mexican Ch. Antar Great Duchess Katya, Rakashi today is the winner of C.A.C.I.B. certificates, with a total of 36 to his credit. This is the record for any dog in any breed for the entire Iberian Peninsula. Rakashi is not only an international champion but has completed individual champions in Spain, Portugal, Monaco, Chile and Italy. He has sired seven champions to

date and was proclaimed the Top Afghan Hound in Spain in 1975 by the Spanish Afghan Club.

When Rakashi arrived in Chile from California, a blue bitch, Ch. Antar Fi-Gun Morning Glory, also arrived from Mexico, after having been bred to Int. Ch. Antar Grand Koriolan. Their first litter, whelped in Chile, produced three champions, all of which won Best In Show awards. One of Glory's daughters, Ch. Huilacos Zolah, was bred to Spanish Ch. Branwen Kamat and

161

produced what Senor Huidobro considers one of the finest homebreds: International, Portugese and Spanish Ch. Huilaco's Rakhasta, proclaimed the best bitch in Spain for both 1975 and 1976 by the Spanish Afghan Club.

By the middle of the 1970's, two more Afghan Hounds were imported for the Huilaco Kennels. One was a black dog, Antar Likos of Crown Crest, sired by American Ch. Lippizan Big Red Machine out of Int. and Mex. Ch. Antar Tihui of Crown Crest. The other was a grey brindle, Ch. Antar Tizoc of Crown Crest, International, Mexican, Venezuelan and Colombian champion. Shortly after his arrival in Spain, Tizoc also completed his title in Portugal and was Best of Breed at the Afghan Hound Specialty Show in Madrid. He has been proclaimed the Best Afghan Hound in Spain for 1976 by the Spanish Afghan Club.

Top-winning dog all breeds in Spain for 1975 was Chilean, Portugese, Spanish, Italian and International (FCI) Ch. Huilaco's Antar Rakashi. Sired by Ch. Taj Arru of Grandeur ex Mexican Ch. Antar Great Duchess Katya, Rakashi was the winner of Best In Show awards in several European countries and was the top Afghan Hound in Europe for both 1974 and 1975. He is owned by Norman Huiolobro of Madrid, Spain, who has bred over 35 champions to date.

French Champion Huilaco's Pineview Granada, owned by the Huilaco Kennels in Madrid, Spain.

The American-bred multiple Group winning brood bitch at Norman Huiolobro's Huilaco's Kennels is International, Chilean and Portugese Champion Huilaco's Akaba's Diddi. Diddi is the dam of 11 champions.

Other top show Afghan Hounds at the Huilaco Kennels include Spanish Ch. Huilaco's Rikki-Tikki-Tavi, Spanish Ch. La Quintrala, Int. Ch. Huilaco's Black Shaliman and Huilaco's Liza. Their Huilaca King Midas was proclaimed by the Afghan Hound Club of Spain as the top winning puppy for 1975.

Another prominent kennel in Spain, based on the Huilaco Kennels stock, is the Kalikos Kennels, owned by Andreas Garcia and Carlos Veloza. Their Huilaco's Coimbra was the winner of three Challenge Certificates and a Reserve Best In Show during her early show ring career. These kennels, which also

include some Branwen and some original early Spanish lines, have three stud dogs. Huilaco's El Khoran is one of which they are particularly proud. His sire is Int. Ch. Huilaco's Antar Rakashi out of Ch. Huilaco's Antar Fi-Gun Morning Glory. Coimbra was sired by Ch. Dic-Mar's Silver Satin ex Ch. Huilaco's Black Jamara.

Cynthia Madigan, an American living in Spain for several decades now, was prominent in the United States in both Afghan Hound and Irish Wolfhound circles. Cynthia still breeds Afghan Hounds, and her stock, when she lived in this country, was descended from the Grandeur lines; it was those same bloodlines on which she established her Branwen Kennels in Spain, as well. In the late 1960's she exported Branwen Sheen Shankar to Israel where the dog served as one of the first stud dogs for the breed in that country.

THE AFGHAN HOUND IN GERMANY

Afghan Hounds are a popular breed in Germany. Dog shows in that country fall under both CAC (national) and CACIB (international) rules and qualifications. For German championship titles a dog must win four CAC championships and between the first and fourth certificates at least one year of time must elapse. This is opposed to the requirements of Belgium which calls for three certificates at three shows (one of which must be won in Brussels). In France, three are called for (one of which must be won in Paris). In each country only one show a year is held in the major city, so it is easy to see that it takes a good deal of time to win a championship in these countries.

The largest and most important German show is the Bundessieger show held in West Germany. The title of Federal Champion or Bundessieger is awarded to Best Dog and Best Bitch in each breed. In Germany the Afghan Hound falls into a category referred to as *the windhunds*. All judges eligible to judge Greyhounds are eligible to judge all of the windhunds.

At the national and international shows there are classes for champions, older dogs, racing dogs, couples and youth classes. Exhibitors are obliged to arrive at the opening of the show because class times are not announced and if they wish to receive their awards they must not leave before the closing of the show when the awards are presented, or they are forfeited.

Top-winning Afghan Hound bitch in Spain for 1975 and 1976 was Portugese, Spanish, and International Champion Huilaco's Rakhasta, a multiple Group winner belonging to Norman Huiolobro's Huilaco Kennels.

There is an official German dog magazine, the *Unser Rassehund*, which each month publishes the news of the dog fancy in Germany, as well as neighboring countries, and contains a special section on the windhunds. The judges are obliged to write critiques on their placements, which are published by the magazine.

BREEDING IN GERMANY

The Afghan Hound suffered in Germany as did all dogs in all countries of Europe during World War II. Many were put to death or eaten by starving people. Slowly, but steadily, the Afghan Hound status began to gain in the years that followed the truce, and today the breed has again come into prominence as both companion, show and racing dogs.

Rigid rules still apply to breeding dogs, however. Registration is possible only after a three generation pedigree of parents and grandparents has been approved for breeding by the kennel club. Bitches must be over nine months of age and never over eight years of age to be bred. No more than a specified number of puppies (this changes from time to time) are allowed to be registered from any one litter. If no more than six puppies are produced in a litter, the bitch may be bred again in the same year, otherwise there is a 12 month waiting period. There is no limit on stud service. The Stud Book Warden must be notified within two weeks of the puppies' birth so that he may come to inspect the litter and dispose of any excess puppies.

BREED CLUBS

The club for windhund owners is called the Deutsher Windhundzuchtund Rennverband. While devoted strictly to the windhunds, it is a branch of the all-breed club, Verbandes fur das Deutsche Hundswesan, which is also associated with the FCI.

There is also the League Championship Show, the Verbandsseigerschau, in which only German windhunds are allowed to compete. In this show not only the beauty, but the speed of the animals is compared. Held on a Saturday, championship racing is held the following day.

The highest title a European windhund can attain is the European Championship for Beauty and Performance. The "beauty" applies to their conformation, while the performance refers to their racing skills.

RACING IN GERMANY

Racing has always been a popular sport in Europe and particularly in Germany. One of the most reknowned racing dogs in Germany was an international champion Ophaal son out of a German-bred bitch. His name was Bhakkar's Arapdur and he was whelped in 1954. Arapdur held the racing record during his lifetime by winning over fifty Firsts, seven Seconds and a Third place in important races, including the Derby and World shows. He also did some winning in Switzerland.

Races in that country are usually on oval tracks of 300, 400 and 500 meters in length, sometimes with hurdles at 80 centimeters. These distances could usually be covered in 21, 28 or 39 or less seconds respectively.

SOME GERMAN BREEDERS

In 1956 Arlos Hellman, a United States Air Force man stationed in Germany, and his wife Maria, from Munich, first became interested in the breed. They purchased their first Afghan Hound from Frau Spiegel, owner of the Irminsul Kennels in Weyers uber Fulda. It was the leading kennel in West Germany and they named their dog Lobo. After two months they purchased a mate for Lobo named Herdis. Shortly thereafter they ap-

African Champion Khanabad Love-in-the-Mist, winner of a Best In Show at 18 months of age.

plied for and received the kennel name of Valley Ridge Afghans from the German Kennel Club. The Hellmans were relatively active in the breed in Germany until they returned to the United States in 1958.

Another of the long-time German breeders and exhibitors is Mrs. Erika Rodde. While she was active in the breeding and showing of the Afghan Hounds, her husband pursued the racing sport. Mrs. Rodde has been an official of the Windhund Club and her Katwiga Kennel lines are based on Eta Pauptit's von de Orange Manege lines.

Frau Eva Kemper of Grosskrotzenburg, West Germany, has perhaps produced the most winners during the past decades, even though she breeds as a hobby rather than maintaining a kennel. Frau Kemper has many important bloodlines behind her dogs, including Crown Crest, Grandeur, Holly Hill and Ammon Hall from America as well as the Horningsea lines from England and the Pandjah from Belgium.

One of the most important sires in Germany was Ozorba de Pandjah, imported by Eva Kemper to improve her "de domis animula" line. One of his daughters that later came to America with a new owner became an International Champion before departing. She won 22 CACIB certificates and 24 CAC certificates. There were also three other international champions sired by Ozorba.

Over the years there have been quite a few prominent kennels in Germany. Franz Fleisher owned the Maiwana Kennels in Berlin, the Granhenburgers showed under the El Kaira name and Ursula Schulze owned the Pachacumac Afghan Hounds.

AFRICA

It is an established fact that Afghan Hounds have long been known to Northern and Eastern Africa and they were used extensively as hunting dogs. The man credited with having introduced the breed to Southern Africa and Rhodesia as a show dog and companion was Mr. Benjamen R. Spencer of the Transvaal. This was during the early 1950's.

In 1957, while on a trip to the United States and Canada to judge at several dog shows, Mr. Spencer revealed that in Africa the Afghan Hound is still regarded first and foremost as a hunting and coursing dog. At one time, Mr. Spencer was Chairman of the South African Gun Dog League. He also told us that he had finished four Best In Show Afghan Hounds of his own breeding in that country.

During the 1960's and 1970's I learned of other Afghan Hound fanciers that have owned, and in some cases have bred, Afghan Hounds, though not all of them were used to hunt. Some of the major kennels in Africa are the Haller-Quell, and those owned by Neil Fry, Eddie Melhiush and Mr. and Mrs. A. Swanepoel. Their dogs are shown at the dog shows held at the Eastern Districts Kennel Club Show in the Transvaal.

African Champion Kalif of Mozsgo, photographed at 20 months of age.

Yabat el Chilab's Famika is pictured at three months of age. She is a daughter from an African bred litter of Fatima of Shahidan and Davlen Siptha Pasha.

African show winner Shirekhan Nasik Sol, owned by June James of Parrow, Africa. Sol has 4 Challenge Certificates and 2 Reserves. The sire Ch. Abu Raman of Shirekhan ex Shirekhan Hilwi.

165

Cinderelle and one of Juliette de Bairacli-Levy's hand-raised hawks were photographed at her home on the sea of Galilee in Israel.

7 month old Jumbo, a black Afghan Hound owned by Amron Agmon, Israel. This photograph was taken in June, 1972.

AFGHAN HOUNDS IN ISRAEL

Afghan Hounds were first introduced to Israel in the second half of the 1960's. In a 1969 dog show catalogue there were six entries listed, four of which were owned by one person. Her name is Hagar Weintraub and her stock was from the kennels of Juliette de Bairacli-Levy, who was an established breeder in Europe and whose Turkuman line was recognized all over the world.

Juliette de Bairacli-Levy presented Hagar with her first Afghan. It was a blue dog which she had received from Cynthia Madigan in Spain. Hagar in turn gave this young male to Amron Agmon. Mr. Agmon had expressed interest in the breed and raised this dog in a kibbutz. Hagar also received a bitch which, in time, was bred to the male and the first Israeli-bred Afghan Hounds were born.

By 1970 the Afghan Hound was popular in Israel and the breed was suddenly very much in demand. Other Afghan Hounds were imported from England and a German dog came to Israel with his master to settle in this country. A great deal of cross-breeding was done and inevitably dreaded juvenile cataracts became evident. This condition presented a serious problem which only careful breeding would eventually breed out.

In 1972, through the efforts of Amron Agmon and an Israeli veterinarian, Dr. Rita Trainin, Elise Abraham of the Ariston Kennels in New Milford, New Jersey, was invited

Juliette de Baircli-Levy of Israel is a long-time Afghan Hound breeder and owner of the famous Turkuman Kennels. She is shown with her Turkuman Nissim's Sea-Campion, photographed in 1972. Her book *The Complete Herbal Book for the Dog,* a handbook of natural care and feeding of dogs, is known the world over. She is the breeder of Ch. Turkuman Nissim's Laurel, the dog imported to the U.S. by Sunny Shay and Sol Malkin that won the Group at Westminster many years ago and helped to popularize the breed in this country.

American visitor and Afghan breeder-exhibitor Elise Abraham visits in Israel with her friend Juliette de Bairacli-Levy. The two ladies walk Kaftan and Sandina's Star of David at Tiberias by the Sea of Galilee. Mrs. Abraham, of the Ariston Afghan Kennels in New Milford, New Jersey, was the judge at the Israel Sight Hound Kennel Club Show during April, 1972.

to Israel to judge one of their sight hound shows. On April 8th of that year "Lee" attended the races which precede the judging at a desert site about 45 minutes outside of Tel-Aviv. The Afghan winner that day was a dog named Scotty, owned by the Weintraubs and whelped by their bitch by a British dog.

After the races on the desert sands, they went into a park where Lee judged Borzois, two Greyhounds and several Salukis. She was faced with 35 to 40 Afghan Hounds, which she was told was the largest entry they had ever had. Lee reports that the ring behavior was utter chaos, since obviously the training, or even the setting-up of the dogs, is practically unheard of in that country. Her 6 to 12 month old puppy class was not to be believed.

Amron Agmon had just acquired Sandina's Star of David, a black 4½ month old puppy, which had lived with her for about a month before being exported to Amron in Israel. Lee co-owned the puppy and had a chance to start training the puppy. Fortunately, she could use Amron and the puppy as a model (since obviously all the other dogs had forgotten the training lesson given by Sunny Shay on her visit to Israel the year before!)

Sandina's Star of David, photographed in Israel in October, 1972 with his owner, Amron Agmon. David is co-owned by Elise Abraham of New Milford, New Jersey.

Juliette de Bairacli-Levy and Kaftan were photographed by the Sea of Galilee in Israel in the summer of 1972. A dedicated breeder of Afghan Hounds from their first days in Europe, she now resides in Israel and continues to breed her world-famous Turkuman dogs.

By the end of the show, Lee Abraham had formed some very definite opinions on the Afghan Hounds in Israel. Aside from the lack of ring training, the grooming was almost non-existent, even though the dogs were well-muscled, with good depth of brisket and good shoulders. She would have preferred to see darker eyes, better toplines, hindquarters and finer heads and was distressed by the white patches on the faces. It was difficult to determine gait since the dogs were virtually not leash-trained.

A British dog imported by David Kramerman was her Best Adult. Best Adult bitch belonged to Hagar Weintraub and was a light cream named Turkuman Wild Sea Lilly El Judea. Best Afghan Hound was a black bitch, Shibas Prinz, owned by a Dr. Levinison, a veterinarian with the Israeli Army.

At a meeting with the group a few days after the show, Lee Abraham made her feelings known to them, knowing that they were well aware that the breed is still in the pioneer stage in their country.

THE AFGHAN HOUND IN AUSTRALIA

Several years ago Barbara Skilton began researching the history of the breed in Australia and learned that the Afghan Hound was probably introduced to that country by the Afghan camel-train drivers in the 1800's who came over to mine in the gold fields. She reported that there are still evidences of some descendents from these early dogs out in the wilds. In investigating, she had had correspondence with a Mrs. Annie Bannan, who claims to be the first girl born in the gold field of Coolgarlie, Western Australia. Mrs. Bannan says her mother was "adopted" by a pale gold bitch named Vashti that had deserted from a camel train in the early 1890's. Vashti would always be at the opening of the tent and Mrs. Bannan remembers her mother always spoke so proudly of Vashti with her "deep, beautiful brown eyes, so full of adoration that you couldn't see the depths of them."

Her letter to Mrs. Skilton went on to say, "Vashti had a long, soft, silky coat and long ears covered with long silky hair, a long head slightly raised from the nostrils to the eyes, a Roman nose, as mother called it, and a wispy tail like a Greyhound's. She must have been a tall dog, Mother was 5'5" and did not have to stoop to pat her side. Sometimes mother would ride away from the mining area for Quongdongs, and Vashti loved that, her speed was amazing and she was lovely to watch playing about the saltbush."

FIRST AUSTRALIAN IMPORTS

In 1935 Dr. Betsy Porter sent Farkhoonda el Kabul to Mr. and Mrs. J. Macdougall in Australia. Farkhoonda was sent in

Branwen Sheen Shankar, a blue Afghan Hound owned by Amron Agmon. This photograph was taken in November, 1969 in Israel. The dog was bred by Cynthia Madigan of the Branwen Kennels in Spain.

whelp by Lakki Marwat. In January, 1936 the Macdougalls imported Dharma-Raja of Geufron, and at the end of that year they imported another bitch named Morita. She arrived in whelp by Tash Garift of Pushtikuh. Morita was sired by Ch. Firdausi of Geufron ex Safiya and was a full sister to Int. Ch. Chota Sahib. The Macdougalls were off to a good start with their Kandahar Kennels, bringing to Australia some valuable English bloodlines.

However, there was considerable opposition to the breed after its arrival. Their reputed hunting instincts and the possibility that they might breed with the dingos was believed to present a danger to livestock. It was some time before this fear was overcome. While Afghan Hounds were entered at the 1935 Melbourne Royal Show, the early prejudice and the war years were responsible for those bloodlines dying out. Not even a trace of these lines could be found in that country until the fifties.

FIRST AUSTRALIAN SHOW DOGS

Afghan Hounds returned once again to Australia with the arrival of Norah Ward in 1950. She brought with her to the Western section of the continent Devilkin Dasti Pasha, son of the well-known English dog, Ch. Netheroyd Alibaba. Before leaving England, Norah Ward also purchased from breeder Barbara Skilton a daughter of Ch. Bletchingley Tajomeer, Devilkin Datoobhos. She was shipped to Australia in whelp to the black and fawn dog, Meshki Baz-i-Pushtikuh. Both attained their championships quickly and became the basis of Norah's Goliath Kennels.

Datoobhos arrived in quarantine in Perth in December of 1950 and whelped twelve puppies. She was helped with their feeding by a Cocker Spaniel and a Dashshund, who served well as foster mothers so that all puppies survived. When grown, these Afghans were responsible for the regeneration of the breed in the Australian show rings. Mustapha, one of these puppies, was later chosen Best In Show at the first all-breed championship show he attended. He not only obtained his championship title in four shows, but held the breed record record for Best In Show wins in Australia with a total of thirteen.

In 1954 Barbara Skilton and her husband arrived in Tasmania with their black and tan dog, Aghai of Hawkfield. He was a superb dog, sired six champions, earned his championship in Tasmania, Victoria and New South Wales, and was the only Afghan Hound at that time to win in all three places. He won Challenge Certificates in 1954 and 1955 at Melbourne and the Challenge and Hound Group at the Sydney Royal Show in 1956. This was one of the first major wins for the breed in Australia. One of the last of the pure Pushtikuh breeding, his sire was Meshki Bar-i-Pushtikuh and his dam Ragsider-i-Pushtikuh.

In 1958 Mrs. Skilton imported a puppy, Taj Amigo of Chaman, from the Chaman Kennels. She later imported Dutch and Int. Ch. Badin von de Orange Manege from the Dutch Kennels of Eta Pauptit. Taj Amigo was an immediate success going all the way to Best Opposite Sex In Show at the Hobart Royal when he made his ring debut. He followed this with a Challenge Certificate at the Melbourne Royal in 1959 over other imports under the Earl of Northesk who was the judge. While not widely campaigned, he won seven Bests In Show and was behind many future generations of Best In Show winners.

In addition to Taj Amigo and Badin VDOM, Mrs. Skilton also obtained a daughter and a granddaughter of Datoobhos from Norah Ward, and her el Tazzi Kennels was successfully established.

Another English breeder arrived "down under" and settled in New South Wales at about the same time the Skiltons came to Tasmania. Mr. F. Long brought two home-breds with him to continue his Hookstone Kennels. They were Hookstone Habibula and Hookstone Humaire. However, the most successful of the Hookstone dogs was Nadir Shah, who won several Challenge Certificates at the Sydney Royal shows and has sired several champions.

THE FIRST AFGHAN HOUND CLUB

In 1956 when Mrs. Skilton was in Sydney she instigated a meeting of Afghan Hound fanciers for the express purpose of starting a breed club. A few months later the Afghan Hound Club of New South Wales was founded. It was slow going at first, but as the breed grew, so did the club and it is still functioning. Patroness of the club was Mrs. Macdougall who held the position for many years.

The first President was Mr. B. Boddington, who owned the Westghan Kennels. Mrs. Stella Heaton-New was the first Secretary.

Litter look-alikes! These puppies were bred and owned by the Withingtons, Stormhill Kennels, and photographed by Joan Ludwig.

Mr. Boddington bred to Mrs. Skilton's famous Aghai line and owned and showed his Ch. Westghan Kinsuka to a Hound Group win at the 1960 Sydney Royal Show.

In 1957 Mr. and Mrs. James Abbott arrived in Melbourne from England with their black and cream dog, Zarusseff Zso Zso, descended from Bletchingley breeding. He was sired by English Ch. Usseff of Carloway ex English Ch. Bletchingley Zara. They also brought two gold bitches with them, Radiant of Carloway and Horningsea Khorrassan Tarbouka. Each became champions in their new country at the Abbott's Khyber Kennels.

While only two litters were bred by the Abbotts, they made a considerable mark in the breed in Victoria with Ch. Khyber Khorran when he won eleven Bests In Show. Their Ch. Khyber Anakh also won Best Opposite Sex honors in the Hound Group at the Melbourne Royal Show in 1960.

In Southern Australia in 1959, Mrs. Marie Hewitt imported Viper of Davlen and Mrs. Catt imported Scheherezade. Both dogs

produced well and Viper, a showy, blackmasked cream son of the Am. Ch. Horningsea Khanabad Azreefa out of Ch. Fantasia of Carloway, won several top show awards.

American bloodlines were also introduced by way of the progeny of Wazir of Desertaire, and Spanish blood through Cynthia Madigan's Branwen Kennels through Ajman Branwen Kandahar and Branwen Kamri. In the 1960's Lynette Schelling was showing her Ch. Astrajud of Kazan, a Waliwog daughter; while Ros Batchelor, Joyce Davey with her Shaaltarah dogs, and Alan Henrie and Michael Lawrence were also exhibiting during this time. Norman Langdon and Barbara Skilton were keeping America posted on their progress by writing various breed columns in dog publications.

In 1966 Graham Paelchem imported Chandhara Tardis Arrakesh, a dog who won Best In Show after his arrival under English judge Stanley Dangerfield at the Adalaide Royal Show. His Shahzada Kennels are one of the oldest in Australia and are co-owned with

Lyle Dally. Kenneth Cutbush was President of the Afghan Hound Club of Queensland when it was formed, and he has been well known for his art work featuring the breed.

While entries at the first shows hovered around a half dozen or so, by the mid-fifties, when noted American judge Percy Roberts judged them at the Royal Easter Show in 1958 there were 27 entries for his approval. When Gini Withington judged the specialty show held by the Afghan Hound Club of New South Wales in the mid-seventies, she had an entry of 516! This is proof positive of the popularity in the breed today—and all in less than a quarter of a century since the first Afghan Hound set foot on Australian soil. Her Best In Show award went to a black and tan, Ch. Calahorra Turban, owned by Mr. and Mrs. R. Kohry, and Best of Opposite went to Raushan Kennels' Ch. Raushan Jamil.

Lt. Col. (Ret.) Wallace Pede has also judged in Australia, and during the early 1970's, along with Tom Stevenson, judged an entry of 300 in September, 1976.

Ch. Coastwind Holy Man, exported by Kay Finch to David Roache in Australla, is a top-winning sire and winner of Specialty and all-breed Bests In Show.

DAVID ROCHE AND HIS FERMOY KENNELS

Along with Barbara Skilton, another dedicated breed advocate on the continent is David Roche, who also became interested in the breed in the mid-1950's. David Roche today is a Counselor/Director of the South Australia Canine Association and is an international all-breed judge. In 1969 he became not only the youngest person to judge Best In Show at Crufts, but also the first person outside of England to have the honor. He has also judged at the 1955 Morris and Essex Show, the Northern California Afghan Hound Club Specialty, as well as other top U.S. shows, and he is well-known in his country as a successful breeder of Afghan Hounds and twelve other breeds. He was the youngest all-breed judge in the world—he had his license by the time he was 21 years of age.

David's kennel prefix is Fermoy and his own breeding, based on some significant imports over the years, has made a major contribution to all the breeds with which he is associated. His first breed was an English Cocker Spaniel, followed by a Kerry Blue, which became his first champion.

Aghar of Hawkfield was the first Afghan Hound he admired, seeing it when it won the Group at the Melbourne Royal Show back in the fifties. When he went to England to judge Best In Show, he made Sheila Devitt's Mazari of Carloway his choice for the top award and tried to buy the dog on the spot. At first Sheila Devitt refused, offering the litter brother. Back in Australia, he later received a cable offering the dog to him. David and his mother co-owned Mazari, who went on to win four Royal Shows in all—three within one year. Mazari's son won the Melbourne Royal the next year, and Mazari came out of retirement once again the following year to win it himself again!

David Roche, who had by this time hired Sheila Devitt's kennel maid who relocated in Australia, was encouraged to get further involved with Afghan Hounds, and he imported Ch. Jill of Carloway. Unfortunately she died shortly after her arrival. She was followed by imports from other kennels, such as the Hatfield's Kinjan Kennels, and later from Kay Finch's American Crown Crest Kennels. David imported two Mr. Universe daughters, Crown Crest Miss Carousel and later Australian Ch. Crown Crest Miss Capriole.

New Zealand Ch. Hassi Baba of Kazah (left), bred in New Zealand, is pictured with three Australian bred and owned dogs: Kaniska My Fair Lady, Kazah Shaz Rachelle and New Zealand Ch. Cregdaca Starmist. This photograph was taken in 1972.

When Sheila Devitt stopped breeding, David imported her Ch. Waliwog of Carloway, though many of the English breeders felt that the dog should not have been allowed to leave the country and should have been purchased by the English parent club to prevent it. Later still, David imported Coastwind Holy Man. After 15 months in quarantine, his first show was the Afghan Hound Club of New South Wales Specialty Show where he went Best In Show under judge Dr. Harry Spirer! David's influence on the breed, along with Holy Man's, Mazari's and Golliwog's, was tremendous. Mazari sired 27 champions and Holy Man will undoubtedly surpass that number.

HELEN FURBER AND FURBARI

Following her marriage, Helen Furber and her husband purchased their first Afghan Hound and started their Furbari strain in the suburbs of Sydney. Westglen Knamba was a gold domino whelped in 1956, one of only about 50 Afghans in Australia at the time to have this distinctive, dark "widow's peak." Descended from the English Bell-Murray line, their next Afghan Hound was Khyber Amanulla from the Ghazni Kennels. Amanulla for many years held the Australian record for being the top producing sire in that country, and his get included 15 champions of which five were Best In Show winners. Knamba produced eight champions.

When Lynne Nichols joined Fubari as a partner, she brought with her an interest in racing dogs. Ch. Furbari Sole Mio is one of a few Australian Afghan Hounds to be both a Best In Show winner and a top racing dog. Their Furbari Theodora was also an excellent racer.

The Furbers next Afghan Hound lived into her teens and was named el Tazzi Gesihie. A black-masked red, she and Amanulla and Knamba brought to Australia all the top English bloodlines. All three gained their champion titles.

Furbari has produced more than fifty champions in Australia with 17 of them having won a Best In Show. Best known of these is Ch. Furbari Shalakhan, owned by Ray and Tatian Lenton. A black-masked gold, he is a multiple Specialty and all-breed Best In Show winner, including the 1969 top award at the PAL International Show. In 1970 he was Best In Show at the Sydney Royal Easter Show.

Ch. Furbari Ulysses, owned by Corinne Kelly, is perhaps the biggest winner, since before reaching the age of three he had scored nine Bests In Show and ten Runners-Up to Best In Show. His sire was Ch. Furbari Sole Mio, out of a Shaaltarah daughter bred by Lynne Schelling.

Ch. Fubari Kusan Kabul, a black-masked, blue brindle import with Crown Crest and Grandeur lines (as well as Carloway and Khorassan from England) was their most recent top-producing sire for Australia. Helen Furber is also a judge of Afghan Hounds (and has been for many years now) and more recently has added other breeds to her list. She has judged Afghans in New Zealand, Ireland, England and in the U.S.A., as well as in her own country.

Helen Furber holds the longest membership in the Afghan Hound Club, the first formed in Australia back in 1956. At the club's first championship show in 1961 there were 31 Afghan Hounds entered. During this decade the entry has risen to over 500! Helen is also an honorary life member of the Afghan Hound Club of New South Wales, a Patroness of the Hound Club of New South Wales, a member of the New South Wales Women's Dog Club and Ladies Kennel Association, a Vice-President of the Sydney Kennel Club and a member of the administrative body of the Kennel Control of New South Wales.

AFGHAN HOUNDS IN MEXICO

The Afghan Hounds migrated "south of the border down Mexico way" in the early 1950's. This was due to the extreme interest of

Pictured is the beautiful Mex. Ch. Crown Crest Great Mogul, owned and handled by Dr. A.L. Jenines of Weslaco, Texas. He is pictured here winning Best In Show in Guadalajara, Mexico, under judge Raul Gamboa. This black-masked silver Afghan took three Bests In Show in Mexico and was the first dog ever to win three Bests In Show in three consecutive days under three different judges—one from Mexico, one from Germany and one from the United States. He was presented with a special award for this achievement.

Senor Rodrigo Quevedo, Jr., who imported several dogs that he had purchased from Kay Finch at her Crown Crest Kennels in Corona del Mar, California.

Rodrigo's dogs competed extensively at the Mexican dog shows and generated much interest in that country in this breed. His dogs did a lot of winning under his kennel name of Antar, and within due time the popularity of the breed began to grow.

In the past two decades there have been other active breeders and exhibitors: Senor Eduardo Ruiz Madrigal and Senor Elias Zacarias, to name two, as well as the Empire Kennels of Dr. Jose Luis Payro.

By 1974 there was enough interest and enthusiasm in the breed to warrant the formation of a breed club, and The Afghan Hound Club of Mexico was organized. Dr. Antonio Eisenhut served as the first President, and since its formation the club has held three very successful specialty shows with just under one hundred dogs competing at each event. This support forecasts a promising future for the breed in Mexico, with dedicated breeders and exhibitors maintaining the high quality of a substantial breeding program originally introduced by Rodrigo

Mex. and Int. Ch. Empire Ginger Golden Passion is pictured winning Best in the Sight Hound Group at the 1976 Hound Specialty Show in Mexico. Judge Irene Khatoonian Schlintz is presiding. The handler is Dr. Antonio Eisenhut, and presenting the trophy is Lic. Fernando Galan, the club's president.

Quevedo 25 years ago, using his imports from both the U.S. and England.

Rodrigo Quevedo saw his first Afghan Hound in 1945 and decided he "always wanted one of these precious things by my side." Since then, he has bred or owned a succession of international champions representing the very top quality in the breed—Group, Specialty and Best In Show winners that were to set the pace in the breed in his country over the next quarter of a century. His dogs, with their Antar prefix, are winning in many foreign countries, including Venezuela, Canada, Columbia and the U.S.A. He also has a Best In Show winner in Australia: David Roche's Crown Crest Maya de Mexico, which is a litter mate of his Tizoc and Tihui. Quevedo's Mexican Ch. Antar Fi-Gun Shooting Star was a Best In Show winner in Mexico City in April, 1973 under judge Betty Francis.

Other Antar winners with championship titles include Grand Rorilian, Crown Crest

Zarak of Antar, his English import Horningsea Aida, Af-Zar Xochiquetzal, Fi-Gun Morning Glory, Great Duchess Katya and Kar-Cae Fine Ending. Rodrigo is also an accredited judge in the U.S. of Afghan Hounds and several Non-Sporting Group breeds.

With this firm foundation and enthusiastic start, there is little wonder that the breed has taken hold in a country where dedicated breeders take their dogs very seriously.

THE AFGHAN HOUND IN PUERTO RICO

In 1957, after Ch. Shirkhan of Grandeur won Best In Show at the Westminster Kennel Club Show, Mr. and Mrs. Harley Miller of Puerto Rico invited Sunny Shay to bring the now-famous dog to their island for exhibition.

Afghan Hounds were virtually unknown on the island and the Millers, who had come to admire the breed on visits to dog shows in the U.S., thought they would like dog fanciers

174

in their club to see this great hound. Mrs. Shay responded, arriving with the blue brindle Afghan Hound and some other dogs that the Millers purchased from her to help establish the breed on their island. The Afghan Hounds created quite a stir among dog owners in Puerto Rico, and soon the Millers were winning Groups and Best In Show awards with their first Afghan Hound, Ch. Chinah of Grandeur.

Fortunately for Afghan Hounds, Mrs. Ileana Miller, President of the Puerto Rico Kennel Club, chose the Afghan breed as her very favorite at her Harleana Kennels outside San Juan. Ileana is interested in all breeds, most especially Whippets, Beagles and Dachshunds, but she holds the Afghan Hound in highest regard. No other person in the history of the dog fancy on that beautiful tropical island has been so influential or has done more toward the betterment of dogs and dog shows than she has.

On her frequent visits to the United States over the years to see our dog show procedures and to observe and purchase the best breeding stock for her kennel, Ileana has seen to it that the Puerto Rico club maintains the highest quality performance in the staging of

Top:
Mex. Ch. Horningsea Aida, imported from England by Rodrigo Quevedo, Jr., has proven herself to be a top-producing bitch. Her sire was Ch. Horningsea Khanabad Subaraj *ex* Afa of Westfieldledge.

Middle:
Mex. Ch. Crown Crest Zarak of Antar was imported to Mexico by Rodrigo Quevedo, Jr., to be used as a stud force at his Antar Kennels in Mexico. Bred by Kay Finch, the sire was Ch. Crown Crest Zardonx *ex* Mexican Ch. Crown Crest Taejaona. Zarak won a Best In Show from the classes while being shown to his championship.

Bottom:
Ch. Khan Dar Khan of Scheherezade, C.D., CACIB , CACM, was photographed at the F.C.I. Mexican International Show in 1974. Khan, pictured at 8 years of age, was Best of Breed and Group Third at this show. The previous day Khan was coursed in open fields after jack rabbits. He is owner-handled by Kathleen M. O'Brien of Willingboro, New Jersey, and was bred by Lt. Col. and Mrs. Wallace Pede. The judge was Winifred Heckmann.

Best In Show winner at the 1964 Puerto Rico Kennel Club Show under judge Marie Meyer was Ch. Harleana's Mukhalla El Wahid, owned by Harley A. Miller, Jr. El Wahid was handled by Ben Burwell and completing the picture is Mukhalla's breeder, Mrs. Harley Miller. Photo by Roberto Mora.

Opposite, top photo:
Sandina Sassafras is shown winning the Breed and her first CACIB win towards her international championship title under all-breed judge Howard Tyler at a 1975 show in the Dominican Republic. "Frownie" is co-owned by Ileana Miller, handling her here, and Lyda Ramirez of Puerto Rico.

Opposite, bottom photo:
Love-in at Harleana Kennels. . . and we see Ileana Miller as we know her best—surrounded by her beloved Afghan Hounds! Left to right are Ch. Chinah of Grandeur, Harleana's Kasim, Shammar of Grandeur and Harleana's Khali of Grandeur. All these dogs helped establish the breed in Puerto Rico during their lives, and live on in the heart of Mrs. Miller, president of the Kennel Club of Puerto Rico.

their point and match shows. Both Ileana and her late husband, Harley Miller, former United States Commissioner for the island, have served as President of the club and as show chairman and official hostess to some of the top dogs, dog owners and handlers.

Her Ch. Chinah of Grandeur became the first Afghan Hound Best In Show winner on the island in 1962. At the time of his retirement from the show ring, Chinah's show record also included five Group Firsts, a Group Third and eight Bests of Breed. His success was topped by a glorious brindle home-bred named Ch. Harleana's Mukhalla El Wahid, the first and only dog of any breed, bred in Puerto Rico, to become a champion and a Best In Show winner. His record at retirement was one Best In Show, four Group Firsts, six Group Placements and 15 Bests of Breed.

In 1972 Ileana Miller's beautiful brindle bitch and third generation Best In Show winner, American and Dominican Ch. Harleana's Arahbezk Del Wahid, won Best In Show from the classes at the Puerto Rico Kennel Club Show and was Best In Show from the classes in Santo Domingo in 1970. Her grand sire was Best In Show at the Puerto Rican show in 1962 and her sire in 1964. She repeated her Best In Show win in 1972. Some of Mrs. Miller's other top show dogs, frequently handled for her by Ben Burwell, were Ch. Harleana's El Calico Cat, Harleana's Kasim, Shammar of Grandeur and Harleana's Khali of Grandeur.

Sandina's Sassafras was Reserve Winners Bitch at the 1976 Afghan Hound Club of America Specialty Show in New York City and is co-owned by Ileana Miller and Lyda Ramirez. Lyda is also of San Juan and for many years was very active working in the kennel club with Mrs. Miller. Lyda's Best In Show-winning Pomeranians are also much to her credit in the fancy on the island.

Miss Ramirez and Mrs. Miller purchased Sandina Skylark in 1977 from the Sandina Kennels. This lovely pale brindle bitch was Reserve Winners bitch at the parent club

Right:
Ch. Harleana's El Kalico Kat is pictured winning the Breed under judge Jim Trullington at the 1974 Kennel Club of Puerto Rico Show. The Kat went on to win Group Second with his handler Bill Trainor. He was bred and owned by Mrs. Ileana Miller of San Juan, where her Harleana Kennels have been the bulwark of the breed on that island for two decades.

178

Ch. Harleana's Mukhalla El Wahid, the first and only dog of *any breed* bred in Puerto Rico to become a champion and a Best In Show winner. His show record included 1 Best In Show, 4 Group Firsts, 3 Seconds, 2 Thirds, 1 Fourth and 15 Bests of Breed. Mukhalla is handled here by Anne Goodwin for late owner Mr. Harley A. Miller, Harleana Kennel, San Juan, Puerto Rico.

Ch. Chinah of Grandeur was one of the first Best In Show Afghan Hounds on the island of Puerto Rico. Chinah won Best In Show in 1962 under judge Maxwell Riddle at the Kennel Club of Puerto Rico Show and is pictured here with Mrs. Harley A. Miller, who co-owned Chinah with Sunny Shay. Chinah's show record also included 5 Group Firsts, 1 Group Third and 8 Bests of Breed.

Mrs. Ileana Miller was the guiding light behind the dog fancy in Puerto Rico. Past and present president of the Kennel Club of Puerto Rico, no one there has done more for all dogs than she has. She is pictured here with her Am. and Dom. Champion Harleana's Arahbezk Del Wahid, a multiple Best In Show winner.

American and Bermudian Ch. Varuna of Ekselo is pictured winning the Hound Group at a Bermuda Kennel Club Show in the early 1970's. Varuna, co-owned by Ellen O'Leske and Dr. Sally Frank, both of Massachusetts, also won the 1969 Colonial Afghan Hound Club Specialty Show under judge Wally Pede. The sire was Ch. Sahadi Commanche Brave Eagle. Handling for the owners was George Alston. Bermuda News Bureau photograph.

specialty that year and will be part of the breeding program at the Harleana Kennels.

By 1976 an Afghan Hound club was being formed on the islands. In February of 1977 I was invited to judge their first sanctioned match show, but had to decline.

THE AFGHAN HOUND KENNEL IN CURACAO

In Curacao, Netherland Antilles, the Afghan Hound is supported by a devoted fan-

cier of many years duration. Dutch-born Anne C. Van Der Vlis, a lawyer specializing in corporate law in Curacao since 1964, has always loved the Afghan Hound. She imported several dogs from the Dutch kennels of Eta Pauptit, and is the only Afghan Hound owner and breeder on this beautiful Dutch colonial island. Anne has an acre of land, shaded with trees on which the Afghans run and swim in the ocean.

Since there are no dog shows on the island, Anne is an exhibitor in both Puerto Rico and the United States on occasion. She is very much interested in canine genetics, and uses the kennel name of Caravanserai. She has also been one of the editors of the quarterly newsletter that was circulated among over forty other Afghan fanciers that have owned Miss Pauptit's dogs. Started in 1971, it was entitled *v d OMer's Newsletter* and sold for one dollar.

In 1964 Anne imported her first Afghan Hound from Holland. It was a puppy bitch named Pepie and when Pepie died, Mrs. Pauptit sent Anne Netherland and Int. Ch. Juno v d Oranj Manege as a gift, who was co-owned by Mrs. Karen Armistead of Brooklyn, New York. Anne's most recent dog is Chahar v d Oranje Manege, a three time great grandson of Miss Pauptit's most famous dog, Int. Ch. Ophaal of Crown Crest, owned and imported to California by Kay Finch.

AFGHAN HOUNDS IN SOUTH AMERICA

By the 1950's small numbers of Afghan Hounds had become scattered in various countries of South America.

In Venezuela the Crown Crest fame had spread, along with Carl Rapps' imported Crown Crest Taejahmen, a Taejon son out of the imported Feeks von de Oranje Manege.

A vdOM dog, bred in 1948 and owned by Senor Pedro M. Campon, was winning the breed and placing in the Group at various shows. Venezuelan Ch. Sirdar of Done was sired by Ch. Shikari of Donde out of Jaba Maleke.

A Majara Menelek son, a brindle dog whelped in 1956 and named Majara Majid, was imported to Venezuela by Maria de Mueller, but went into a decline after his arrival in his new country. It was quite some time after his arrival before he was back in condition to be shown. However, he won Best of Breed and Group Second at the 12th all-breed show of the Afghan Hound Club de Caracus.

Also in Venezuela, the Baroness de Saint Marque imported a dog bred in Belgium by F. Esmans named Emmy de Samarkand for her Maharadjas Kennels. This bitch was responsible for several litters, but nothing of quality came from the breedings with the stock they had on hand. Because of this, coupled with the realization that the market for Afghan Hound puppies in that country was small (if not non-existent), the Baroness found herself with more puppies than she cared to have as a necessary part of any future breeding program.

American, Bermudian and Canadian Ch. Cyndar of Ekselo poses for this stately portrait taken in 1973. "Cyn" is co-owned by Sally B. Frank and Ellen O'Leske of Brookline, Massachusetts.

After the death of Senor Campon, show entries declined still further at the Associacion Canina de Caracas all-breed show and the breed reached a standstill in that country.

AFGHAN HOUNDS IN SOME OTHER EUROPEAN COUNTRIES

The Sigurd Bruun Tonnessens own the Khasru Kennels in Oslo, Norway. They were famous for their Afghan Hounds, which were shown all over the country. In 1946 at the first post-war dog show in Norway, their kennel accounted for 16 of the entries! Their stock is behind many of the other kennels that have been showing the breed in that country.

181

Venezuelan Ch. Antar Ko-Chac Prometeus was sired by Crown Crest Chactaw *ex* Mex. Ch. Antar Af-Zar Xochiquetzal. The owner is Blanca Y Vivian De Jory of Caracas, Venezuela, who is pictured showing Ko-Chac to this win at the 1975 Exposicion Canina under American judge Mel Downing.

8-month-old Mon Ami Morrissa is owned by Pedro Salles, who is the son of the former Brazilian Ambassador to the U.S. Morrissa lives at the Brazilian Embassy in Rio de Janeiro and will start her show career in that country in 1977. The sire was BIS Ch. Ninth Turn Argus and the dam was Am. and Can. Ch. Tinkerbelle of Stormhill. Morrissa was bred by Carol and Martin Kutnyak.

In Belgium, Mariette Decker's kennel produced Amanullah Khan of Acklum, a beautifully marked black and tan dog distinguished for his impressive wins at both the French and Belgian shows. Mariette Decker was one of the earliest supporters of the breed in her country and M.J.A. Appels, President of the Belgian Afghan Hound Club, owned the Kaboul Kennels.

THE AFGHAN HOUND IN AFGHANISTAN IN MODERN TIMES

Today in Afghanistan the majority of the Afghan Hounds are owned by the rocky mountain farmers and the nomads and are referred to as *Thasis*.

These dogs seldom bark, are quite shy and wary of strangers. They go out of their way to avoid fights either among themselves or with other dogs. However, all these questionable or undesirable traits in no way detract from their superior hunting instincts for which they are owned, bred and respected.

They "hunt free," that is, without command from their owners, and act on their instincts alone. This instinct has become so inherent over the centuries that once the game is sighted the Thasis can be depended on to outlast and outwit any and all prey that enters their territory.

The mountain farmers, who sometimes hunt with their dogs at altitudes exceeding 6,000 feet, are so poor they cannot afford weapons or guns, so they often must rely on the dogs to provide their food. The dogs are depended upon for their speed and surefootedness to kill the Chamois and mountain goats, which are their chief source of meat. Their proficiency at this has earned them the name of Thasi, while the other dogs are referred to as szack, the Afghan name for dogs that are low, dirty creatures in the eyes of the Mohammedans.

While the szack are held in contempt by the natives, there are, of course, evidences of many cross-breedings visible on the hills and valleys of the Hindu-Kush mountains along the old rocky caravan roads. In the cities, a few of the wealthier Afghan people breed excellent dogs that have been obtained from the kennels of the Maharajas. There are no dog clubs and no records are kept on breeding programs or linear descent.

Indian Ch. Sans Craintes Super Star, owned by Raj Pathy, Coimbatore, India.

Am. and Dom. Ch. Harleana's Arahbezk Del Wahid is pictured winning the Hound Group on the way to Best In Show at the 1972 Kennel Club of Puerto Rico event under judge Mrs. Paul Silvernail. Arahbezk was also Best In Show from the classes at just 18 months of age at this event in 1970, and Best In Show from the classes in Santo Domingo in 1970. Her sire was also Best In Show at this event in 1964 and *her* grandsire in 1962. She was bred and is owned by Ileana Miller of Puerto Rico.

Top-winning Afghan Hound in the history of the breed! Ch. Holly Hill Desert Wind is owned by Mrs. Cheever Porter of New York City. Windy's handler during most of his illustrious show career was Jane Forsyth, pictured with him here. His total record was 258 Bests of Breed, 126 Best Hound awards and 36 Bests In Show.

Chapter V

The Top Ten Afghan Hounds
In the History of the Breed

True, records are made to be broken, and we can all look to the day when another magnificent Afghan Hound comes on the scene and cuts a path through the crowds to triumph as the top-winning dog in our breed! There is always room for another great dog to bring additional glory to the Afghan Hound and just as naturally as night follows day, we all hope that that extra special specimen will be our own!

As this book goes to press in the second half of the 1970's, we have a remarkable list of sensational dogs that can already claim fame as being at the top of the list of ten of the all-time show winners in the history of the breed—to date! This book would be less than complete if it did not pay tribute in both word and picture to those dogs which have earned their titles by accumulating outstanding wins over the years. These records, of course, are based on the accumulation of Phillips System points, the first and most fairly compiled system of achievement for the nation's top dogs.

WHAT IS THE PHILLIPS SYSTEM?

In the mid-1950's Mrs. John Phillips, a woman famous for her Haggiswood Irish Setter Kennels and a judge of many breeds, devised a point system based on show records published in the *American Kennel Gazette* to measure the successes of the nation's show dogs.

As in all sports, competition and enthusiasm in the dog fancy run high, and Irene Phillips—now Mrs. Harold Schlintz—came up with a simple, yet certainly the most fair, method of measuring wins for this competition, which over the years has provided many thrills for dog lovers interested in the good sportsmanship so essential to a competitive sport.

The Phillips System which Mrs. Phillips compiled herself during the early years was sold as an annual feature to *Popular Dogs* magazine, whose editor at that time, Mrs. Alice Wagner, did much to make it the most important rule of success for a show dog. Later, when I took over as editor of *Popular Dogs* in 1967, I carried on and did the compiling of the figures as well. For the five years I was tallying the finals for the Phillips System, it was a constant source of enjoyment for me to watch the leading dogs in this country, in all breeds, climb to the top. Because I knew that so many others felt the same way, and since the competition increases with each passing year, I felt that a healthy sampling of the Afghan Hounds which have achieved honors should be represented in this book so that they may become a matter of permanent record.

HOW THE SYSTEM WORKS

The Phillips System is designed to measure with fairness the difference between a dog show win scored over many dogs and one scored over just a few dogs. For example, a Best In Show won over 1,000 dogs should obviously have more significance than a Best In Show scored over 200 dogs. The Phillips System acknowledges this difference by awarding points in accordance with the number of dogs over which the win was scored. Points are awarded for Best In Show and Group Placings only. Best of Breed wins do not count.

The Best In Show dog earns a point for each dog in actual competition. (Absentees or obedience dogs are not counted.) The first Place winner in each of the six Groups earns a point for each dog in his group. The dog which places Second in the Group earns a point for each dog in the Group less the total

Ch. Holly Hill Desert Wind, the top-winning Afghan Hound in the history of the breed, is pictured winning the Hound Group at the 1968 Boardwalk Kennel Club Show in Atlantic City, New Jersey, under judge William Acklund. Robert Forsyth handled Holly for owner Mrs. Cheever Porter of New York City. Dr. Irving Botwinick, show chairman, presented the trophy.

dogs in the breed which were First. Third in the Group earns a point for each dog in the Group less the total of the breeds which were First and Second. Fourth in the Group earns a point for each dog in the Group less the total of the breeds which were First, Second and Third.

Source for the count is the official records for each dog show as published each month in the *American Kennel Gazette* magazine, the official publication for the American Kennel Club. An individual card is kept on each and every dog which places in the Group or wins a Best In Show during the entire year. Figures are tallied for publication at the end of each 12-month period.

In the beginning only a few of the top dogs were published, but starting in 1966 the phrase "Top Ten" in each breed was established. The published figures include the total number of points (or number of dogs defeated), the number of Bests In Show and the number of Group Placements. It is extremely interesting to note that as the years passed there was a tremendous increase in the number of points accrued by the big winners. This is proof positive of the amazing increase in the number of entries at the dog shows from the mid-1950's when the System was first created by Irene Phillips to the mid-1970's. It is a matter of record that the #1 dog in the nation has had to amass over 50,000 points to win the title of top show dog in the United States!

ALL TIME TOP WINNERS IN AFGHAN HOUNDS

#1 Am. and Can. Ch. HOLLY HILL DESERT WIND

Windy was campaigned during the height of his ring career by his owner, Mrs. Cheever Porter of New York City, and was cord-total of 39 Bests In Show, four Specialty wins, 126 Group Firsts and 258 Bests of Breed to earn him this title of top-winning Afghan Hound in the history of the breed to date. Windy was sired by the Sheldon's Ch. Khabiri of Grandeur out of the Kauffman's top-winning bitch, Ch. Samaris of Moornistan.

Windy was campaigned during the height of his ring career by his owner, Mrs. S. Cheever Porter of New York City, and was her first Afghan Hound. Many other of her dogs have also been top winners during her over 35 years in the fancy, and Windy's clownish behavior in the ring was a joy to her and everyone else at ringside. He was always a crowd pleaser and brought much attention to the breed. Windy is the official receptionist at the Forsyth Kennels where he is now past 14 years of age. He is still kept in top show condition and still conducts himself as a showman.

#2 Ch. SAHADI SHIKARI

I am proud to say that I do not know of anyone else in the fancy that can say that they bred a Westminster Group Winner in their first home-bred litter in any breed—except me. The shiny, beautiful black Sheik came from a breeding with Ch. Shirkhan of Grandeur, the 1957 Best In Show winner at the Garden out of my magnificent bitch, Ch. Crown Crest Kahlifah. The nine puppies they produced on January 21, 1959 were to make Afghan history.

The litter of one bitch and eight dogs were all brindle and blacks; at that time, before their Dad made breed history, these were not popular colors. I had difficulty in selling them because of their color. As a result three went to non-show homes, and I later tried to buy them back, without success. They were Sahadi Sinni, Sahadi Serge and Sahadi Sukarno. The rest, Sahadi Sequin, Sinbad, Scaramouche, Satan and Sessu all entered the show ring and found acclaim. All but Satan achieved championship and Satan had many points and both majors before his owners found it impossible to continue showing. And then there was Sahadi Shikari!

Ch. Sahadi Shikari was the top-winning Afghan Hound in America for 1963 and ranked fifth for all hound breeds that year, according to the Phillips System. This glorious black dog, owned by Dr. and Mrs. Earl Winter and bred by Joan Brearley, is the second top-winning Afghan Hound in the history of the breed in America! "Sheik" is a son of Ch. Shirkhan of Grandeur *ex* Ch. Crown Crest Khalifah.

Owned by Dr. and Mrs. Earl F. Winter of Oshkosh, Wisconsin, Sheik was to soar to all-time heights as #2 in the breed. His first time shown, he was Best of Winners under Dr. William Waskow at the Mid-West Afghan Hound Club Specialty Show, and finished with a 5-point major shortly thereafter under judge Gini Withington at a Greater Chicago Afghan Hound Specialty.

From 1963 through 1966 he won 10 Specialty Shows and had a total of 32 Bests In Show. During one year he won 57 Hound Group Firsts to take the Quaker Oats Award. This was more than twice the number of Groups won over a similar period by any Afghan Hound up to that time. The Winters graciously invited me to attend the Quaker Oats Dinner that year, but I had to decline because this was the same year my lilac-point Siamese cat won the same honors in the feline fancy! Since he had no escort to his presentation ceremoney and Sheik did, I felt obliged to attend the cat banquet since my cat was an "old man" and Sheik still in his prime! However, this did not lessen my extreme pride in either of my "top contenders." It's nice to win—but it's even better to win in two categories!

Sheik was seldom used at stud outside his own kennel and not shown outside the United States, so there is no telling what additional claims to fame he might have achieved, but suffice it to say that in his first home-bred litter, five out of seven puppies achieved championship!

Int. Ch. Crown Crest Mr. Universe, one of the greatest winning Afghan Hounds in the breed. He had 35 Best In Show wins, 4 specialty show wins and 100 Hound Group Firsts. Mr. U has over 20 champion sons and daughters that are winning at the shows all over the country. He was bred and owned by Kay Finch, Crown Crest Kennels, Corona del Mar, California.

The illustrious Ch. Shirkhan of Grandeur was the Best In Show winner at the 1957 Westminster Kennel Club Show at Madison Square Garden in New York City. The ultimate in show win success, Shirkhan is pictured with judge Mrs. Beatrice Godsol, Mr. William Rockefeller, president of the club, and his breeder and handler, Sunny Shay, who co-owned the dog with Dorothy Chenade. Evelyn M. Shafer photograph.

#3 Am. and Can. Ch. CROWN CREST MR. UNIVERSE

Kay Finch considers her beloved Mr. U the "ultimate" in Afghan Hounds. This impressive black-masked golden was the sire of 40 champions and had a supreme show record, including 35 Bests In Show, all breeds, 100 Hound Group Firsts and four National Specialty Show wins, always owner-handled by Kay herself. She considered him the most perfect example of her Crown Crest Kennels breeding and it will be a long time before any dog will top his total achievements. Mr. U. was nominated for the *Kennel Review* magazine Hall of Fame, won the 1974 Beaters Club Award and placed in the Top Ten polls in 1959 and 1960. He was whelped in June, 1957 and died in February, 1968.

#4 Ch. SHIRKHAN OF GRANDEUR

Shirkhan is the only Afghan Hound to win Best In Show at Westminster in the history of the breed! This was accomplished in February, 1957 and eventually lead to his being named the top-producing sire in the breed, as well. Shirkhan won 26 Bests In Show during his career and received the Quaker Oats Award for Top Hound dog in 1957. He was also named to *Kennel Review* magazine's Hall of Fame. Bred by Sunny Shay, at the time of his Westminster win he was co-owned by her and Dorothy Chenade. He was always owner-handled by Sunny and was solely responsible for the popularity and "acceptance" of the dark brindle color in the breed show ring. He was sired by the great Ch. Blue Boy of Grandeur out of Mahdi of Grandeur.

189

#5 Ch. TAEJON OF CROWN CREST

Kay Finch and her husband Braden made a special trip to Decatur, Illinois, to see "Johnnie" after his breeder, Mrs. Leo Conroy, sent them his photograph. After the purchase, Johnnie (named after the battle of Taejon in Korea that was launched on the day he was born) was shipped to Kay in September, 1951. I quote here Kay's own words commemorating their initial meeting:

"After a stop at a wide beach where he breathed in the fresh ocean air, his tail came up and he made an unforgettable picture against the clear blue sky. . . seeming to sense that he would have every chance to prove his worth. I felt deeply proud and grateful to own this glorious and promising young Afghan Hound, which I loved at first sight."

Taejon was 16 months old when Kay first showed him. He won Best of Breed over Group-winning champions. He won his first Best In Show one month later, which he celebrated by jumping up onto the judge's table when the judge pointed to him as the winner! In May, 1952 he won Best of Breed at the Morris and Essex Show under what Kay considers to be "the father of the breed in America," Q.A. Shaw McKean, owner of the Prides Hill Afghan Hound Kennels.

His total show record was 19 Bests In Show, four Specialty wins, 49 Hound Groups and 72 Bests of Breeds in 77 times shown for Crown Crest. He was undefeated in the breed for three consecutive years and won 14 consecutive Hound Groups in a row. His sire was Ch. Elcoza's Ponder and his dam was Ch. Winomana of Rreks. He was born on May 12, 1950 and died in July, 1961 in Kay's arms. When asked in an interview one time what was the saddest thing that ever happened to her in dogs, Kay replied, "Johnnie dying in my arms."

Johnnie was the sire of 34 champions, received the Will Judy Award in 1954 and was featured on the cover of the March 12, 1956 issue of *Sports Illustrated* magazine, along with the story of his show career.

Taejon can be said to be responsible for bringing much attention to the breed. I know he is largely responsible for me being in the breed. I had always followed the progress in the breed and felt they were the most beautiful of all dogs, but it was while sitting in the Garden and watching Kay Finch and Johnnie win the Hound Group that I made a decision: I vowed on the spot that no matter how long I

Ch. Taejon of Crown Crest appears to be having a good laugh for himself! Johnnie was owned and shown throughout his illustrious ring career by Kay Finch, Crown Crest Kennels, Corona del Mar, California.

had to wait I would have a Taejon son that looked just like his dad and that I would show him at the Garden, too! I wrote Kay a letter that very day and sent a deposit and the eventual result was my first Afghan Hound, Ch. Crown Crest Jesi Jhaimz who completed his championship at the Garden in 1957! Dreams do come true. . . I later purchased my brood bitch, Ch. Crown Crest Khalifah, in whelp to Johnny and we finished three champions from this litter.

I feel it is a fitting tribute to Johnny that we won so many hearts and brought so many people into the wonderful world of Afghan Hounds. He was always a credit to the breed in and out of the show ring. Next to Kay, I think Johnnie is remembered most by me. . .

#6 Ch. DAHNWOOD GABRIEL

Gabriel was a showman and to prove it he went Best In Show the very first time he was shown at the age of 2½ years. In 1968 he won Best of Breed at the Afghan Hound Club of America Specialty Show in New York City under breeder-judge Cyrus Rickel and went on to win the Quaker Oats Award for Top Hound. Sired by Ch. Crown Crest Zardoni out of El Amron Tarquin, Gabriel was owned

Ch. Dahnwood Gabriel wins Best In Show under judge Percy Roberts at the 1968 Albany, Georgia, Kennel Club Show. Handling here is Michele H. Leathers for owners Herman and Judith Fellton, Mandith Kennels. Dr. Lewis E. Richardson presented the trophy.

by the Herman Feltons of Georgia and handled for them by Michelle Leathers Billings. Together they brought his show record up to a total of 14 Bests In Show, three Specialty Show wins and 46 Group Firsts. He has sired 11 champions, show winners in their own right.

#7 Ch. COASTWIND GAZEBO

Ezra's record is exceptional when one considers that the dog was only campaigned for 18 months—but what an 18 months! He captured 14 Bests In Show, four Specialty wins, 52 Groups and 99 Bests of Breed. After his retirement he was entered in competition

The great Ezra at play. . . ! Ch. Coastwind Gazebo displays his fantastic personality during an informal moment in the show ring. He is owned by the Coastwind Kennels, Salinas, California.

on two other occasions and on both outings won the California Specialties! Owned by Mike Dunham and Richard Souza, this glorious dog was sired by Akaba's Allah Kazam out of Ch. Shaadar's Blajnhe of Karlyle and rates as a Phillips System Top Ten dog and Top sire as well. I was privileged not only to be in the audience for his first Best In Show win at the Beverly Hills Show in California on

January 5, 1969, but was invited to present the Best In Show trophy to him as well. I told his handler, Marvin Cates, that at the time he was one of the most magnificent Afghan Hounds I had ever seen. In all the years that have followed, I have not changed my mind. Many of his get carry his great quality and I pride myself on being able to "pick them out in a crowd!"

Multiple Best In Show winner Ch. Taralane's Carpetbagger, owned by Mr. S. Howard Ruback, is pictured winning at the 1970 Grand Island Kennel Club Show with his handler Rex Vandeventer. The judge was Sally Keyes, and Dr. Robert Kreycik presented the trophy.

#7 Ch. TARALANE'S CARPETBAGGER

Tying for the #7 place, also, is Faye and Howard Ruback's Ch. Taralane's Carpetbagger. "Shu" was purchased by them to replace a much loved 15-year-old Boxer. One of the highlights of his career was winning back-to-back Bests In Show—which he repeated later on during his ring career. In addition to 13 Bests In Show, he won 42 Hound Groups and 69 Bests of Breed while handled by Rex Van Deventer and his wife Leota. On several occasions he was shown by 12-year-old Cindy Ruback, who won a Group with him and a Group Placement on another venture into the ring. His sire was Ch. Musket Fire of Cobb's Web ex Longlesson Summer Shadow.

Shu retired with a Best In Show win in his native city of Omaha on the same day Leota Van Deventer was retiring as a handler to become a judge. Both dog and handler were well known in the area and upon the awarding of the Best In Show they both received a five-minute standing ovation! How wonderful for them to quit while they were ahead!

#8 Am, Mex. and Can. CH. CROWN CREST ZARDONX

Zar's first show was at the Golden Gate Kennel Club on January 21, 1956 where he won a 4-point major under judge Marie Meyer. It was the start of a brilliant show career for this heavily black-masked true-hound and his championship was completed in five straight shows, including three 4-point majors. Zar was born in July, 1954; his sire was American, German, Belgian and Holland Ch. Ophaal of Crown Crest and his dam was Kay Finch's beautiful Ch. Crown Crest Taejoan. When Zar died in January, 1968, he had produced 15 champions and his show record stood at 13 Bests In Show, 57 Hound Group Firsts, 98 Bests of Breed and three Specialties. He was the top breed winner in 1957 and this same year his littermates, Ch. Crown Crest Rubi and Ch. Crown Crest Topz, were ranked 3rd and 9th respectively.

The wonderful Zar was another personal favorite of mine and it was a joy to have Kay and Zar stay at my home on their various trips to the East to compete at the shows during the height of his show career. It was a sad time for me when he died in January, 1968.

This magnficient wind-blown headstudy of Am. and Mex. Ch. Crown Crest Zardonx was featured on one of breeder-owner Kay Finch's Christmas cards. The fantastic Zar won Best of Breed at the 1957 Afghan Hound Club of America Specialty Show in New York City under judge Mrs. Lauer Froelich. He repeated the win the following year under judge Anna Katherine Nicholas.

Ch. Sandhihi Joh-Cyn Taija Baba is pictured winning at the 1967 Westchester Kennel Club Show under judge Fred Hunt. Brandt Houtsma handled Taija, who he co-owns with Dorothy Houtsma.

Ch. Shangrila's Pharahna Phaedra, owned and shown by Dr. Gerda Maria Kennedy, is pictured winning Best In Show at the 1970 S.E. Missouri Kennel Club Show under judge Henry Stoecker. William E. Busch, show chairman, presented the trophy. Earl Graham photograph.

#8 CH. SANDHIHI JOH-CYN TAIJA BABA

A striking black-masked silver dog, Baba was owned by Mr. and Mrs. Brandt Houtsma of California, and always shown by Mr. Houtsma. Always beautifully presented, Baba's show record included 11 Bests In Show and 60 Hound Group Firsts. He also won four Specialty Shows and 150 Bests of Breed. His sire was Ch. San-Dhi's Hatim Tai of San Dhihi, C.D., out of Ch. Dominja Joh-Cyn. Shown during the second half of the 1960's, Baba gained additional recognition as the sire of the all-time top-winning Afghan Hound bitch, Ch. Sangrila Pharahna Phaedra with whom he shares a tie for the #8 spot in this Top Ten listing of the breed.

#8 Am. and Can. Ch. SHANGRILA PHARAHNA PHAEDRA

Born on December 10, 1967, Phaedra won her first all-breed Best In Show at Del City Kennel Club under Albert Van Court in 1969 when she was not yet two years old. In February, 1970 she won the parent club specialty show in New York City under judge Herman Fellton over an entry of 205. This win classified her as being not only the youngest bitch ever to win this show, but the first bitch to do it in over a quarter of century. When her owner, Dr. Gerda Maria Kennedy, retired Phaedra in December, 1972, her show record listed 13 All-breed Bests In Show, four Specialty wins, 49 Group Firsts, 21 Group Placings and 80 Bests of Breed. Her dam was Ch. Shangrila Pharahna Cleopatra.

Ch. Ali Khyber of Khanhassett is shown winning Best In Show at a February, 1944 kennel club show under judge Major Joseph C. Quirk. John Hill was handler and Lt. E. Boswell, the club president, presented the trophy. Percy T. Jones photograph.

Ch. Ammon Hall Nomad, owned by J. Playfair and M.P. Gray, is pictured winning Best In Show under judge Virginia Hampton at the 1971 Spartanburg, South Carolina, Kennel Club Show Handler was Tom Glassford and Margaret Burchette presented the trophy. Earl Graham photograph.

#9 Ch. ALI KHYBER OF KHANHASSETT

We go back to the 1940's for our #9 dog, the winner of ten Bests In Show under the handling expertise of John Hill. Ali Khyber was owned by Mrs. Leah McConaha of Great Neck, New York, one of the early advocates of the breed. Mrs. McConaha handled the dog herself on occasion. His complete show record is unavailable, but it was an impressive one considering that Afghan Hounds were relatively new to the country in the 1940's and were not always given their share of the awards. Ali Khyber is acknowledged within the breed, however, as being one of the early and all-time greats.

#10 Ch. AMANULIAH OF KANDAHAR

Tying for the #10 spot on the list is Amelia White's Ch. Amanuliah of Kandahar, winner of 10 Bests In Show back in the days when these awards were not as numerous as they are today. Therefore, his complete show record and a photograph are not available.

However, the prominence of the Kandahar Kennels and the record amassed by this dog are remembered and figured in the list of the all-time winners in the history of the breed.

#10 Ch. AMMON HALL NOMAD

Bred by Jay Ammon and owned by the Grayfair Kennels, Nomad was the 1971 Quaker Oats Award winner for being the hound that won the most Groups during that year. It was this same year that he was shown at the Canadian National Sportsman Shows and won five straight Bests In Show! He also won Best of Breed for two consecutive years at Westminster in 1969 and 1970 with handler Tom Glassford as his pilot. His total record reads nine Bests In Show, five Specialty Shows, 57 Group Firsts and 180 Bests of Breed. He is the sire of two Best In Show winning dogs, Ch. Khayam's Apollo and Ch. Kalamazoo El Achmed, and is himself sired by the #1 dog, Am. and Can. Ch. Holly Hill Desert Wind. His dam was Ch. Holly Hill Lorna Doone.

With the exception of the dogs from the early days, Ali and Amanuliah of Kandahar, I have had the great privilege of having seen all of these top show dogs and can attest to their excellence and great beauty. All of them are breathtakingly beautiful, worthy of both championships and the name of Afghan Hound, and are a credit to their breeders and owners. We have come a long way with the breed since they first reached our shores in the early 1930's and we can be proud of the work that went into preserving the breed and bringing it up to its present standard.

While I am thrilled at having bred and enjoyed the #2 dog, I think a special tribute is due Kay Finch who has bred and/or owned *three* out of the ten, and her breeding is behind some of the others as well!

THE TOP TEN THROUGH THE YEARS

While the Phillips System was first published in 1956, we present here listings starting with 1960, which unfortunately do not give the number of dogs defeated. However, by the 1965 finalists we see not only names of some of the top kennels still winning, but the remarkable tally of 16,440 points won by Shikari—twice the number of dogs defeated by the #2 ranking Afghan, Desert Wind. Starting with 1967 we present the yearly tally of the Top Ten Afghan Hounds in the nation. They make interesting comparisons on a year-to-year basis as well as represent a permanent record for those who enjoy breed statistics.

TOP TEN AFGHAN HOUNDS—1957

Dog	BIS	1	2	3	4
1. Ch. Shirkhan of Grandeur	4	17	9	3	1
2. Ch. Crown Crest Zardonx	4	18	8	5	2
3. Ch. Crown Crest Rubi	2	18	8	2	2
4. Ch. Shahzenan of Moornistan	1	4	1	5	2
5. Ch. Conners Mill Jeffara		9	5	10	3
6. Ch. Ben Ghazi's Kaman		4	2	4	1
7. Ch. Khabiri of Grandeur		3	1	0	1
8. Ch. Desert Chieftan of Mikai, C.D.		3	0	1	0
9. Ch. Majara Menelek		2	5	1	2
10. Ch. Crown Crest Topaz		2	1	2	1

TOP TEN AFGHAN HOUNDS—1960

Dog	BIS	1	2	3	4
1. Ch. Crown Crest Mr. Universe	7	23	6	1	0
2. Ch. Shirkhan of Grandeur	1	12	2	4	2
3. Ch. Hassan-Ben of Moornistan	1	7	3	3	0
4. Ch. Pamir Storm Ho	1	4	4	0	0
5. Ch. Majara Metaab		4	1	1	1
6. Ch. Tajmir's Bhijupiter		3	5	5	2
7. Ch. Radizar of Azad		2	1	0	0
8. Ch. Javelin of Camri		2	0	0	0
9. Ch. Crown Crest Bongo Bongo		2	0	0	0
10. Ch. Holly Hill Talisman of Kismet		1	6	4	6

TOP TEN AFGHAN HOUNDS—1965

Dog	BIS	1	2	3	4	POINTS
1. Ch. Sahadi Shikari	17	57	18	3	0	16,440
2. Ch. Holly Hill Desert Wind	9	23	10	5	1	8,423
3. Ch. Pandora of Stormhill	1	11	8	2	1	4,760
4. Ch. Shahmirs Sampson	2	7	1	1	1	1,936
5. Ch. Ammon Hall Judas	2	7	2	2	4	1,673
6. Ch. Cha Cha Cha of Shamalan	1	5	0	0	0	1,555
7. Ch. Smoke Dream of Stormhill	1	9	0	1	1	1,539
8. Ch. Sandhihi Joh-Cyn Taija Baba		2	2	2	0	1,392
9. Ch. Tajmir Gunsmoke of Mecca		3	5	3	2	1,235
10. Ch. Silverstone Witch Doctor		2	4	1	5	1,067

TOP TEN AFGHAN HOUNDS—1967

Dog	BIS	1	2	3	4	POINTS
1. Ch. Holly Hill Desert Wind	7	28	8	4	2	11,355
2. Ch. Sandhihi Joh Cyn Taija Baba	2	25	6	6	6	8,822
3. Ch. Dahnwood Gabriel	2	9	9	8	4	3,753
4. Ch. Shahmirs Sampson	2	12	10	4		3,648
5. Ch. Altai Ataturk		8	6	3	5	2,248
6. Ch. Rujhas Windman of Grandeur	1	4	5		3	1,928
7. Ch. Duchess Royal Grey Mystic		4	5	1	3	1,487
8. Ch. Akabas Sterling Silver		2	1		1	1,018
9. Ch. High Hos Moon Majesty Obahara		1		1	2	917
10. Ch. Mahabbis Continental Sytar		4		1	3	909

TOP TEN AFGHAN HOUNDS—1968

Dog	BIS	1	2	3	4	POINTS
1. Ch. Holly Hill Desert Wind	8	16	5	2		9,974
2. Ch. Sandhihi Joh-Cyn Taija Baba	4	13	9	5	5	9,185
3. Ch. Dahnwood Gabriel	4	26	21	8		8,492
4. Ch. Altai Ataturk	2	8	3	3		2,803
5. Ch. Balkhwood Banknote	1	5	4	2	1	2,219
6. Ch. Abashaghs Mr. Tambourine Man	1	5	1	2		1,573
7. Ch. Coastwind Gazebo		5	3	2	1	1,523
8. Ch. Shahmirs Sampson		8	2	2	1	1,504
9. Ch. Ammon Hall Nomad		2	8	3	1	1,453
10. Ch. Artemus of Province	1	2	3	2	1	1,430

TOP TEN AFGHAN HOUNDS—1969

Dog	BIS	1	2	3	4	POINTS
1. Ch. Coastwind Gazebo	8	34	19	4	4	17,458
2. Ch. Dahnwood Gabriel	4	19	7	4	3	8,902
3. Ch. Ammon Hall Nomad		8	16	2	6	4,143
4. Ch. Kismets Red Baron	1	7	10	6	1	3,625
5. Ch. Altai Ataturk	2	7	7	2	1	3,548
6. Ch. Akabas Royal Flush	1	5		1	3	2,217
7. Ch. Dahnwood Season of Bluemarc	2	3				2,046
8. Ch. Shangrilas Pharahna Phaedra	1	5	2	1		1,983
9. Ch. Taralanes Carpetbagger	1	8	2	1		1,696
10. Ch. Pamir Ho Chester		2	3	1		1,475

199

TOP TEN AFGHAN HOUNDS—1970

Dog	BIS	1	2	3	4	POINTS
1. Ch. Ammon Hall Nomad	5	25	17	10	7	13,350
2. Ch. Taralanes Carpetbagger	9	19	3			10,528
3. Ch. Coastwind Gazebo	5	18	2	1		9,624
4. Ch. Shangrilas Pharahna Phaedra	5	15	3	1		7,925
5. Ch. Mandith Salute	2	15	7		1	4,360
6. Ch. Ammon Hall Ter Caj of Tajmir		8	4	11	5	3,841
7. Ch. Pamir Ho Chester	1	3	3	2	2	3,426
8. Ch. Westwinds Dorian of Grandeur		3	2	2	2	2,171
9. Ch. Akabas Blue Bonnet of Sandina		2	3	3	2	1,998
10. Ch. Altai Ataurk		2	2	1	3	1,252

TOP TEN AFGHAN HOUNDS—1971

Dog	BIS	1	2	3	4	POINTS
1. Ch. Ammon Hall Nomad	4	23	20	3	3	10,601
2. Ch. Shangrilas Pharahna Phaedra	1	16	4			5,577
3. Ch. Coastwind Jubilan Tiger Paw	2	7	3	1	1	4,090
4. Ch. Belamir's High Tide	1	10	6	6		4,020
5. Ch. Taralanes Carpetbagger	2	11	4	3	1	3,588
6. Ch. Ammon Hall Ter Caji of Tajmir	1	7	6		3	2,903
7. Ch. Pandora's Shiek of Stormhill		2	6	5	3	2,716
8. Ch. Mandith Salute	1	10	2		3	2,581
9. Ch. Westwinds Dorian		2	2	4	2	2,040
10. Ch. Akabas Unsinkable Molly Blue		3	3		4	1,575

TOP AFGHAN HOUNDS—1973

Dog	BIS	1	2	3	4	POINTS
1. Ch. Khayams Apollo	3	14	4	2	1	8,141
2. Ch. Pandoras Shiek of Stormhill		5	7	7	5	6,525
3. Ch. Benvikkis A Bit Of Harmony	2	10	2	5	3	6,412
4. Ch. Rajahs El Cid		8		4	3	3,628
5. Ch. Shangrila Pharoah Bhima	1	4	8	4		3,380
6. Ch. Geyms Shades Of Bou	1	4	4	2	3	2,552
7. Ch. Hollyhill Genie Ace Of Spades	1	4	4	2	1	2,549
8. Ch. Ninth Turn Argus		4	4	1	3	2,272
9. Ch. Ambrosia Bon Nanza	1	1	1			2,126
10. Ch. Dea Zenga Quinton			3	1	1	2,010

TOP AFGHAN—1974

Dog	BIS	1	2	3	4	POINTS
1. Ch. Kings Royal Kaluku	3	5	4	5	6	5,848
2. Ch. Sandina Starstream	2	13	9	3		5,277
3. Ch. Gold Coast Calcutta		5	8	3	4	4,043
4. Ch. Khayams Ares		8	8		3	3,887
5. Ch. Ninth Turn Argus	1	7	3	5	1	3,691
6. Ch. Pandoras Sheik of Stormhill	1	8			1	3,492
7. Ch. Shiloh Addis Abebe	1	6	7	2		3,491
8. Ch. Amulets Pinball Wizard	2	5	2	1	1	3,451
9. Ch. Meccas Mission Impossible		4	4	2	3	2,354
10. Ch. Wildenaus Bonvivant		1	5		1	2,272

TOP TEN AFGHAN HOUNDS—1975

Dogs	BIS	1	2	3	4	POINTS
1. Ch. Sandina Starstream	12	31	11	4	4	17,170
2. Ch. Khayams Ares	8	28	3	6	3	13,600
3. Ch. Alpha Friendly Guy	6	13	4	5	1	3,562
4. Ch. Mandith Pericles	3	12	4	4		6,985
5. Ch. Wildenaus Bonvivant	2	8	2	4	1	6,421
6. Ch. Lippizans Big Red Machine	4	12	4	1	2	5,425
7. Ch. Kings Royal Kaluku	1	10	5	5	3	5,107
8. Ch. Amulets Pinball Wizard	2	6	6	2	2	4,388
9. Ch. Shiloh Addis Abeba Superstar	1	11	5	2	3	4,317
10. Ch. Kalamazoos Zeus Of Rehotpe	1	4	6	4	1	3,829

TOP TEN AFGHAN HOUNDS IN CANADA

The Phillips System is known and acknowledged in Canada as well, since many of the dogs compete in both countries. This competitve spirit is equally welcomed north of our border and while full statistics are not required here, nor a full year-by-year record, we present here a list of the Top Ten Canadian Afghan Hounds in 1975 along with their total points, which under the Canadian rules also indicate a point for each dog defeated in competition:

AFGHAN HOUNDS—1975

1. Ch. Amberhall Aquarius (D)	6,648
2. Ch. Mirabad's Caiphas of Spectrum (D)	1,259
3. Ch. Amberhall Serpents Tooth (D)	1,222
4. Ch. Amberhall Scorpio (D)	1,035
5. Can. Am. Ch. Sandina Starstream (D)	808
6. Ch. Khyber Khans Nathan (D)	664
7. Ch. Rokeish Sorocco (D)	579
8. Am. Ch. Pamir Sweet William (D)	463
9. Ch. Koibaba's Hylas Khinjii (B)	442
10. Ch. Mandith Pericles C.D. (D)	417

We hasten to add that a few of the dogs listed above are American owned and bred dogs which competed enough in Canada during the year to earn places on their list, while earning their Canadian championship titles.

Ch. Mirabad's Caiphas of Spectrum was whelped in 1971 and owned by Mrs. Ingeborg James of Vancouver, Canada. In 1973 he was #11 Afghan in Canada, #5 in 1974 and he was #2 in 1975. He has one all-breed Canadian Best In Show, one Canadian Specialty Best Canadian-Bred In Show and has points toward his U.S. championship title. He is the sire of champion get with many more pointed and is a keen and speedy lure coursing dog.

Ch. Bakali Cymbeline of Zuvenda, owned by Karen Usry and G. Cumberland, her breeder. Their kennel is located in Owings Mills, Maryland. Cymbeline is a Group-winning bitch and was Best of Breed at the 1974 Afghan Hound Club of America show when just over one-year old. She is the youngest bitch to ever win this honor.

Top-winning dog all breeds in Spain for 1975 was Norman Huiolobro's Int. Ch. Huilaco's Antar Rakashi. Rakashi is a champion in Chile, Portugal, Spain, Italy and Monaco.

Ch. Empire Gazebo Jr., Best In Show winner at the 3rd Afghan Hound Specialty Show held in Mexico in December, 1975. Judge for this major dog show event was Mrs. Cynthia Guzevich from the United States. This lovely black-masked golden dog was also Best Hound Dog in Mexico for the year 1975 and is owned by Lic. Jorge Martinez. He is handled here by Mariano Fuster. Presenting the trophies are Mrs. Thelma Von Thadden and Dr. Antonio Eisenhut, first president of the Afghan Hound Club of Mexico.

Khyanti's Moon Bandit, Field Champion, illustrates the perfect form of the coursing Afghan Hound in action! Bandit was the #1 coursing Afghan in the country for 1975. Owned by Kate Relick, Team Sunarise, San Jose, California.

BEST OF BREED
OR VARIETY

THE AFGHAN HOUND
CLUB OF AMERICA, INC.

FEB. 12, 1977

KLEIN

Ch. Shangrila Pharahna Kunasata was the winner of the 1977 Afghan Hound Club of America Specialty Show under judge Mrs. Herman L. Fellton. Handling for Dr. and Mrs. Thomas C. Burger of Evansville, Indiana, was Ray Brinlee. Club president Diane LaGreca presents the trophy. This win was followed by a Best of Breed win at the Westminster Kennel Club Show.

Chapter VI

The Afghan Hound Club of America

In 1935 the parent Afghan Hound club was formed in the United States with Q.A. Shaw McKean as its first president. It was not until 1938 that it was recognized by the American Kennel Club. In spite of a limited membership—only five attended that first meeting—the club members worked diligently to increase their membership and establish a headquarters for a breed club, so that they might also stage the first of their specialty shows.

Actually, the very first Afghan Hound specialty show was held in 1938, but by the Mid-West Afghan Hound Club held in conjunction with the Detroit Specialties Group. The winner was Garrymhor Pearie, imported from England.

The Specialty is just what the name implies—a special show for our special breed. And the ingredient that makes it so special, such a very great honor to win, is that this show of shows affords Afghan Hound lovers and exhibitors the opportunity to support and promote a show especially dedicated to the glorification of the breed.

The first of the national Afghan Hound Specialty Shows was held in the month of June in 1940, with Dr. Eugene Beck awarding Best In Show honors in accordance with the Standard for the breed used in England. It wasn't until September of 1948 that the Afghan Hound Club of America submitted and had accepted a clarification of the English Standard which became our American Standard for the breed.

The Afghan Hound was a comparatively new and different breed to this country back in 1940 when the entrants at the first specialty show were seen by the public at the North Westchester Kennel Club Show. It was only through the concentrated efforts of such loyal and devoted supporters as Mrs. Sherman Hoyt, Mrs. Pamela Porter, Mrs. Jack Oakie, Mrs. Marion Foster Florsheim, Mrs. Leah

McConaha, Mr. and Mrs. Robert Boger, Mr. and Mrs. Cyrus Rickel, Mr. and Mrs. Charles Wernsman, Dr. Eugene Beck and Q.A. Shaw McKean that the breed began to flourish and grow to the extent it has today.

Charlotte Coffey and Mrs. Robert Boger, until her death in 1956, had served for many years as the club's secretaries. Miss Coffey, until her death in January, 1975, had been our incomparable Specialty Show Chairman, bringing much beauty to the show dedicated to our beautiful breed. Charlotte Coffey was singularly responsible for the breath-taking array of silver trophies, the signing of contracts, etc., even during the years she served in other capacities and the title of show secretary was held by someone else. One could sense the strong guidance of Charlotte behind the scenes, giving the show of shows its touch of class!

Charlotte served as the Secretary-Treasurer of the AHCA from 1946 through 1950, as its President from 1951 through 1954, first

Ch. Tanyah Sahib of Cy Ann, bred and owned by Cyrus K. Rickel of Fort Worth, Texas, was the first AHCA Best of Breed winner in 1940. Photographed for the owner by Tauskey.

Mrs. Sherman Hoyt is captured on film while judging a class at the 2nd Annual Specialty Show of the Afghan Hound Club of America on the estate of the H.A. Florsheims in September, 1942.

Vice-President from 1955 until 1971, Show Chairman from 1955 until 1970. She was said to be significantly responsible for the writing of the Standard for the breed, revised and adopted in 1948 and still in use today.

The 38th National Specialty Show of the Afghan Hound Club of America was dedicated to the memory of Charlotte Coffey, the dedication to her was written by Donald A. Smith. I particularly liked his final two paragraphs, as follows: "So great was her involvement that for years some members used to worry about how the show could possibly go on 'if something were to happen to Charlotte.' Now the 'something' has happened to Charlotte, but the show goes on. She could ask no better memorial than for it to continue in the elegant format and tradition of excellence which she created for it."

I personally knew and loved Charlotte Coffey. It happened that I came into the breed as a novice and her telephone calls and great plethora of correspondence helped set me straight on both the breed and club activities. She was an enormous help to me in writing the first of my Afghan Hound books, and I was extremely pleased to be associated with her from 1959 when I took over the catalogue advertising committee from Marge Lathrop and until I passed it on to Karen Armistead in 1962. Charlotte taught me a lot of AHCA "ropes," for which I shall always be grateful.

It was always gratifying to notice that each year the show's entries increased noticeably because everyone wanted to be a part of this marvelous pageant staged by the gentle lady as a showcase representing the social register of Afghandom!

Ch. Karach of Khanhasset was the winner of both the 1946 and 1947 Afghan Hound Club of America Specialty Shows under judges Robert F. Boger and Charles A. Wernsman. Karach's owner was Leah P. McConaha. Photographed by famed dog photographer Tauskey.

Champion Karli ben ghaZi is shown winning Best of Breed from the Bred by Exhibitor Class at the 1952 Afghan Hound Club of America Specialty Show under judge Alex Scott. Karli was owned and handled by Ruth Tongren of Bloomfield, Connecticut.

Ch. Karan of Khanhasset was the winner of the February, 1948 Afghan Hound Club of America Specialty Show. The judge was E.E. Ferguson. Karan was handled by John H. Hill for owner Leah P. McCohaha. Shafer photograph.

Best of Breed at the February, 1951 Afghan Hound Club of America Specialty Show in New York City was Ch. Blu Arabis of Kuvera, owned by Lee and Howard Iverson of San Francisco, California. Paul Mountz handled for the owner. This important win was under judge Cyrus Rickel.

1. Ch. Yev-Rah Silhouette is pictured finishing for championship at a Salinas Kennel Club Show under judge Len Carey. Handled by Bill Liles for owner-breeders Mark and Geaniel Harvey of Watsonville, California.

2. Ch. Tai-Ahmus of Jhabhul is pictured finishing his championship under judge Joan Brearley. He is handled by Bill Maseth of Timonium, Maryland, who co-owns Tai with Jane Slusher.

3. In this jubilant scene Elmo's Blue Graffiti wins the Best Puppy In Show award from Kay Finch at an Afghan Hound Club of Greater Houston Specialty Show. While being shown only 5 times as an adult, he was still ranked #11 according to the National Dog system of show ratings. Blue Graffiti is owned, bred and handled by Peter Belmont, Elmo Kennels, Kansas City, Missouri.

4. 7-week-old Suni's Golden Raintree was captured on film by photographer Stu Bolin for owners M. Van Woert and Lynda Rabyn. "Kenya's" sire was Ch. Khayams Gold Dust ex Starlanes Suni Fantasy.

5. Starlanes Standing Ovation, C.D.X., is currently working toward her utility title. "Tassel" is owned, trained and handled by artist Marcia Van Woert of Brookville, Ohio. Her sire was Ch. Mohammed Ali of Scheherezade ex Starlanes Holli Lulah Baby. This lovely photograph was taken by Stu Bolin.

6. One of the Tongren's most beautiful bitches, Ch. Ben ghaZi's Apryl, was photographed by Life magazine while draped around Guy Tongren's neck at the Sighthound Coursing Exhibition in Connecticut many years ago.

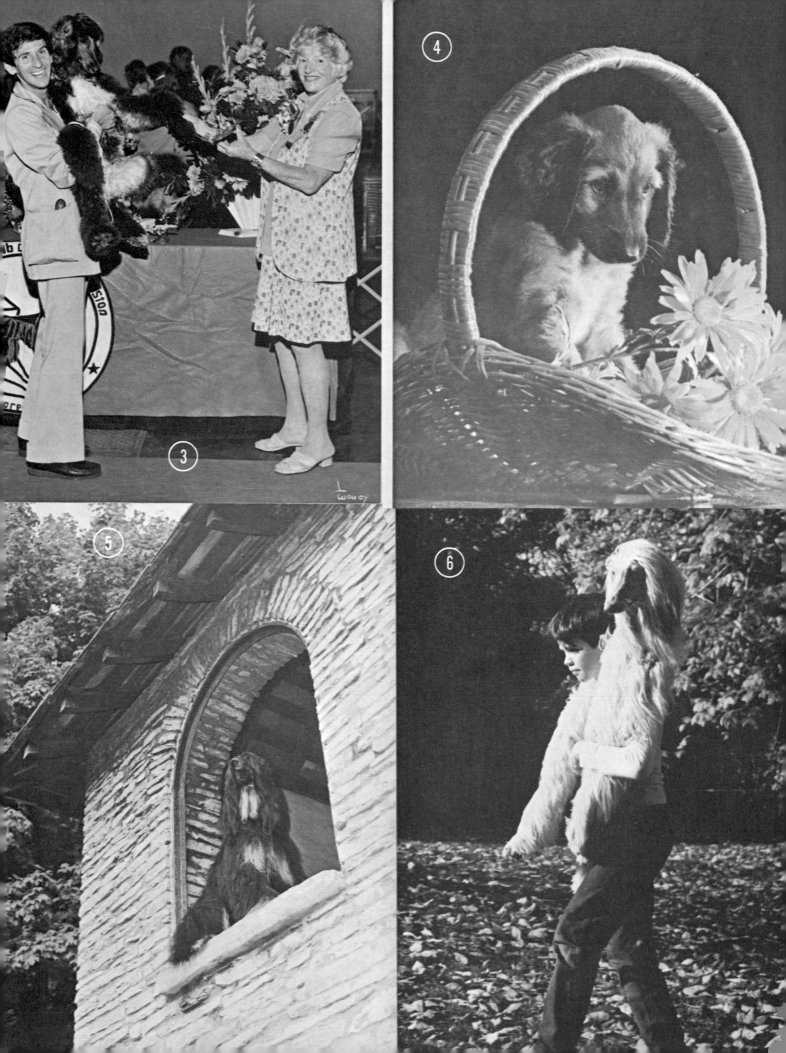

7. June F. Boone, owner of the Kassan Kennels in Kokomo, Indiana, poses with two of her favorite Afghan Hounds, Ch. Ambrosia Bon-Dir and Ch. Kassans Nina-Nerina.

8. This lovely headstudy portrait is of two 7-month-old Afghan Hounds owned by Joseph Kluchinsky of Spotswood, New Jersey. They are Bokhara Taj-Akbar and his litter sister, Bokhara's Blueberry Muffin.

9. *The glorious Ch. Coastwind Phobos is pictured finishing his championship title under breeder-judge Herman Fellton at a Silver Bay Kennel Club Show. The sire was Ch. Coastwind Abraxas ex Coastwind Jubilan Butterfly. He is shown by Richard Souza and owned by the Coastwind Kennels, Salinas, California.*

10. *Am. and Can. Ch. Esfahan Echo Hawk of Apache, a beautiful domino Afghan Hound, is owned by Charles and Virginia Robinson, Apache Kennels, Wichita, Kansas. Hawk finished his American championship with four majors and his Canadian championship in three shows, undefeated in the breed and including a Hound Group First win from the classes over Best In Show Specials. He has numerous other Group placements in Canada as well. Hawk has done more winning than any other domino in history, with the exception of Cynthia Guzevich's Tanjore Domino who was campaigned several years ago.*

11. *Ch. Khan Shah of Grandeur is pictured winning the Breed at the 1973 Elm City Kennel Club Show under Joan Brearley. Damon is co-owned by his breeder and handler, Sunny Shay, and Loraine P. Munter of Rye, New York.*

BEST OF
BREED

GILBERT PHOTO

12. Ch. Briarhill Denarius is owned by Ms. Sandra Terry and was sired by Ch. Coastwind Gazebo ex Ch. Sultana Irisa. The breeder was Barbara Craddock, Briarhill Afghans, Houston, Texas.

13. Ch. Dynasty's Supercharger is pictured with breeder, owner, handler Frederic M. Alderman. Sired by Ch. Coastwind Gazebo ex Ch. Dynasty's Wildcard, this black-masked red brindle bitch won one of her majors at a specialty and has a Group placement to her credit. She is also a Breed winner from the classes.

14. A 1976 acrylic painting of two Afghan Hounds was created by artist Peter Belmont. This detail of a 16" x 30" painting is another of the magnificent works devoted to our breed by this talented artist and college professor. Mr. Belmont teaches art and breeds, judges and exhibits Afghan Hounds in the Midwest.

15. Am. and Can. Ch. Honiego's Ambassador to Fram, Am. and Bda. C.D., is breeder-owned by Nancy Eisaman of Jeanette, Pennsylvania. "Amir" is a multiple Group winner and top obedience performer. He is the sire of obedience and conformation winners in both the U.S. and Canada, and is pictured winning the breed at the 1976 Fort Steuben Kennel Club Show under Kurt Mueller. Amir went on to win the Group at this show under judge Robert Braithwaite.

16. Sura's Silver Sundown and owner Suzanne J. Neill are pictured high on a windy hill!

BEST OF **BREED**
OR **VARIETY**

FORT STEUBEN
KENNEL ASSOC., INC.
MAR. 21, 1976   KLEIN

17. *A darling little oriental boy and his Afghan Hound puppy were the subject of this magnificent painting by Nancy Turner Rea. This photo is courtesy of Steve and Susan Sakanye of Santa Barbara, California.*

18. *The incomparable Kay Finch relaxes with Karima's Silver Meteor in a photograph taken in April, 1977 by Said Mughabghab.*

19. *Canadian Ch. Hi Vandal of Rokeish, C.D., owned by Rena Kirkham of Alberta, Canada, was captured in this fascinating photograph by T.D. Lindsay. Remy finished his obedience title with scores of 192, 192 and 191 and his championship title in three straight shows, including two Best of Breed wins. All this was accomplished after having been severely injured when hit by a car and his owners were told he would not walk again without a severe limp. His great spirit pulled him through and he earned not one but two titles before being retired from the rings.*

20. *The beautiful Ch. Shangrila Pharoah Kongatoh was whelped in 1972 and is owned by Otto and Erika Soeding of Troy, Michigan. His sire was Ch. Shangrila Pharaoh Gandharra ex Shangrila Pharahna Elektra.*

21. The magnificent Ch. Coastwind Gazebo is pictured winning his 100th Best of Breed at 10 years of age under Kay Finch at the Santa Barbara Kennel Club Show. He is handled by Richard Souza, who co-owns Gazebo with Michael Dunham. Gazebo is one of the author's all-time favorite Afghan Hounds!

22. Jubilan's Silver Shotgun is pictured going Best of Winners at the 1974 Westchester Kennel Club Show under judge Joan Brearley. He is handled by L. Garrett Lambert, who co-owns him with Joe and Lill Inguaggiato, Jebel Musa Afghans, Rochester, New York.

Best Team In Show at the Afghan Hound Club of America Specialty Show under judge Alyce Carlsen was composed of Am., Can. and Mex. Ch. Pamir Ho Chester and three of his sons, Ch. Pamir's One and Only Felix, Am., Can., Mex. Ch. Pamir Ho Sweet William Chester, and Ch. Pamir Shahdoro. All four black-masked silvers were handled by Donald Jensen of Bonita, California.

THE CLUB IN THE MIDDLE 1970'S

Much progress—in addition to increases in entries at the Specialty—took place in the 1970's. By 1975, much thanks due to the new blood among the officers and Board of Directors, the Afghan Hound Club of America had many accomplishments to its credit. Besides holding their first Judges' Seminar, the club instituted an annual award to be given to the highest scoring Afghan in obedience work, published a booklet entitled *Introduction to the Afghan Hound* to serve as a primer for newcomers to the breed, formed a standing committee to study biological defects and instigated a library to collect photographs, books and memorabilia on the Afghan which are now stored as permanent records.

Pictured is the lovely Ch. Huzzah Epic, owned by Dr. and Mrs. E. Conrad Monson of Ogden, Utah. Epic was Winners Dog at the 1974 Afghan Hound Club of America Specialty Show while competing for his championship title.

REGIONAL CLUBS

By 1975 the Afghan Hound Club of America recognized no less than 25 specialty-giving regional clubs across the nation that were interested in the promotion and advancement of the breed. Just as the parent club supports the annual and, in some cases, a semi-annual specialty show , these other clubs are also dedicated to educating the public to our breed through specialty and match shows. Some clubs also participate in racing and lure coursing, while some areas do rescue work on behalf of the Afghan Hound.

Almost from the beginning when the Afghan Hound (in all its elegance and beauty) began to take a strong foothold in the dog fancy, the formation of these regional clubs became inevitable. These clubs were needed to serve members who could not make the annual pilgrimage to the New York headquarters each February to take guidance from the parent club.

One of the largest and most active of all the regional clubs has been the Afghan Hound Club of California. They held their first annual specialty show in 1948. There is also a Northern California Afghan Hound Club that held their first annual specialty show in conjunction with the Golden Gate Kennel Club event at the Civic Auditorium in San Francisco in January of 1958.

In the Mid-West there was, appropriately enough, the formation of the Mid-West Afghan Hound Club; this organization, which held its first Specialty Show in 1958, holds its annual specialty the day of the Ravenna (Ohio) Kennel Club Show. In 1959 the Afghan Hound Club of Greater Chicago was formed with a large and active membership.

The Potomac Afghan Hound Club, originally called the Eastern Afghan Hound Club, staged its early specialties along with the National Capital Kennel Club Show in Washington, D.C. This club was formed on August 15, 1948 at the home of Mr. and Mrs. Ward M. French, with 16 members present. Mrs. Howard Jackson was elected first President. In 1949 the club sponsored the Afghan Hound entry at National Capital, but their first specialty show was in 1950, held in conjunction with the Old Dominion Kennel Club Show.

The Tara Afghan Hound Club had its beginnings in Atlanta, Georgia, and held their first annual specialty in 1956. In the early 1960's we saw the formation of the Afghan Hound Club of Detroit, and it was my

Best Obedience Dog In Show at the 2nd Annual Specialty Show of the Afghan Hound Club of America, held on the estate of Mr. and Mrs. H.A. Florsheim in Darien, Connecticut, was Renee. She was owned by Miss Elizabeth D. Whelen of Fairview Village, Pennsylvania. The date was September 20, 1942 and the willingness to work shown by Renee did much to dispell the rumors that Afghan Hounds cannot be obedience trained.

distinct pleasure to judge this annual specialty show for them in 1976!

The Colonial Afghan Hound Club was another early club serving many members in the New England area. This was soon followed by, though not in the order of their formation, the Delaware Valley Afghan Hound Club, Afghan Hound Association of Long Island, Afghan Hound Club of Southwestern Ohio, Afghan Hound Club of Central Indiana, Afghan Hound Club of Dallas (which I judged in the 1970's, AHC of Omaha, AHC of Toledo, AHC of St. Louis, AHC of South Florida, AHC of Oklahoma City, the AHC's of Northern and Southern New Jersey, Afghan Hound Clubs of Greater Baltimore, Pittsburgh, Chicago, Columbus, Houston and Portland, the Alamo Area Afghan Hound Club, the Greater Twin Cities Afghan Hound Club of Minnesota and the Mohawk-Hudson Afghan Hound Association. The newest to my knowledge are the Afghan Hound Club of Hawaii and the Evergreen Afghan Hound Club in Seattle, Washington, whose first licensed specialty show on July 31, 1976 I was invited to judge and had to decline with regrets!

Many members of these regional clubs are also members of the parent club, thereby assuring a very close association with breeders, owners and exhibitors in all parts of the nation. This alliance has been especially stressed since the mid-seventies when, for the first time, elected delegates from all clubs were invited to meet in New York for an exchange of ideas with the parent club serving as host.

Most of the regional clubs publish high quality newsletters or bulletins which are most informative for both newcomers to the breed and the seasoned fancier. These papers aim to keep their members abreast of the activities in the area regarding shows, matches and obedience training programs and sometime contain a directory listing of puppies for sale, available stud service and notices of club meetings.

INTRODUCTION TO THE AFGHAN HOUND BOOKLET

While the copyright date on the AHCA's booklet entitled *Introduction to the Afghan Hound* reads 1973, in actuality the idea of such a presentation had been talked about and planned for quite a few years before. This booklet, designed and created to be sent by the club to those in the market for a new puppy, is the result of the tireless efforts of Karen Armistead, Judith Fellton, Sheila Mc-Crimmon and Selma Tenenbaum.

Its contents include a brief discussion of Afghan Hound temperament and interpretation of the Standard as well as information on feeding, lead training, exercising, grooming and a thoughtful discussion on "to breed or not to breed" your dog. It concludes with a bibliography on Afghan Hound books and magazines where additional information about the breed can be obtained. The booklet is available through the parent club at a cost of $1.50 each.

THE CLUB EMBLEM

Even though the Afghan Hound Club of America was established in 1937, during the years no club seal or emblem had been accepted to be the hallmark for the parent organization. In 1971, however, the situation changed. The club accepted as their official logo a circular medallion which will be used on catalogues, club tie-tacks, gold pins and car window stickers. Originally open to all artists' conceptions, the club adopted the

Insignia of the Afghan Hound Club of America, designed for the parent club by Kay Finch of Corona del Mar, California. This insignia appears on official documents of the club and is available only to club members.

magnificent wind-blown headstudy created by Kay Finch, bearing the name of the club and "est. 1937" as its seal. These are available to club members only, and are carefully given and proudly displayed. How appropriate that the breed's greatest artist should be the designer behind them!

MEMBERSHIP IN THE PARENT CLUB

Membership in the Afghan Hound Club of America, Inc., is by sponsorship of two current members in good standing (not serving as an officer), with at least one member who has been a guest in the aspiring member's home and able to vouch for the proper facilities for owning an Afghan Hound. Election by the Board of Directors follows after a review of the answers to a written questionaire designed to establish the pledge's ability to uphold the rules and regulations of the club, its constitution and by-laws and the payment of a membership fee. As of 1975, this fee was fifteen dollars.

As in most clubs, annual dues or membership fees are required. There is an annual meeting covering the general activities of the club, as well as four annual meetings of the club's officers and Board of Directors. The annual meeting, open to all regular members, is held following the judging of the national specialty show each February in New York City, on the weekend preceding the Westminster Kennel Club Show.

THE AHCA MATCH SHOWS

In addition to the national specialty, the parent club usually holds an annual Fall match show with A.K.C. sanction. The first of these match shows was held on September 26th, 1941 at Marion Foster Florsheim's Five Mile Kennels in Connecticut. John H. Hills was the judge at this initial event. Mrs. Sherman Hoyt's Rudika of Blakeen was named Best In Match.

AFGHAN HOUND CLUB OF AMERICA
Specialty Show Winners

1940 Ch. Tanyah Sahib of Cy Ann
     Owners, Mr. and Mrs. Cyrus K. Rickel
     Judge, Dr. Eugene C. Beck

1941 Ch. Hazar
     Owner, Dr. Gertrude Kinsey
     Judge, Dr. Arthur W. Combs

1942 Ch. Rajah of Arken
     Owner, Charles A. Wernsman
     Judge, Mrs. Robert F. Boger

1943 Ch. Rajah of Arken
     Owner, Charles A. Wernsman
     Judge, Dr. Gertrude Kinsey

1944 Ch. Rajah of Arken
     Owner, Charles A. Wernsman
     Judge, Mrs. Jack Oakie

Ch. Bakali Cymbeline of Zuvenda was bred by Geraldine Cumberland and is co-owned by Karen Usry of Pennington, New Jersey, and Geraldine Cumberland. She was photographed here at 14 months of age shortly after winning Best of Breed at the Afghan Hound Club of America Specialty Show in 1974. She is the youngest bitch to attain this honor and finished out 1974 as the top-winning Afghan Hound bitch. The sire was Ch. Mecca's Falstaff *ex* Adrienne of Shirkden. Photo by Terri Jordan.

Ch. Eljac's Dragon Lady of Dureigh is pictured winning under the late Cyrus Rickel at the 1959 Afghan Hound Club of America Specialty Show. The Dragon Lady was best in the Bred by Exhibitor class her second time shown. Her owners are Reigh and Dewey Abram of Ohio.

1945 No Specialty Show
     (Govt. war restrictions on travel)

1946 Ch. Karach of Khanhasset
     Owner, Leah P. McConaha
     Judge, Mr. Robert F. Boger

1947 Ch. Karach of Khanhasset
     Owner, Leah P. McConaha
     Judge, Mr. Charles A. Wernsman

1948 Ch. Karan of Khanhasset
     Owner, Leah P. McConaha
     Judge, Mr. E.E. Ferguson

1948 Ch. Majara Mahabat
     Owners, Mr. and Mrs. Fred A. Jagger
     Judge, Mrs. E. Ferguson McConaha

1948 Ch. Majara Mahabat
     Owners, Mr. and Mrs. Fred A. Jagger
     Judge, Mr. E. Ferguson McConaha

1950 Ch. Turkuman Nissim's Laurel
     Owners, Sunny Shay and Sol Malkin
     Judge, Alva Rosenberg

Akaba's Moonlight Sonata, winner of the Brood Bitch Class at the 1972 Afghan Hound Club of America Specialty show, and foundation bitch at the Caravan Kennels of Betty and Vincent Leap of Hicksville, New York.

1951 Ch. Blu Arabis of Kuvera
Owners, Lee and Howard Iverson
Judge, Cyrus K. Rickel

1952 Karli ben ghaZi
Owners, Ruth H. Thom and J.E. Baird
Judge, Alex Scott

1953 Ch. Majara Mihrab
Owners, Mr. and Mrs. Fred A. Jagger
Judge, Dr. Arthur W. Combs

1954 Ch. Taejon of Crown Crest
Owner, Kay Finch
Judge, Chris Shuttleworth

1955 Ch. Karli ben ghaZi
Owners, Ruth H. Tongren and Josephine Baird
Judge, Dr. Eugene C. Beck

1956 Ch. Lala Rookh of Estioc
Owner, Patricia D. Leary
Judge, Mrs. Warner S. Hays

1957 Ch. Crown Crest Zardonx
Owner, Kay S. Finch
Judge, Mrs. Lauer J. Froelich

1958 Ch. Crown Crest Zardonx
Owner, Kay S. Finch
Judge, Miss Anna Katherine Nicholas

1959 Ch. Shirkhan of Grandeur
Owners, Sunny Shay and Dorothy Chenade
Judge, Mr. Cyrus K. Rickel

Ch. Tajmir's Redstone Rocket, co-owned by breeder Patricia Sinden and Joan Fantl of Chicago, Illinois, was the winner of the Afghan Hound Club of America Specialty Show in 1964 under judge Mrs. Sherman Hoyt. Rocket also had 27 Hound Group Firsts and 55 Bests of Breed to his credit.

Ch. Akaba's Top Brass was the winner of the 1962 Afghan Hound Club of America Specialty Show in New York City. He was owner-bred and handled by Mrs. Lois Boardman of Calabasas, California. The judge was Dr. William Waskow. Brassy is a son of the famous Ch. Shirkhan of Grandeur *ex* Gigi in White. Shafer photograph.

1960 Ch. Crown Crest Mr. Universe
    Owners, Kay S. Finch and Chas. A.
      Costabile
    Judge, Mr. Robert F. Boger
1961 Ch. Holly Hill Draco
    Owner, Sue A. Kauffman
    Judge, Mr. Percy Roberts
1962 Ch. Akaba's Top Brass
    Owner, Lois R. Boardman
    Judge, Dr. Wm. L. Waskow
1963 Ch. Sahadi Shikari
    Owner, Dr. and Mrs. E.F. Winter
    Judge, Mrs. Braden Finch

1964 Ch. Tajmir's Redstone Rocket
    Owners, Patricia Sinden and Joan Fantl
    Judge, Mrs. Sherman R. Hoyt
1965 Ch. Majara Muzaffar
    Owner, Majorie A. Lathrop
    Judge, Mrs. Dale R. Carlsen
1966 Ch. Ammon Hall Judas
    Owner, Dr. Joseph Pois
    Judge, Mr. Stanley Dangerfield
1967 Ch. Akaba's Sterling Silver
    Owners, Donna M. Bandy and Lois R.
      Boardman
    Judge, Mr. W. Frank Hardy

1968 Ch. Dahnwood Gabriel
Owners, Mr. and Mrs. Herman L. Fellton
Judge, Mr. Cyrus K. Rickel

1969 Ch. Coastwind Gazebo
Owners, Michael Dunham and Richard Souza
Judge, Mrs. Louise Snyder

1970 Ch. Shangrila's Pharahna Phaedra
Owner, Dr. Gerda Maria Kennedy
Judge, Mr. Herman L. Fellton

1971 Ch. Khayam's Apollo
Owners, Dr. and Mrs. Doyle N. Rogers
Judge, Mrs. William H. Withington

1972 Ch. Ammon Hall Ter-Caj of Tajmir
Owner, Patricia Wallis
Judge, Mrs. Major H. Godsol

1973 Ch. Rajah's El Cid
Owners, Frances and George Bruning
Judge, Dr. William L. Waskow

1973 Ch. Panjhet of Stormhill
Owner, Virginia R. Withington
Judge, Mrs. Dale R. Carlsen

1974 Bakali Cymbeline of Zuvenda
Owners, Karen B. Usry and Geraldine Cumberland
Judge, Mrs. David (Jay) Ammon

1975 Ch. Lipizzan's Big Red Machine
Owners, Faye S. and S. Howard Ruback
Judge, Mrs. James Edward Clark

1976 Ch. Khayam's Ares
Owner, Walter Greene
Judge, Mrs. James Prior

1977 Ch. Shangrila Pharahna Kunasata
Owners, Mr. and Mrs. Thomas Burger
Judge, Mrs. Herman Fellton

Winners Bitch at the 1964 Afghan Hound Club of America Specialty Show was Khabira Shady Lady. Judge Mrs. Sherman Hoyt, one of the first to own Afghan Hounds in this country, presents the ribbon to Jennifer Sheldon, daughter of breeder-owners Werner and Mary Sheldon. Shady Lady's sire was Ch. Khabira Khan *ex* Laurel Ridge Siah of Grandeur.

Ch. Sandina Sweet Gypsy Rose was photographed here at 10 months of age with her breeder-owner Glorvina Schwartz. Gypsy Rose finished her championship in just 17 days, and was Best Puppy at the 1974 Afghan Hound Club of America Specialty Show.

Ch. Bakali Macbeth, a breed winning male, is pictured winning Reserve Dog at the 1974 Afghan Hound Club of America Specialty Show. He is owned by G. Cumberland, Owings Mills, Maryland.

Ch. Karistan Shirka of Grandeur is pictured as a youngster winning the Puppy Class at the 1967 Afghan Hound Club of America Specialty show. The sire was Ch. Shirkhan of Grandeur ex Monarc's Durrani. Owner is Joseph Kluchinsky. Shirka was also Best of Opposite Sex at Westminster in 1968.

Ch. Monarc's Nubia was photographed with her owner, Gloria Britain of Winthrop, Maine, shortly after finishing her championship at just 13 months of age. She was Best of Opposite Sex at the parent club specialty show in New York City in 1964.

Best of Breed at the 1965 Afghan Hound Club of America Specialty Show was Ch. Majara Muzaffar, owner-handled by Marjorie Jagger Lathrop. Mrs. Dale R. Carlsen was the judge.

233

An informal portrait of Am. and Can. Ch. Crown Crest Mr. California at 18 months of age. Mr. C. is co-owned by Forrest Hansen and Donald McIlvain of Seattle, Washington and was top dog in Canada for 1963. He was the winner of five all-breed Best In Show awards during his ring career.

Chapter VII

The Standard for the Breed

The following Standard for the Afghan Hound was approved by the American Kennel Club in September, 1948 after having been submitted by the Afghan Hound Club of America.

THE STANDARD

GENERAL APPEARANCE—The Afghan Hound is an aristocrat, his whole appearance one of dignity and aloofness with no trace of plainness or coarseness. He has a straight front, proudly carried head, eyes gazing into the distance as if in memory of ages past. The striking characteristics of the breed—exotic or "Eastern" expression, long silky topknot, peculiar coat pattern, very prominent hip bones, large feet, and the impression of a somewhat exaggerated bend in the stifle due to profuse trouserings—stand out clearly, giving the Afghan Hound the appearance of what he is, a King of Dogs, that has held true to tradition throughout the ages.

HEAD—The head is of good length showing much refinement, the skull evenly balanced with the foreface. There is a slight prominence of the nasal bone structure causing a slight Roman appearance, the center line running up over the foreface with little or no stop, falling away in front of the eyes so there is an absolutely clear outlook with no interference; the underjaw showing great strength, the jaws long and punishing; the mouth level, meaning that the teeth from the upper jaw and lower jaw match evenly neither overshot nor undershot. (This is a difficult mouth to breed. A scissors bite is even more punishing and can be more easily bred into a dog than a level mouth, and a dog having a scissors bite, where the lower teeth slip inside and rest against the teeth of the upper jaw, should not be penalized.) The occipital bone is very prominent. The head is surrounded by a topknot of long, silky hair.

EARS-The ears are long, set approximately on level with the outer corners of the eyes, the leather of the ear reaching nearly to the end of the dogs nose and covered with silky hair.

EYES—The eyes are almond shaped (almost triangular), never full or bulgy, and they are dark in color.

NOSE—The nose is of good size, black in color.

Faults—Coarseness; snipiness; overshot or undershot; eyes round or lacking in substance.

BODY—The back line appears practically level from the shoulders to the loin, strong and powerful loin and slightly arched, falling away toward the stern, with the hip bones very pronounced; well ribbed and tucked up in flanks. The height at the shoulders equals the distance from the chest to the buttocks; the brisket well let down and of medium width.

Faults—Roach back; sway back; goose rump; slack loin; lack of prominence of hip bones; too much width of brisket causing interference with elbows.

TAIL—The tail is set not too high on the body, having a ring or a curve on the end. It should never be curled over, or rest on the back, or be carried sideways, and is never bushy.

LEGS—The forelegs are straight and strong with great length between elbow and pastern; elbows well held in; forefeet large in both length and width; toes well arched; feet covered with long, thick hair, fine in texture; pasterns long and straight; pads of feet unusually large and well down on the ground. Shoulders have plenty of angulation so that the legs are well set underneath the dog. Too much straightness of shoulder causes the dog to break down in the pasterns, and this is a serious fault.

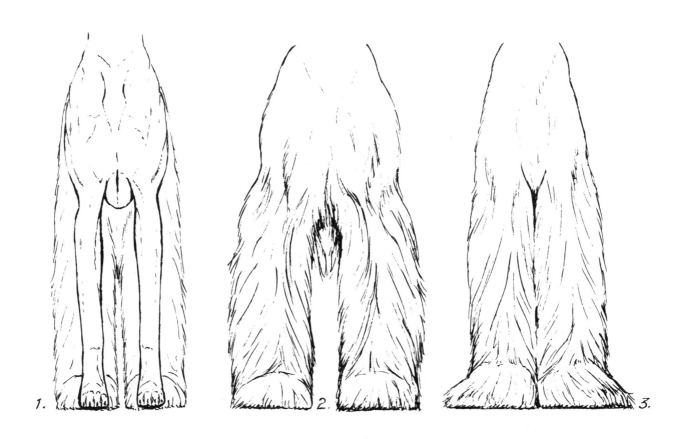

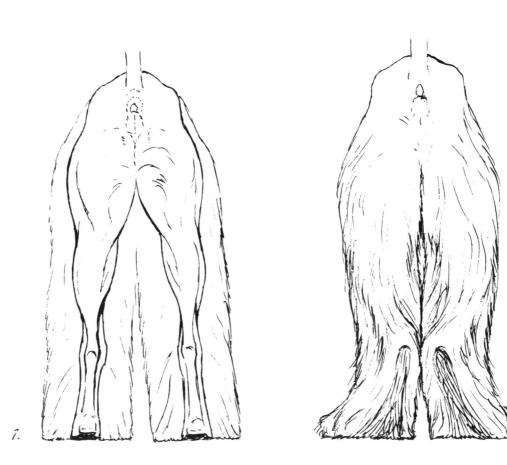

All four feet of the Afghan Hound are in line with the body, turning neither in nor out. The hind feet are broad and of good length; the toes arched, and covered with long, thick hair; hindquarters powerful and well muscled with great length between hip and hock; hocks are well let down; good angulation of both stifle and hock; slightly bowed from hock to crotch.

Faults—Front or back feet thrown outward or inward; pads of feet not thick enough; feet too small; or any other evidence of weakness in the feet; weak or broken down pasterns; too straight in stifle; too long in hock.

COAT—Hindquarters, flanks, ribs, forequarters and legs are well covered with thick, silky hair, very fine in texture; ears and all four feet well feathered. From in front of the shoulders, and also backwards from the shoulders along the saddle from the flanks and ribs upwards, the hair is short and close, forming a smooth back in mature dogs—this is a traditional characteristic of the Afghan Hound.

The Afghan Hound is shown in its natural state; the coat is not clipped or trimmed; the head is surmounted (in the full sense of the word) with a topknot of long, silky hair—this also an outstanding characteristic of the Afghan Hound. Showing of short hair on cuffs on either front or back legs is permissible.

Faults—Lack of short haired saddle in mature dogs.

HEIGHT—Dogs, 27 inches, plus or minus one inch. Bitches, 25 inches, plus or minus one inch.

WEIGHT—Dogs, about sixty pounds. Bitches, about fifty pounds.

COLOR—All colors are permissible, but color or color combinations are pleasing. White markings, especially on the head, are undesirable.

GAIT—When running free, the Afghan Hound moves at a gallop, showing great elasticity and spring in his smooth, powerful stride.

When on a loose lead, the Afghan can trot at a fast pace. Stepping along, he has the appearance of placing the hind feet directly in the foot prints of the front feet, both thrown straight ahead. Moving with head and tail high, the whole appearance of the Afghan Hound is one of great style and beauty.

TEMPERAMENT—Aloof and dignified, yet gay.

Faults—Sharpness or shyness.

Opposite:

Upper drawings:

1. Dog with legs well under body, feet pointing straight ahead. Excellent front, showing the proper conformation hidden by coat.
2. Out at the elbows, loaded in shoulder, too wide with legs set too far apart.
3. Narrow front, feet pointing out "east and west," elbows pinched in.

Lower drawings:

1. Well-muscled hindquarters, can have slightly "bowed" appearance above hocks. Excellent rear.
2. Faulty rear; cowhocked, with feet pointing outward.

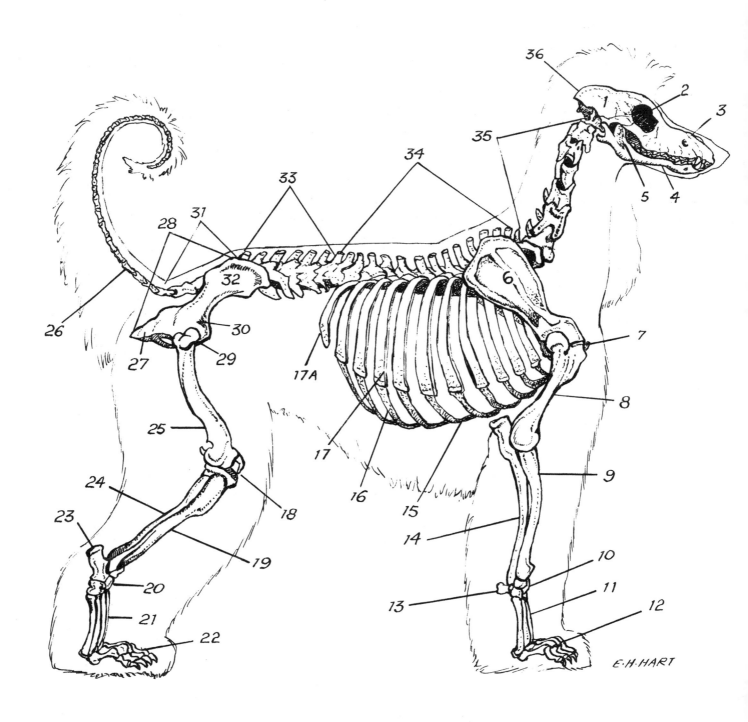

1. Cranium (skull). 2. Orbital cavity. 3. Nasal bone. 4. Mandible (lower jaw). 5. Condyle. 6. Scapula (shoulder blade). 7. Prosternum (front end of sternum). 8. Humerus (upper arm). 9. Radius (front forearm bone). 10. Carpus (pastern joint). 11. Metacarpus (pastern). 12. Phalanges (toes). 13. Disciform. 14. Ulna. 15. Sternum. 16. Costal cartilage. 17. Rib bones. 17A. Floating rib. 18. Patella (knee joint or stifle). 19. Tibia. 20. Tarsus. 21. Metatarsus. 22. Phalanges. 23. Os calcis (point of hock). 24. Fibula. 25. Femur (thigh bone). 26. Coccygeal vertebra (tail bones). 27. Pubis. 28. Pelvic bone entire. 29. Head of femur. 30. Ischium. 31. Sacral vertebra. 32. Illium. 33. Lumbar vertebra. 34. Thoracic vertebra. 35. Cervical vertebra (bones of neck). 36. Occiput.

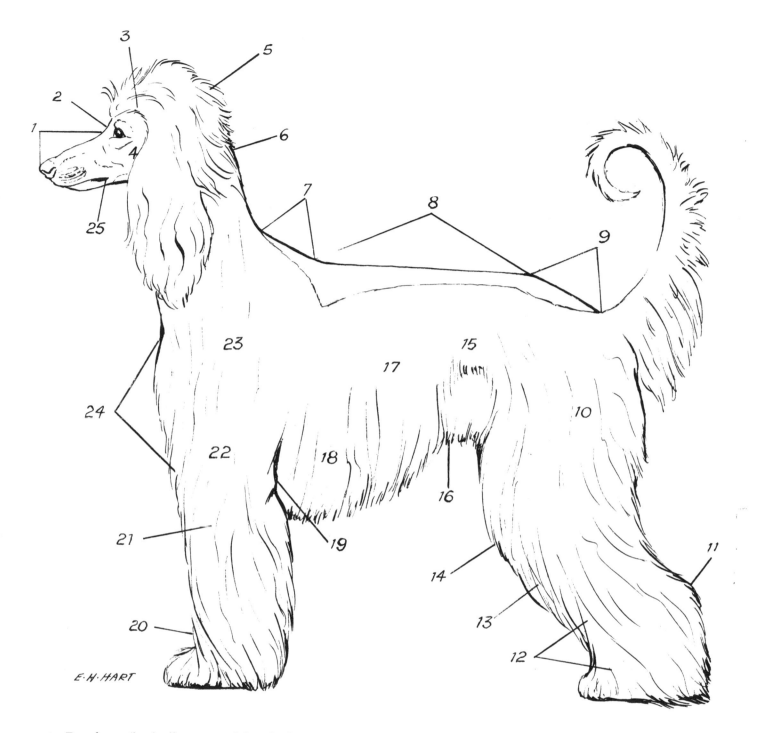

1. Foreface (including muzzle). 2. Stop. 3. Skull. 4. Cheek. 5. Occiput. 6. Crest of neck. 7. Withers. 8. Back (or saddle). 9. Croup. 10. Thigh. 11. Joint of hock. 12. Metatarsus (front of hock). 13. Lower thigh. 14. Stifle joint (knee). 15. Loin. 16. Tuck up (abdomen). 17. Ribs. 18. Brisket. 19. Elbow. 20. Pastern. 21. Forearm. 22. Upper arm. 23. Shoulder blade. 24.Forechest. 25. Lip corner (flew).

AKC Registrations and Breed Rank
Beginning 1926

Year	Reg.	Rank
1926	4	65
1927	2	70
1928	3	67
1929		
1930	1	83
1931		
1932	1	79
1933	17	63
1934	25	59
1935	12	76
1936	82	53
1937	55	80
1938	125	48
1939	148	45
1940	135	49
1941	217	40
1942	218	39
1943	138	46
1944	134	44
1945	310	42
1946	462	40
1947	444	45
1948	417	42
1949	465	43
1950	377	46
1951	472	45
1952	449	45
1953	470	45
1954	386	48
1955	469	46
1956	524	46
1957	636	43
1958	794	41
1959	691	44
1960	668	42
1961	831	40
1962	889	43
1963	1,092	40
1964	1,242	43
1965	1,820	38
1966	1,922	39
1967	2,660	37
1968	3,408	37
1969	4,605	37
1970	6,127	35
1971	8,049	31
1972	9,023	30
1973	10,549	28
1974	10,918	28
1975	10,412	28
1976	10,045	30

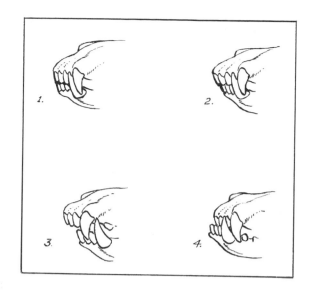

1. Desired level bite.

2. Acceptable scissors bite.

3. Overshot bite—undesirable.

4. Undershot bite—undesirable.

Ch. Tazi Talaii of Phedana, bred and owned by Huldah and Edward M. Segal of Rensselaer, New York.

Ch. Sonali of Shajawn, co-owned by Blossom and Norman Shuman, Man Shu Kennels, Brooklyn, New York.

Ch. Majara Marfu and Ch. Holly Hill Ara of Moornistan, both owned by Mrs. Donald Patterson, wait to go into the show ring.

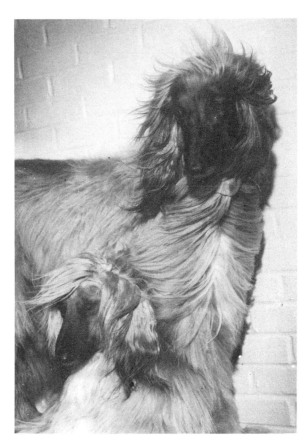

Ch. Bacha Khiva of Kubera, Best In Show winner at the 1961 North Country Kennel Club Show. owned by the Erman M. Moores, Kubera Kennels. Klein photograph.

Int. Ch. Felt's Thief of Bagdad. This pale silver-blue Afghan Hound male was one of the famous foundation stud dogs at Kay Finch's Crown Crest Kennels in Corona del Mar, California. This photograph was the cover photo on the 1948 Christmas issue of *Dog World* magazine.

Ch. Prism's Akbar Khan of Grandeur is pictured winning on the way to championship at the 1975 Somerset Hills Kennel Club Show under judge Joan Brearley. Bred by Marcia Stoll and handled by Sunny Shay, he is co-owned by the James Crawfords and Sunny Shay. The sire was Ch. Khan Shah of Grandeur *ex* Ch. Dic Mar's Blue Dhimond.

Artist George Finch painted this oil entitled *Evensong at Timu-Ka* in 1976 at the summer home of Dr. and Mrs. Philip Haims in the Almaden Valley in California. This sunset scene includes the Haims' blue and gold Macaw Timu-Ka Chica and their Afghan Hounds: Timu-Ka Michal, Timu-Ka Tamir and Timu-Ka Hamuda. This painting was the cover of the *Afghan Hound Review* magazine for the November-December, 1976 issue.

Demo's Silver Cloud wins Best Puppy In Show at the Afghan Hound Club of Northern New Jersey's first independent specialty show under the famous Molly Sharpe, owner of the Chaman Kennels in Scotland. Silver Cloud was bred and is owned by Thomas C. Lauridia and J. Kluchinsky.

Xzora's Black Onyx has points toward championship in both the U.S. and Canada and was Winners Dog at the 1975 Afghan Hound Club of Canada Specialty Show. Owned by M. Wolfe of Huron, Ohio.

Ch. Alcara's Aida Alif was photographed at rest in 1955. Aida's owners were Mr. and Mrs. T.J. O'Connor of Madison, New Jersey.

Ch. Infashia of Grandeur is pictured winning under judge Ruth Tongren. James Stewart was the handler for Infashia's owners, Mr. and Mrs. Warren Fenn.

Lifestyle Illumination, a 3-month-old cream bitch puppy, was whelped in November, 1975 by breeder-owners Paul and Jean Ravinski, Lifestyle Kennels, Kingston, Massachusetts. "Ghost" was shown once as a puppy at the Colonial Afghan Hound Club Match Show and won Best In Match over an entry of 70 puppies.

244

Chapter VIII

The Afghan Hound as a Breed

When someone asks you what breed of dog you have, it is incorrect to say, "an Afghan." An Afghan is a native of Afghanistan, a crocheted or knitted blanket or wrap, the chief language of Afghanistan or a Turkoman carpet of large size, long pile, woven in geometric design with the dominating color being wine red. There is also an Afghan stitch, and there are Afghan Foxes. The dog we know and love is an Afghan *Hound.* That is its full and proper title, and the name recognized by the American Kennel Club. And that is what we should call it. . .

No matter what other nickname you give it, Af, Affie or whatever call name you have bestowed upon your own dog, it really deserves to be referred to—especially when talking with newcomers to the breed—by its official name. When the word Afghan is used as an adjective, it can mean anything relating to Afghanistan, but we must remember that the dog did not originate in Afghanistan, but was merely the adopted, though official, dog of that country, so it still does not apply.

Since our Afghan Hounds are such a noble breed, we should all be sure that they are referred to by their full and proper name as a breed, since so many of the registered and call names given them by their owners are completely lacking in dignity!

AFGHAN HOUND INTELLIGENCE

Haven't we all heard someone say, "I hear that Afghan Hounds aren't too smart. ." Some come right out with it and say they understand that Afghan Hounds are downright stupid.

Anyone who has ever owned one knows that nothing could be further from the truth. If these people had taken the trouble to read the Standard they would see that it states that the Afghan Hound is "aloof." They obviously mistake the aloofness for indifference and indifference for stupidity. Actually, it is these people who are "stupid" for not realizing that the Afghan Hound is *so smart* that he is more often than not fooling them into thinking he is indifferent or stupid.

The great and ever-increasing number of obedience-titled Afghan Hounds bear this out, and all that needs to be done is to keep our breed working, racing, coursing and showing, and to present them in the best possible light to put these rumors to rest. Next time your Afghan Hound gives one of these people the "aloof" treatment and looks right through them, tell them that is "the look of eagles" or "eyes gazing into the distance as if in memory of ages past." It sounds impressive and just happens to be included in the Standard for the "King of Dogs."

One of the best examples of their superior intelligence can be proven by an Afghan Hound named Aggie. Aggie distinguished herself during World War II in the military service. Cy Rickel sent four of his Cy-Ann dogs to be trained for guard duty with the Army. He lost track of the two males, and one of the females was given a corpsmen when she could not adjust to rigors of the training. But Aggie made the grade!

Upon completion of her duty with the War Dog K-9 Section of the Quartermaster

Elmo's Portiananka typifies the Afghan Hound gazing into the distance in memory of ages past. Portiananka has won majors under top judges in tough competition, and is near her championship title. Co-breeders were Gordon McDowell and Peter Belmont, who owns her.

Corps she was given a certificate of honorable discharge which read: "The War Dog Aggie, Tattoo No.19a, having served with the Armed Forces of the United States of America, is hereby awarded this Certificate of Faithful Service and Honorable Discharge. Enlisted: August 29, 1942. Discharged April 20, 1944. Service: Sentry Duty."

Aggie was sent home to the Rickels in Texas to rest on her laurels. She died in 1955 at the age of fifteen.

AFGHAN HOUND TEMPERAMENT

There is no denying that in the early days when Afghan Hounds were imported here and abroad, there were dogs that were sharp.

This was a recognized fact both in their native lands and in the kennels where they were being bred. Some of this quite naturally continued down through the bloodlines over the years, and during the early years in this country it was at times even attributed to certain specific bloodlines.

However, as the breed became more and more popular, selective breeding all but eliminated this trait. This is not to say that *all* Afghan Hounds have good dispositions. It means that a great deal of the sharpness has been eliminated, owing heavily to our new knowledge of canine behavior, obedience training, socialization of young puppies and the aforementioned selective breeding. In other words, it has been "bred out."

246

therefore, it is safe to say that the temperament of the Afghan Hound, with rare exception, is stable. They are good with children of all ages and fit in well with city or country living. When talking about Afghan Hound temperament today it can be said that "There are no bad dogs, only bad owners," if there is trouble in the breed!

AFGHAN HOUND SIZE

We are beginning to hear more and more discussion about Afghan Hound size—or more specifically, Afghan Hounds that are *over*-sized!

While we are all aware of the importance of adhering to the Standard when considering our breeding programs, we must also be aware that the Standard for our breed size was written in the 1930's when dogs were fed table scraps and not nutritionally perfect diets that contribute to growth and good health. When the Standard was reviewed in 1948 it was not deemed necessary to make any change regarding their size.

While I do not personally know of any judge who has not put a good dog up because it was over-sized, I must admit that a great majority of today's Afghan Hounds, both male and female, are frequently found to be over the measure called for in the Standard. Size can be controlled in a breeding program if this condition is taken into consideration without having to jeopardize a sound nutritional diet.

Hopefully, the judges are more inclined to judge the dog on its symmetry and over-all balance than on a shoulder measurement that is becoming more and more impossible to maintain.

Perhaps in the not too distant future the Standard will be adjusted to allow for this "natural" increase in size. Certainly not as a crusade for a change in the Standard as some believe is indicated, I nevertheless offer the following information as food for thought. . . During the writing of this book I measured at random one hundred Afghan Hounds: fifty males and fifty females. Twelve males came within the Standard and 22 females. Less than half met the Standard reviewed more than a quarter of a century ago.

AFGHAN HOUND COLORS

People who admire the glamorous Afghan Hound have also come up with some truly "glamorous" names for the colors they

Pictured is Ch. Cathay's Aspasia, a lovely blue bitch co-owned by Pat Horner and Bill Maseth, who handled her to this win at the 1974 Finger Lakes Afghan Hound Club Specialty Show under judge Romayne Switch.

Ch. Belamir's High Tide wins the coveted top award of Best In Show at the 1971 Agathon Kennel Club Show under judge Dr. Frank Booth. Elizabeth Kohn handled for owner Roger M. Bell.

Kassan's Johann Sebastian, who grew up to be a champion and his sister Kassan's Victoria were photographed at 8 weeks of age. They are owned and bred by June Boone, Kassan Kennels, Kokomo, Indiana.

wear! Ordinary terms like red, gold, cream, white, brindle, blue or black don't seem to be descriptive enough for some fanciers. We hear words like champagne, apricot, smoke, steel, blond, ashen—and worse—applied to our silky coated beauties! The more unique they can make the color sound, the better they like it, and the more convinced they become that such an exotic color will bring additional attention to their dogs.

Actually, such widely variant descriptions of Afghan Hound color only confuses other breeders when trying to make comparisons in pedigrees and confuses newcomers trying to learn the intricasies of the breed. Afghan owners would do themselves a favor if they would get a little deeper into the actual color genetics connected with our breed by reading a few books written by proper authorities.

While the Afghan Hound Standard allows for all colors or combinations of color that are pleasing, it does present a wide spectrum of hues. However, achieving these various colors depends very much on genealogical facts.

DOMINOS ANYONE?

In the early days of the Afghan Hound in this country, the vast majority of Afghan Hounds were reds and golds. This was not only the most popular color, but certainly the most prevalent. Occasionally, as in any breed where the Standard states "any color allowed," there were many exceptions as to color and color patterns. The same held true for the amount of mask. Since some of the early dogs carried what is called a "domino" pattern, it was inevitable that sooner or later the dominos would show up in U.S. breedings. Basically, a domino Afghan has a distinct dark widow's peak down the forehead above the eyes. It is so distinctive that if you ever see a good domino you will recognize it immediately.

However, since the most popular colors in early dogs were solid reds, the domino pattern was regarded as a "reverse mask." We began to hear of more and more dominos being culled since they were believed to be impossible to sell or show.

One of the original Ghazni imports was reported to be a domino, though now we also learn that almost all of the lines carried this gene and dominos cropped up in litters every now and then. The famous Int. Ch. Tanjores Domino did much to popularize this rare and remarkable pattern and they are being seen and shown more and more.

Apache's Free Spirit of Ahrana is a domino foundation bitch for Gilda Barton's Ahrana Kennels in Wichita, Kansas.

This all domino litter was whelped by Apache's Free Spirit of Ahrana and sired by Ch. Mecca's Falstaff. These four 5-month-old puppies were bred and owned by Gilda Barton, Wichita, Kansas.

The domino pattern is usually very evident at the moment of birth and again at maturity. Since domino markings are both hair color and hair pattern, they are sometimes indistinct during the growing up period of development.

THE LEGENDARY PROMINENT HIPBONES

Over the years there has been discussion on the Afghan Hound's legendary "pivotal hip joints" and their prominent hipbones.

Countless fanciers can recall incidents where Afghan Hounds, while running free, have truly seemed to "turn on a dime." These maneuvers have almost made us believe they *do* have pivotal hip joints. Needless to say, there is actually no mention of pivotal hip joints in our Standard. However, there are two mentions of "prominent hipbones" and a "lack of prominence of hipbones" is a definite and specific *fault*.

The term "pivotal hip joints" must then be regarded as just another aphorism applied to the breed by a lay person who has only observed the dog in action, rather than by anatomical study.

My friend, Wayne H. Riser, D.V.M., at the University of Pennsylvania, is the author of a book on hip dysplasia and bears this out. His contention is that all long-legged, thinboned sporting hounds have comparable pelvis and thigh bones, and it is rather a lack of gluteal muscles (to cover the crests of the iliums, or hipbones, in the Afghan Hound) that make them as prominent as they are.

Therefore, we must not claim that Afghan Hounds have pivotal hip joints, but instead we must be aware of the reason why the hip bones are visible and must judge them according to our Standard which calls for them to be prominent.

SCENTED AFGHAN HOUNDS

"It takes one to know one" is a phrase that may well apply to anyone who has ever been exposed to a scented Afghan Hound. There is no mistaking the distinct odor they give off around their heads, and more specifically, between the corners of their mouths and the base of their ears. It has been likened to sandalwood, as being vaguely reminiscent of musk and several other exotic, oriental fragrances.

249

Ch. Majara Mustapha enjoys the snow at the Majara Kennels in Somerville, New Jersey, in 1955. Her sire was Ch. Karach of Khanhasset *ex* Far Away Loo. Her four champion get are Majar Mardan—I—Ghayb, a Best In Show winner; Majara Mulihah; Majara Mudarris and Majara Mamrak.

I have had several scented Afghan Hounds over the years and the odor was so pronounced that without turning around I would become acutely aware that the scented puppy had come into the room. For me, the odor was marvelous, and I couldn't get enough of it. I wished that all my Afghan Hounds would carry it. Other people that I have discussed this condition with state that they find the odor highly offensive, and I have even heard it referred to as being "sickening."

During the 1940's scented Afghan Hounds were reported to have been found in the El Myia lines in Canada. Scented dogs in those early days were also traced back and attributed to the descendants of the Ch. Turkuman Pomegranite and Ch. Westmill Bayezid Ansari dogs. I found it in my Crown Crest breeding during the 1950's.

This by no means indicates that the scent was restricted to these lines. Actually, we have no way of knowing how many lines carried it since in those early days not enough attention was given to recording this phenomenon to constitute anything resembling research or the establishment of a specific "pattern." As a matter of fact, there seems to be no scientific explanation—even today—for these scented Afghan Hounds.

From the information gathered by those of us interested in the subject, there seems to be no proof of any relation between sex, color or bloodlines, nor does it seem to be possible when considering the Mendelian law.

When I first discovered my scented dogs I discussed the condition with my veterinarian. He put me in touch with William Montagne, Director of the Oregon Regional Primate Research Center. In his book, *The Structure and Function of Skin*, he wrote about the musk glands found in the cheeks of male elephants and the Stump-tailed Macaques. He also stated in correspondence with me that these glands disappear at maturity.

While some of the other Afghan Hound owners I discussed this with claim that the odor either disappeared or faded considerably at maturity, it was my experience that it re-

Ch. Turalanah Tajah, owned by Donald E. Clark of Dallas, Texas. She finished her championship with a 4-point major at 7 months of age and had previously garnered two 5-point majors at Dallas and Ft. Worth shows.

mained throughout their lifetime. Others claimed that it usually disappeared around nine to twelve months of age. This does present the possibility that it may be "sex" oriented or of a glandular nature as in the elephants and monkeys mentioned in the Montagne book.

In his correspondence with me, William Montagne concluded that the skin from the jowls of Afghan Hounds would have to be studied for the presence of special glands which might be responsible for special secretions which would provide such an odor as has been reported.

TATTOOING

Ninety per cent success has been reported on the return of stolen or lost dogs that have been tattooed. More and more this simple, painless, inexpensive method of positive identification for dogs is being reported all over the United States. Long popular in Canada, along with nose prints, the idea gained interest in this country when dognapping started to soar as unscrupulous people began stealing dogs for resale to research laboratories. Pet dogs that wander off and lost hunting dogs have always been a problem. The success of tattooing has been significant.

Tattooing can be done by the veterinarian for a minor fee. There are several dog "registries" that will record your dog's number and help you locate it should it be lost or stolen. The number of the dog's American Kennel Club registration is most often used on thorough-bred dogs, or the owner's Social Security number in the case of mixed breeds. The best place for the tattoo is the groin. Some prefer the inside of an ear, and the American Kennel Club has rules that the judges officiating at the AKC dog shows not penalize the dog for the tattoo mark.

The tattoo mark serves not only to identify your dog should it be lost or stolen, but offers positive identification in large kennels where several litters of the same approximate age are on the premises. It is a safety measure against unscrupulous breeders "switching" puppies. Any age is a proper age to tattoo, but for safety's sake, the sooner the better.

The buzz of the needle might cause your dog to be apprehensive, but the pricking of the needle is virtually painless. The risk of infection is negligible when done properly, and the return of your beloved pet may be the reward for taking the time to insure positive

The true picture of Afghan Hound aloofness and dignity! Amir, owned by Nancy Elsamen of Jeannette, Pennsylvania, was sired by Ch. Holly Hill Riptide *ex* Lynncrest Little Bit Of Honey, C.D. His official name is Am. and Can. Ch. Honiego's Ambassador to Fame, and he is a C.D. obedience title holder in both the U.S. and Bermuda.

identification for your dog. Your local kennel club will know of a dog registry in your area.

ROAD WORK

Some Afghan owners, no matter how long they have been in the breed, continue to be guilt-ridden about the amount of exercise the breed requires and go to all lengths to see that their dogs are getting plenty of running. More often than not, this takes on the form of road work, or running behind a car for mile after mile, whether the dog likes it or not, until they are satisfied that their coursing hound has "coursed."

While they mean well, and while we must acknowledge that even the average Afghan Hound requires more than a walk on the end of a leash twice a day, road work can be too strenuous and not at all necessary if not handled properly or gauged in accordance with the individual dog's requirements. Some Afghan Hounds are so active that they get

Siesta on the patio! Sura's Fire Cracker was bred by S.J. Neill of Torr, California. The sire was Huzzah Ozymandias *ex* Taz Mahal Sahr-I-Kha.

Ch. Mandith Alexander the Great was the three-year-old winner of the Tara Afghan Hound Club Specialty Show in 1964. Alex also has five Group placings to his credit. He is owned by Judith Fellton of the Mandith Kennels, Marietta, Georgia.

Ch. Shikari's Gingilier is pictured winning under judge Peter Knoop at a recent show. The sire was Ch. Mecca's Falstaff *ex* Ch. Nadja Sheba of Byalitine. He is handled here by Mary Lou Benjamin, who co-owns Gingilier with Norman Benjamin.

A lovely show winner owned by Dale and Alyce Carlsen.

Fantasis High Card of Alijon is pictured winning on the way to championship at the Shasta Kennel Club Show under judge Dr. Gerda Kennedy. Dana Plonkey handled High Card for owner Mr. A.J. Gagliana of Seattle, Washington.

Off and running. . . the black in the lead is Houn' Hollow Purli Victorious, owned by Dennis and Ida Di Fromcesco, and the close-second cream is Pasha of Desperation, owned by Mary Drueding. The location of the race was the Vale Vue Kennels in West Chester, Pennsylvania.

their required exercise running around in their fenced in yards or jumping around on the furniture.

I have heard of too many incidents where Afghans pull up lame or get burned feet from asphalt roads or panic and run off when other cars come up too close behind them, etc. It simply is not possible for one person to handle a car and a dog running beside it safely. If road work is to be done at all, one person should drive the car while another sits on the tail gate to watch the dog at every moment. The distance must be increased slowly, tried in the coolest part of the day, on the most deserted roads and only when the dog looks forward to it as an adventure and not as a required part of a training regimen. It is far safer to risk having an Afghan Hound which could use a little more activity than to end up with one that is defeated because of trying in vain to keep up with his owners idea of physical fitness based on ancient history when they were expected to course for miles and miles across the desert.

TREADMILLS

I disapprove of treadmill training of Afghan Hounds as much as I disapprove of roadwork behind a car—for all the same reasons, plus a few more. People have been known to walk off or answer the telephone or otherwise forget the dog on the treadmill and all sorts of dire consequences have resulted (overexertion, exhaustion, heart attacks, etc.).

These facts were borne out when I was editor of *Popular Dogs* because deaths and injuries were reported. I absolutely refused to take treadmill advertising, but would still hear about cases where dogs had succumbed or been injured on treadmills because of "forgetful" owners. From what I see at the dog shows, it might do owners a lot of good to leave the car at home and run alongside their dog and get in shape themselves. The cost of a treadmill invested instead in a pair of sneakers and a sweatsuit will do both dog and owner a lot more good! Either one can stop when they've had enough.

TRAVELING WITH AFGHAN HOUNDS

Afghan Hounds are good travelers. This goes for the automobile or the mobile home where they can stretch out on the bunks and give the distinct impression that they were designed and included for their exclusive accomodation!

Ch. Patrician Tulu-I D'Khardahn, better known at Tuli, is owned by Helen and Barney Cardan of Sherman Oaks, California. The sire was Patrician's Sharif *ex* Ch. Patrician's Bad Penny.

When traveling with an Afghan Hound, on short jaunts around town, to and from a dog show or on an extended vacation trip, there are certain "courtesies" which should be provided for them to assure comfortable and safe conditions for them and pleasure for everyone.

It is safest to include an adequate-sized crate for the dog so that it does not jump around in the car and distract the driver. The crate will protect the dog from getting thrown off its feet while the car is going fast, stopping or starting suddenly or swerving through traffic. If your dog is not a restless rider, you may prefer to let it sit on the seat, or perhaps you prefer to tie it in the rear of the car or station wagon. Above all, do not tie it to a door handle!

There are many people who allow their dogs to ride with their heads out the window since all dogs seem to love to "sniff the breeze." Others fear a stone might fly up from the road and hit the dog or injure it. This is a remote possibility. As long as the window is not open so far that they could jump out, but

Mrs. James M. Austin's Lakshmi of Geufron, photographed shortly after winning Best In Show at a Mohawk Valley Kennel Club event several years ago.

is open far enough for them to pull their head in and out with ease, I can see no reason for denying them this pleasure anymore than you would forbid your children from riding next to an open window.

The exception might be while shopping at gas stations where the dog might snap at the attendant while "guarding" the family car, at toll booths where strange hands are extended toward owners they are inclined to protect or at fast food stands where the smell of food adds to their survival instincts.

If you are traveling any great distance, some thought must be given to feeding and watering the dog. When a long drive is involved, wait until evening when you have reached your destination before feeding. They will

sleep better, take more time to eat and digest their food properly, and can be exercised at greater length after the meal. The packaged, semi-moist food is best for traveling since there is no spoilage and no cans to be opened. If you do not feed this as a regular diet at home, introduce it a few days before your departure so you can be sure the dog will eat it.

Water is a most important consideration. Water must be offered at various intervals during the day. In small amounts, of course, and neither too cold nor too warm. Leave the water down overnight.

Remember to stop at intervals to exercise the dog during the day. Frequently rest stops for humans will also offer water and exercise areas for dogs. Be sure collars and leashes are secure so that the animal doesn't run off if they should slip away. *NEVER* exercise off leash in strange places or in unfamiliar ground, and make it a strict rule with the children that the dog's leash is held tightly in someone's hand before the car doors are opened!

If you are to put your dog in a pen or an enclosure of any kind while temporarily visiting, resting, eating, etc., make sure all gates have secure catches and/or locks, that there are no tunnels under the fences and that shade is provided against sun and shelter against rain. No matter how much you love your dog, it is *not* pleasant to travel with a wet Afghan Hound.

It is a good idea to bring along a toy or rawhide bone to relieve boredom, especially if you are traveling with a young dog or puppy. If your dog doesn't get car sick, you might also include a few dog biscuits so that they can also snack on them after playing with them.

Bring along a large towel and sufficient water for drinking, and saturate a towel to cool off the dog if heat gets intense. You can leave the towel on him or put it in the bottom of the crate while traveling through particularly hot country.

When registering at a motel always request a room with parking right outside the door so you can watch the dog at all times and leave it in the car or crate while loading or unloading. Always inform the registration clerk that you have a dog, or dogs, and whether or not you intend to take the dog into the room. If you meet any resistance offer to put up a deposit (many motels ask $25.00) and suggest they inspect the room before your departure the next day. If the dog will be sleeping in the car, tell them that, or if you intend to bring the crate into the room, they might be relieved to hear the dog will be sleeping in it. Start proving your good intentions by telling them that you intend to walk the dog beyond their lawns and gardens!

There are two unpardonable sins when traveling with your dog. The first I will mention only briefly because the mere thought of it is so cruel that I cannot bear to discuss the consequences. That is, *NEVER* leave your dog behind to fend for itself when you leave for home at the end of your vacation. The second unpardonable sin—and this applies every time you leave your dog in the car—is *NEVER, EVER* leave the dog inside with all the windows closed! Heat buildup in a car can kill the dog within a matter of minutes.

Traveling with a dog, or even a couple of them, can be fun and very little trouble if some previous thought is given to their comfort as well as your own.

AFGHAN HOUND PUBLICATIONS

An important way of acquiring knowledge and maintaining the cooperation of those active in the breed is through the written word. The aforementioned club bulletins and newsletters are one way, of course, as are the breed columns in the dog magazines. Some of the magazines can be purchased at the newsstands, but most require a paid subscription from the magazine itself. These are:

American Kennel Gazette, 51 Madison Ave., New York, New York 10010

Kennel Review, 828 North LaBrea Ave., Hollywood, California 90038

Dog World, 10060 West Roosevelt Road, Westchester, Illinois 60153

Other important dog magazines which are of interest to all and feature the Afghan Hound on occasion are:

Showdogs, 257 Park Avenue South, New York, New York 10010

Dogs, (address the same as above)

Two publications, for which I have the very highest praise and which I consider to be essential for every Afghan Hound owner are:

The Afghan Hound Review, P.O. Box 1369, Watsonville, California 95076

The Gazehound, 16258 Lovett Place, Encino, California 91436

These latter two are of the highest quality and coverage, and are beautiful to see— even if you don't have Afghan Hounds! There are other magazines, of course, worth having if your interests go beyond the breeding and showing.

Unfortunately we no longer have, but must acknowledge in passing, *Popular Dogs* magazine. Few magazines, if any, have given so much coverage to our breed over the years, not only through the monthly column which I wrote myself for many years, but through the compilation and presentation of the annual results of the Phillips System. We can see through our chapter on "The Top Ten Afghan Hounds in the History of the Breed" just how important a part *Popular Dogs* played in the shaping of our nation's great show dogs. It

23. *Scobeta Keekorok Ru, C.D., owned by Susan Bell of Shreveport, Louisiana, is shown relaxing in the midday sun.*

24. *Headstudy of Rakala's Tempest in a Teapot, daughter of Am. and Can. Ch. Rokeish Sorroco and Esfahan Apache Fire. Tempest is owned by C. Pearson and L. Andrews, Canada.*

25. *Canadian Ch. Thaon's Kashta of Ekselo is pictured winning at the 1973 Green Mountain Dog Club Show in Stowe, Vermont. William Trainor handled Kashta for co-owners Sally B. Frank and Ellen O'Leske of Brookline, Massachusetts.*

26. *A field champion and specialty show winner!!! Ch. Wita Vail of Nightwatch, Field Champion, is pictured at 9 months of age winning the Best of Winners title for a 4-point major at the Buckhorn Valley Kennel Club Show. Vail is owned by Robert and Denyce Verti of LaPorte, Colorado. Vail's excellence in both field and conformation was further proven when she won Best of Breed at the first Afghan Hound Club of St. Louis Specialty Show in May, 1974.*

27. Ch. Mecca's Falstaff is shown with owner Barbara Guidebeck of Marietta, Georgia. "Hap" is the sire of 15 champions in three years and has been a top producer since he was put at stud.

28. Caravanserai Chahar, whelped in Holland in January, 1971, holds both the CAC and CACIB titles. Co-owned by Anne C. van der Vlis of Curacao and Karen Armistead of New York, the sire was Nazim van de Oranje Manege ex Dutch and Int. Ch. Juno van de Oranje Manege. This photograph by Studio Tramm was taken in August, 1975 and is a beautiful example of the vdOM dogs.

29. Kalizma's Chi Chi of Kaja is shown capturing the Best of Opposite Sex title at the 1975 Ramapo Kennel Club Show. She was named Best Puppy at the 1973 Afghan Hound Club of America Specialty Show, and is co-owned by Karen Armistead with Bob Philbin and B. Proctor. Mrs. Armistead is handling.

30. Ch. Sandina Sparkling Champagne and his breeder-owner Glorvina Schwartz pose for this lovely photograph at their home in Tuxedo Park, New York. "Pinky" is a multiple Best In Show winner and one of the top-winning Afghan Hounds in the U.S. after beginning his Specials career in 1976.

31

32

33

THE AFGHAN HOUND CLUB
OF SOUTHWESTERN OHIO, INC.
MAY 28, 1976
JUDGE: MRS. SUSAN HAMLIN
SPECIALTY
WINNERS
DOG

B.O.S.
Photo by Gilbert

34

35

GROUP
FIRST

GILBERT PHOTO

BEST OF
OPPOSITE

GILBERT PHOTO

31. Bakali Sleuth, co-owned by Margo Kato and G. Cumberland, is shown in this stately pose outside his home.

32. Am., Bda. and Can. Ch. Varuna of Ekselo is pictured winning at the 1971 Hockomock Kennel Club Show under judge Wallace Pede. "Jazz" is handled by Ellen O'Leske of Brookline, Massachusetts, who co-owns him with Sally Frank.

33. Ch. Shikari's Streak of Blue is shown going Winners Dog from the Bred by Exhibitor Class at the 1976 Afghan Hound Club of Southwestern Ohio Specialty Show under judge Susan Hamlin. This win gave Streak a 5-point major and finished his championship. His sire was Ch. Ninth Turn Argus ex Shikari's Ghandira. He is co-owned by Norman and Mary Lou Benjamin, St. Peters, Missouri, and handled here by Mr. Benjamin.

34. Dureigh's Phoebe Snow is pictured winning Best of Opposite Sex on the way to her championship at the Penn Ridge Kennel Club Show under judge Mary Stephenson. She is owner-handled by Bill Maseth of Timonium, Maryland.

35. Ch. Mandith Pericles, C.D., is pictured winning a Hound Group under judge Gerhardt Plaga at a recent Lewiston-Auburn Kennel Club Show. Jane Forsyth handled for owner Mrs. Cheever Porter of New York City.

36. Sura's Royal Charger, C.D., and Aaron Lobenberg are pictured enjoying the first signs of Spring in March, 1973. Charger is co-owned by Mike and Pat Lobenberg of Oxnard, California, and Suzanne Neill.

37. On the sands of time... Ch. Dureigh's Tall, Dark'n Hansum, bred and owned by Reigh and Dewey Abram of Wellington, Ohio. This photograph was taken in November, 1967.

38. Sura's Wild Amber Sundown, C.D.X., scored a 195 at the January, 1975 Ventura County Dog Fanciers Association Obedience Trial to win the Highest Scoring Dog in Trial Title. This top obedience dog is owned by Mike and Pat Lobenberg of Oxnard, California.

39. This pastel portrait is of Am. and Can. Ch. Rujha's Mohhammed of Kyber Khann, owned by the William Greens and Jay Ruiz. The artist was Rene H. Folmer of Alberta, Canada.

40. This lovely head study is of Ch. Harleana's El Kalico Kat, another home-bred owned by Ileana Miller of San Juan, Puerto Rico. The Kat is 7 months old in this photograph.

41. The beautiful Ch. Charaj Golden Wind is the most recent champion finished at Bob Stein's Charaj Kennels in Dayton, Ohio.

42. Frederic Alderman, owner of the Afghans of Dynasty, runs with his Ch. Dynasty's Wild Streak and Ch. Dynasty's Wild Goose Chase. These litter brothers were sired by Ch. Coastwind Abraxas ex Dynasty's Wild Card.

43. Philip Haims, D.V.M., and Dolores Haims pose elegantly with Timu-Ka Yehuda, Ch. Regalia Blue Dalhia, Timu-Ka Zahov and the beautiful white bird, Timu-Ka Cockatoo Cookie. They were photographed at their home in San Jose, California.

44. Ch. Sandina Sparkling Champagne, handled by owner Glorvina Schwartz, is pictured winning at the 1975 Boardwalk Kennel Club Show along with his multiple breed-winning litter sister, Ch. Sandina Stainless Steel, handled by Jim Rathbun. Both Afghans were bred at the Sandina Kennels, Tuxedo Park, New York.

45. *Ch. Montrose Azul Dominga is pictured winning under judge Kay Finch at the 1975 Colorado Springs Kennel Club Show. Owned by Linda Case of the Linmara Afghans, Littleton, Colorado, Dominga's sire was Coastwind The Hermit ex Gabriella of Grandeur.*

46. *Sandina Sun Bonnet of Ariston is pictured winning Reserve Winners Bitch at the 1976 Chenango Valley Kennel Club Show under the handling of Karen Armistead. Sun Bonnet is owned by Mrs. Kurt "Lee" Abraham of New Milford, New Jersey.*

47. *Ch. Dynasty's Wildfire is pictured with owner Sue Andris after capturing a Winners Dog decision. The sire was Ch. Coastwind Abraxas ex Ch. Dynasty's Wildcard. He was bred by Frederic Alderman.*

48. *Ch. Aatiks Cerulian Blue is pictured winning Best of Breed under judge James Trullinger at a 1976 show with handler Jeri Cates. Blue finished his championship in March, 1976 under judge Joan Brearley. He is owned by Denise Cushenberry of Thousand Oaks, California.*

49. *Ch. Four Socks Thief of Man Shu is pictured taking a 5-point major win under judge Stanley Hanson at a recent Chagrin Falls Kennel Club Show. Owners are Blossom and Norman Shuman, Man Shu Kennels, Brooklyn, New York. Mr. Shuman is handling.*

RESERVE
WINNERS
CHENANGO VALLEY
KENNEL CLUB, INC.
JUNE 25 1976

WINNERS
DOG
PHOTO BY
BOOTH

WINNERS
PHOTO Graham

50. Annette S. Constantine is shown relaxing with her Ch. Dynasty's Wild Goose Face. This photo appeared on the July-August, 1976 cover of The Afghan Hound Review magazine.

51. Am. and Can. Ch. Karamoor's Karoun of Gwalior was photographed in a rustic setting with Richard Dean Albee, who co-owns Karoun with Dr. Gareth Morgan-Jones of Auburn, Alabama.

52. Ch. Majestic Knight of Stormhill was named Best of Breed at the 1976 Sun Maid Kennel Club Show by judge Joan Brearley. His sire was Mecca's Zeus ex Ch. Pandora's Xotica of Stormhill, and he was bred and is owned by the Withingtons, Stormhill Kennels, Pasadena, California. Handled by Sandy Withington.

53. Ch. Dynasty's Wild Streak, bred and owned by Frederic Alderman, Afghans of Dynasty, Mundelein, Illinois. This lovely silver-blue brindle dog won one of his majors at a specialty show. The dog's sire was Ch. Coastwind Abraxas ex Ch. Dynasty's Wild Card.

54. Specialty Best In Show winner Ch. Bella-Mu Ivory Tower is pictured with judges Marion Mangrum and William Bott. Bred by Dr. and Mrs. Robert Sergio, Ivory Tower is handled by Madelyn Lacar, who co-owns him with John Lacar.

55. Ch. Briarhill Demetrius is shown winning the points on the way to his championship in 1972. Bred and owned by Barbara Craddock of Houston, Texas. Demetrius' sire was Ch. Coastwind Gazebo ex Ch. Sultana Irisa.

56. *Four beautiful examples of the top Afghan Hounds in Spain. . . Norman Huiolobro's Int. Ch. Antar Tizoc of Crown Crest, Int. Ch. Huilaco's Rakhasta, Int. Ch. Huilaco's Black Shaliman and Int. Ch. Huilaco's Antar Rakashi. These four dogs, all champions in many countries, are the breeding force behind the Huilaco Kennels in Madrid.*

57. *Linda Case of the Linmara Afghans in Littleton, Colorado, poses for this charming informal photograph with two blue Afghans. These two puppies were sired by the multiple Best In Show winner, Ch. Wildenau's Bonvivant. Their names are Linmara's Debja and Linmara's Levanter.*

58. *Canadian Ch. Oranje Anisette was photographed along the Oregon sea coast in July, 1975. Sired by American Ch. Red Rock Brandishi ex Canadian Ch. Janine vdOM, Anisette is owned by The Volant Hounds, Seattle, Washington. Photo by Art Priddy.*

59. *"A thing of beauty. . . ." Pictured is one of the all-time greats, Ch. Taejon of Crown Crest, owned by Kay Finch of Corona del Mar, California, who handled him through his fabulous show career.*

60. *Pandahari's Copper Kid, a field champion owned by Hazle and Chester Hickok, Vale Vue Kennels, West Chester, Pennsylvania, is shown in action. "Topper's" photograph was taken by C.A. Grove at one of the coursing sessions held in Pennsylvania.*

61. *A lovely head study of Cairo, owned by Steve and Linda Smith of San Jose, California.*

Ch. Kaftan Korrigan, a multiple Group and multiple Specialty winner, is owned and bred by Carol Esterkin of Tarzana, California and co-owned and handled by Carol Reisman of Woodmere, New York. The sire was Ch. Kaftan Khan of Grandeur *ex* Anastasia Johar. Korrigan is pictured here winning at the 1975 Pasadena Kennel Club Show under judge and Afghan Hound fancier Mrs. Betsy Prior.

was always a source of great interest to me, while compiling the statistics for the Phillips System and putting together that special "Phillips System Issue" each July, to watch our great dogs compete and climb to the top.

We must also be grateful to *Popular Dogs* magazine for the fine special issues published on the Afghan breed down through the years. These issues have become collectors' items and bring high prices when available for sale. I refer specifically to the June 1950, 1952 and 1956 issues. Much of the ancient breed history and rare photographs of the old-time great dogs were presented on the pages thanks to editor Alice Wagner, who also greatly admired the breed. The "Rights and Wrongs" photographs and the excellent anatomical drawings of veterinarian Robert F. Way should be part of every Afghanites' education. While these three issues stand out above all others, each June issue of *Popular Dogs* was devoted to the hound breeds and presented much of value to dog owners. It will always be a great sadness to me to have been a witness to the demise of this most worthy publication created by the late George F. Foley, one of dogdom's greatest men. He was not only great because of his publication of this magazine of integrity, but because he created, shaped and ruled over the entire dog fancy as we know it today. I was proud to

have worked for him and with him toward the welfare of dogs and the dog shows we all enjoy so much.

Over the years there have been attempts at other magazines devoted to the Afghan Hound which sadly enough have gone into oblivion. During 1957 and 1958 a worthy publication called *Afghan Hound Parade* came out and offered some valuable information to the fancy. *Afghan International* made its appearance in 1973 and is no longer, but available back issues can provide some valuable insight into our breed and breeders.

BOOKS ON THE AFGHAN HOUND

The list of books, starting with the American Kennel Club's official publication entitled *The Complete Dog Book* right on down to this particular book you are now reading, is far too long to be presented here. My bibliography for the writing of this updated book on the breed would require far too many pages to list in its entirety. However, for those who might wish to extend their knowledge to include books on dogs in general or Afghan Hounds in particular, I would suggest writing to the American Kennel Club library and requesting a copy of their up-to-date list of reading on our breed which at the time of this writing will be supplied upon request.

This typical profile photo of an 8-month-old puppy is of future Ch. Crown Crest Devikkrokit, owned by Gertrude T. Curnyn of Hanson, Massachusetts and bred by Kay Finch. The sire was Ch. Taejon of Crown Crest *ex* Ch. Breezealong of Kandabar.

Chapter IX

Buying Your Afghan Hound Puppy

In searching for that special puppy, there are several paths that will lead you to a litter from which you can find the puppy of your choice. If you are uncertain as to where to find a reputable breeder, write to the parent club and ask for the names and addresses of members who have puppies for sale. The addresses of Afghan Hound breed clubs can be obtained by writing directly to the American Kennel Club, 51 Madison Avenue, New York, N.Y. 10010. They keep an up-to-date, accurate list of breeders from whom you can seek information on obtaining a good, healthy puppy. The classified ad listings in dog publications and the major newspapers may also lead you to that certain pup. The various dog magazines generally carry a monthly breed column which features information and news on the breed that may aid in your selection.

It is advisable that you become thoroughly acquainted with the breed prior to purchasing your puppy. Plan to attend a dog show or two in your area at which you can view purebred dogs of just about every breed at their best in the show ring. Even if you are not interested in purchasing a show-quality dog, you should be familiar with what the better specimens look like so that you will at least purchase a decent representative of the breed for the money. You can learn a lot from observing the show dogs in action in the ring, or in a public place where their personalities can be clearly shown. The dog show catalogue is also a useful tool to put you in contact with the local kennels and breeders. Each dog that is entered in the show is listed along with the owner's name and address. If you spot a dog that you think is a particularly fine and

This trio of Afghan Hound puppies is from the Stormhill Kennels. They are Shenn's Tikatu of Stormhill, Sno-Foolin of Stormhill and Majestic Knight of Stormhill.

pleasing specimen, contact the owner and arrange to visit their kennel to see the types and colors they are breeding and winning with at the shows. Exhibitors at the dog shows are usually more than delighted to talk to people interested in their dogs and the specific characteristics of their breed.

Once you've decided that the Afghan Hound is the breed for you because you appreciate its exceptional beauty, personality and intelligence and you have a place in your home for an Afghan Hound, it is wise to thoroughly acquaint yourself by reading some background material on owning the breed. When you feel certain that this puppy will fit in with your family's way of life, it is time to start writing letters and making phone calls and appointments to see some puppies.

Some words of caution: don't choose a kennel simply because it is near your home and don't buy the first "cute" puppy that romps around your legs or licks the end of your nose. All puppies are cute, and naturally some will appeal to you more than others. But don't let preferences sway your thinking. If you are buying your Afghan Hound to be strictly a family pet, preferences can be permissible. If you are looking for a top-quality puppy for the show ring, you must evaluate clearly, choose wisely and make the best possible choice. Whichever one you choose, you will quickly learn to love your Afghan puppy. A careful selection, rather than a "love at first sight" choice will save a disappointment later on.

To get the broadest idea of what puppies are for sale and the going market prices, visit as many kennels as possible in your area and write to others farther away. With today's safe and rapid air flights on the major airlines, it is possible to purchase dogs from far-off places at nominal costs. While it is safest and wisest to first see the dog you are buying, there are enough reputable breeders and kennels to be found for you to take this step with a minimum of risk. In the long run, it can be well worth your while to obtain the exact dog or bloodline you desire.

It is customary for the purchaser to pay the shipping charges, and the airlines are

Int. Ch. Crown Crest Eve Queen poses with four of her puppies that were whelped in June, 1966. The breeder was Kay Finch, Crown Crest Kennels, Corona del Mar, California.

most willing to supply flight information and prices upon request. Rental on the shipping crate, if the owner does not provide one for the dog, is nominal. While unfortunate incidents have occurred on the airlines in the transporting of animals by air, the major airlines are making improvements in safety measures and have reached the point of reasonable safety and cost. Barring unforeseen circumstances, the safe arrival of a dog you might buy can pretty much be assured if both seller and purchaser adhere to and follow up on even the most minute details from both ends.

WHAT TO LOOK FOR IN AN AFGHAN HOUND PUPPY

In few other breeds will you notice a change as remarkable as the one you will see in your Afghan Hound puppy and adult dog. Many breeds such as Dalmatians, Pointers, Ascob Cocker Spaniels, Harlequin Danes, etc., have their colors and markings pretty well established at birth. Each is recognizable as a puppy of its specific breed. To the uneducated eye, the Afghan Hound puppy is said to resemble a smooth-coated cross between a Cocker Spaniel and a Collie, but certainly not the silky-coated, glamorous Afghan Hound it grows up to be.

Anyone who has owned an Afghan Hound as a puppy will agree that the most fascinating aspect of raising the pup is to witness the complete and extraordinary meta-

Young Stephen Mason of Lancaster, California, was photographed several years ago with two of his puppy pals. . . Diane and Astrea of Windswept.

Coastwind Mistletoe wins a Hound Puppy Group First at a match show under Diana Allen. Owned by Coastwind Kennels, the puppy's sire was Ch. Coastwind Phobos *ex* Ch. Coastwind Bijou of Highland.

morphosis that occurs during its first year of maturing. Your puppy will undergo a marked change in appearance, and during this period you must also be aware of the puppy's personality for there are certain qualities visible at this time that will generally make for a good adult dog. Of course, no one can guarantee nature and the best puppy does not always grow up to be a great dog. However, even the novice breeder can learn to look for certain specifics that will help him to choose a promising puppy.

Should you decide to purchase a six- to eight-week old puppy, you are in store for all the cute antics that little pup can dream up for you! At this age, the puppy should be well on its way to being weaned, wormed and ready to go out into the world with its responsible new owner. It is better not to buy a puppy that is less than six weeks old; they simply are not ready to leave their mother or the security of the other puppies. By eight to twelve weeks of age you will be able to notice much about the behavior and appearance of the dog. Afghan puppies, as they are recalled in our fondest childhood memories, are amazingly active and bouncy— as well they should be! The normal puppy should be alert, curious and interested, especially about a stranger. However, if the puppy acts a little

reserved or distant, don't necessarily construe these acts to be signs of fear or shyness. It might merely indicate that he hasn't quite made up his mind whether he likes you as yet! By the same token, though, he should not be openly fearful or terrified by a stranger—and especially should not show any fear of his owner!

In direct contrast, the puppy should not be ridiculously over-active, either. The puppy that frantically bounds around the room and is never still is not especially desirable. And beware of the "spinners"! Spinners are the puppies or dogs that have become neurotic from being kept in cramped quarters or in crates and behave in an emotionally unstable manner when let loose in adequate space. When let out they run in circles and seemingly "go wild." Puppies with this kind of traumatic background seldom ever regain full composure or adjust to the big outside world. The puppy which has had the proper exercise and appropriate living quarters will have a normal, though spirited, outlook on life and will do his utmost to win you over without having to go into a tailspin.

If the general behavior and appearance of the dog thus far appeal to you, it is time for you to observe him more closely for additional physical requirements. First of all, you cannot

277

A family portrait of 10-week-old future Best In Show winners. This litter, named the "jubilee litter," was sired by Am. and Can. Ch. Felt's Thief of Bagdad, one of the greatest dogs in the history of the breed. This was the first litter whelped at Kay Finch's famous Crown Crest Kennels in Corona del Mar, California.

expect to find in the Afghan puppy all the coat he will bear upon maturity. That will come with time and good food, and will be additionally enhanced by the many wonderful grooming aids which can be found on the market today. Needless to say, the healthy puppy's coat should have a nice shine to it, and the more dense at this age, the better the coat will be when the dog reaches adulthood.

Look for clear, dark, sparkling eyes that are free of discharge. Dark eye rims or lids are a most desirable trait. They should also be small and almond shaped. From the time the puppy's eyes open until the puppy is about three months old the eyes might have a slight blue cast to them. The darker the blue, the better are the chances for a good dark eye in the adult dog. The eyes should slant slightly upwards at the outer corners and should not be set too far apart. The head should not be too domed, but should give a strong indication, even at this age, of a long, lean muzzle.

It is important to check the bite. Even though the puppy will cut another complete set of teeth somewhere between four and seven months of age, there will already be some indication of how the final teeth will be positioned. Too much of an overshot bite (top teeth are positioned too far *over* the bottom teeth) or too much of an undershot jaw (bottom teeth are positioned too far out *under* the top teeth) is undesirable as they are considered faults by the breed Standard.

Puppies take anything and almost everything into their mouths to chew on, and a lot of diseases and infections start or are introduced in the mouth. Brown-stained teeth, for instance, may indicate the puppy has had a past case of distemper, and the teeth will remain that way. This fact must be reckoned with if you have a show puppy in mind. The puppy's breath should be neither sour nor unpleasant. Bad breath can be a result of a poor mixture of food in the diet, or of eating too low quality of meat, especially if fed raw. Some people say that the healthy puppy's breath should have a faint odor vaguely reminiscent of garlic. At any rate, a puppy should never be fed just table scraps, but raised on a well-balanced diet containing a good dry puppy chow and a good grade of fresh meat. Poor meat and too much cereal or fillers tend to make the puppy grow too fat. Puppies should be in good flesh, but not fat from the wrong kind of food.

Even as a puppy, the ears should be well furred with the leather reaching to the end of the nose. There is little or no topknot at this age and there is no saddle, with perhaps only the suggestion of a shade of color down the middle of the back. The feet should be exceptionally large, with thick pads and little wisps of fur beginning to show between the toes.

The overall impression of the puppy should be that he is a true hound, meaning that he is a dog of great depth of brisket, with good tuck-up and long, slender legs. His topline should be level, and the puppy should possess great reach of neck. The hip bones will be prominent even at this young age, and the tail should not be set too high on the body. The front legs should run straight down from shoulders and well under the body; the rear legs should be well angulated and in line directly behind the front legs. The puppy, when viewed from the side, should give a general "squarish" appearance.

It is difficult to predict the final form of an Afghan Hound's tail while the dog is still a puppy. While it is all but impossible to expect the strong erect tail carriage of the grown dog

Salem Darrick Elsazy Lim Ti, or Elsa, is pictured with her litter of 2 sired by Jaune's Victory. Elsa is co-owned by Mary Sioussat and Sharon R. Watson of Burlington, North Carolina. The three-week-old puppies are named Salem Jack Rex and Salem Jill Rex.

in a puppy, there should be a definite indication of a curl or at least a curve into the desired ring at the end. If there is a curl at this age, so much the better! The tail will not have its feathering yet, and should *never* curve up over the body and touch down onto the back. When stretched out to its full length it should reach down at least to the hocks.

Needless to say, the puppy should be clean. The breeder that shows a dirty puppy is one to steer away from! Look closely at the skin. Make sure it is not covered with insect bites or red, blotchy sores and dry scales. The vent area around the tail should not show evidences of diarrhea or inflammation. By the same token, the puppy's fur should not be matted with excretion or smell strongly of urine.

True enough, you can wipe dirty eyes, clean dirty ears and give the puppy a bath when you get it home, but these things are all indications of how the puppy has been cared for during the important formative first months of its life, and can vitally influence its future health and development. There are many reputable breeders raising healthy puppies that have been reared in proper places and under the proper conditions in clean housing, so why take a chance on a series of veterinary bills and a questionable constitution.

MALE OR FEMALE?

The choice of sex in your puppy is also something that must be given serious thought before you buy. For the pet owner, the sex that would best suit the family life you enjoy would be the paramount choice to consider. For the breeder or exhibitor there are other vital considerations. If you are looking for a stud to establish a kennel, it is essential that you select a dog with both testicles evident, even at a tender age, and verified by a veterinarian before the sale is finalized if there is any doubt.

This magnificent 4-month-old puppy, Bokhara's Regalia, is owned by Joseph Kluchinsky of Spotswood, New Jersey.

The visibility of only one testicle, known as monorchidism, automatically disqualifies the dog from the show ring or from a breeding program, though monorchids are capable of siring. Additionally, it must be noted that monorchids frequently sire dogs with the same deficiency, and to introduce this into a bloodline knowingly is an unwritten sin in the fancy. Also, a monorchid can sire dogs that are completely sterile. Such dogs are referred to as cryptochids and have no testicles.

An additional consideration in the male versus female decision for the private owners is that with males there might be the problem of leg-lifting and with females there is the inconvenience while they are in season. However, this need not be the problem it used to be—pet shops sell "pants" for both sexes, which help to control the situation.

THE PLANNED PARENTHOOD BEHIND YOUR PUPPY

Never be afraid to ask pertinent questions about the puppy, as well as questions about the sire and dam. Feel free to ask the breeder if you might see the dam, the purpose of your visit to determine her general health and her appearance as a representative of the breed. Ask also to see the sire if the breeder is the owner. Ask what the puppy has been fed and should be fed after weaning. Ask to see

Spectrums Iceblue Tiffany poses with "friend." The sire was Chaka's Calico Boy of Spectrum *ex* Ch. Mirabad's Byrones of Spectrum. The breeder-owners are Art and Inger James of Vancouver, Canada.

the pedigree, and inquire if the litter or the individual puppies have been registered with the American Kennel Club, how many of the temporary and/or permanent inoculations the puppy has had, when and if the puppy has been wormed and whether it has had any illness, disease or infection.

You need not ask if the puppy is housebroken. . . it won't mean much. He may have gotten the idea as to where "the place" is where he lives now, but he will need new training to learn where "the place" is in his new home! And you can't really expect too much from puppies at this age anyway. Housebreaking is entirely up to the new owner. We know puppies always eliminate when they first awaken and sometimes dribble when they get excited. If friends and relatives are coming over to see the new puppy, make sure he is walked just before he greets them at the front door. This will help.

The normal time period for puppies around three months of age to eliminate is about every two or three hours. As the time draws near, either take the puppy out or indicate the newspapers for the same purpose. Housebreaking is never easy, but anticipation is about 90 per cent of solving the problem. The schools that offer to housebreak your dog are virtually useless. Here again the puppy will learn the "place" at the schoolhouse, but coming home he will need special training for the new location.

A charming photograph of a little girl and her dog, both "bred and owned" by Said and Suzanna Mughabghab of Sayville, New York.

A reputable breeder will welcome any and all questions you might ask and will voluntarily offer additional information, if only to brag about the tedious and loving care he has given the litter. He will also sell a puppy on a 24-hour veterinary approval. This means you have a full day to get the puppy to a veterinarian of your choice to get his opinion on the general health of the puppy before you make a final decision. There should also be veterinary certificates and full particulars on the dates and types of inoculations the puppy has been given up to that time.

PUPPIES AND WORMS

Let us give further attention to the unhappy and very unpleasant subject of worms. Generally speaking, most puppies—even those raised in clean quarters—come into contact with worms early in life. The worms can be passed down from the mother before birth or picked up during the puppies' first encounters with the earth or their kennel facilities. To say that you must not buy a puppy because of an infestation of worms is nonsensical. You might be passing up a fine animal that can be freed of worms in one short treatment, although a heavy infestation of worms of any kind in a young dog is dangerous and debilitating.

The extent of the infection can be readily determined by a veterinarian, and you might take his word as to whether the future health and conformation of the dog has been damaged. He can prescribe the dosage and supply the medication at this time and you will already have one of your problems solved.

VETERINARY INSPECTION

While your veterinarian is going over the puppy you have selected to purchase, you might just as well ask him for his opinion of it as a breed as well as the facts about its general health. While few veterinarians can claim to be breed-conformation experts, they usually have a good eye for a worthy specimen and can advise you where to go for further information. Perhaps your veterinarian could also recommend other breeders if you should want another opinion. The veterinarian can point out structural faults or organic problems that affect all breeds and can usually judge whether an animal has been abused or mishandled and whether it is oversized or undersized.

I would like to emphasize here that it is only through this type of close cooperation between owners and veterinarians that we can expect to heap the harvest of modern research in the veterinary field.

Most reliable veterinarians are more than eager to learn about various breeds of purebred dogs, and we in turn must acknowledge and apply what they have proved through experience and research in their field. We can buy and breed the best dog in the world, but when disease strikes we are only as safe as our veterinarian is capable—so let's keep them informed breed by breed, and dog by dog. The veterinarian can mean the difference between life and death!

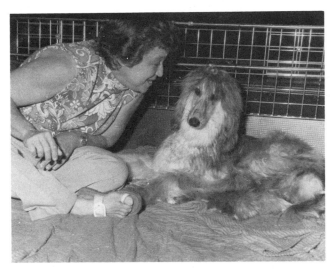

"You won, you won!" is what owner Ileana Miller is telling Sandina Sassafras after having just been chosen Best Puppy In Show at the 1975 Afghan Hound Club of America Specialty Show. One year later Sassafras was Reserve Winners at the same show and finished her American championship in strong mainland competition, handled by her breeder Glorvina R. Schwartz. "Frownie" is co-owned by Mrs. Miller and Lyda Ramirez.

THE CONDITIONS OF SALE

While it is customary to pay for the puppy before you take it away with you, you should be able to give the breeder a deposit if there is any doubt about the puppy's health. You might also (depending on local laws) postdate a check to cover the 24-hour veterinary approval. If you decide to take the puppy,

The call of the wild! This very vocal little puppy grew up to be Ch. Yenghiz Khan of Five Mile. By the time he reached 18 months of age he had been a Hound Group winner 18 times and had won 2 Bests In Show. Originally owned by Marion Foster Florsheim, he was later owned by Mrs. Clarke of Ohio. Ylla photograph.

the breeder is required to supply you with a pedigree, along with the puppy's registration papers. He is also obliged to supply you with complete information about the inoculations and American Kennel Club instructions on how to transfer ownership of the puppy into your name.

Some breeders will offer buyers time payment plans for convenience if the price on a show dog is very high or if deferred pay-

ments are the only way you can purchase the dog. However, any such terms must be worked out between buyer and breeder and should be put in writing to avoid later complications.

You will find most breeders cooperative if they believe you are sincere in your love for the puppy and that you will give it the proper home and the show ring career it deserves (if it is sold as a show quality specimen of the breed). Remember, when buying a show dog, it is impossible to guarantee nature. A breeder can only tell you what he *believes* will develop into a show dog. . . so be sure your breeder is an honest one.

Also, if you purchase a show prospect and promise to show the dog, you definitely should show it! It is a waste to have a beautiful dog that deserves recognition in the show ring sitting at home as a family pet, and it is unfair to the breeder. This is especially true if the breeder offered you a reduced price because of the advertising his kennel and bloodlines would receive by your showing the dog in the ring. If you want a pet, buy a pet. Be honest about it, and let the breeder decide on this basis which is the best dog for you. Your conscience will be clear and you'll both be doing a real service to the breed.

BUYING A SHOW PUPPY

If you are positive about breeding and showing your Afghan, make this point clear so that the breeder will sell you the best possible puppy. If you are dealing with an established kennel, you will have to rely partially, if not entirely, on their choice, since they know their bloodlines and what they can expect from the breeding. They know how their stock develops, and it would be foolish of them to sell you a puppy that could not stand up as a show specimen representing their stock in the ring.

However, you must also realize that the breeder may be keeping the best puppy in the litter to show and breed himself. If this is the case, you might be wise to select the best puppy of the opposite sex so that the dogs will not be competing against one another in the show rings for their championship title.

THE COLOR OF YOUR PUPPY

The color of your Afghan Hound is a matter of personal preference, as are the contrasting colors on the ears and mask. Black on the muzzle and ear fringes is referred to as the "points." Puppies may be born with white feet or tail tips, but they usually bend in; however, if you intend to show your dog in the breed ring, white on the face is most undesirable.

THE PURCHASE PRICE

Prices vary on all puppies, of course, but a good show prospect at six weeks to six months of age will usually sell for several hundred dollars. If the puppy is really outstanding, and the pedigree and parentage is also outstanding, the price will be even higher. Honest breeders, however, will all be around the same figure, so price should not be a strong deciding factor in your choice. If you have any questions as to the current price range, a few telephone calls to different kennels will give you a good average. Reputable breeders will usually stand behind the health of their puppies should something drastically wrong develop, such as hip dysplasia, etc. Their obligation to make an adjustment or replacement is usually honored. However, this must be agreed to in writing at the time of the purchase.

THE COST OF BUYING ADULT STOCK

Prices for adult dogs fluctuate greatly. Some grown dogs are offered free of charge to good homes; others are put with owners on breeders' terms. But don't count on getting a "bargain" if it doesn't cost you anything! Good dogs are always in demand, and worthy studs or brood bitches are expensive. Prices for them can easily go up into the four-figure range. Take an expert with you if you intend to make this sort of investment. Just make sure the "expert" is free of professional jealousy and will offer an unprejudiced opinion. If you are reasonably familiar with the Standard, and get the expert's opinion, between the two you can usually come up with a proper decision.

Blu Tazi of Grandeur, co-owned by Roger Rechler and Sunny Shay, is pictured here going Best Puppy In Breed at the 1975 Brookhaven Kennel Club Match Show.

Chapter X

Grooming the Afghan Hound

GROOMING METHODS AND EQUIPMENT

All dogs, especially long-coated dogs such as the Afghan Hound, require good grooming. A beautifully-coated dog which proudly wears the thick, silky coat that his owner has taken time and trouble to cultivate is a joy to behold, both in and out of the show ring. Once ruined or cut off, the coat of the Afghan Hound requires two years' time and daily care to come to its original length and luster. Therefore, it is wise to take a little time each day to groom the coat and keep it in top condition rather than have to work diligently on the dog for days to make the coat presentable for the show ring.

Take the time to establish grooming as a common practice in the daily routine. You'll find matters simplified by choosing one particular spot for grooming your dog each time. Be sure to place the grooming table in a spot where the light is good and where the dog will have relatively few distractions. Eliminate temptations by keeping toys, food, other dogs, etc., out of sight. Make the dog understand that there is work to be done and that you mean to do it. Be gentle, yet firm.

Opposite:
Ready for the ring! The ultimate in grooming perfection, the glorious Afghan Hound stands poised on the grooming table waiting for his moment in the show ring! This beauty is owned by Jim and Joyce Saarinen of Astatula, Florida. The dog is Best In Show Winner Ch. Harun Al-Rashid II.

As soon as the dog is capable of jumping safely onto the table by himself, encourage him to do so. Give him the command to "stand" so that it becomes clear that the time for grooming has come. How you choose to position your dog while grooming is not merely a matter of choice or convenience. A thorough grooming will require the dog to both stand and recline on each side. In the beginning you should encourage your dog to stand long enough to stand at ease. He will have to stand at the end of the grooming session for the finishing touches, so do your best to teach him to enjoy all the attention you are lavishing on him.

A sturdy table is a must for grooming. Don't use one that tips from side to side or wobbles even slightly. Dogs are comfortable only when they are sure of their footing. As for the height of the table, make it easy on yourself. In the areas where you do the most work you will not want to have to reach too far up or down. Set the height to your convenience, and the narrower the table the better. A rough surfaced table will allow the dog to get a good grip with his feet, yet you do not want it so rough that it is not easily wiped off after each use.

Since each dog and each coat differ, there is no set amount of time recommended for grooming. Heavily coated dogs will naturally require more grooming time. Be sure, however, to allot enough time for going over the entire dog *each time* he is put up on the table. The area you skip over one time will be twice as hard to remedy the next! The spots you miss will show up all too soon.

The correct brush for grooming the Af-

This original Afghan Hound grooming chart was conceived and created by the author. The arrows indicate the direction in which the Afghan coat should be combed.

ghan Hound's coat is one made with soft bristles—*not nylon!* The hair should be brushed in layers from the skin out to the very ends of the hair. If you notice that your brush is gathering hair on one side of the brush only, you are not holding it correctly. The strokes must be gentle, and the entire stroke should be straight, with no twist of the wrist. It is generally easier to begin with the legs and work up to the body, all the while holding the layers of hair up with one hand and the flat of your arm while brushing with the other hand. As time goes by you will develop your own grooming pattern, deciding just where to start and finish to make it easier for both you and your dog.

On the whole, the brushing should be done to follow the lay of the hair. With puppies it is sometimes stimulating to the skin and the hair for it to be brushed directly opposite. Since you are dealing with the puppy coat, this "going against the grain" does no serious harm to the hair and stimulates the hair cells to encourage growth of the permanent coat.

The hair on the head should be brushed both up and back and then down forward over the eyes. This wild appearance of the topknot is characteristic of the Afghan Hound. The ears require considerable brushing because this is one of the major tangle areas. The inside of the ears can best be brushed by laying the leather against the length of the neck.

The tail should always be brushed in the direction of its natural curl. Start at the base and brush outward and move on up to the tip from the curve outward. Be aware that the tail, when in a direct line from the saddle, will be covered with flat, smooth hair while the feathering grows from underneath. You will find this presents two "sides" of the tail to be brushed.

The feet are usually the first part of the dog to get dirty. They should be brushed in a semi-circular direction along with the anatomy of the foot and from the leg outward. The hocks and elbows should receive special attention, since bones are prominent in these areas and the friction and wear on these spots makes the hair tend to tangle and mat.

At approximately one year of age the Afghan Hound begins to get his saddle. This is a smooth strip of differently colored hair (except in all-black dogs) that is another distinguishing feature characteristic of the breed.

The saddle is usually a few inches wide and runs from the base of the neck down the back and past the prominent hip bones to the end of the croup. Once in evidence, the saddle should be brushed with the lay of the hair—down the back from the neck toward the tail.

The puppy hair may fall out completely and all at once, or this may be a slow process taking several months, with more and more of the soft puppy coat falling away with each brushing. It might be necessary to brush a little harder to get out the dead hairs completely, but usually the excess hair will clear in the normal course of brushing.

Your biggest problem in grooming, particularly while your dog is shedding his puppy coat, will be mats. Little bits of debris that work their way into the coat, accompanied by bits of dead hair that don't get brushed away completely, will cause these tangles. If not taken care of promptly these tangles will develop into mats. Mats have a way of getting even "mattier" and will eventually have to be cut out if allowed to remain too long.

It is next to impossible to hide or cover up the unmistakable hole left in the coat when it has been necessary to cut out a mat. At its best, the Afghan Hound's amazing silky coat gives the glorious illusion of "floating" when the dog is in action, and this illusion is broken if the coat has become damaged or cut in any way.

Should you find a bad tangle or mat, brush away the surrounding hair and take the mat in your hand. Take a little bit at a time and shred it gently with your fingers, working it apart. When you use a comb, carefully and gently work the mat apart a little bit at a time, starting at the end of a tangle and shredding it up toward the body. When you get the hair separated, start brushing very gently from the ends of the hair gradually up toward the body until all the hair is free. When the tangle is completely combed out, brush the hair back in with the rest of the coat.

There are various kinds of coat conditioners on sale at all pet shops that can help you keep your dog well groomed. Which of these you use, if any, should be a matter of which will best suit your dog's needs. Some of these preparations are strictly cleaning aids, and others help keep the coat free of "electricity," help retard tangles, etc. One thing is certain, they all make the dogs smell divine. Dogs with skin that is inclined to be dry or scaly should have dressings that contain more lanolin or other oils. These conditioners are applied with an atomizer and brushed into the coat.

If your Afghan Hound is exceptionally active in the woods or fields or is a city dog where excessive dirt and soot plague him, you will more than likely want to use a dry shampoo or lather dry bath between actual tub baths. These are also for sale at all pet shops. Whatever products you use, do not expect miracles from these preparations. You must groom and feed properly to maintain the good health that will normally give your Afghan Hound the lustrous coat he is meant to have.

BATHING THE ADULT AFGHAN HOUND

There are probably as many theories on how, and how often, to bathe a dog as there are dog owners. However, there is no set rule on bathing frequency or method. Show dogs, or dogs that are outdoors a great deal in all kinds of weather and still spend time indoors with the family, will require an occasional bath. In dealing with dogs the size of the Afghan Hound, you'll make things easier for

Ch. Khabira Zabrula, photographed at 2 years of age, is owned by Diane LaGreca, Afghan Hounds of Gran Salaam, West Hempstead, New York.

yourself if you use the bathtub. Good drainage is essential for the several rinsings that will be necessary, and for convenience a hand spray or length of hose can be attached to the faucet to aid in the washing and rinsing.

Before placing the dog in the tub you might wish to place bits of cotton in the dog's ears to prevent soapy water from entering them. You might also put a few drops of mineral oil in his eyes to prevent them from burning should some soap suds splash in. Be sure your dog has good footing. A ribbed rubber bath mat placed in the bottom of the tub will prevent him from slipping, and you'll find the dog will be much less troublesome and easier when he's on firm footing.

Dog shampoos are preferable to cake soap, and two thorough soapings should be sufficient. Before the first application of shampoo, thoroughly wet the coat until it has been soaked to the skin with water. Rinsings should continue until *every last bit* of shampoo has been washed away. This thorough rinsing cannot be stressed enough; any soapy residue or shampoo that is left behind will make the hair gummy, dull and lifeless, and will dry the skin as well.

It is best to use a wide spray when rinsing. Start at the head, rinsing down the neck to the body, all the while taking care to lift and separate the hair by layers. By spreading your fingers through the coat, you will allow the water to reach all the way to the skin. Don't just dump the water over the dog's head. Grab the muzzle firmly in one hand, tilt the head up and back, and pour the water down the head and neck from a point just *behind* the eyes.

After the head, body and tail have been done, pay additional and particular attention to the feet and legs since the rinsing water that runs off the dog will remain in the bottom of the tub and cling to the feet. Continue rinsing them until you are convinced the soap has gone completely. Then do it once again for good measure!

Now is the time to apply a hair rinse, if you choose to use one on your Afghan Hound. Many people prefer creme rinses, others lemon or vinegar. Any of these conditioners will give the coat an extra sheen and luster. Another light rinsing follows the conditioning and you are almost ready to start the drying process. Let the dog drip-dry for a few minutes first (not long enough for him to get a chill, of course, but long enough to prevent a water

Love-in! Young Sandra Withington and Koh-I-Baba, U.D., express their love and admiration for each other. Both "owned by" Virginia Withington, Stormhill Kennels, Pasadena, California.

trail between the tub and the grooming table). Now stand back. It's time for him to shake himself. If you can get a towel over him before he does, so much the better for your walls!

THE DRYING PROCESS

While your dryer (or vacuum cleaner attachment) is warming up, gently towel dry the dog and get rid of the excess water that will be dripping from his coat. Pressing the hair flat against the body and rubbing your hands down over the dog will take off a great deal of the excess water. Above all, try to avoid any circular motions with the towel as this is definitely conducive to tangling the hair, which can cause considerable problems later on.

When your dryer has reached room temperature, start using the brush, working within the current of warm air. You should always keep the dryer *at least* twelve inches away from the coat to avoid scorching it. Brush the hair downward in layers, separating the hair completely down to the skin as you go. Be careful that you never leave your Afghan Hound dry on the outside and wet next to the skin. The entire bathing and drying process may take several hours, so never bathe your dog unless you are fully prepared to finish the job once you've started it. Allow for plenty of drying time. Move the dryer frequently all over the body, so that the dog will dry evenly and not just in one area. He will brush out much better if he is uniformly dry—not too wet in one spot and too dry in another.

Xanadu of Gran Salaam, co-owned by Steven T. Black and Frank LaGreca of West Hempstead, New York. The sire was Ch. Ninth Turn Argus ex Gran Salaam Carte Blanche.

True enough, there are dogs that just never get to like being groomed. These dogs require extra patience and, quite possibly, extra work, since they will employ every scheme known to canines to put you off and hamper progress. More often than not, if you meet resistance to grooming it's because the dog is genuinely uncomfortable.

The main thing is to be gentle; be even more gentle in the sensitive areas such as the groin, the feet, under the tail, around the eyes, etc. The calmest of dogs will flinch when he sees the bristles of a brush or the shiny teeth of a steel comb flashing overhead. You can be pretty brisk when grooming the body, the chest, saddle, etc., but such fervor in the tender regions can resemble Chinese torture.

Grooming your dog will probably never seem easy, but it can be a gratifying experience for both dog and master if approached with common sense and patience. Let your dog see that you take a definite pride in taking care of him. He will appreciate this interest and gentleness, and it will result in a closer communication between you and your dog through this personal relationship. He'll certainly look a lot better for the correct care!

BATHING THE PUPPY

There are two schools of thought on the advisability of bathing the very young puppy. If you are an advocate of the bath, the same technique can be used for the puppy that is advised for the grown dog. The younger the puppy, however, the more vulnerable they are, so pay special attention to keeping them free of drafts and *never* leave a puppy only partially dry.

If you believe a bath endangers a puppy unnecessarily, it is wise to know about the dry shampoos when a cleaning job seems necessary. These dry shampoos, plus regular brushings, will keep the puppy clean as well as stimulate the hair follicles and encourage the natural hair oils and coat growth.

GROOMING BEHAVIOR

If your Afghan Hound wiggles and squirms, backs off and fights you every bit of the way when grooming time rolls around, chances are you're being a little too rough.

Opposite, top photo:
The lustrous coat of Best In Show winner Ch. Harun Al-Rashid II is shown after his daily grooming session. He is owned by Jim and Joyce Saarinen, Afghans Al Rashid, Austatula, Florida. Whelped in 1969, Harun is also a multiple Group winner.

Opposite, bottom photo:
Ch. Harmony's Jack Frost, bred and owned by Joyce and Joseph Messineo, Jamal Afghans, River Vale, New Jersey. Photo by Ashbey.

Exotic headstudy of Mrs. Stephanie Johnson's Ch. Eastern Star of Stormhill. The sire was Ch. Mecca's Zeus *ex* Ch. Pantomine of Stormhill. Star finished his championship with 3 majors, including a 5-point major as Winners Dog at the 1975 Afghan Hound Club of California Specialty Show. He is always owner-handled by Mrs. Johnson of Palatine, Illinois. Photograph by Joan Ludwig.

Chapter XI

The Dog Show World

Let us assume that after a few months of tender loving care, you realize your dog is developing beyond your wildest expectations and that the dog you selected is very definitely a show dog! Of course, every owner is prejudiced. But if you are sincerely interested in going to dog shows with your dog and making a champion of him, now is the time to start casting a critical eye on him from a judge's point of view.

There is no such thing as a perfect dog. Every dog has some faults, perhaps even a few serious ones. The best way to appraise your dog's degree of perfection is to compare him with the Standard for the breed, or before a judge in a show ring.

MATCH SHOWS

For the beginner there are "mock" shows, called match shows, where you and your dog go through many of the procedures of a regular dog show, but do not gain points toward championship. These shows are usually held by kennel clubs, annually or semi-annually, and much ring poise and experience can be gained there. The age limit is usually reduced to two months at match shows to give puppies four months of training before they compete at the regular shows when they reach six months of age. Classes range from two to four months, four to six months, six to nine months, and nine to twelve months. Puppies compete with others of their own age for comparative purposes. Many breeders evaluate their litters in this manner, choosing which is the most outgoing, which is the most poised, the best showman, etc.

For those seriously interested in showing their dogs to full championship, these match shows provide important experience for both the dog and the owner. Class categories may vary slightly, according to number of entries, but basically include all the classes that are included at a regular point show. There is a nominal entry fee and, of course, ribbons and usually trophies are given for your efforts as well. Unlike the point shows, entries can be made on the day of the show right on the show grounds. They are unbenched and provide an informal, usually congenial atmosphere for the amateur, which helps to make the ordeal of one's first adventures in the show ring a little less nerve-wracking.

THE POINT SHOWS

It is not possible to show a puppy at an American Kennel Club sanctioned point show before the age of six months. When your dog reaches this eligible age, your local kennel club can provide you with the names and addresses of the show-giving superintendents in your area who will be staging the club's dog show for them, and where you must write for an entry form.

The forms are mailed in a pamphlet called a premium list. This also includes the names of the judges for each breed, a list of the prizes and trophies, the name and address of the show-giving club and where the show will be held, as well as rules and regulations set up by the American Kennel Club which must be abided by if you are to enter.

A booklet containing the complete set of show rules and regulations may be obtained by writing to the American Kennel Club, Inc., 51 Madison Avenue, New York, N.Y., 10010.

When you write to the dog show superintendent, request not only your premium list for this particular show, but ask that your name be added to their mailing list so that you will automatically receive all premium

The first Afghan Hound brace shown in this country: Ch. Meheronee Kahlifafa and Int. Ch. Rudiki of Pride's Hill.

lists in the future. List your breed or breeds and they will see to it that you receive premium lists for specialty shows as well.

Unlike the match shows where your dog will be judged on ring behavior, at the point shows he will be judged on conformation to the breed Standard. In addition to being at least six months of age (on the day of the show) he must be purebred for a point show. This means both of his parents and he are registered with the American Kennel Club. There must be no alterations or falsifications regarding his appearance. Females cannot have been spayed and males must have both testicles in evidence. No dyes or powders may be used to enhance the appearance, and any lameness or deformity or major deviation from the Standard for the breed constitutes a disqualification.

With all these things in mind, groom your dog to the best of your ability in the specified area for this purpose in the show hall and *exercise your dog before taking him into the ring!* Too many Afghan Hound owners are guilty of making their dogs remain on their crates so they do not get dirty, and the first thing they do when they start to show is stop to empty themselves. There is no excuse for this. All it takes is a walk *before* grooming. If your dog is clean, well groomed, *empty* and leash trained you should be able to enter the show ring with confidence and pride of ownership, ready for an appraisal of your dog by the judge.

The presiding judge on that day will allow each and every dog a certain amount of time and consideration before making his decisions. It is never permissible to consult the judge regarding either your dog or his decision while you are in the ring. An exhibitor never speaks unless spoken to, and then only to answer such questions as the judge may ask—the age of the dog, the dog's bite, or to ask you to move your dog around the ring once again.

However, before you reach the point where you are actually in the ring awaiting the final decisions of the judge, you will have had to decide in which of the five classes in each sex your dog should compete.

POINT SHOW CLASSES

The regular classes of the AKC are: Puppy, Novice, Bred-by-Exhibitor, American-Bred, Open; if your dog is undefeated in any of the regular classes (divided by sex) in which it is entered, he or she is *required* to enter the Winners Class. If your dog is placed second in the class to the dog which won Winners Dog or Winners Bitch, hold the dog or bitch in readiness as the judge must consider it for Reserve Winners.

PUPPY CLASSES shall be for dogs which are six months of age and over but under twelve months, which were whelped in the U.S.A. or Canada, and which are not champions. Classes are often divided 6 and (under) 9, and 9 and (under) 12 months. The age of a dog shall be calculated up to and inclusive of the first day of a show. For example, a dog whelped on Jan. 1st is eligible to compete in a puppy class on July 1st, and may continue to compete up to and including Dec. 31st of the same year, but is not eligible to compete Jan. 1st of the following year.

THE NOVICE CLASS shall be for dogs six months of age or over, whelped in the U.S.A. or Canada which have not, prior to the closing of entries, won three first prizes in the Novice Class, a first prize in Bred-by-Exhibitor, American-Bred or Open Class, nor one or more points toward a championship title.

THE BRED-BY-EXHIBITOR CLASS shall be for dogs whelped in the U.S.A. which are six months of age and over, which are not champions and which are owned wholly or in part by the person or by the spouse of the person who was the breeder or one of the breeders of record. Dogs entered in the BBE Class must be handled by an owner or by a member of the immediate family of an owner, i.e., the husband, wife, father, mother, son, daughter, brother and sister.

First in the Hound Group at the 1964 Grand River Kennel Club Show was Balkwood Kennel's Ch. Balkwood Colonel Mosby. Handled by Jerry Rigden, this win was under judge Edith Nash Hellerman. Presenting the trophy is Edgar Risley. Glenn photo.

Turkara of Grandeur is pictured finishing her championship at the 1954 Westchester Kennel Club Show. She finished with four major wins. Turkara was owned and handled by Alice E. Schmidt of Somers, New York.

The beautiful Ch. Coastwind Nassim Pasha was bred by the Coastwind Kennels and owned by Susan Bahary of the Kennels of Bay Winds in Huntington Bay, New York. Owner-handled, Nassim was a breed winner from the classes and Best of Winners at both the Afghan Hound Club of S.W. Ohio and the Finger Lakes Afghan Hound Club Specialty while earning his championship. His sire was Ch. Coastwind Gazebo *ex* Regalia's Ebony.

Ch. Bokhara's Zartic is pictured winning Best of Winners under judge Anna Katherine Nicholas on the way to his championship. Sired by Cadburyhill Infashia's Image *ex* Baijais Meditation, he is owned and shown by Joseph Kluchinsky of Spotswood, New Jersey.

Opposite:
Ch. Kabul's Crown Crest Khachmi, owned by Patricia Sinden of Illinois. Kachmi is pictured here winning a Best In Show under Dr. A.A. Mitten at the 1962 Sandemac Kennel Club Show with handler Jack Funk.

Ch. Morningcall Candy Man of Dic Mar is pictured winning at a recent show under judge Judith Fellton. Marcia Stoll is handling for owner Dr. Bernard Rogers of Dallas, Texas.

Bokhara Taj Akbar, bred by Joe Kluchinsky and Sunny Shay, is pictured winning at the 1975 Afghan Hound Club of Northern New Jersey Specialty Show under judge Kay Finch. He is shown by Joe Kluchinsky and is owned by Linda and Howard Levine.

A nice win for William Walsh's Ch. Siah Nayd of Shahi-Taj at a 1962 dog show in Charleston, South Carolina, under judge Derek Rayne.

THE AMERICAN-BRED CLASS is for all dogs (except champions) six months of age or over, whelped in the U.S.A. by reason of a mating that took place in the U.S.A.

THE OPEN CLASS is for any dog six months of age or over, except in a member specialty club show held for only American-Bred dogs, in which case the class is for American-Bred dogs only.

WINNERS DOG and WINNERS BITCH: After the above male classes have been judged, the first-place winners are then *required* to compete in the ring. The dog judged "Winners Dog" is awarded the points toward his championship title.

RESERVE WINNERS are selected immediately after the Winners Dog. In case of a disqualification of a win by the AKC, the Reserve Dog moves up to "Winners" and receives the points. After all male classes are judged, the bitch classes are called.

BEST OF BREED OR BEST OF VARIETY COMPETITION is limited to Champions of Record or dogs (with newly acquired points, for a 90-day period prior to AKC confirmation) which have completed championship requirements, and Winners Dog and Winners Bitch (or the dog awarded Winners if only one Winners prize has been awarded), together with any undefeated dogs which have been shown only in non-regular classes; all compete for Best of Breed or Best of Variety (if the breed is divided by size, color, texture or length of coat hair, etc.).

BEST OF WINNERS: If the WD or WB earns BOB or BOV, it automatically becomes BOW; otherwise they will be judged together for BOW (following BOB or BOV judging).

BEST OF OPPOSITE SEX is selected from the remaining dogs of the opposite sex to Best of Breed or Best of Variety.

OTHER CLASSES may be approved by the AKC: STUD DOGS, BROOD BITCHES, BRACE CLASS, TEAM CLASS; classes consisting of local dogs and bitches may also be included in a show if approved by the AKC (special rules are included in the AKC Rule Book).

The MISCELLANEOUS CLASS shall be for purebred dogs of such breeds as may be designated by the AKC. No dog shall be eligible for entry in this class unless the owner has been granted an Indefinite Listing Privilege (ILP) and unless the ILP number is given on the entry form. Application for an ILP shall be made on a form provided by the AKC and when submitted must be accompanied by a fee set by the Board of Directors.

All Miscellaneous Breeds shall be shown together in a single class except that the class may be divided by sex if so specified in the premium list. There shall be *no* further competition for dogs entered in this class. Ribbons for 1st, 2nd, 3rd and 4th shall be Rose, Brown, Light Green and Gray, respectively. This class is open to the following Miscellaneous dog breeds: Australian Cattle Dogs, Aus-

Ch. Jisnah of Arken is pictured winning at a show years ago after being purchased by Miss Virginia Hare from Charles Wernsman. Miss Hare campaigned Jisnah on the Southern and California circuits with handler Charles Long.

tralian Kelpies, Border Collies, Cavalier King Charles Spaniels, Ibizan Hounds, Miniature Bull Terriers, Spinoni Italiani and Tibetan Spaniels.

OBEDIENCE TRIALS

Some shows also offer Obedience Trials, which are considered as separate events. They give the dogs a chance to compete and score on performing a prescribed set of exercises intended to display their training in doing useful work.

There are three obedience titles for which they may compete. First, the Companion Dog or C.D. title; second, the Companion Dog Excellent or C.D.X.; and third, the Utility Dog or U.D. Detailed information on these degrees is contained in a booklet entitled Official Obedience Regulations and may be obtained by writing to the American Kennel Club.

JUNIOR SHOWMANSHIP COMPETITION

Junior Showmanship competition is for boys and girls in different age groups handling their own dogs or ones owned by their immediate family. There are four divisions: Novice A (10 to 12 year olds) and Novice B (13 to 16 year olds) for competitors with no pre-

Ch. Zaamarakuri of Ghazni was named Best In Show at the 1955 Dayton, Ohio, Kennel Club Show. Owner was Mary Kenney of Dayton. Frasie photo.

Ch. Farah's Autumn Frost is pictured finishing for championship under judge Kent Delaney in July, 1975. Silvy was the 25th champion sired by Ch. Akaba's Royal Flush. Whelped in 1972, Silvy is handled by Andrea Poore, and owned by Robert and Dorothy Poore.

vious Junior Showmanship wins, Open A (10 to 12 year olds) and Open B (13 to 16 year olds) for competitors with one or more JS awards.

As Junior Showmanship at the dog shows increased in popularity, certain changes and improvements had to be made. As of April 1, 1971, the American Kennel Club issued a new booklet containing the Regulations for Junior Showmanship which may be obtained by writing to the A.K.C. at 51 Madison Avenue, New York, N.Y. 10010.

DOG SHOW PHOTOGRAPHERS

Every show has at least one official photographer who will be more than happy to take a photograph of your dog with the judge, ribbons and trophies, along with you or your handler. These make marvelous remembrances of your top show wins and are frequently framed along with the ribbons for display purposes. Photographers can be paged at the show over the public address system, if you wish to obtain this service. Prices vary, but

This photo of two glorious Afghan Hounds waiting in the benched area before entering the show ring was featured on the February, 1957 cover of the *American Kennel Gazette* magazine.

you will probably find it costs little to capture these happy moments, and the photos can always be used in the various dog magazines to advertize your dog's wins.

TWO TYPES OF DOG SHOWS

There are two types of dog shows licensed by the American Kennel Club. One is the all-breed show which includes classes for all the recognized breeds, and groups of breeds; i.e., all terriers, all toys, etc. Then there are the specialty shows for one particular breed which also offer championship points.

BENCHED OR UNBENCHED DOG SHOWS

The show-giving clubs determine, usually on the basis of what facilities are offered by their chosen show site, whether their show will be benched or unbenched. A benched show is one where the dog show superintendent supplies benches (cages for toy dogs). Each bench is numbered and its corresponding number appears on your entry identification slip which is sent to your prior to the show date. The number also appears in the show catalog. Upon entering the show you

should take your dog to the bench where he should remain until it is time to groom him before entering the ring to be judged. After judging, he must be returned to the bench until the official time of dismissal from the show. At an unbenched show the club makes no provision whatsoever for your dog other than an enormous tent (if an outdoor show) or an area in a show hall where all crates and grooming equipment must be kept.

Benched or unbenched, the moment you enter the show grounds you are expected to look after your dog and have it under complete control at all times. This means short leads in crowded aisles or getting out of cars. In the case of a benched show, a "bench chain" is needed. It should allow the dog to move around, but not get down off the bench. It is also not considered "cute" to have small tots leading enormous dogs around a dog show where they might be dragged into the middle of a dog fight.

IF YOUR DOG WINS A CLASS. . .

Study the classes to make certain your dog is entered in a proper class for his or her qualifications. If your dog wins his class, the rule states: *You are required* to enter classes for Winners, Best of Breed and Best of Winners (no additional entry fees). The rule states, "No eligible dogs may be withheld from competition." It is not mandatory that you stay for group judging. *If your dog wins a group*, however, *you must stay for Best In Show competition.*

THE PRIZE RIBBONS AND WHAT THEY STAND FOR

No matter how many entries there are in each class at a dog show, if you place first through fourth position you will receive a ribbon. These ribbons commemorate your win and can be impressive when collected and displayed to prospective buyers when and if you have puppies for sale, or if you intend to use your dog at public stud.

All ribbons from the American Kennel Club licensed dog shows will bear the American Kennel Club seal, the name of the show, the date and the placement. In the classes the colors are blue for first, red for second, yellow for third and white for fourth. Winners Dog or Winners Bitch ribbons are purple, while Reserve Dog and Reserve Bitch ribbons are purple and white. Best of Winners ribbons are blue and white; Best of Breed, purple and gold; and Best of Opposite Sex ribbons are red and white.

In the six groups, first prize is a blue rosette or ribbon, second placement is red, third yellow and fourth white. The Best In Show rosette is either red, white and blue or incorporates the colors used in the show-giving club's emblem.

QUALIFYING FOR CHAMPIONSHIP

Championship points are given for Winners Dog and Winners Bitch in accordance with a scale of points established by the American Kennel Club based on the popularity of the breed in entries, and the number of dogs competing in the classes. This scale of points varies in different sections of the country, but the scale is published in the front of each dog show catalog. These points may differ between the dogs and the bitches at the same show. You may, however, win additional points by winning Best of Winners, if there are fewer dogs than bitches entered, or vice versa. Points never exceed five at any one show and a total of fifteen points must be won to constitute a championship. These fifteen points must be won under at least three differ-

ent judges, and you must acquire at least two major wins. Anything from a three to five point win is a major, while one and two point wins are minor wins. Two major wins must be won under two different judges to meet championship requirements.

PROFESSIONAL HANDLERS

If you are new in the fancy and do not know how to handle your dog to his best advantage, or if you are too nervous or physically unable to show your dog, you can hire a reliable professional handler who will do it for you for a specified fee. The more successful or well-known handlers charge slightly higher rates, but generally speaking there is a pretty uniform charge for this service. As the dog progresses with his wins in the show ring, the fee increases proportionately. Included in this service is professional advice on when and where to show your dog, grooming, a statement of your wins at each show, and all trophies and ribbons that the dog accumulates. Any cash award is kept by the handler as a sort of "bonus."

When engaging a handler, it is advisable to select one that does not take more dogs to a show than he can properly and comfortably handle. You want your dog to receive his individual attention and not be rushed into the ring at the last moment because the handler has been busy with too many other dogs in other rings. Some handlers require that you deliver the dog to their establishment a few days ahead of the show so they have ample time to groom and train him. Other handlers will accept well-behaved and trained dogs that have been groomed from their owners at ringside, if they are familiar with the dog and the owner. This should be determined well in advance of the show date. NEVER expect a handler to accept a dog at ringside that is not groomed to perfection!

There are several sources for locating a professional handler. Dog magazines carry their classified advertising. A note or telephone call to the American Kennel Club will also put you in touch with several in your area.

DO YOU REALLY NEED A HANDLER?

The answer to that question is sometimes yes, sometimes no! However, the answer which must be determined first of all is, "But can I *afford* a professional handler!" or, "I want to show my dog myself. Does that mean my dog will never do any big winning?"

Ch. Coastwind Ultra Violet, owned by Marguerite Terrill and the Coastwind Kennels. The sire was Ch. Coastwind Nepenthe ex Ch. Regalia's Blue Dhalia.

Ch. Arabi's Dark Secret is owned, bred and handled by Richard Mauro. Secret finished at a recent Afghan Hound Club of Northern New Jersey specialty and was also Best of Opposite Sex at a Colonial Afghan Hound Club Specialty. The sire was Ch. Akaba's Royal Flush ex Al Quahid's Moonmist.

Shirekhan Duktar Abarb was Afghan Hound of the Year for 1976 in Africa. This Best In Show winner had three Challenge Certificates by the time she was 20 months old. Owned by June James, Parow, Africa.

Can. Ch. Karamoor's Isis of Gwalior is pictured winning at the Ottawa Kennel Club Show. Gary McDonald is handling for owner Dr. Gareth Morgan-Jones, Auburn, Alabama.

302

Ch. Tora Nado of Faith, owned by Dave and June Suttie of Wheat Ridge, Colorado, is handled here by John Thysen. The sire was Ch. Ajax The Greater of Camri *ex* Kabul's Tjani of Naranjal.

Spanish Ch. Huilaco's Kabiz is owned by Norman Huiolobro of Madrid. Kabiz traces his ancestry back to American lines which include Grandeur and Akaba breeding.

Dynasty's Rising Star is pictured winning a 3-point major on the way to championship at the 1976 Lexington Kennel Club Show. Star is handled by Mike Bagley, co-owner with Vikki Highfield of Birmingham, Alabama.

Rubyyat's Prelude of Khan Khel was bred by Donna Ruby and is owned by Rhonda and Effie Yeates of the Okura Kennels, Lee's Summit, Missouri. The sire was Chaka's Tomahawk Chev-Charise *ex* Rubyyat's Blu Kristol.

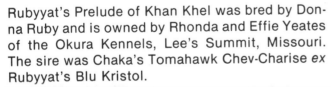

Isfahan's Silver Godspell, owned by John and Rosemary Jordan and Frank and Robbin Vasquez of San Diego, California, is shown in action. The sire was Isfahan's Azul De Coupe *ex* Charikar Krystal. Godspell was whelped in 1971 and died as a result of the dreaded bloat in March, 1976.

Do you *really* need a handler to win? If you are mishandling a good dog that should be winning and isn't because it is made to look bad in the ring by its owner, the answer is yes. If you don't know how to handle a dog properly, why make your dog look bad when a handler could show it to its best advantage?

Some owners simply cannot handle a dog well and still wonder why their dogs aren't winning in the ring, no matter how hard they try. Others are nervous and this nervousness travels down the leash to the dog and the dog behaves accordingly. Some people are extroverts by nature, and these are the people who usually make excellent handlers. Of course, the biggest winning dogs at the shows usually have a lot of "show off" in their nature, too, and this helps a great deal.

THE COST OF CAMPAIGNING A DOG WITH A HANDLER

At present many champions are shown an average of 25 times before completing a championship. In entry fees at today's prices, that adds up to about $200. This does not include motel bills, traveling expenses or food. There have been dog champions finished in fewer shows, say five to ten shows, but this is the exception rather than the rule. When and where to show should be thought out carefully so that you can perhaps save money on entries. This is one of the services a professional handler provides that can mean a considerable saving. Hiring a handler can save money in the long run if you just wish to make a champion. If your dog has been winning reserves and not taking the points and a handler can finish him in five to ten shows, you would be ahead financially. If your dog is not really top quality, the length of time it takes even a handler to finish it (depending upon competition in the area) could add up to a large amount of money.

Campaigning a show specimen that not only captures the wins in his breed but wins Group and Best In Show awards gets up into the big money. To cover the nation's major shows and rack up a record as one of the top dogs in the nation usually costs an owner between ten and fifteen thousand dollars a year. This includes not only the professional handler's fee for taking the dog into the ring, but the cost of conditioning and grooming, board, advertising in the dog magazines, photographs, etc.

There is great satisfaction in winning with your own dog, especially if you have trained and cared for it yourself. With today's enormous entries at the dog shows and so many worthy dogs competing for top wins, many owners who said "I'd rather do it myself!" and meant it became discouraged and eventually hired a handler anyway.

However, if you really are in it just for the sport, you can and should handle your dog if you want to. You can learn the tricks by attending training classes, and you can learn a lot by carefully observing the more successful professional handlers as they perform in the ring. Model yourself after the ones that command respect as being the leaders in their profession. But, if you find you'd really rather be at ringside looking on, then do get a handler so that your worthy dog gets his deserved recognition in the ring. To own a good dog and win with it is a thrill, so good luck, no matter how you do it.

Ch. Connors Mill Jeffara, owned by Eunice B. and Evelyn A. Clarke, Hughcliffe Kennels, Brunswick, Ohio. Handled by James B. Stewart, Jeff is pictured winning Best In Show at the 1958 Muncie Kennel Club Show.

Ch. Ociana Nightsong is pictured winning under judge Alfred Treen at a recent show. This bitch is owned by James R. and Sharon A. Roseland of Marshalltown, Iowa.

Ch. Wielki Sezlem of Nightwatch F. Ch. (Field Champion) is pictured winning on the way to his conformation championship under judge Dr. Gerda Maria Kennedy. He is owned by the Robert Vertis of Colorado.

305

Portrait of a magnificent puppy owned by Lee Everson of California. This photo was taken by Joan Ludwig, the famous West Coast photographer.

Chapter XII

Showing and Judging the Afghan Hound

Ever since I started judging Afghan Hounds in 1961, I never enter a show ring to begin an assignment without thinking back to what the late, great, judge Alva Rosenberg told me when he discussed my apprenticing under him. His most significant observation I find still holds true today. . . that a judge's first and lasting impression of a dog's temperament and bearing will be made the moment it walks into the ring.

It has always been a source of amazement to me the way many exhibitors ruin that important first impression of their dog before the judge. So many are guilty of dragging their dogs along behind them, squeezing through the ringside crowds and snapping at people to get out of their way, just to arrive in the ring with the dog having had ladies' handbags banged into their faces, their feet stepped on by those pushing to get closer and splashed with children's food. After all this they are expected to turn on the charm, fascinate the crowds, captivate the judge and bring home the silverware! All this on a day that invariably is either too hot or too cold—or too rainy—and after a couple of hours of standing rigidly on a crate being sprayed in the face and all over their bodies with a grooming substance that doesn't smell or taste too good, and then brushed until dry to their handler's satisfaction. Add this to the five-hour bath and grooming session the day before the show and the bumpy ride to the show grounds. Alva Rosenberg had a point! Any dog that can strut into the ring after what they must regard as a 48-hour torture treatment DOES have to have excellent disposition and a regal bearing!

There is no reason an exhibitor cannot allow sufficient time to get to ringside with a few minutes to spare, in order to wait calmly somewhere near the entrance to the ring. They need only walk directly ahead of the dog, politely asking the people along the way to step aside with a simple statement to the effect that there is a "dog coming through." It works very well. I have seen spectators promptly step aside, not only to oblige this simple request, but also to observe the beauty of the show dog going by.

The exhibitor making such a request not only clears a path in the aisle, but allows for the dog to follow behind in their steps without being pulled along side them and getting bumped on the way. If enough time is allowed to get ringside before the class is actually called it is then possible to *walk* into the ring so the judge can see your dog at its best.

I have actually observed dogs entering the ring limping because in the last-minute haste to get into the ring their own handlers have stepped on them! I cannot emphasize too strongly the importance of allowing your dog to set his own pace in a crowd where only he can properly appraise the space he requires to navigate safely. We must remember we are dealing with sight hounds and an Afghan cannot see much if its head is being pulled into the folds of a skirt or the seat of your pants.

The short waiting period at ringside also allows time for the dog to gain his footing and prospective and gives the exhibitor time to get his armband on securely so it won't drop down their arm and hit the dog on the head during their first sprint around the ring. These few spare moments will also allow a great deal of the "nervousness" that travels down the leash to your dog to disappear as the realization that you have arrived at your class on time occurs to you and you can both relax.

ENTERING THE RING

When the ring steward calls out the numbers for your class there is no need for you to try to be first in the ring. There is no prize for being first! If you are new at the game, you would do well to get behind a more experienced exhibitor or professional handler where you can observe and perhaps learn something about ring behavior. The judge will be well aware of your presence in the ring when they make a small dot or a small check in their judge's book, as they must also mark all absentees before starting to judge the class.

Simply enter the ring as quickly and calmly as possible with your dog on a loose lead, and at the first opportunity make sure you show your armband to the judge. Then take a position in the line-up already forming in the ring (usually at the opposite side from the judge's table). Set your dog up in the show pose, so that once the judge has checked in all the dogs in the class he will have an immediate impression of the outline of your dog in show stance.

The judge will then go up and down the line of dogs in order to compare one outline with another, while getting an idea of the symmetry and balance of each profile. This is the time when you should see that your dog maintains the show stance, and don't be nervously brushing, constantly adjusting feet, tilting the head, primping the tail, etc. This all should have been done while the judge was walking down the line with his eyes on the other dogs.

By the time the judge gets to your dog it should be standing as still as a statue, with your hands off of it. Far too many exhibitors handle show dogs as if they were puppets with strings attached to all the moving parts. They are constantly pushing it in place, prodding it to the desired angle for the judge, placing the head and tail and feet according to their idea of perfection. More often than not their fingers are covering the dog's muzzle or they are employing their thumbs to put a curl in the tail because there is none there and they know there should be! Repeatedly moving a dog's feet tends to make the judge believe the dog can't stand correctly by itself. If a dog is

After checking all dogs in, the judge stands back and takes a look at each dog. At this time all the dogs are positioned in show stance by their handler and the judge gets a chance to evaluate the dogs in accordance with the Standard for the breed.

After evaluating each dog in show stance, the judge has them gait around the ring. When the gaits have been appraised, the judge goes over each dog individually. Starting with the head, the judge checks for expression and checks the eyes, muzzle and entire head for excellence. During this examination the handler makes sure the dog remains perfectly still and in correct show stance.

standing incorrectly the judge might assume that it just happened to be standing incorrectly at that moment and that the exhibitor couldn't imagine such a thing and therefore never notices it!

Fussing over a dog only calls attention to the fact that the exhibitor has to do a lot to make the dog look good, or is a rank amateur and is nervously mis-handling the dog. A free, natural stance, even when a little "off base," is still more appealing to the judge. To me, all Afghan Hounds are beautiful on their own, and unnecessary handling can only be regarded as a distraction, not as indulgence on the part of the exhibitor. Do not get the mistaken idea that if the judge thinks you are working hard with your dog that you deserve to win!

MOVE THEM OUT!

Once the judge has compared the outlines, or profiles, of each dog, they will ask the exhibitors to move the dogs around the ring so that they may observe the dogs in action. This usually means two complete circles of the ring, depending upon the size of the ring and the numbers of dogs competing in it. This is the time when the judge must determine whether or not the dog is moving properly or if it is limping or lame. They check the dog out for the proper gait, observe the dogs to see if they are reaching out in front and are moving in the true tradition of coursing hounds. Hopefully, they can observe the dog moving freely on its own—not strung up on the end of a lead obeying a handler's demand to gait with head held high.

With our breed, there is seldom a ring big enough to get a true picture of movement or a handler with legs long enough to move the dog at its natural gait. Even at the outdoor shows the rings are usually too small and the Afghan Hounds have to adjust their gait to that of the handler. It is still possible for a judge, even in a small ring, to determine the gait, though it will not be the beautiful flowing motion we envision as they course the deserts and fields, or run free in their fenced yards at home.

With these two restrictions in mind, you must be sure that you do not hamper your dog in any way in the limited time and space you have to show the judge how your dog moves. This means gaiting on a loose lead. Run next to your dog at a safe distance to the side so that you do not step on it going around cor-

ners or pull it off balance on a turn (all the while try not to run into the judge's table on the next circling of the ring!). You must also keep in mind that you should not get too close to the dog ahead of you and that you must also keep far enough ahead of the dog behind you so that your dog doesn't get spooked—or that you don't break their gait!

Once the judge has had the time to observe each of the dogs in motion, the signal will be given to one person to stop at a specific spot in the ring, forming the line-up for closer inspection of each dog by the judge. Starting with the first dog in the line, the judge will go over each dog, completely evaluating it according to the Standard for the breed.

JUDGING THE HEAD

As the judge approaches your dog, he will get his first close look at the expression. The judge wants to see that "far away" look in the dark, triangular eyes that is so characteristic of the aloof and dignified Afghan Hound. He does NOT want to see any sign of fear or shrinking back or turning of the head to one side; that would indicate shyness. At this time the judge also looks for the typical long, narrow head with a flat, or slightly arched Roman nose. There is little or no stop when observing the profile, and the strong jaws should have a level or scissors bite.

Am. and Bda. Ch. Kai's Turkhan of Grandeur is a Best In Show, multiple Group and specialty winner that was bred, owned and handled by Carol A. Reisman, Afghans of Kai, Woodmere, Long Island, New York. Turkhan is pictured here being judged by Louise French Snyder, one of the earliest Afghan Hound fanciers in the U.S.

The walls of "the Johnnie Bar," named after Kay's fabulous Ch. Taejon of Crown Crest, are lined with glass shelves and the hundreds of silver trophies won by the fabulous hounds of Crown Crest. Kay keeps them shined by lending the various pieces to friends who bring them back polished!

Ch. Ky's Sheik was Best In Show under judge William H. Pym at a past Tanana Valley Kennel Club Show in Fairbanks, Alaska. Sheik was handled by Mrs. Robert Fulton of Anchorage, Alaska, and is owned by Mr. and Mrs. A.B. Nosky of Anchorage. Edward A. Jacobs photo.

Best Junior Showman at the 1965 Westminster Kennel Club Show in New York City was Jennifer Sheldon, handler of Khabira Shady Lady. Leonard Brumby, Jr., was the judge. Shafer photograph.

This prize-winning Best Brace In Show is caught on film just prior to winning at a recent Kennel Club of Beverly Hills show. This exotic brace consists of Ch. Tantalus and Ch. Majestic Knight of Stormhill, and they have been named Best Brace In Show at the Silver Bay show and the Afghan Hound Club of California Specialty. The dogs are co-owned by the Stormhill Kennels and Robert and Susan Lund. Handling is Sandy Withington.

In the Afghan Hound breed the occiput should be prominent and the ear set in a line with the outer corners of the eye. The closer the ear leather reaches the end of the nose the better. The judge will check to see that the head is surmounted with the characteristic and beautiful top knot, the true crowning glory of the Afghan Hound!

This top knot should be very much in evidence with the long, silky hair flowing free, not parted and combed down into the ear feathering, hiding the length and profusion of this characteristic found only in the Afghan Hound. When going over the head the judge will take a step backward to get the full profile and to observe the "straight ahead" placement of the front feet and to note the distance or space between the front legs.

The head should be on top of a long, graceful and strong neck that leads to well laid-back shoulders. The judge will lift up the ears to see just how long the neck really is and how well placed it is on the shoulders. The short or coarse neck is to be avoided at all costs since they detract so obviously from the "aloof" head carriage in the breed. The judge will check the angle of the shoulders very carefully since the shoulders are important to the proper placement of the long front legs and strong pasterns.

Running hands down the front leg, the judge will go all the way to the foot. Picking up the paw they will check for the huge thick paws and paw pads that are meant to enable the dog to both course the desert sands or climb rocky mountain paths. The judge should notice particularly whether the dog puts its foot down correctly when released.

The brisket should be well let-down. Hopefully, as far down as to be level with the elbows. Depth of brisket is important in a coursing hound since the chest cavity must provide enough space for the lungs and enough air for the dog to sustain over long distances. This trait can also be observed in the Greyhounds which have great depth of brisket and good tuck-up for running. This is important to all coursing dogs. Depth of brisket does not mean barrel chested, but rather depth of brisket to allow for good healthy lungs. Just ask any racing Greyhound or Whippet owner how important depth of brisket is!

After judging the brisket and tuck-up the judge moves to the saddle and topline. The topline should be level from the shoulders to

After going over the head and ears carefully, the judge then checks for length of neck. By pulling the ears forward the judge is also able to see if the correct coat pattern is present on the neck, i.e. feathering on the front with a smooth coat on the back.

Here the judge can be seen checking out the shoulder bone placement. Notice how the handler assists the judge by pulling the dog's long hairy ears out of the way to afford the judge a clear picture of both the length of neck and the side view of the front of the dog. At this point the judge will also exert a little pressure on the dog and move it back and forth slightly to make sure the dog is strong on its feet. The dog should not move its feet or falter under this action.

The handler now steps out in front of the dog in order not to obscure the judge's view. From this position the judge is able to check the placement of the front legs and will move around to the front of the dog to check whether or not the legs are well under the body with the proper amount of space between the front legs.

After checking to see that both feet are properly placed and pointing straight ahead, *i.e.* neither pointing inward or outward, the judge runs her hand down the leg and checks the feet. The Afghan Hound is supposed to have large feet, well-padded for both coursing the desert or crossing rocky terrain. When the judge drops the foot she checks to see that the dog puts its foot back in the proper position.

the prominent hipbones. By prominent it is meant that the hipbones should be *visible*! This characteristic can be found in the Afghan Hound breed only, and far too many of our dogs today are covered with fat.

The saddle should be natural with no evidence of having been shaved or shaped in any way! Those who have shown under me will attest to the fact that I always rub my thumbs against the natural growth of the saddle hair (which grows from the neck toward the rear) to be sure there is no evidence of razor stubble or stripping. The only permissible clearing of the saddle pattern is by plucking with the fingers. This usually is only necessary when the dog goes from puppy to adult coat. At all other times a good brushing will remove any unnecessary hair or fuzz.

I have heard it said over the years that three of the backbones should also be visible along the topline, as are the two prominent hipbones. However, there is nothing in the Standard indicating this, and it has been my experience that when backbones are visible the dog is thin to the point that some ribs are also in evidence. While I require the hipbones to be showing, I would rather have the dog in proper weight *without* backbones or ribs showing. With today's good nutrition for dogs it can be difficult to keep an Afghan Hound in proper weight. If they are sufficiently active they can hold their own, but most of them either run-off weight or are pampered housedogs and are inclined to be lethargic and go to fat.

THE WONDERFUL AFGHAN HOUND TAIL

The judge will next procede to the tail section where we observe yet another of the characteristics found only in our Afghan Hounds! They possess the wonderful, long, curved tail with the ring at the end! Hopefully, the tail will have the "doughnut" at the end of the curve to leave no doubt at all that this is an Afghan Hound. The tail should be set in the lower third of the "square" which falls away from and is formed by the prominent hipbones and the rear end.

The judge will also check to see if the top surface of the tail is smooth and of the same quality as the saddle hair, with the underside of the tail providing the *thin* feathering. The tail should never be bushy. It is always a source of constant amazement to me to see

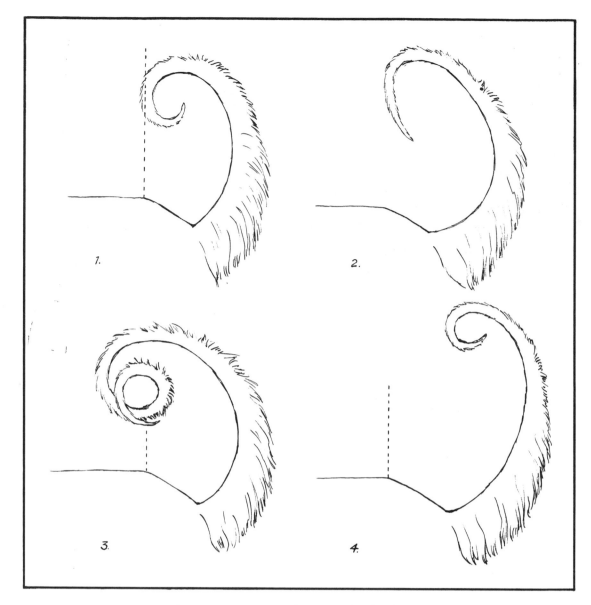

1. Proper Afghan Hound tail carriage, erect and in line with hip bones.
2. Faulty, wrong curve in tail.
3. Faulty, double ring. The tail is carried too far over the back.
4. Undesirable. Not in line with hip bones, but acceptable ring at the end.

how many exhibitors either "thin out" the hair on the tail, or groom it as part of a profuse coat! While those who "thin out" at least know how it should really be, they are equally guilty, since the Afghan Hound coat should not be altered in any way by scissors or stripping!

While discussing the tail it should be pointed out that the tail is only required to be "up" when the Afghan Hound is in motion. It should never be up over the back farther forward than the hipbones or pushed down to touch the back. Worse still, the tail should not be carried off to either side.

I firmly believe that if more handlers would stop primping tails, chucking chins and poking thumbs into stomachs to try to level out toplines we would soon see more Afghans in the ring with the required gay temperament!

HINDQUARTERS

Judging the hindquarters on the Afghan Hound is a most serious consideration. Remember that the breed is a coursing hound and that while the front legs reach out ahead of it, it is from the rear that the dog with powerful hindquarters will get the strength, the

With the feet in their proper position, the judge checks for breadth and depth of brisket which will hopefully reach to the elbow. The elbows should not point inward or outward nor in any way deter from the straight forward, far-reaching gait that is proper for the breed.

After checking the brisket and tuck-up, the judge moves around to the rear end to check the croup and tail set. By making a "square" of the prominent hip bones and the end of the pelvic bones, the tail should be set on the lower third of the square. At this point the judge may do well to exert a little pressure on the hindquarters of the dog. The dog should not move its feet or "fall under" at this pressure, but rather push back up under the judge's hand to give the impression of strength in the rear legs. At this point the judge will also check, in the case of male dogs, for testicles.

Once the croup and tail set have been evaluated, the judge runs her hands down the legs, checking for correct angulation and, once again, feeling to see if the legs are strong and well-muscled. Notice how the handler keeps the dog in show stance to give the judge every opportunity to check out the dog at her own direction.

After checking for rear angulation the judge checks on the height and strength of the hocks. Afghan Hound hocks should be low to the ground and when the judge moves them firmly from side to side there should not be too much play in them. While the hindquarters of the Afghan Hound should give sort of a wishbone shape from the anus to the ground, the hocks are straight down. Here again the judge should get the feeling of strength in the hindquarters.

Kay Finch poses the 2½-month-old future Int. Ch. Crown Crest Mr. Universe for some early show ring training.

push, the speed and the distance necessary to chase, catch and bring down prey.

The extent of angulation in the hindlegs can best be observed from the side, but the strength can best be determined when the judge runs his hands down the legs to feel the muscletone and to observe whether or not the dog pushes back against the pressure of his hands rather than buckle under. The judge should also step back a bit to note what resembles a slightly bowed or "wishbone" appearance from the base of the tail to the feet. The hocks should be strong and when moved gently back and forth, or lightly "twanged," should respond to the touch, and not falter.

When judging the male dogs the judge will also check for testicles when evaluating the hindquarters. At this point I also run my hand down the length of the tail against one of the back legs hoping it will reach at least to the hock to assure desired length. This is usually not necessary, however, since the Afghan Hound carries its tail so proudly there is usually ample opportunity to observe its length during the course of the examination, or when the dog is moving.

At this point I usually stand up over the dog and, with both my hands, smooth down the coat on both sides of the body. With this "view from above" I can usually get a good idea on the weight and "breadth" of the dog. I also place my hands on the rear end and gently apply pressure to see if the dog falters or moves its feet. Hopefully it will stand firmly in place; I do the same at the shoulders to see if the dog can easily stand up under the slight pressure.

PROPER COAT TEXTURE

At some point during the examination, usually when checking the saddle hair, I check the dog for the proper silky coat texture. It should be glorious, with all the good food and remarkable grooming aids we have today. Good breeding also provides for a good coat and today there is really no excuse for an Afghan Hound not being well put down. While a good coat is both hereditary and dietary, it can be additionally enhanced by the grooming aids to present the ultimate in beauty, but not to the point where a judge's hands get "sticky," even on a clear day!

Today it almost seems to be contest to see who can spray the most conditioner on their dogs before they enter a show ring. If I had my way, I would like to judge Afghans soaking wet, with handlers forbidden to bring brushes or combs into the ring! I would miss the spectacle of the beauty of those flowing coats but a multitude of faults that escape many other judges' eyes would not—could not—be overlooked!

Once a judge has gone over the dog completely, they will usually step away from the dog and give it a final over-all side view, keeping a complete picture in their mind before moving on to compare that image with the next dog or a previous dog in the line that has come under their consideration. This "last look" is one of the primary reasons for always having to keep your dog and yourself on your toes! You don't want the judge to suddenly take another look at your dog and find it sitting down or chasing butterflies or lifting its leg on the number markers. On the contrary, this does not mean that at every moment you have to have your dog strung up by the neck, or be grooming hairs individually, or constantly placing feet in position. That is a form of over-handling and can be a distraction to the judge and a nuisance to the dog. But surely during the time spent in the ring the dog should be able to stand on its own, look alive and be ready for the next command that may be required during judging. If it isn't trained to this degree it is not ready for the ring! Training is done at home—*performance* is required at the show!

INDIVIDUAL GAITING

Once the judge has gone over each dog individually he will go to the end of the ring and ask each handler to gait his dog. It is important at this point to pay strict attention to the judge's instructions as to how they want this done. Some judges require the "T" formation, others the half-triangle. Further observation of your dog may bring a request for you to repeat the pattern, especially if your dog did not show well during the first trip. It is important that you hear whether the judge wants you to repeat the entire exercise or merely to gait your dog "down and back."

When each dog has been gaited, the judge will want a last look at all of them lined up together before making his final decisions. Usually the procedure will be to once again present the left side of your dog with the judge then weaving in and out of the line to check once more the fronts or rears or other individual points of comparison. Some dogs may be asked to gait a third time, or to gait side by side with one of the other dogs, should he want to "break a tie" on which dog is the better mover. Because such deciding factors can not be predicted or anticipated, it is necessary for the handler to always be ready to oblige once the request is given by the judge.

After the decisions are made, the judge will point to his four placements and those four will set their dogs up in front of the designated number markers on the side of the ring. Be ready at this point to show the numbers on your arm band so that the judge can mark his judge's book accordingly. The judge then presents the winners with the appropriate color ribbons and any trophies won, and you may leave the ring.

Contrary to popular opinion it is not necessary, or even correct, to thank the judge for the ribbon. It is to be assumed that the dog *deserved* the ribbon or the judge would not have awarded it. Handing you the ribbon is part of the procedure and does not warrant a thank-you. The club, not the judge, is responsible for the donation of the trophies. It is not called for that the exhibitor speak to the judge, but if the win is significant enough so

After examining the entire dog and individually evaluating its gait, the judge proceeds to repeat the entire process with every dog in the class. After all have been thoroughly evaluated, the judge makes her placements. She directs the dogs and handlers to the proper award markers and marks her book.

After the judge has made her placements and marked the judge's book accordingly, it is time to award the ribbons, rosettes and/or trophies. It is not necessary to thank the judge, since it is assumed that the dog deserved the win he was awarded. Merely accept the ribbon and leave the ring so that the next class can be called into the ring. If desired, photographs of the judge awarding the ribbon should be taken after all the classes in the breed have been judged or at the discretion of the judge. Judge Joan Brearley wishes to thank Glorvina Schwartz and Pinky (Ch. Sandina's Sparkling Champagne) for being the handler and entry in these photographs and she sends special thanks to Sandy Schwartz for taking this series of pictures.

Am. and Can. Ch. Pandora's Sheik of Stormhill is stepping out! Sired by Ch. Mecca Tajma Khan of Tajmir *ex* Am. and Mex. Ch. Pandora of Stormhill, his show record included 1 Best In Show, 3 Specialty Bests of Breed, more than 20 Group Firsts and over 80 Bests of Breed. He is owned and bred by Virginia and Sandy Withington, Stormhill Kennels, Pasadena, California.

that you feel compelled to say *something*, a simple and not overly exhuberant "I'm so pleased that you liked my dog," or something similar is still more than is necessary.

The "thank you" for the ribbon has on occasion become what some exhibitors like to think of as a "weapon." At ringside you can sometimes hear words to the effect that, "I didn't even thank him for that rotten red ribbon!" As if the judge had even noticed! However, it *is* expected that you take with you from the ring a ribbon of *any color*. To throw it on the ground or leave it behind in the ring so that the steward is obliged to call you back into the ring for the judge to hand it to you again is most unsportsman-like. You must play the game according to the rules. Your entry fee is to obtain the opinion of your dog by the judge. You must take their opinion and

behave accordingly. If you do not like it, do not give them another entry, but you owe the judge the courtesy of respect for their title.

After this juding procedure is followed in the five classes for dogs, and Winners Dog and Reserve Winners Dog have been determined, the bitches are judged in this same manner. After Winners Bitch and Reserve Winners Bitch awards have been made, the Best of Breed judging follows. Class procedures here are discussed in another chapters on showing. Once the judged has completed his assignment and signed his judge's book, it is proper to request any photographs which you may wish to have taken of your wins.

At this time it is also permissible to ask the judge his motives in his judging of *your* dog. If you do so, it should be done in a polite, calm and unquestioning manner. It must be remembered that the judge is not going to make comparisons rating one dog *against* another, but can, if he chooses, give a brief explanation as to how he evaluated your dog. More often than not, on the way home in the car or back at the bench when you have given the decisions some thought, it will occur to you why the judge did what he did without your having to have asked.

It is always helpful to remember that no one wins them all. You will win some and lose some no matter how good your dog is. Judges are human and, while no one is perfect, they have earned the title of "judge" for some mighty good reasons. Try to recall that this is a sport and should be fun, and tomorrow is another day!

THE GAMES PEOPLE PLAY

If you are new to the game of dog show exhibiting there are a few things you should know about, like how to protect youself and your dog so that you do not get too discouraged and disillusioned right at the start.

For an example, the first time I exhibited in the show ring I became convinced, with good reasons, that I had a wonderful dog because so many of the competitors in the class with me tried so hard to make us look bad! I'm sure my nervousness was obvious because I was trying so hard to remember what my mentor, Kay Finch, had told me and had shown me, and I wanted so desperately to exhibit my dog properly.

Perhaps that was part of the problem, but the other part was that he *was* a good dog, and posed a threat to the others competing and they decided to do something about it. It was nothing personal, of course, I hadn't been around long enough for the other Afghanites to either like or dislike me, but this beautiful black-masked silver of the great Ch. Taejon of Crown Crest was an obvious contender for the ribbons, and they thought they *could* do something about that!

Two of the old-time breeders decided they would "initiate" me and really gave my dog the business. One got ahead of me and the other behind me in the lineup. Gaiting around the ring one ran up on top of us and the other stopped short in front of us. This followed an episode at ringside earlier when another exhibitor, under the pretense of going over my dog and saying (so quietly that no one else could hear the compliment) that my dog had "nice hindquarters," squeezed his testicles! It was hoped that this would make my dog spook in the ring when the judge later checked him out.

Another trick was that while stacking the dogs as the judge came down the line they would block my dog by walking in front of

A champion brood bitch poses with some of her champion offspring. . . Fourth from the left is Ch. Sultana Irisa owned by Barbara Craddock of Houston, Texas. Starting from left to right are Irisa's get: Ch. Mahadi's Que Sera of Briarhill, Briarhill Sabra of Kirsch, Ch. Briarhill Denarios, the lady herself, Ch. Briarhill Demetrius and Briarhill Natasha.

him, all the while pretending to get their dog ready for the judge to look at next. While supposedly giving the judge a better look at their dog, the woman next to me "accidentally" stepped on my dog's back foot! The second time I saw it coming and I gave her a nudge with my hip and threw her off balance before she could come down hard enough to make him go lame and get us excused from the ring. I might have been new in the game, but she got the message and never tried it again. Fortunately, a very discerning and "show-wise" judge saw what had been going on and gave us Best of Winners anyway!

Before our next appearance in the show ring for our next points toward championship, a youngster poured beer all over my almost-white dog. The girl was prompted by a parent who happened to be entered in our class at the show that day. Just so you do not think it was only my misfortune that day, the incident was witnessed by another woman who had also been a victim of this vicious woman. She had had a cigarette rubbed out in her dog's coat; the singing left a large hole in the coat. Over the years there have been fatal and near fatal poisonings, and thefts as well. I cannot emphasize too strongly about looking after you dogs at the shows. We all know that the more winning a dog does, the more competitors become jealous. As Shakespeare once wrote, "Jealousy is the green-eyed monster which doth make the meat it feeds upon!" So protect your dogs against the green-eyed monsters!

Fortunately, my story had a happy ending. Crown Crest Jesi Jhaimz made his championship in short order, finishing as Best of Winners at the 1957 Westminster Kennel Club Show. However, he was also "retired" the same day, since it was the year Ch. Shirkhan of Grandeur went all the way to Best In Show at the Garden and was entitled to all his future wins at the shows in the following years that brought so much favorable attention to our breed!

Needless to say, most judges are aware of these nasty tricks people play and do not tolerate them. For instance, a judge will ask the handler to move his dog aside so he can observe another dog without interference or he will inform the handlers to keep enough space between the dogs as they gait around the ring if he sees there is crowding. A judge may ask a handler to pull his dog out of the line so that

he might get an unobstructed view. YOU must also be aware of those around you that might be trying to make you and your dog look bad. Be pleasant at ringside and at the benches, but in the ring you must remember it is "all business" and the competition is keen. You have to think of everything, including showing your dog. Some of the professional handlers can be guilty of these practices also, so stay on your toes and always keep in mind the games people play!

CHILDREN IN THE SHOW RING

No one is more approving than I am of children learning to love and to care for animals. It is beautiful to see a child and an animal sharing complete rapport and companionship, or performing as a team in the show ring. Those of us who have been around dog shows for any length of time have all been witness to some remarkable performances by children and their dogs. Junior showmanship is one example; dogs virtually caring for or standing guard over babies and infants is another example.

However, there is nothing "cute" about a child being allowed to handle a dog where both the welfare of the child and the general public are in danger. I have been witness to scraped faces when large dogs have pulled children to the floor and dragged them along behind as they pursued another dog. I have seen a male take off after a bitch in season, and I have had the horrible experience of seeing a child unable to restrain a large dog simply let go of the leash allowing the dog to attack another dog. Worse still was the incident where the child itself became entangled in the dropped leash and became the central figure in a three way battle that left all three scarred for life in spite of the wonders of today's plastic surgery.

If a child shows the natural desire to exhibit a dog after having attended handling classes where they are taught how to show the dog, they must also be taught ring procedure. It is not fair to expect other exhibitors to show patience while a judge or the steward informs the child where to stand, or waits for them to gait the dog several times before they do it in the formation requested. Lack of knowledge or repeated requests delays the judging, looks bad to the ringside crowds and certainly doesn't make the dog look good.

If necessary, parents might stay late after dog shows are over and actually train the chil-

Pictured winning the Hound Group under judge Louis Murr at a 1972 show is Ch. Caravan's Mandarin Blue, bred and owned by Betty and Vincent Leap of Hicksville, New York.

Ch. Patterson's Artemis, a beautifully coated, black-masked red bitch owned by Mrs. Donald Patterson of Shawnee Mission, Kansas. Artemis was Winners Bitch at the 1964 Westminster Kennel Club Show.

Michael Madden and his living fur coat were photographed in 1974 in Bradenton, Florida.

Coastwind Scarpia is a brother to Ch. Coastwind Graffiti, Tar N' Feathers and Nassim Pasha. The sire was Ch. Coastwind Gazebo *ex* Regalia's Ebony. He is owned by Mr. and Mrs. R. Tracy and was handled to this Best of Winners award by Rosemarie Crandahl.

Ch. Mecca's Zeus, owned by Michael Koss and Jim Nesbitt of the Hoffman Estates, Illinois. The sire was ben ghaZi's The Silver Shadow *ex* Ch. Mecca's Melancholy Baby.

Am., Can. and Mex. Ch. Pamir Ho Chester was bred, owned and handled to his many show ring successes by Donald A. Jensen of Bonita, California. Chester is pictured here earning a win under judge Dorothy Sweet.

Far Corner So Black Ninth Turn, owned by Joe and Lill Inguaggiato, Rochester, New York.

dren in an empty ring. This can help. Parents might try sitting at ringside near the judges table with their young handlers to explain each process to them as it is performed. Doing this a few times will certainly acquaint the child with proper procedures that they will have to follow once they enter the ring.

We have to assume that any small child that wishes to show a dog is a bit precocious, so make sure you channel this tendency in the right direction. Many match show appearances should certainly precede any appearance in a regular show where serious contenders are vying for those important points. Even if the child doesn't actually win, their presence can still delay matters and detract from normal procedure. Certainly no parent could possibly expect a judge to give them a win just because they are a cute pair—even though they are!

BAITING

No matter how one feels about baiting a dog in the ring, we must acknowledge that almost everyone at one time or another has resorted to it in the show ring. Certain breeds are particularly responsive to it, while others show little or no interest in baiting with so much going on all around them.

There is no denying that baiting is an aid to basic training and there is no rule against it. Aside from the fact that it is disgusting to observe handlers popping small bits of boiled brown liver into their mouths and then wagging it about in the air before popping it into their dog's mouth, baiting is an indication that the training of the dog for the show ring is not yet complete. It becomes obvious to the judge that the dog still needs an incentive to respond to what other dogs are doing in the name of performance and showmanship.

Also, so many of the exhibitors are inept at handling the bait that more often than not pieces of liver end up all over the ring floor and turn out to be a distraction for other dogs that can't help but pick up the scent. I have found that Afghan Hounds, which aren't always the most enthusiastic eaters in the dog world anyway, are more responsive to squeaky toys, though I disapprove of these as well. If you are in the habit of talking to your dog you have surely come to recognize certain sounds you can make that will bring a genuine response, even in the show ring, without resorting to the toy chest or the kitchen stove.

DOUBLE HANDLING

While it may not seem probable, you can rest assured that the competent judge becomes aware of any double-handling to which some of the more desperate exhibitors may resort!

Double handling is both unfair and frowned upon by the American Kennel Club. Nonetheless, some owners go to all sorts of ridiculous lengths to get their apathetic dogs to perform in the ring. They hide behind trees or posts at ringside, or may lurk behind the ringside crowd until the exact moment when the judge is looking at or gaiting their dog and then pop out in full view emitting some familiar whistle or make some sort of clucking noise, or wave a crazy hat, or squeak a pet toy, all in the hopes that the dog will suddenly become alert and express a bit of animation.

It calls to mind my early days in dancing school when during recitals some of the children couldn't remember the time step until they spotted Mommy in the front row keeping time with her foot and clapping her hands to the music. Double-handling, no matter what form it takes, is against the rules and stupid. Many of us can recall the woman who sneaked her dog's favorite companion—the family cat—to ringside to encourage a spirited gait. She had neglected to inform her handler about what she intended to do and the dog took off to greet the cat leaving the surprised handler in the ring by himself!

If your dog needs you as a security blanket in order to go through a few formations in a show ring, it shouldn't be shown! Don't be guilty of double handling. The day may come when you finally have a great show dog, and the reputation of an owner guilty of double handling lives on forever! They will still accuse you of the same shady practices and your new show dog is apt to suffer for it!

APPLAUSE APPLAUSE!

Another "put-on" by some of our "less secure" exhibitors is the practice of bringing their own cheering section to applaud vigorously every time the judge happens to cast an eye on their dog.

The judge that is truly dedicated and concentrating on what he is doing will not hear or be influenced by the claques set up by those trying to push their dogs over the top, supposedly by popular approval. One of my earliest revelations at the dog shows was my

Winning a championship isn't always a bed of rosettes! Ch. Sultana Irisa is pictured winning a 5-point major under very wet conditions at the 1970 Houston Kennel Club Show. This win was under judge Ellsworth Gamble and marked Irisa's first appearance in the Open class. Owner-handler Barbara Craddock, the judge and Irisa seem to be taking it very well!

In all fairness we feel it only fitting and proper that we picture Irisa at her best winning at another show under judge Raymond Beale. Her sire was Ch. Jan's Goldfinger v Zerulistan *ex* Ch. Nomad's Asiri of Tuxedo. Owner-handler is Barbara Craddock, Briarhill Afghans, Houston, Texas.

sheer astonishment at one woman who was instructing in a loud whisper a little cluster of assorted friends and relatives as to where to stand at ringside during the judging. "Spread out," she told them, "so it doesn't look as if you are a group of my friends." During the actual judging, she looked around the crowd after setting her dog up in the ring to check and see if everyone was in their designated position and ready to burst forth with appropriate applause. By the time the judge was ready to make his final placements the situation had almost gotten out of hand. . . the applause was more than obvious and included whistles and yeas from kids who were trying to become part of the drama.

As far as I am concerned the only legitimate time for applause is during a Parade of Champions, during the gaiting of an entire specialty Best of Breed class or during the gaiting of an entire Stud Dog, Brood Bitch or Veterans Class. At these thrilling moments the tribute of applause—and the many tears—are understandable and well received, but to try to prompt a win or stir up interest in a particular dog during the normal course of judging is amateurish. If you have ever observed this

A winning brace in the Midwest during the late 1950's consisted of Leo Goodman's Ch. Crown Crest Sancy and Ch. Crown Crest Vegas Ghambler of Belden. The judge for this 1959 International Kennel Club Show of Chicago was J.H. Aldrich. These two striking black-masked silvers were the foundation stock for Mr. Goodman's Belden Kennels in Chicago. Mr. Goodman is pictured handling the brace.

practice you will almost always see that the dogs being applauded are the poorest specimens in the class. Their owners seem to subconsciously realize they can not win under normal conditions.

In conclusion here is a list to check off before entering the show ring:

Cardinal Sins when Showing an Afghan Hound

1. *DON'T* forget to exercise your dog before entering the ring! Do it before grooming if you are afraid they will get wet or dirty after getting off the grooming table.
2. *DON'T* be late for your class and enter the ring with both you and your dog in a nervous state.
3. *DON'T* drag the dog around the ring on a short lead and destroy its proud carriage.
4. *DON'T* shape the hair or alter the coat pattern on your dog. This means not shaping the feet, shaping or stripping the saddle, neck or tail. The Standard makes this perfectly clear.
5. *DON'T* part the topknot down the middle and comb it into the ears. The Standard clearly calls for a "topknot" so let it fly free to add to the true Afghan Hound expression.
6. *DON'T* talk to the judge in the ring. Watch the judge closely and follow instructions. Don't talk to people at ringside, either.
7. *DON'T* strike or in any way abuse your dog—especially not in the ring! The time and place for training and discipline is at home and not in front of the judge or the public. Even outside the ring we know that the reward system, not punishment, is the most successful method of training a dog.
8. *DON'T* be a bad loser! Win or lose, be a good sport. You can't win 'em all, so if you win today be gracious, if you lose, be happy for the one who won today.
9. *DON'T* shove your dog in a crate or leave him on the bench and forget him until it's time to go home. A drink of water or something to eat and a little companionship will go a long way toward making dog shows more enjoyable for him so that he will show even better next time!

The Best of Breed winner at the 1958 Afghan Hound Club of California Specialty Show was Ch. Crown Crest Kabul, owned by Mary Nelson Stephenson. The judge was the well-known Marion Foster Florsheim. John Buchanan handled Kabbie to his victory over an entry of 74 Afghan Hounds which included thirteen other champions.

Am., Mex. and Can. Ch. Coastwind Graffiti, for several years on the Top Ten list, finished his American title in 10 shows, his Canadian in 4 and won a Best In Show from the classes at the Vera Cruz show In Mexico while gaining his championship there! Graffiti is a Group, Specialty and all-breed Best In Show winner under many of the top breeder-judges in the country. He is owned and handled by Peter Belmont, Elmo Afghans, Kansas City, Missouri. The sire was Ch. Coastwind Gazebo *ex* Regalia's Ebony.

Ch. Karamour's LaRogue of O'Havoc is pictured winning the Best of Breed honors under judge Winifred Heckmann before going on to Group Third at a recent Midwest show. The sire was Ch. Scharlau O'Havoc *ex* Stumpy Acres Karamoor Zadja. Andrea Poore is pictured handling for owners Robert and Martin Poore, Hoffman Estates, Illinois.

Crown Crest Raffles, a striking black masked silver dog owned by Charles Farley of Long Beach, California several years ago.

Ch. Princess Shanti of Remcroft, owned and shown by Gail and Charles Peek of Millville, New Jersey. Shanti is pictured here winning the points at the 1974 Bucks County Kennel Club Show on the way to her championship.

Chez Rancho Shoshoni, C.D., holds the reins on his palomino friend, the Golden Sunshine Lady II. Shoni completed his obedience title in August, 1975 with three high qualifying scores of 194, 195½ and 197½, earning him the honor of being one of the highest scoring Afghan Hounds in the past ten years. Shoni's owner is Mr. Raymond C. Tracy of Sandy, Utah.

Chapter XIII

The Afghan Hound in Obedience

There are those obedience buffs who will tell you that the Afghan Hound is not too well suited to obedience training. In some instances this is absolutely true. There is nothing more frustrating than trying to train an Afghan Hound that just doesn't "get the call." It is uphill work all the way to train them and always with the doubt lingering in the back of your mind whether they will do it or won't do it, which is a far cry from the satisfaction one gets from *knowing* that your dog is as anxious as you are to put on a perfect show after weeks of training.

More and more Afghan Hounds are receiving their degrees, and more and more training methods and devoted owners are succeeding where others failed, proving that Afghan Hounds are intelligent and can be trained—especially if they want to be! Some Afghan Hounds do seem to take a special delight in convincing their owners that they aren't suited for obedience, when actually it is just that they don't happen to *want* to and convince their owners that it is a hopeless cause. Others just need to be coaxed.

While it is not advisable to force a dog into working for a degree, basic training is good for every dog just for the sake of his good manners. If approached correctly, training will not make the dog stubborn or unresponsive. This much training should be given starting at an early age. Those who wish to go further should make sure that their dog has the natural desire to "please" its owner and both owner and dog can take pleasure from the experience.

Those of us who have owned or observed Afghan Hounds at work are the first to admit that it is a delight to see and proves that titles can be won by these highly intelligent and independent dogs when properly done. It was my original intent to list all the obedience titlists in the breed in this chapter, but I am happy to say—if only to prove my point—that they are too numerous to mention!

THE DELANEY SYSTEM

For those who love the challenge and who do pursue the obedience work there is a fine newspaper which publishes only news of the obedience rings, and it is called *Front and Finish*. This fine publication is edited and published by Robert Self and A.J. Harler, in Galesburg, Illinois. In addition to publishing what they call "the dog trainer's news" each year, they publish the Delany System of top-winning obedience dogs. Much like the Phillips System for show dogs, Kent Delaney has devised a rating system designed to balance the difference between obedience wins scored over a few dogs as compared with wins scored over many dogs by way of a point system.

The Delaney System is open to all dogs, Novice, Open and Utility, and points are awarded for High In Trial or class placements only, based on published scores from the American Kennel Gazette. High In Trial winner, for instance, receives one point for each dog in actual competition; First place in each class receives one point for each dog competing in the class. Second place winner in each class earns a point for each dog competing less one, Third place winner in each class earns a point for each dog competing less two, Fourth place dog earns a point for each dog competing in the class less three.

There is a list of the Top Ten Dogs in All Breeds at the end of each year, as well as a list of the Top Ten in each of the six Groups. They also present, as does the Phillips System, a list of the Top Ten Obedience Dogs in each breed.

TOP TEN OBEDIENCE AFGHAN HOUNDS

For 1975 there were no Afghan Hounds listed either in the Top Ten all-breeds, or the Top Ten in the Hound Group. However, we present here, with congratulations to each Afghan Hound and its owner, the list of winners for the 1975 season:

1. Sheimars Harvest Gold, CD—L. Nelson
2. Eaziz Sharik—J. & L. Thomson
3. Chez Rancho Shoshoni—R. Tracy
4. Dawning of Tajmahal—D. Burns
5. Mirkwood Thorin Oakenshield—P. Matzinger
6. Maggie May—T. Howard
8. Chaparral Soylent Blue Ro Jan, CDX—S. Hennessy
9. Schernova Tiara of Pierce, CD—B. & K. Pierce
10. Ficeks Hookah—C. Serbin & C. Fiecek
    Sheba Mehsu, CD— T. & L. Pirnie

Chandar Ghazni of Rahsaan, C.D., a blue Afghan Hound, and Xanadu's X'Plorer, C.D., finished their obedience degrees on the same weekend. They are owned by Ms. Kay Nuzenski of Friendswood, Texas.

Bowman's Jhazbeau, C.D.X., finished his title in 1970 and was on the way to his U.D. when he suddenly died. An eager obedience worker, he was the first and much missed Afghan Hound owned and trained by Annemarie Greenberg, Jhaz-Beau Afghans, Alameda, California.

BASIC TRAINING FOR YOUR AFGHAN HOUND

There are few things in the world a dog would rather do than please his master. Therefore, obedience training or even the initial basic training will be a pleasure for your dog, if taught correctly, and will make him a much nicer animal to live with for the rest of his life.

WHEN TO START TRAINING

The most frequently asked question by those who consider training their dogs is, naturally, "What is the best age to begin training?" The answer is "not before six months." A dog simply cannot be sufficiently or permanently trained before this age and be expected to retain all he has been taught. If too much is expected of him, he can become frustrated and it may ruin him completely for any serious training later on, or even jeopardize his disposition. Most things a puppy learns and repeats before he is six months of age should be considered habit rather than training.

THE REWARD METHOD

The only proper and acceptable kind of training is the kindness and reward method which will build a strong bond between dog

Thunder Bays Heather, an American and Canadian C.D.X., is pictured here going through her paces with owner-trainer Fred Sarmiento of Mt. Clemens, Missouri. Heather was always a high scoring contender in U.S. obedience, and was retired at 8½ years of age.

Needless to say, whatever the distractions, you never lose control. You must be in command at all times to earn the respect and attention of your dog.

HOW LONG SHOULD THE LESSONS BE?

The lessons should be brief with a young dog, starting at five minutes, and as the dog ages and becomes adept in the first lessons, increase the time all the way up to one-half hour. Public training classes are usually set for one hour, and this is acceptable since the full hour of concentration is not placed on your dog alone. Working under these conditions with other dogs, you will find that he will not be as intent as he would be with a private lesson where the commands are directed to him alone for the entire thirty minutes.

If you should notice that your dog is not doing well or not keeping up with the class, consider putting off training for awhile. Animals, like children, are not always ready for schooling at exactly the same age. It would be a shame to ruin a good obedience dog because

and owner. A dog must have confidence in and respect for his teacher. The most important thing to remember in training any dog is that the quickest way to teach, especially the young dog, is through repetition. Praise him when he does well and scold him when he does wrong. This will suffice. There is no need or excuse for swinging at a dog with rolled up newspapers or flailing hands. This will only tend to make the dog hand shy the rest of his life. Also, make every word count. Do not give a command unless you intend to see it through. Pronounce distinctly with the fewest possible words, and use the same words for the same command every time.

Include the dog's name every time to make sure you have his undivided attention at the beginning of each command. Do not go on to another command until he has successfully completed the previous one and is praised for it. Of course, you should not mix play with the serious training time. Make sure the dog knows the difference between the two.

In the beginning, it is best to train without any distractions whatsoever. After he has learned to concentrate and is older and more proficient, he should perform the exercises with interference, so that the dog learns absolute obedience in the face of all distractions.

Highest Scoring Sighthound In Match at the 1975 Southern California Sighthound Association Show with a score of 196 was Sura's Wild Amber Sundown, C.D.X. The judge was Addie Bryant. Owners are Mike and Pat Lobenberg.

Three obedience title holders pose for this lovely photograph! To owner Nancy Eisaman's knowledge, these are the only three consecutive generations of obedience title holders in the breed in this country. Lying down in the foreground is Lynncrest Little Bit of Honey, C.D., owned by Nancy Eisaman; on the right is Eaziz Sharik, C.D., (with 9 points in conformation), owned by Jim and Lesley Thomson; and sitting on the left is Am. and Can. Ch. Honiego's Ambassador to Fame, an obedience title holder in both this country and Bermuda. Sharik was the second highest scoring Afghan Hound in the country according to *Afghan Review* magazine in 1975. Bit of Honey is the dam of 2 obedience title holders and a Canadian champion.

you insist on starting his training at six months rather than at, say, nine months, when he would be more apt to be receptive both physically and mentally. If he has particular difficulty in learning one exercise, you might do well to skip to a different one and come back to it again at another session. There are no set rules in this basic training, except "don't push!"

WHAT YOU NEED TO START TRAINING

From three to six months of age, use the soft nylon show leads, which are the best and safest. When you get ready for the basic training at six months of age, you will require one of the special metal-link choke chains sold for exactly this purpose. Do not let the word "choke" scare you. It is a soft, smooth chain and should be held slack whenever you are

not actually using it to correct the dog. This chain should be put over the dog's head so that the lead can be attached over the dog's neck rather than underneath against his throat. It is wise when you buy your choke collar to ask the sales person to show you how it is put on. Those of you who will be taking your dog to a training class will have an instructor who can show you.

To avoid undue stress on the dog, use both hands on the lead. The dog will be taught to obey commands at your left side, and therefore, your left hand will guide the dog close to his collar on a six-foot training lead. The balance of the lead will be held in your right hand. Learn at the very beginning to handle your choke collar and lead correctly. It is as important in training a dog as is the proper equipment for riding a horse.

WHAT TO TEACH FIRST

The first training actually should be to teach the dog to know his name. This, of course, he can learn at an earlier age than six months, just as he can learn to walk nicely on a leash or lead. Many puppies will at first probably want to walk around with the leash in their mouths. There is no objection to this if the dog will walk while doing it. Rather than cultivating this as a habit, you will find that if you don't make an issue of it, the dog will soon realize that carrying the lead in his mouth is not rewarding and he'll let it fall to his side where it belongs.

Let the puppy walk around by himself for a while with the lead around his neck. If he wants to chew on it a little, that's all right too. In other words, let it be something he recognizes and associates with as readily as he does a collar. In other words, do not let the lead be just something he is "pulled around on" from the first moment it is put around his neck.

If the dog is at all bright, chances are he has learned to come on command when you call him by name. This is relatively simple with sweet talk and a reward. On lead without a reward and on command without a lead is something else again. If there has been, or is now, a problem, the best way to correct it is to put on the choke collar and the six-foot lead. Then walk away from the dog, and call, "Pirate, come!" and gently start reeling him in until the dog is in front of you. Give him a pat on the head and/or a reward.

Walking, or heeling, next to you is also one of the first and most important things for him to learn. With the soft lead training starting very early, he should soon take up your pace at your left side. At the command to "heel" he should start off with you and continue alongside until you stop. Give the command, "Pirate, sit!" This is taught by leaning over and pushing down on his hindquarters until he sits next to you, while pulling up gently on the collar. When you have this down pat on the straightaway, then start practicing it in circles, with turns and figure eights. When he is an advanced student, you can look forward to the heels and sits being done neatly, spontaneously, and off lead as well.

THE "DOWN" COMMAND

One of the most valuable lessons or commands you can teach your dog is to lie down on command. Some day it may save his life,

and is invaluable when traveling with a dog or visiting, if behavior and manners are required even beyond obedience. While repeating the words, "Pirate, down!" lower the dog from a sitting position in front of you by gently pulling his front legs out in front of him. Place your full hand on him while repeating the command, "Pirate, down!" and hold him down to let him know you want him to *stay* down. After he gets the general idea, this can be done from a short distance away on a lead along with the command, by pulling the lead down to the floor. Perhaps you can slip the lead under your shoe (between the heel and sole) and pull it directly to the floor. As the dog progresses in training, a hand signal with or without verbal command, or with or without lead, can be given from a considerable distance by raising your arm and extending the hand palm down.

THE "STAY" COMMAND

The stay command eventually can be taught from both a sit and a down position. Start with the sit. With the dog on your left side in the sitting position give the command, "Pirate, stay!" Reach down with the left hand open and palm side to the dog and sweep it in close to his nose. Walk a short distance away and face him. He will at first, having learned to heel immediately as you start off, more than likely start off with you. The trick in teaching this is to make sure he hears "stay" before you start off. It will take practice. If he breaks, sit him down again, stand next to him, and give the command all over again. As he masters the command, let the distance between you and your dog increase while the dog remains seated. Once the command is learned, advance to the stay command from the down position.

THE STAND FOR EXAMINATION

If you have any intention of going on to advanced training in obedience with your dog, or if you have a show dog which you feel you will enjoy showing yourself, a most important command which should be mastered at six months of age is the stand command. This is essential for a show dog since it is the position used when the show judge goes over your dog. This is taught in the same manner as the stay command, but this time with the dog remaining up on all four feet. He should learn to stand still, without moving his feet and without flinching or breaking when ap-

The great Ch. Crown Crest Koh-I-Baba, U.D., was the first Utility Dog winner in this country in our breed and was featured on the cover of *Dog World* magazine in July of 1955. He was owned and trained by Gini Withington of Pasadena, California.

Left:
Su-Ric's Safar, C.D.X. She is pictured in front of owner Robert Luzietti's home in Elmwood Park, Illinois.

Right:
Ivardon Tufan Khan, U.D., won his Utility Dog title in July of 1953, one of the few U.D. title Afghan Hounds ever to accomplish this feat. Bred by Dr. William Ivens, he is co-owned by him and Ruth Thompson, his trainer.

proached by either you or strangers. The hand with palm open wide and facing him should be firmly placed in front of his nose with the command, "Pirate, stand!" After he learns the basic rules and knows the difference between stand and stay, ask friends, relatives and strangers to assist you with this exercise by walking up to the dog and going over him. He should not react physically to their touch. A dog posing in this stance should show all the beauty and pride of being a sterling example of his breed.

FORMAL SCHOOL TRAINING

We mentioned previously about the various training schools and classes given for dogs. Your local kennel club, newspaper or the yellow pages of the telephone book will put you in touch with organizations in your area where this service is performed. You and your dog will learn a great deal from these classes. Not only do they offer formal training, but the experience for you and your dog in public, with other dogs of approximately the same age and with the same purpose in mind, is excellent. If you intend to show your dog, this training is valuable ring experience for later on. If you are having difficulty with the training, remember, it is either too soon to start—or YOU are doing something wrong!

"Look, Ma, I'm sitting!" Bandars Brando has major points in the conformation classes and also has Open Field and Lure Coursing points. He is pictured here on the Long Sit in the obedience classes at the 1972 Ventura Dog Fanciers Show in California. He was the first Afghan Hound owned by Robert and Denyce Verti, Nightwatch Afghans, La Porte, Colorado.

ADVANCED TRAINING AND OBEDIENCE TRIALS

The A.K.C. obedience trials are divided into three classes: Novice, Open and Utility.

In the Novice Class, the dog will be judged on the following basis:

TEST	MAXIMUM SCORE
Heel on lead	40
Stand for examination	30
Heel free—on lead	40
Recall (come on command)	30
One-minute sit (handler in ring)	30
Three-minute down (handler in ring)	30
Maximum total score	200

THE COMPANION DOG EXCELLENT DEGREE

There are seven exercises which must be executed to achieve the C.D.X. degree, and the percentages for achieving these are the same as for the U.D. degree. Candidates must qualify in three different obedience trials and under three different judges and must have received scores of more than 50% of the available points in each exercise, with a total of 170 points or more out of the possible 200. At that time they may add the letters C.D.X. after their name.

If the dog "qualifies" in three shows by earning at least 50% of the points for each test, with a total of at least 170 for the trial, he has earned the Companion Dog degree and the letters C.D. (Companion Dog) are entered after his name in the A.K.C. records.

After the dog has qualified as a C.D., he is eligible to enter the Open Class competition, where he will be judged on this basis:

TEST	MAXIMUM SCORE
Heel free	40
Drop on recall	30
Retrieve (wooden dumbbell) on flat	20
Retrieve over obstacle (hurdle)	30
Broad jump	20
Three-minute sit (handler out of ring)	30
Five-minute down (handler out of ring)	30
Maximum total score	200

THE UTILITY DOG DEGREE

The Utility Dog degree is awarded to dogs which have qualified by successfully completing six exercises under three different judges at three different obedience trials, with

Scobetha Keekorok Ru, C.D., plays with "friend" Tiffany, a Shih Tzu just 3 months old. Both are owned by Susan Bell of Shreveport, Louisiana. Keeko's sire was Shangrila Pharoah Aksata *ex* Shangrila Unah Ru of Sandhihi.

a score of more than 50% of available points in each exercise, and with a score of 170 or more out of a possible 200 points.

Again he must qualify in three shows for the C.D.X. (Companion Dog Excellent) title and then is eligible for the Utility Class, where he can earn the Utility Dog (U.D.) degree in these rugged tests:

TEST	MAXIMUM SCORE
Scent discrimination (Article #1)	30
Scent discrimination (Article #2)	30
Directed retrieve	30
Signal exercise (heeling, etc., on hand signal)	40
Directed jumping (over hurdle and bar jump)	40
Group examination	30
Maximum total score	200

For more complete information about these obedience trials, write for the American Kennel Club's *Regulations and Standards for Obedience Trials*. Dogs that are disqualified from breed shows because of alteration or physical defects are eligible to compete in these trials.

THE TRACKING DOG DEGREE

The Tracking Dog trials are not held, as the others are, with the dog shows, and need be passed only once.

The dog must work continuously on a strange track at least 440 yards long and with two right angle turns. There is no time limit, and the dog must retrieve an article laid at the other end of the trail. There is no score given; the dog either earns the degree or fails. The dog is worked by his trainer on a long leash, usually in harness.

SCHUTZHUND TRAINING

There has been much talk these last years about the remarkable feats many of the working breeds have been accomplishing in Schutzhund training. There is no doubt about it, it is the training "of the future" as well as the present. What part our Afghan Hounds will play in the future remains to be seen. As of yet, only one Afghan Hound has been listed by the Schutzhund organization. Anyone interested in this advanced training may get full details by writing to the North American Working Dog Association, the parent club for recognized Schutzhund clubs at 1677 North Alisar Avenue, Monterey Park, California 91754. They publish a bulletin entitled *NASA NEWS* every other month that reports fully on the subject.

The beautiful Crown Crest Koh-I-Baba, C.D., was owned and trained by Virginia Withington, Storm Hill Kennels in California. Photograph by Joan Ludwig.

Opposite:
Picasso's Tam-Teri, C.D., was the number two obedience Afghan Hound in the U.S. for the first half of 1976. This lovely black and tan bitch was from the first litter bred by John and Barb LoCascio of Barrington, Illinois, and finished her title with three straight qualifying scores. Whelped in September, 1973, her sire was Picasso's Mystery, C.D., and her dam Dari Ali Scherezade.

Crown Crest Behapi Goluke breaks first from the starting box at an early racing event in California in 1959. Marianna Burrows, one of the racing enthusiasts in the Palo Alto area, waves the starting flag. Luki was owned by Betty and Earl Stites, Hullabaloo Afghans. The sire was Ch. Crown Crest Zardonx *ex* Crown Crest Queen of India.

Chapter XIV

Afghan Hound Racing

One of the most exciting aspects of Afghan Hound ownership is the sport of racing.

Since the first Shikari watched his pack of hunting Afghan Hounds race across the desert or scale the rocky tors of the Arabian desert tracking prey, the striking beauty of the dog "in flight" has kindled a desire to see this great coursing hound in action. The fact that entirely too many of today's Afghan Hounds are content to sit in metropolitan apartments merely adorning brocade couches is leading many people to believe that this is now their sole purpose in life. To those who truly enjoy these dogs as sporting companions there is forever the lingering desire to see them at their best—in pursuit of game or after the lure.

Some of the first people to import these dogs to England back in the early 1900's used them to hunt and to race. Mrs. Molly Sharpe of Dumfries, Scotland, had a team of racing Afghan Hounds back before World War I. Her Garrymhor Faiz-Bu-Hassid was one of the best and fastest racers of his day. No accurate records were kept of the various distances and timings, however. We have only word-of-mouth accounts of Afghanites getting together on private estates and racing their hounds for sheer love of watching them on the run.

Even in those early days the keen interest in this sport was by no means confided to England. Coursing hound fanciers all over Europe enjoyed racing their dogs. The various clubs were constantly on the lookout for larger and larger tracks to accommodate the crowds of spectators that wanted to come to share the excitement. These races were, of course, in addition to the tremendous crowds that turned out for the official Greyhound races. Crowds appeared even at the everyday

training sessions for the dogs. Small clubs grew to be official national clubs and were then required to adhere to strict rules and regulations when competing for trophies at the cup races and official derbies.

Fees from membership and race entries were often used to improve conditions at the track, to perfect the "U" or oval tracks, to purchase more complicated equipment and to offer bigger purses and prize money. Oftimes the great amounts of money garnered from these events were given to charity. On many occasions the profits were used to cover travel expenses because the events were often held in different countries on a rotation basis.

One of these racing organizations was called the Union Internationale des Clubs de Levriers, or the UICL. At one of the Europa-Rennen events held in Switzerland there were just under 200 entries representing dogs from Sweden, Holland, Austria, Germany and Finland. Many of the dogs competed the first day in the conformation classes and stayed on for the races the next day. During a Lantern Fest race in the 1960's, an American Afghan Hound, Ch. Kuano Lavas, owned by Joan Stepanaukas, ran off with a bronze medal!

AFGHAN HOUND RACING COMES TO AMERICA

Afghan Hound racing was discouraged in the United States in the early days, lest it interfere with the Greyhound racing, which was big business for a long time, and still is. By the middle of the 1970's, Greyhound racing was being held in nine states but was pulling an attendance count of over 16½ million people annually.

It wasn't until the 1950's that Earl Stites started Afghan Hound racing in the San Francisco area by founding a racing club there. In the fall of 1959 Bill and Gini Withington got "hooked" on racing. Betty and Earl Stites were visiting them in southern California when a bunch of their Afghans took off down a 400-foot straightaway after a lure. That day a love of Afghan racing was born. Immediately the Withingtons began to get a club together and began practice sessions on a fenced portion of their Stormhill Kennels property. Together with the Mikas, the Robinettes and the Guthries, the Racing Associates Club was formed officially at their first meet on January 3, 1960, and a new exciting sport had come to southern California.

Thirty or more Afghans competed at that first event, racing along a 450-foot course at the Sawtelle Veterans Home in the Los Angeles area. The club was later lucky enough to find a Greyhound track complete with a mechanical lure in Gardena, California, where they were to hold their meets for quite some time. In the next years many other coursing clubs were invited to compete as both membership and interest increased. The first official Afghan race to be held in conjunction

Headstudy of Christy, a one-year-old Afghan Hound owned and bred by the Curnyns, Devi Baba Kennels. Christy is known for his great racing speed. The Curnyns are the proud owners of their own home track in Hanson, Massachusetts.

Ryng Tayl Lynx is shown winning the run-off at a Kalamazoo dog show where she went on to set her speed record of 110 yards in 8 seconds. On another occasion Lynx raced in Milwaukee against Whippets and held the track record for five days, during which time five races per day were run for each dog. In obedience, Lynx has her C.D. title and is now working toward her C.D.X.

342

One of Georgiana Guthrie's racing Afghan Hounds was caught on film in mid-air. The Guthries are active in the sport of racing in the Los Angeles area, and are avid exhibitors at the dog shows.

with an AKC recognized show was at the 1960 Santa Barbara Kennel Club Show, and the interest in the racing made it an annual event through 1969.

The Afghan Coursing Associates, originally called the Racing Associates, and the Orange County Hound Coursing Association really launched the sport for the entire country. These two organizations had over 100 members and over 150 dogs; together they generated enough enthusiasm and publicity to call attention to the fun involved in seeing their dogs do what they were intended to do, and were most helpful in educating the rest of the country to successful racing.

Afghan Hound races were held at the Chicago International Show as early as 1962. In the same year Lou and Warren Fenn were instrumental in putting on an exhibition of Afghan Racing at the August Chagrin Valley Kennel Club Show in Ohio. After consulting with the Withingtons and getting the benefits of their experience with the California contests, the Fenns gathered together all the necessary ingredients. Lou whipped up silks and Warren devised a lure-pulling device from bicycle parts, while Margaret Waskow provided the pattern for a muzzle. Six starting boxes were constructed and 18 Afghans and

their owners appeared to try racing just two weeks before the show. The results were the same as the California groups had endured. Some dogs sat down, some ran off, some rolled in the grass, but by the day of the show things went a bit better.

There were eight elimination races with four dogs in each race, with several running twice, and three final heats. In just two of the heats did the dogs not choose to run! Twenty out of the 28 present ran as was intended and 15 of these had not run before. The fastest head was a tie between Charaj J-Mela of Dureigh and Majara Mapuh of Balkhwood, but Ch. Majara Murtanjui stole the show by coming in second in her heat and she was eight years old! Such was the beginning of the Ohio Afghan Hound Racing Associates, which then began further plans for race meetings to further the sport in their area.

In 1965 an eastern club was organized to encourage racing and to enjoy the sport that was catching on all across the country. This group included Afghans and Salukis. Frank Holder was the secretary of the Eastern Afghan and Saluki Coursing Club and meetings were held at Robert Tongren's home in the summer of that year. Bob was the club's president for the first five years. Their first exhib-

RROR IMAGE

#4 wins by a head! Or so it seems in this photo finish race at the 1975 Afghan Hound Club of Greater Denver Racing Meet in Brighton, Colorado. A crowd of thousands watched this photo finish race in which #4, Dhandi Musa Shafig, C.D.X., was the winner in an elapsed time of 42.5 seconds. Dhandi is owned by Peter and Daphone Lowe of Englewood, Colorado. The #2 dog is Hector Son of Prime, owned by Jan and Darina Juhas. Note that this is only a two-dog race, with the official finish line photograph showing at top a mirror image of these dogs as they reach the line.

ition of Afghan racing was held in conjunction with the June 26, 1965 Mid-Hudson Kennel Club Show in Rhinebeck, New York. An open house party to celebrate the event was held immediately following at the home of George and Carol Duffy.

This eastern coursing club was headquartered in Pleasant Valley, New York, and was also granted permission to hold a racing meet along with the June, 1966 all-breed Greenwich Kennel Club Show. Practice sessions for the event were held at the home of Frank Holder, where the dogs rehearsed chasing a lure for 180 yards. Profits from the meet went toward construction of starting boxes, muzzles, walkie-talkies and other necessary equipment.

Also during the 1960's the east coast saw the beginning of the Liberty Hound Racing Association on Long Island. In June of 1966

they issued a bulletin entitled *Chase News* in which they heralded their first meet held on Sunday, June 19th, when 150 people and 55 dogs turned out. The original directors of the club were Felix and Pat Cruz, Linda and George Trucknett and Sally and Wally Storch.

Ken Downs' Afghan named Sam won the top Afghan prize, and in addition to the 42 Afghans competing there was a Borzoi, a Saluki, a Greyhound, seven Whippets and several Deerhound puppies competing. At the chicken and beer party hosted by the Storches after the races plans were made for the date of the next event on July 4th. This group first hosted a racing exhibition at the Westbury Kennel Club Show that year.

Joan Brearley was writing the Afghan Hound column for *Popular Dogs* magazine at this time and immediately caught the enthusiasm and growing popularity for this sport and helped to promote it still further through her column. When a November, 1966 issue of *Life* magazine ran a photographic feature called "Shaggy Dog Racing—A Rising New Sport for Non-Greyhounds," this new sport hit a new high and racing clubs all over the country became almost too popular to imagine. Will anyone ever forget the magnificent full page color photograph of nine year old Guy Tongren carrying the beautiful race-winning Apryl as a fur necklace through the autumn leaves after winning the Millbrook, New York event the day *Life* paid us a visit! This photograph is one of the all-time "classics" in the history of this breed.

Much has been learned and improved upon since those early beginnings. The various clubs began to establish rules and regulations with an eye toward a future national racing and coursing association. Experienced fanciers met to discuss such topics as whether the most satisfactory tracks were those being 400 feet or more, whether more speed can be attained on a straight track than on an oval

and whether the dogs were more inclined to maintain interest on the oblong or oval tracks. Muzzles, it was agreed, are a must, since the most even-tempered dogs have been known to lose their heads in the excitement of completing a race. Owners prefer to prevent the scuffles that might ensue and ruin their valuable dogs.

Starting boxes are safest for a fair start. In this way no leash-held dog is given a head start by an over-zealous owner. Some of the racing clubs have applied a cooperative effort in building these starting boxes and supply them for the entrants. Other members prefer to build their own, as well as make their own muzzles out of soft leather.

A fur lure is the surest way to keep your race keen, though it need not necessarily be a scented one. Afghan Hounds, remember, are primarily sight hounds and it's the movement of an object more than the scent of an object that piques their interest.

No definite conclusions have been reached as to speed in relation to the sex of the animal. There are many—if not more—bitches

Ch. Crown Crest Bongo Bongo was a speedy and eager racing hound back in the late 1950's in California. Whelped in 1958, he was co-owned by Kay Finch and Betty Stites. This photograph was taken by J. Barry O'Rourke.

which lead the pack as there are dogs. Nor does the size of the individual dog make an appreciable difference. Sheer love of the race seems to motivate the swiftness of foot, and only the most spirited and the best-conditioned of them can maintain their speed as the heats continue during a racing event.

An alert dog will do well in the first heat, but it takes a dog that is in top condition and has had plenty of exercise in its training curriculum to consistently maintain speed as the races continue. The number of heats is determined by the number of entries, and the winner of each heat then competes against the others until the top winner is determined. Four to six dogs racing at one time seem to be about the most comfortable limit for these events.

The speed these dogs attain in any given race quite naturally varies. Each individual proud owner of a consistent winner can reel off individual timings reached by their dogs on various occasions, since most owners can be found at track-side with stopwatches in their hands. But club averages vary, because track lengths vary from club to club.

Dick and Georgiana Guthrie, who were so instrumental in the formation of the Afghan Coursing Club in California in 1960 (mentioned earlier), claim that an avid racer in pursuit of a lure can attain a speed of twenty-nine miles an hour. On a 450-foot track an Afghan Hound can do the distance in 10.5 seconds. The less eager dog, which merely enjoys "running with the pack" averages only about twenty-five miles an hour, or 450 feet in 13.3 seconds.

EARLY RULES AND REGULATIONS

When racing was first begun in earnest, most clubs used the regular Greyhound racing rules. Time and experience have made certain modifications necessary for our particular breed. Most clubs have their own rules or use those sent out by the clubs sponsoring the racing events at the all-breed kennel club shows. An example of such rules which would probably apply and which would accompany any request for an entry form might be:

RACING RULES FOR
AFGHAN RACING EXHIBITIONS

1. All dogs must wear muzzles and collars while racing.

346

A fast break for the number two slot dog may be all the lead he needs to gain the advantage on this clear track! Sheer love of the race seems to motivate these dogs to oftentimes reach speeds of twenty-nine miles an hour.

They're off! A group of California racing enthusiasts are shown at the starting boxes during a three-dog race. Some racing clubs have applied a cooperative effort in building starting boxes which they supply to all entrants. Other members still prefer to build their own boxes for use in both practice and competition. Local trials such as this one were the forerunners of today's track events which create such interest in racing Afghan Hounds.

The racing line-up at the Devi Baba Kennels is shown waiting for their chance to run on their private racetrack in Hanson, Massachusetts. Bucky, Christy, Bobbi, Mojud, Davy and Tina watch the track being put in readiness for the first race of the day. The clubhouse can be seen above the living quarters of these fortunate racing and show dogs.

2. All dogs must be on lead except when racing.
3. No dogs or handlers shall be allowed on the track except those participating in the race actually being conducted.
4. It is the responsibility of the owner or handler to retrieve his dog at the finish of a race, or at any time the dog stops running.
5. A bitch in season shall not be allowed to race or be anywhere on or near the track.
6. The stewards have sole discretion to determine which dogs will run in any race, and to remove any dog from any race for misbehavior.
7. No dog will be allowed in any race unless a release form has been properly signed.
8. No person shall be allowed on the track at any time without permission of the stewards.
9. All Afghan Hounds must be AKC registered or eligible to be registered.
10. Entry fee must accompany racing entry. Dogs need not be entered in conformation to be eligible for racing.
11. Choke collars are acceptable as racing equipment, and entrants must furnish their own collars.

Racing clubs must be made responsible for providing adequate training sessions prior to letting their members enter all-breed exhibitions so that we put our best foot forward in bringing Afghan Hound racing to the forefront as an exciting sport. Unreliable entrants that act up during the heats can spoil things for the experienced dogs as well as make the performance confusing and lackluster to those at ringside.

THE PERFECT HOME TRACK

During the late 1950's and early 1960's when Afghan Hound racing was incubating in our minds and our initial efforts were being concentrated on forming clubs to further these endeavors, a brother and sister team, Pat and Gertrude Curnyn of Hanson, Massachusetts, were hatching their own plans for a race track in their own backyard. This plan did, indeed, come to fruition amid a woodland setting where their guests where also invited to race their dogs in "guest silks" at their Devi Baba Kennels.

Some day, perhaps, some of us who are still caught up in the enthusiasm of Afghan Hound racing will be as fortunate as Pat and Gert were in seeing their dream come true. Designed and supervised by the late Pat Curnyn, this private track has been photographed on many occasions for many publications, and was the subject of a television program that brought additional publicity to racing and called attention to the track's complete accuracy and perfection of design.

This oval track is smoothed between races by a special tractor, and there is a fountain that graces the center area. A tack room is provided complete with a wardrobe rack to hold the racing silks, special wire schooling muzzles and numerous grooming aids. A

347

The "home" track at the Devi Baba Kennels. As professionally equipped as any major track could be, this home race course is complete with nightlights and an electrical squirrel lure named Ignition. Guests of owners Gertrude and the late Pat Curnyn are invited to race their Afghan Hounds in guest silks.

The squirrel lure named Ignition is mounted on this car, moves in either direction and can do a lap in 5 seconds flat. It also operates the starting bell and starting box doors.

Felix Cruz, co-founder of the Liberty Hound Racing Association in the 1960's, is pictured operating the hand lure during a racing heat.

This close-up shows the starting boxes and the starting bell that is located at the corner of the chute. The bell is synchronized with the doors and sounds off for 1 second while the doors are opening and starts the lure on its way.

Central Control at the track. This photo shows the coursing slip and the "stop curtains," as well as the gate for entering the track.

Bucky is posed and ready to run in his leather muzzle and silks. Owned by the Curnyns of Hanson, Massachusetts, Bucky had the privilege of training and racing on their own private track.

squirrel lure named Ignition is also in residence. There is a huge porch off the back of the main house that overlooks the entire track, and the open runs for each of the dogs overlook the racing area. The track is completely and properly lighted so that night racing is also a part of the entertainment.

Anyone who has been at the track has come away with the thought that it would be wonderful if we could all have such facilities available for our own dogs that love to race. Those of us interested in racing our Afghans know that the sport of racing is here to stay and wish that some day there may also be a national racing and coursing club exclusively for Afghan Hounds. This wish is becoming closer to a reality and is no longer just a dream as more and more interest is being expressed by the parent Afghan Hound club toward both racing and coursing. . .

Chapter XV

Lure Coursing with Afghan Hounds

Coursing is one of the oldest dog-oriented sports, dating back centuries. Some 2,000 years ago Ovid wrote, "the impatient greyhound slipped from far, bound o'er the glade to course the fearful hare," giving written testimony to the pursuit of coursing even that far back. In those early times coursing was usually conducted to capture food to sustain life, only down through the years did the chasing after game become a means for both food and fun.

While the Mid-West Coursing Club and the Delaware Valley Afghan Hound Club began coursing during the 1960's, it was in 1972 that Lyle Gillette, a Saluki breeder in California, had the great foresight to realize the inevitable growth of the sport and to see the necessity for unity and organization. Lyle Gill-

ette and 20 or so other coursing enthusiasts met at the home of Annette and Arthur McConnel in Walnut Creek, California, on May 21st, 1972 and the American Sighthound Field Association became a reality. Lyle Gillette has served as President of ASFA since its beginning and is due the major portion of credit for having made lure coursing the safe, humane and regulated sport it is today.

The first official ASFA licensed Lure Field Trial was held in August of that year after Art McConnel, as Rules Chairman, worked up an initial set of general rules on which the club could operate. The first Annual ASFA Conference was held on March 9, 1974; at this time officers were elected and the constitution adopted.

Their Statement of Purpose read as follows: "The American Sighthound Field Association is an organization of sighthound fanciers dedicated to the common goal of preserving and further developing the natural beauty, grace, speed and coursing skill of the gazehound. We will endeavor to promote a recognized system of lure field trials for sighthounds throughout the United States and governed by rules that can be accepted by the American Kennel Club. To allow uniformity in administering these lure field trials, a lure coursing system will be used."

At this first meeting it was also decided that ASFA would grant authorizations to ASFA clubs elsewhere in the country to hold their own lure coursing trials. By the end of 1974 there were many of them. Two of the most prominent were The Delaware Valley Afghan Hound Club and the Borzoi Club of Delaware Valley. In November they held an ASFA licensed Lure Field Trial in the Phila-

Opposite:
Tamora's Image of Ali, C.D., F. Ch., the top lure coursing Afghan Hound for 1976, is better known as Bandit! Winner of the first Lure Coursing award given by the Afghan Hound Club of America, he was also the winner at the Grand National Lure Course, the Eastern Invitational, the Colorado Lure Coursing Association meet, the Connecticut Sighthound Club, the Ibizan Hound Club of U.S. Lure Trials, and others. He has run at field trials from Vermont to California to defeat more Afghan Hounds in the field during 1976 than any other Afghan in one year since lure coursing became an organized sport under the American Sighthound Field Association. Bandit was also in the top twenty Afghan Hounds in obedience for 1976. He is flown to most of the field trials in a private plane owned and operated by his owner, Gary Forrester of York, Pennsylvania.

351

Ch. Wielki Sezlem of Nightwatch, F. Ch., is pictured enroute to winning the Highest Scoring Afghan title at the 1975 Grand National competition in Denver over an entry of 27 Afghan Hounds. This 3-year-old was ranked 4th in the all-breed entry of 101, and is owned by Robert and Denyce Verti, Nightwatch Afghans, LaPorte, Colorado.

delphia suburbs. Highlight of the event was the attendance of His Excellency Abdullah Malikyan, Afghanistan's Ambassador to the United States. He and several members of his family journied up from Washington, D.C., especially to watch the coursing.

On March 8 and 9, 1975 another annual ASFA Conference was held, this time in San Jose, California. Later that year on September 20 and 21st, the Colorado Lure Coursing Association played host to The Grand National in Denver, Colorado. 95 entries competed on a 660 yard course, 27 of which were Afghan Hounds. A banquet was held at which the owners shared their experiences and planned future activities, which included a 1976 Grand National.

The Grand National was another example of the growing popularity for Lure Coursing, and there is no doubt that the members of the American Sighthound Field Association look toward recognition by the American Kennel Club as well as continued growth of their organization through licensed ASFA coursing clubs.

As of 1975 there were over 75 coursing clubs functioning all over the United States. There is also a Canadian Sighthound Association in Victoria, B.C. They frequently use AFSA judges and get full benefit of their experience and moral support. ASFA provides a rule book available without cost for the first copy, from which any clubs or groups interested in forming a coursing club can learn all about it. The ASFA Corresponding Secretary, Mrs. Royce Northcott, can be reached at 9590 Trenton Way, Stockton, California 95205.

LURE FIELD TRIALS

Lure coursing trials are held in large fenced areas or fields in which all sighthound breeds registered or listed with the American Kennel Club compete in Open breed stakes for championship points toward a field champion title. A field championship entitles them to the addition of the initials "F.CH." after their names. In order to earn the title each coursing hound must have one first or two second place wins to their credit. The maximum number of points which can be won at any single trial is 40, which means that competition in at least three trials is necessary in order to amass the total number of 100 points required for the title. Since the entries are usually large, this is not easily accomplished.

Drawings are held to determine which dogs will course together, and each wears a colored blanket for identification. Muzzles are optional. Each dog is scored by two judges in two separate courses. Points are awarded on four requirements: 30 points for enthusiasm and following the lure, 25 points for speed, 25 points for agility and 20 points for endurance. There can also be a 10 point deduction from each judge for a "pre-slip" or a zero to 10 point deduction from each judge for delaying the course in any way.

The dogs run anywhere from 375 to 880 yards—ASFA allows no more or no less—and are based on ASFA approved zigzag courses which must be described in the premium list sent to applicants along with their entry form. The dogs are released, or "slipped," from their collars to the cry of "Tally Ho!" given by the Huntmaster. It is also the Huntmaster who calls "Retrieve your dogs!" at the end of each course. The lure is kept between 10 and 30 feet ahead of the dogs, and any time a dog touches or catches the lure a "no course" is declared.

The two judges and the Field Clerk stand in the center of the course where they can best observe the dogs in action. The judges do not discuss their ratings before handing them over to the Field Clerk. All the hounds entered in the stakes are divided into braces or trios by a drawing which precedes the course. After all entries have run their first heat, the winners are then re-drawn by number and compete again in a second heat. Preliminary and final scores are totalled and the highest scoring dog is declared the top winner.

Championship points in all regular stakes, both open and field champion, are awarded by the following method:
First place: four times the number of hounds competing in the stakes with a maximum of 40 points. Second place: three times the number of hounds competing in the stake with a maximum of 30 points. Third place: two times the number of dogs competing in the stakes with a maximum of 20 points. Fourth place: point equal to the number of dogs competing with a maximum of 10 points. The "Next Best Qualified" or 5th place winner gets no points, but is designated by a notation of NBQ.

VARIOUS KINDS OF COURSES

In addition to the Open Field Stakes for which the dogs compete for their Field Champion titles, there is also a Field Champion Stake in which dogs that have already earned their titles compete against one another. A Grand Field Champion title, or G.F. Ch., may be added to the name of any Field Champion that has earned, in addition to the first title requirements, four first placements against competition in any regular stake, and a total accumulation of 300 points in regular stakes. However, this title and the winning of it was only open to competitors from May 1, 1975 until it was abolished in August, 1975.

In the Non-Regular Stakes, where there is only one winner declared and no championship points awarded, there can be (at the

Wita Rosie von der Oranje Manege, F. Ch., and kennel mate Ch. Wielki Sezlem of Nightwatch, F. Ch., are pictured in action during the summer of 1975 at the Geeley, Colorado, racing site. Their owners are Robert and Denyce Verti of LaPorte, Colorado.

option of the host club) a Puppy Stakes in which only dogs under one year of age on the day of the meet may compete.

Each host club holds two regular stakes specifically for their particular breed, and may also hold Individual Stakes for each of the other sighthound breeds present that day.

Also at the option of the host club, a Best In Field course may be run by the First Place or Best of Breed winners in each breed present. There is only one stake run for this event and also no championship points are awarded.

A Kennel Stake is for entries of an individual breed which consist of two hounds participating in the regular stakes that are owned and kenneled by the same person.

Breeder Stakes are for any breeds which shall have two or more entries of dogs bred by the same owner.

Veteran Stakes are for entries of any dogs that are more than six years old.

Bitches in season or hounds which are declared lame by the Field Trial Committee at the time of the roll call are barred from competition and entry fees are returned. The de-

cisions of the Field Trial Committee are final when in agreement with the rules of ASFA. Entry fees for events are determined by the host clubs and are forfeited when dogs are dismissed from the field with cause. A hound is disqualified, or dismissed, if it is guilty of fighting, or being the aggressor in a fight in the field.

Xanadu's Xixith is taking off after the prey! The 19-month-old Xixith was bred and owned by Johanna Tanner of Friendswood, Texas.

Ch. Wita Vail of Nightwatch, F. Ch., is owned by Robert and Denyce Verti. Vail is pictured winning under judge Dr. Robert Turner. She won her field title in four trials and her conformation championship with all majors at just 17 months of age.

THE COURSING "TOP TEN" CONTENDERS

Lure Coursing News, a magazine which was published in the early days of ASFA, evolved a point system to determine the Top Ten Lure Coursing Sighthounds each year, starting in 1972 when the ASFA began holding licensed trials. Each of the Top Ten was awarded an Award of Achievement certificate to comemorate their performance in the field, and was based on the following point system:

LURE COURSING NEWS TOP TEN POINT SYSTEM

TOTAL means the total Top Ten Points received by the hound.

1   means the number of first placements
2   means the number of second placements
3   means the number of third placements
4   means the number of fourth placements
NBQ means the number of Next Best Qualified

Points are awarded to sighthounds who place in Open Breed Stakes, Open Mixed Stakes or non-regular Field Champion Stakes held at ASFA licensed lure field trials as follows:

ONE Top Ten point is awarded for placing

This lovely black and tan bitch enjoys lure coursing. This 1-year-old Afghan Hound was rescued from a pound and is now a happy member of Kathleen O'Brien's kennel in Willingboro, New Jersey.

1st, 2nd, 3rd, 4th, or NBQ in one of the above stakes.

TWO Top Ten points are awarded for each placing hound beaten, including Field Champions and non-field champions who are judged by the same judges.

FOUR Top Ten points are awarded for each placing Field Champion beaten who is judged by the same judges.

Statistics for the Top Ten point system are complied by Linda Blalock & Wendy Waller.

TOP TEN LURE COURSING AFGHAN HOUNDS
TOP TEN—1973

Dogs	Total	1	2	3	4	NBQ
1. Reddy To Love Thru Kindness, F. Ch.	51	2	0	2	2	1
2. Elrey's Saschi Of Saschaar	37	0	2	1	0	0
3. Kaa's Keana of Sanmac	25	0	1	1	0	1
4. Chaka's Circe of Sesame	19	0	1	0	0	2
5. Skol, C.D.X.	19	0	0	1	2	0
6. Sachi of Chaka	18	1	0	0	1	0
7. Tanis King Of Hearts	12	0	0	0	1	1
8. High Life Sweet Sunday	11	0	0	1	0	0
9. Camri's Sea Idol of Sesame	6	0	0	1	0	1
10. Santana's Little Oaks Mimi	3	0	0	0	1	0

TOP TEN—1974

Dogs	Total	1	2	3	4	NBQ
1. Chaka's Circe Of Sesame, F.Ch.	52	1	2	1	0	0
2. Reddy To Love Thru Kindness, F.Ch.	49	2	0	1	0	0
3. Elrey's Saschi Of Saschaar, F.Ch.	36	1	3	0	0	0
3. Ch. Wita Vail Of Nightwatch, F.Ch.	36	1	2	1	0	0
4. Camri's Sea Idol Of Sesame	34	0	1	2	1	2
5. Shiva's Sebrina Of Ta Deva, F.Ch.	34	2	0	2	0	0
7. Ballywash Mishra	27	1	0	0	0	0
7. Pasha Of Desperation	27	1	0	0	0	0
7. Saahn-Mac Magic Christian	27	2	0	0	1	0
10. Muscat Of Vale Vue	25	1	0	0	0	0

TOP TEN—1975

Dogs	Total	1	2	3	4	NBQ
1. Kyanti's Moon Bandit, F.Ch.	197	3	1	2	1	0
2. His Majesty's Liberty Belle, F.Ch.	161	2	4	2	1	0
4. Yev Rah Parmahansa Nataraja, C.D., F.Ch.	151	2	2	3	0	2
5. Kaychuck's Amber Lace Of Olympus, F.Ch.	142	3	1	0	0	0
7. El Mari Shasta La Grandeur	132	1	2	1	0	4
8. Reddy To Love Thru Kindess, F.Ch.	126	2	0	1	1	0
9. Sesame's Streaked Lightning	114	0	0	2	3	1
10. Chaka's Circe of Sesame, F.Ch.	92	2	1	1	0	2

Running free! Many California owners run their dogs on the beach for both exercise and conditioning for racing. Suzanne Neill's Charger, Amber and Crecia were photographed taking off down the beach in July, 1972.

#1 LURE COURSING HOUND FOR 1976

Tamora's Image of Ali, C.D., F.Ch., was the #1 Lure Coursing Afghan Hound for 1976. Known best in coursing circles as "Bandit," Gary and Marietta Forrester's beautiful black and tan dog had the distinction of being named the winner of the Afghan Hound Club of America's first Annual Lure Coursing Award.

Bandit was the Afghan Hound winner at the Grand National Lure Course, the Eastern Invitational, Colorado Lure Coursing Association, the Connecticut Sighthound Club, Ibizan Hound Club of the United States Lure Trials, and on and on his record goes! Bandit has run in field trials from Vermont to California to earn his #1 position, and had defeated more Afghan Hounds in the field during 1976 than any other Afghan in any one year since lure coursing became an organized sport under the American Sighthound Field Association rules.

Bandit was whelped March 16, 1972—the very year ASFA was established—and was sired by Ch. Native Dancer of Scheherezade out of Ch. Tamora's Salome. He was also listed among the Top Twenty Afghan Hounds in Obedience for 1976. He earned his C.D. title in three consecutive shows. Bandit hates the conformation ring so in deference to his amazing achievements in all the other rings his owners do not force the issue. However, it is a shame that he just lacks this one additional title to become the "perfect" all-around Afghan Hound!

Bandit is flown from his home in York, Pennsylvania, to most of the Field Trials in his owners' private plane, in which he sits on the back seat very self-assuredly, gazing out of the windows as if searching for the site of his next grand chase! How wonderful it would be if all our Afghan Hounds could be as talented as Bandit, as well as having his exceptional temperament and good manners. The Forresters are both proud—and fortunate!

PUTTING ON A LURE COURSING TRIAL

For local groups wishing to course their dogs, the staging of a lure coursing trial can be relatively simple and lots of fun. There are lure coursing kits available for around two to three hundred dollars. The kits include a lure machine with electronic speed control, a couple of hundred yards of line, several pulleys, lures and a manual describing how to use all of it. Information on how and where to

Wita Rosie vdOM, F. Ch., owned by Robert and Denyce Verti. Rosie was sired by International and Racing Champion Kysyl vdOM *ex* Racing Champion Rosita vdOM. She is pictured here at 4 years of age in 1974.

purchase these kits can undoubtedly be obtained by writing to the ASFA office perhaps at the same time you request their rule book.

Once you have obtained your equipment and appointed a Field Trial Secretary and Chairman, both of whom are members of the host club, it would be wise to inquire of other coursing clubs as to the availability of any movies which they might have taken at their field trials. While viewing these it is usually good to make a check on whether or not you have considered all the necessary aspects for putting on a successful trial.

By this time your Secretary should have obtained your license from ASFA, and, of course, obtained a proper site on which to hold a trial. All premiums should have been printed and mailed after receiving acceptance by the two qualified judges you have invited to preside. Entry fees are usually around three or four dollars and your profits can be used toward more equipment, club activities or toward prizes.

Be certain your coursing grounds are completely fenced, and that you are holding your trial with the full approval of the owners of the property. While there are no laws against coursing that we know of, we do not want to antagonize those who are helping us stage these events. Escaped dogs that might damage property or knock over and injure pedestrians in the fervor of a race can mean lawsuits or restrictions we hope to avoid.

El Citono Del Desierto, or Tono as he is called, is one of Pearson Crosby's hunting Afghan Hounds from his Del Desierto Kennels in New Mexico.

358

You will require the services of additional officials at your trial. In addition to the Field Trial Chairman who heads up the Field Committee of two additional people, your Field Trial Chairman will be responsible for carrying out the roll call and official drawings, checking out all equipment, be responsible for the awards and the cleaning up of the grounds before, during and after the event. The Field Chairman also calls up each succeeding course and, in general, lends any necessary assistance to the Field Clerk and the Field Trial Secretary.

You will need a Huntmaster who can take complete charge of all hounds and their handlers, can precisely explain racing procedures before every course, give a definitive hand signal to the Lure Operator to start the lure and can sound the necessary "Tally Ho" and "Retrieve Your Hounds" commands when the moment comes. The Huntmaster is also required to inspect the lure before each course to determine if a replacement is needed.

The Field Clerk is responsible for the drawing of hounds in each competition and keeps score on the Field Record sheets. The Field Clerk announces the winners of each course as well as the final placements at the conclusion of the trial.

The Lure Operator also plays an important role in a successful trial. He lays out the course in accordance with the approved course plan and is required to hold at least one "practice" run of the lure before the first course is started. At the beginning of each course, the Lure Operator awaits the signal from the Huntmaster to start the lure.

Names of these officials must be included in the Premium List. Any substitute of judges must be declared before the roll call, at which time refunds on entries will be made when requested.

PROTECTING AFGHAN HOUND COATS

During the practice sessions for the coursing trials, there is the ever-present danger that the beautiful silky coats we want to see on our Afghan Hounds can be damaged. This can be aided by racing and schooling the dogs in "long johns." Red underwear on an Afghan Hound viewed by unsuspecting observers from across a field can be a startling sight, but it does protect the coat from twigs, burrs, leaves and other debris, and yet still gives the dogs enough freedom to run. This is also help-

ful in getting the dogs accustomed to wearing their racing and coursing blankets.

In August, 1961 several of the Sunday newspaper supplements all over the country published a color cover story featuring the Withington's Afghan Hound cavorting about the California countryside in their long red underwear. It was wonderful coverage for the sport as well as for the beautiful breed.

COURSING INJURIES

The injuries sustained in lure coursing are few, and usually fall into the same category as those that befall any dog that is allowed to run free. Dog fights or dislocations as a result of quick turns would be one of the most likely, but avoidable if your dog is well trained and in good condition physically.

Good physical condition means that your dog is in excellent health and is used to plenty of proper exercise. Field coursing or racing is an excellent source of exercise in itself, but you can not expect to take an Afghan Hound from the "couch to the course" and come up with a winner. There is a lot of pre-conditioning required to give your dog the proper start if you expect to stick with this exciting sport.

The most prevalent injuries occur to the legs and feet, since they come in direct contact with uneven ground while the animal is running at great speed. These injuries may result in lameness, broken or torn nails, cut paw pads, muscle sprains or tears. Lure coursing is also one of the greatest reasons in the world for removing dew claws on puppies! It is very easy for dew claws to get caught in brush, the fencing or even the lure line itself.

Muscle cramps are also common and are recognizable by the dog changing pace, and finally not moving at all. Actually, the dog should keep moving to walk the cramp out. Pad injuries can be avoided by keeping your dogs in sand or crushed blue stone runs. These help keep hard callouses that can crack or split while coursing from building up.

Nails should be kept short, and if they break the broken portion should be removed. If there is any bleeding, cauterize the exposed area and stop the bleeding. Nails bleed profusely and a break can be painful as well. Cold, wet cotton; vaseline; steptic pencils or powders applied with pressure to the nail will usually control and eventually stop the bleeding.

Toes may be dislocated or ligaments torn in the foot. These should be treated by a vet-

Ch. Wita Vail of Nightwatch, F. Ch., was the winner of the Afghan Hound Field Champion Stakes over 6 competitors at the 1975 Colorado Lure Coursing Association site. This lovely black and tan bitch is 3 years old and shown by her owners, the Vertis, in conformation classes as well. Her score at the September 20, 1975 event was 369.

erinarian; they seldom result in amputation, but can be painful to the dog. Running at the speed required for coursing can also mean broken or fractured bones in the foot or hock. Shoulder injuries can result from collisions if the dogs bump or pile up during the chase.

Other injuries might be tendon sprains, tears, ruptures, muscle cramps or fractures and breaks elsewhere on the body. Aside from the humane aspect of having injuries looked at by a veterinarian, it is common sense that you will want to keep from irritating any injury by neglecting it. Act with caution. Before coursing the dog again, make sure the injury is completely cured and the dog shows the desire to run again.

COURSING AND BEHAVIOR PATTERNS

There is no doubt that our sighthounds are born with an innate ability to sight, course and bring down prey. . . prey in the form of a fleeting object. Whether or not it is hungry, the moving object presents the challenge and the fun of a chase. Our present-day

dogs are fed so often and so well that hunger never enters into it, but while our dogs no longer have to hunt to eat, that instinct may be dormant but is ever-present no matter how long or how well it remains in the background of their personality.

It is sometimes quite obvious just by observing the dogs at the trials whether their particular instinct is for a "kill" or for the fun of the chase. But once the instinct is awakened, with live rabbits, or scented lures, or perhaps just the excitement and competition of the chase, you are going to have to keep your dog away from the family cat or any other small pets you might have living at your house. It is the erratic motion of the moving object that catches their eye. There is a fine line between chasing prey and killing prey, and to the avid hunter they are almost one and the same.

For all who course their hounds it would be wise to notice how seriously the dogs take their coursing. If it is the fun of the chase, with no visible change in disposition toward other moving objects away from the track,

360

coursing trials can be pure joy for both dog and owner. If you notice that predatory look in their eyes, you had better stop coursing, or take a new look at the safety measures provided for the other living things in your home or neighborhood.

OPEN FIELD COURSING AND PARK COURSING

Open Field Coursing is just what the name implies. . . the dogs course live game in open fields and frequently there is a kill. Advocates of this type of coursing argue that the game is on its home ground and is faster than the dogs, so the dog is theoretically at a disadvantage. Park Coursing is conducted in a specified area, or "park," and is limited to the use of captured and then released jackrabbits. Many people feel this definitely puts the rabbits at a disadvantage because they have to run for their lives in unfamiliar territory; here again, advocates of this type of coursing admit to even more frequent kills.

The National Open Field Coursing Association was in existence as early as 1960. In 1963 another club, the New Mexico Dog Racing and Coursing Club decided, by vote of the stockholders, to devote two full days of their meets to Afghan Hound Open Field Coursing exclusively. The first was held on February 23 and 24, 1963. Club member Pearson Crosby reported that the entry fee was ten dollars, two-thirds of which went into purses for winners and one-third to cover the club's expenses. Entries were divided into two classes: over 14 months old and under 14 months old. Name, age, sex, color and markings had to be included on the entry blanks along with the usual pertinent information required at such sporting events.

A field 1,000 feet long and 350 feet in width with escape hatches for the live jackrabbits at the far end was used, with the Afghan Hounds coursing in pairs determined by earlier drawings. The use of live rabbits caused some adverse comments—as it still does in coursing circles—but it was said that escape hatches were numerous, and winners could often be declared by the time many of the rabbits managed to escape the course.

An article by Steve Copold published in a past issue of *The Gazehound* tells of Open Field Coursing at Reese Air Force Base in Texas. Located in the Texas Panhandle, jackrabbits constitute a real hazard as they swarm over the landing field to escape the coyotes. In lieu of past rabbit drives where the rabbits were killed off by shotguns under potentially dangerous conditions, some of the dog owners on the base were invited by the Air Force to try Open Field Coursing to cut down on the jackrabbits. After several weeks the situation was brought under control. They were given the unofficial name of Reese Rodent Control Unit, and the Air Force felt more confident that landing planes were no longer in danger. They felt, especially in this instance, that coursing live game was not only justified but was serving an important purpose.

In spite of the rabbit fatalities and the seemingly useful purpose mentioned above, Open Field Coursing enthusiasts will tell you that the emphasis is definitely not on a kill, because coursing is *not* a form of hunting, but rather a test of the dogs' speed, endurance and agility. Wearing their colored blankets, the dogs and their handlers are led into the field by the Huntmaster who sets the pace and determines the direction they will follow. Other entrants follow 10 or 20 yards behind to put up the rabbits. When a rabbit takes off, the Huntmaster determines if it is able to run well enough, is not too young or lame, and could be considered "fair game." If he approves, he gives the "Tally Ho!" call and the handlers release their dogs.

The judge evaluates the dogs performance during the chase, and after the rabbit either escapes or is killed, the owners recall their dogs and the next brace or trio repeats the same procedure. Once all of the entrants have run, the winners of each course, and perhaps a few others that have run particularly well in the opinion of the judge, get to run again. From this coursing the judge selects the winner.

There are, of course, many other intricacies involved in both Open Field and Park Coursing which any of the club members are always happy to explain to those who wish to try it and do not object to the killing of animals. For instance, there is great significance in the actions of the dogs taking and maintaining the lead position in the chase, the dogs' regulation of their own speed based on their observance of the position of the rabbit's ears, and so forth.

Here again, it must be pointed out that Open Field or Park Coursing is not recognized by the American Kennel Club, or the Afghan Hound parent club, and especially not by the author.

Chapter XVI

The Afghan Hound in Art

Perhaps no other breed of dog lends itself so beautifully to each and every art form as does our exotic, clownish and aristocratic Afghan Hound!

From the earliest days when hieroglyphics were first etched on the walls of Egyptian tombs and scratched onto papyrus with quills from ancient desert birds, slender dogs resembling the Afghan Hound have been part of recorded history. Because of the great beauty and grace of the Afghan Hound, they have managed to capture the eye of artists and art lovers through the centuries.

Through these artistic endeavors on tombstones, papyrus, frescoes on flat stones, woodcuts, carvings, sculptures, oil paintings and other printing processes from the past up to the present day ceramics, jewelry, needlework, tapestries, and other art forms, we have been able to enjoy the ancient gazehounds in all their splendor.

Nearly every book on dogs that touches on ancient history features a copy of the XVIII Dynasty's wall painting of a group of hounds from the tomb of Rekh-mi-Re, which they liken to Afghan Hounds. However, they appear to be hairless and rather short of leg, but we are aware that the Afghan Hound of ancient times more than likely was a smaller dog. We see this in the 1813 painting of "A Meenah of Jajurh with Afghan Hound." This dog is well-coated and the withers reach only to the knee of the Meenah of Jajurh.

Opposite:
Charikar Silver Belle, a
20-month-old bitch owned by Dr. and
Mrs. E. Conrad Monson of Ogden, Utah.

This lovely metal sculpture is by Joanna Tanner of Houston, Texas. This piece was the Best of Opposite Sex trophy at a 1974 Houston Specialty Show.

At the Victoria and Albert Musuem in London there is a miniature circa 1835 entitled, "Maharana Jawar of Mewar Hunts a Boar," that illustrates the hound hunting along with the hunter brandishing a sword, the method of hunting during the Middle Ages. As in most all ancient paintings, the dogs are without the long coat associated with the Afghan Hound. However, the drop ears, curved tail and well-angulated hindquarters give credence to the possibility that the Afghan Hound traits are well represented in the painting.

Afghan Hound enthusiasts are constantly fighting the desire to claim every large hunting dog with curved tail from ancient drawing as being our breed. We are also aware that the Saluki people make the same claim to fame, as do the greyhound people. If the truth be known the chances are most likely that they *are* Greyhounds, though we are equally aware that the British have always labeled this type of dog as being a Greyhound, whether it was or not.

Dorothy MacDonald, in an article entitled "The Afghan Hound in Art," reported that an enormous tapestry hangs in the Worcester Art Museum which actually shows heavy-coated Afghan Hounds. Designed and woven in 1938 by the contemporary French artist Jean Larcat, there are three dogs standing at their master's feet with the Afghan Hound conformation and long hair.

I think it is interesting to note that a retired British Army officer named Major Charles Fitzwilliam, in correspondence with Kay Finch dated 1952, states that his first acquaintance with the breed was a wall painting in an ancient Egyptian tomb attributed to 8,000 B.C. Major Fitzwilliam, who was associated with the breed for over fifty years, received his first pair of Afghan Hounds as a gift from the Emir of Peshawar while he was Captain of his bodyguard. This occurred during his service in the Anglo-Indian forces along the Indian-Afghanistan border.

This pastel portrait of Ch. Amberhall Scorpio was rendered by artist Rene H. Folmer of Alberta, Canada.

Conni Nibarger's beautiful ginger jar features one of her Afghan Hounds. These fifty dollar jars have been awarded as trophies at Afghan Hound specialty shows.

EARLY BRITISH ARTISTS

Back in the early part of this century when Afghan Hounds were first imported to England, the symmetry of the graceful Afghan Hound came to the attention of the British artist Frederick T. Daws. Perhaps among the first to do oil paintings of the Afghan Hound greats of that era, Mr. Daws' works, especially his painting of Zardin, are held in high esteem for their beauty and accuracy, and have become collector's items among the fancy.

Marion Florsheim brought several Afghan Hound paintings to this country years ago, one of which she later passed on to Kay Finch. A beautiful mountain tor is the setting for four of the English-bred dogs, Ch. Westmill Omar, Ch. Badshah of Ainsdart, Ch. Sirdar of Ghazni and Ch. Azri-Havid of Ghazni. Mrs. Florsheim came into possession of a number of Daws' paintings on the death of her good friend Phyllis Robson in England.

A Lenox china service of plates with gold, blue and white borders was presented to Marion Foster Florsheim as a permanent record of the show wins of her three international champion Afghan Hounds. Hand colored by Walter R. Duff, the plates featured Int. Ch. Rudiki of Pride's Hill, Int. Ch. Rudika of Blakeen and Int. Ch. Rana of Chaman of Royal Irish. On the back of each plate was their show ring record.

The late Mrs. Florsheim had expressed intentions of willing her Daws' paintings to the American Kennel Club upon her death, where one of the Daws' paintings already hangs in the office of the editor of the *American Kennel Gazette.*

Another famous artist of the period was Edwin Magargee. The walls of the American Kennel Club are filled with so many of his beautiful oils, many of which have been featured in dog articles in the *National Geographic Magazine.* We also are aware of the works of Maud Earl and Arthur Wardle during this period.

Undeniably the artist who has done the most to immortalize the Afghan Hound in our time, however, is Kay Finch. As an owner, breeder, exhibitor and judge for many years, Mrs. Finch has managed to capture and relate the true conformation and personality of this distinctive hound in many of her art forms.

Mrs. Finch's California studio at Corona del Mar has been the scene for the creation of a multitude of figurines and statuary representing many of our great dogs. Distribution has been wide, with her work being seen in many countries of the world. They are in private collections and have been reproduced as show trophies as well. It is still not unlikely that ringsiders can see Kay Finch make an entrance into the show ring with one of her beautiful Afghan Hounds whose likeness has been painted in brilliant colors on her jacket or skirt! Her Afghan jewelry has become a topic of conversation wherever she goes!

Perhaps the most famous of all her works is the full figure bronze she created of Int. Ch. Rudiki of Pride's Hill. It was given many years ago as a gift to her good friend Marion Florsheim, and only 10 originals were cast from the form, making it truly a collectors' item. Fortunately for the rest of us, it has also been reproduced in ceramic and I am pleased to report one of those is in my personal collection, a gift from Kay Finch during my early days in the breed.

A close second to the Rudiki statue is the head study Kay presented to Sunny Shay and Sol Malkin done in the likeness of their exotic black imported dog, Ch. Turkuman Nissim's Laurel. This was the dog which won the Afghan Hound Club of America Specialty Show and the Hound Group at the Westminster Kennel Club Show in 1950.

As the Afghan Hound becomes increasingly popular, more and more artists are drawn to the breed and introduce their own particular presentation of it. Two other prominent artists that have been breeding and showing the Afghan Hound over the years are

Kay Finch relaxes in her favorite corner of the living room with one real Afghan and one stuffed toy Afghan. Notice the magnificent Afghan Hound paintings on the wall; left is one of the Daws original oils and the other was done by George Finch, Kay's artist son.

Photo below:
An Afghan Hound classic! Three great dogs were captured on canvas by Kay Finch in this beautiful rendition of our breed. The dogs, of course, are Ch. Felt's Allah Baba, Ch. Taejon of Crown Crest and Ch. Crown Crest Jubilee Julian.

Mary Nelson Stephenson and Elisabeth Harvey Treharne. Mary Stephenson is known for her magnificent oil and water colors of the breed; Betty Treharne is also known for her exquisite line of note paper and art of glassware. Her Afghan Hound works are in great demand, as are all the other breeds she presents in her various art forms.

Perhaps Betty Treharne's best known work is the oil painting done of Ch. Shirkhan of Grandeur, painted from life in 1960 after his Best In Show win at the Garden and subsequent successes. Soon after that she painted the 26" x 30" portrait of Am. and Can. Ch. Coastwind Graffiti for fellow-artist Peter Belmont, Jr. However, it was her painting of Black Cyn and Black Rynof Dondi several years ago which originally brought her talent to the attention of breeders, and she has been in demand ever since.

We have enjoyed the work of Helen Bussen who was so proficient with pen and ink, Rutherford Boyd, Marjorie Walker, Diana Fuertes, Diana Thorne, Earl Sherwan, Peter Belmont and Kurt Kroll, to name a few. I'm sure there were other artists who doted on our exotic breed whose work, unfortunately, has not yet come to public attention so that we might include their names with the others.

Today the artistic talents among our breed fanciers are many and varied. One of the most outstanding is George Finch, Kay Finch's son. He has done great paintings of many breeds, and works in oils and bronze as well as other mediums. George's paintings of the Crown Crest dogs are exquisite, and more recently his paintings of the Haims' Timu-Ka Afghan Hounds are marvelous.

Ch. Taejon of Crown Crest was painted by George Finch from the famous photograph of Johnny that had become so well-known and such a favorite with his followers. This painting is in the collection of the artist's mother, Kay Finch.

Vic Tor, whose studio is in Lake Worth, Florida, is producing paintings that are causing wide acclaim. A Navy veteran and graduate of the Art Institute of Chicago, he is known for his sensitive studies of flowers and Afghan Hounds in pastel shades rendered in oil and watercolor. His works have appeared in several magazines and some of his paintings are on continuous exhibition at galleries all over the United States and Canada.

A 1975 exhibition of the paintings of Keith Ingermann at the Hammer Galleries in New York City contained several of his works, which included Afghan Hounds and many other breeds. His "Une Villa de la Conca d'Oro" features a reclining Afghan Hound in the foreground and several Pekingese, and his "Au bord de la Riviere" includes an Afghan Hound, a Poodle and several Yorkshire Terriers.

Pablo Picasso had an Afghan Hound named Kabul. Pictures of Kabul with Picasso and his friend Jacqueline at Vauvenargues Chateau in 1962 have been widely touted by Afghanites. There are many who claim that Picasso's 40-ton structure, five-stories high, at Chicago's Civic Center Plaza is his interpretation of an Afghan Hound. It is Picasso's only civic monument in North America and was a gift to that city. Some liken it to a baboon, others seem to have labeled it with the title of

Entitled *Hound of the Feast,* this oil painting by Vic Tor was the May, 1974 cover of *Our Afghans* magazine. Mr. Tor's studio is in Lake Worth, Florida. The artist is well-known for his paintings, which are shown in many countries of the world at gallerys and private showings. This *Hound of the Feast* painting relates to the ancient custom in Afghanistan of decorating the Afghan Hounds as a tribute to their herding abilities.

Artist Vic Tor and one of his Afghan models relax in his Lake Worth, Florida, studio. Mr. Tor owns two Afghan Hounds which he uses as models for his paintings. The one in the photograph with him is Zahrin; not shown is Ali Ben Zahrin. Mr. Tor is a graduate of the Art Institute of Chicago.

Artist Elizabeth Harvey Treharne is shown in her New Jersey studio doing a pastel of the famous showdog Ch. Ali Khyber. This photo was taken in 1944. In the 1970's Mrs. Treharne still has a thriving business, including painting of the Afghan greats and creating a complete line of stationery and paintings on glass.

369

a woman. Picasso never revealed what it really was. . . So, as the ancient hieroglyphics, the Picasso work shall remain what it represents in the eye of the beholder.

The Museum of Modern Art in New York has a Picasso with a title supplied by the artist which simplifies matters considerably. It is entitled "Girl With Dog" and the dog is easily and definitely identifiable as an Afghan Hound! There is also the very distinct possibility that Picasso owned more than one Afghan Hound over the years. Pictures listing the name of the dog as Kabul indicate a Hound of much heavier stature than the one shown in those photographs where the name is given as Kazbek. A picture of the dog on the floor of the artist's Paris Studio in 1941 was obviously showing the ravages of war-time food rationing. Also, it would have made the 1962 Kabul a very old Afghan Hound!

NANCY TURNER REA

The exquisite work of the young Nancy Turner Rea is well known within our breed and to the art world in general. While Nancy's beginning work centered mainly around animals, she is now including people with the animals. Among the most beautiful is her self-portrait with her Afghan Hound, done in oils with marvelous technique for so young an artist. Her "The Baby Sitter" features a Bulldog and "A Dog's Best Friend" features a Basset Hound, both shown with little children. Her little oriental boy with his six month old Afghan Hound puppy is marvelous.

Nancy was born on a farm in the Kentucky mountains, and her sensitivity in portraying animals obviously stems from her childhood in the bluegrass country. She has had many one-woman shows and has won many awards in the art world. Her paintings can be seen in several select galleries and she is a member of the American Institute of Fine Arts. One of her recent commissions resulted in a magnificent oil for Philip and Dolores Haims, which was featured on the color cover of the December 1975 issue of the *Afghan*

Opposite:
This 40-ton sculpture by Picasso stands in front of Chicago's Civic Center. While Picasso never titled the piece, there are many who maintain that it is an Afghan Hound.

Artist Nancy Turner Rea poses outside her home with her Aladdin of Scheherezade. Bred by Kathleen O'Brien and Wallace Pede, Aladdin's sire was Ch. Shangrila's Pharoah Uhuru *ex* Ch. Kleopatra of Scheherezade, C.D.

This self-portrait of the artist in repose with her Shahndi of Scheherezade is one of the recent paintings of Nancy Turner Rea. This magnificent 30" by 40" work was on exhibition at many prominent galleries all over the United States since being rendered by this talented young artist.

This head study model is of Ch. Patrician Tulu-I D'Khardahn, made by Bossons of England. This picture is of the first wall plaque from the original mold that was sent to owner Mrs. Helen Cardan of Sherman Oaks, California, by Mr. W. Ray Bossons. Special permission was given to include it in this book.

Hound Review magazine. Her Christmas card entitled "Peace" depicts an Afghan Hound discovering a rabbit beneath a Christmas tree and is part of the 1976 line of Mary Rogers Productions.

Among the collections of Afghan art we are apt to find lovely pieces by an artist named Jane Callendar. Jane's work is characterized by solid figures with portions of the dogs done with hair-like attachments that are highly breakable. Jane also does all breeds, not strictly Afghan Hounds.

Years ago, Hazel Kovacs did some fine Afghan Hound figurines. I am pleased to say the work of these creamic artists is included in my collection along with several pieces which are not identified in any way. The signatures on these pieces are too small to make an accurate identification. It is a shame that these artists can not be given proper credit because these figures are very beautiful and were obviously done by artists who knew and loved our breed.

CAROL MOORLAND MARSHALL

Carol Moorland Marshall was first and foremost a portrait painter and concert pianist, later deciding to create her own collection of dog models. Starting with her own breeds, Borzoi and Whippets, she now has every intent of continuing her work until she has created a model of each and every breed!

One of her earliest efforts was the Afghan Hound. She has produced both single models and beautiful groupings that now reside in the private collections of Afghan Hound fanciers all over the country.

These exquisite "noodle" and "hair" sculptures were made by the husband and wife team of Judy and Orvel Sternberg of Dallas, Texas. Much in demand as trophies as well as for private collections, these highly stylized figurines are appropriately mounted on rock, wood or calcite formations to add to their beauty but keep them within the "under one hundred dollars" price category.

Carol's work was first sold in Abercrombie and Fitch, but later was seen at Cartiers as well. Because of their true representation of the breed Standard, her figurines are much in demand as trophies at dog shows as well as for collections in this country, Canada and England. A Basenji model, made in the likeness of Princess Alexandra's dog, "resides" at the Palace in Monaco! Her exhibition at the Bruce Museum in Greenwich, Connecticut, in July, 1971 was an enormous success.

OSAH

Osah is the kennel name adopted by Judy and Orvel Sternberg of Dallas, Texas, but they are certainly better known as the artists creating the fabulous "string" and "noodle" sculptures of Afghan Hounds. They call their studio "The Hair," and all of their distinctive original sculptures of our breed are gloriously mounted on river rock, wood, quartz or crystalized geodes, etc.

Judy is known specifically for the "string" sculptures which are mounted on petrified wood, quartz, calcite, etc., or enclosed in glass within a brass case. Each hair on the dog is hand rolled and made of durable rubber-like clay and fired.

Orvel is the "noodle" artist, with most of his work mounted on river rock. In the near future they will be creating sculptures in porcelain and stoneware so that they may use glazes as well. Since all the sculptures are priced under one hundred dollars, you can well imagine that they are in much demand by private collectors and are often used as trophies at the major specialty shows.

Judy and Orvel first got interested in Afghan Hounds when Orvel's parents gave them an Afghan Hound as a wedding present. The dog was shown from time to time and their interest in the breed heightened. In 1973 they bred Orvel's mother's bitch, Princess Rubaiyat, to Ch. Summerwine's Cuba Libra, a mating that produced three puppies. They kept two and co-own the third with Kathie Ware. All three are being campaigned during the mid-seventies and the one named Rhubarb has already finished his coursing championship.

Their great love and regard for Afghan Hounds is seen in their marvelous sculpture. While extreme and exaggerated to the nth degree of style, the grace and beauty inherent in the breed is presented to perfection!

Other modern day artists that work in

This magnificent hand sculptured Afghan Hound is in the collection of artist Marcia Van Woert, who uses the title *Originals by MosH*.

many mediums, from oils to pen and ink, include Virginia Szekula, Conni Nibarger, Sandy Samardick, Bonita Rabull, Nan Schneider, Elaine Shaw, Cheryl Horn and Nancy Carolyn Wood. Marcia Van Woert is another and signs herself "Mosh." Susan Bahary is one of the latest to try her hand at ceramic figurines and her first Afghan Hound model is *truly* a work of art!

MARY ROGERS

While Mary Rogers of Santa Ana, California, will tell you that she herself is not an artist, she is certainly responsible for *presenting* many of today's top artists featuring the Afghan Hound as an expression of their work.

Mary finds an artist whose designs she admires and purchases them for reproduction and marketing under her title. Sometimes these are in the form of logos or kennel stationery, but her distinctive line includes cocktail napkins, calendars, sweatshirts, aprons, needlepoint, wall hangings, Christmas cards, and the like. Some of her artists are James Conrad, Kurt Kroll, Peter Belmont, R. Garnham Elmore, Nancy Rea, Marianne Wilt, George Mason and Tutti Rogers.

Most items are handscreened at her Rogers Productions and are all popular items that are becoming more and more recognizable within the entire dog fancy, not just within our breed. All are copyrighted, of course, and owned by her or those who have purchased designs from her.

LEATHERWORK

Years back Kay Finch had a magnificent tooled leather handbag which she took with her on judging assignments in Europe and had all her Afghan friends autograph it for a keepsake of her trip. Many names still well-known in the breed were written across that excellent piece of work.

Leatherwork continues to grow in popularity and Santarelli Enterprises in California and customwork by Glenn in Colorado feature the breed in or on their leatherwork.

THE AFGHAN HOUND IN BRONZE

Once again, Kay Finch must be credited for her exquisite work in bronze. The most famous of which is undoubtedly the full-figure of Marion Florsheim's immortal Int. Ch. Rudiki of Pride's Hill, mentioned earlier. Mrs. Florsheim at one time also owned an excellent bronze of Ch. Tufan of Ainsdart.

June Hurrah, who had a studio just off Third Avenue in New York City, was known for her bronzes of horses and champion show dogs. Many showings of her work have been on display around the Westminster Kennel Club Show at the National Art Museum of Sport at the Madison Square Garden Center Gallery of Art in New York. She also works in gold, sterling, watercolor and oils.

After the death of Mrs. Geraldine Dodge and the subsequent auction of the hundreds of

Artist Carol Moorland Marshall's rendering of an Afghan Hound and mallard ducks. This piece is from the collection of the author.

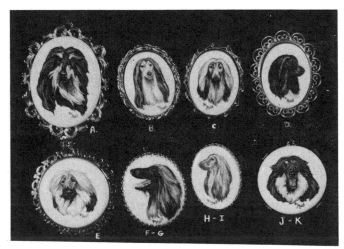

Lovely Afghan Hound portraits on enamel jewelry are made by Marcia Van Woert, who signs her beautiful work *Originals by MosH.*

A hand-screened Garnham Elmore design for a Christmas card series is copyrighted by Mary Rogers.

374

bronzes she possessed, it was most unfortunate to see that there was not a single Afghan Hound represented among them! During her lifetime, on many occasions, I fervently wished that the favor of this great dog woman would eventually settle on our breed. Had this been the case, I am sure she might have commissioned one!

Today, in the 1970's, we can all enjoy the beautiful bronzes of Ric Chashoudian. As of 1976 he had not included an Afghan Hound in the breeds available so far, but he certainly is our hope for the future! If his current models are any indication, we can look forward to another marvelous piece for our collections.

AFGHAN HOUND JEWELRY

The name Drago of Dallas is synonymous with beautiful Afghan Hound jewelry! The marvelous work executed by its creator, Monroe Jackson of Dallas, Texas, has earned him prizes at countless state fairs and has earned him a very special place in the art world. There is hardly an ardent fancier in the breed who doesn't own at least one of the exquisite pieces of Drago jewelry.

Metal sculpture by Johanna Tanner of the Xanadu Kennels in Friendswood, Texas, is always in demand! This particular piece was the Best of Breed trophy at a 1975 Dallas specialty show. Her work is frequently commissioned as trophies for specialty shows as well as by private collectors.

Drago of Dallas are the creators of the world's largest collection (and selection!) of Afghan Hound jewelry, including pieces that are the ultimate in artistry! Encrusted or set with tigereyes, turquoise, etc., these sterling silver pieces range in price from under $100 on up to $700. The pieces at right start at $300 and range up to $675.

The Drago jewelry runs from tie tacs and silver pins all the way up to complicated pieces encrusted with rare gems and costing many hundreds of dollars. Monroe Jackson works in silver, brass, with beads, and at one time produced some ceramic figurines.

Jackson and his wife own the Summerwine Kennels and are breeders and exhibitors of prize-winning Afghan Hounds. It seems only natural that their accent is on Afghan Hound jewelry, but there are Borzoi and Saluki pieces as well.

Jim, Lee and Mike Canalizo of Freeport, Long Island, New York, are also designers and makers of rare and unusual Afghan Hound jewelry. They also own Afghan Hounds and Lee has become an Afghan Hound judge, so their particular feeling for this breed is what comes through so well in their unusual pieces. Necklaces and bracelets predominate their collection and many are studded with stones in modernistic settings.

Beau-J Creations in Colorado also advertise a line of Afghan Hound jewelry, as do many modern commercial jewelry lines whose pins are seen adorning Afghanites wherever you go.

The Afghan Hound jewelry worn by Kay Finch is always a topic of conversation, many created from Kay's own designs and made in the materials of her choice. The most beautiful piece is the gold Crown Crest Afghan Hound insignia set with peridots which was a present from Braden Finch before his death.

THE AFGHAN HOUND ON FABRICS

In 1956 Kay Finch created a fabric design which was so popular it was soon reproduced on skirts, dresses, handkerchiefs and scarves, notepaper, towels, and so on. The fabric also enjoyed popularity as a bench decoration. Since then, other artists have done Afghan Hound caricatures in silkscreen. In 1976 Peter Belmont produced a magnificently colored Batik print of an Afghan Hound.

AFGHAN HOUND NEEDLEWORK

The 1970's were the years that saw the coming of the needlepoint craze! It was only natural that the Afghan Hound would lend itself to this medium as well, and many designs appeared. Virginia Szekula produced a lovely headstudy marketed by Cliff Toye's ETC Enterprises in New Jersey, and Mary Rogers also had designs available for needlepoint enthusiasts. Mary Dee Huntsman of

Poetry in motion. These two Afghan Hounds are created both as a pin and on bracelets by the prize-winning Drago of Dallas jewelry firm. It is evident by the typical Afghan art he turns out that Monroe Jackson owns Afghan Hounds himself.

This magnificent gold jeweled Afghan Hound pin was given to Kay Finch by her husband Braden before his death. Kay had the pin copied as a tie tack for him. After Braden's death Kay presented the tie tack to her friend Rodrigo Quevedo to commemorate the judging of his first specialty show. The significance of the gesture brought Rodrigo to tears and he regards it as one of his most cherished possessions.

Variations on a theme. These two renditions in needlepoint were done by the author from Virginia Szuleka's design that is distributed by Etc. Enterprizes.

Mrs. William Waskow and one of the Afghan Hounds from her Little Fir Kennels in Madison, Wisconsin, pose in front of the state capitol building in their Afghan coats! Mrs. Waskow's coat is made from hair from her dogs, and was carded, spun, woven, cut and sewn by her friend Donna Ellis. Afghan hair has been used for sweaters, but this was the first it was seen as a full coat. The finished cloth has a texture resembling cashmere and is exceptionally soft and warm.

Brookville, Ohio, also created Afghan Hound wall hangings in crewel.

Some of the most exquisite needlepoint ever seen were designed and executed by Dale Levaque, and were donated for trophies in 1974 when I judged at the Dallas Afghan Hound Specialty Show.

PHOTOGRAPHIC ARTISTRY

Let us not forget the art involved in properly capturing the beauty of the Afghan Hound on film!

Retouching aside, the presentation of our dog in photographs is as much an art as the

Afghan Hound statue in terra cotta, and built by Joy Madden, Jamaden Afghans, Bradenton, Florida.

other mediums and deserves its proper recognition.

In the earliest days famous show dogs were taken by their proud owners to regular portrait photographers whose entire clientele consisted of human subjects. Dog photographers, per se, were unheard of. Suddenly men like "Brownie" and Tauskey and Jones appeared on the scene and we began to see our dogs in a new light. The photographer's eye recognized the strong points of each dog and put the emphasis on their finer points to create truly fine pictures of those early dogs. The importance of photographing at its best to further enhance its show career became very important to owners campaigning dogs.

The artistry of Evelyn Shafer, who could appear in a show ring and within a matter of seconds pick out a perfect stance for a dog and

This Afghan
Hound drawing
by Elaine Shaw
is from a limited
edition signed
by the artist. The
complete
portfolio
consisting of 6
drawings is
entitled *Afghans
. . . caught in the
act of being
themselves.*

make the proper noises to catch its interest, has given us a permanent record of several decades of America's show dogs. The same applies to Joan Ludwig on the West Coast whose famous "tossing" of a catalogue in the air has put the proper alert expression on many a show dog. Years ago Athos Nilson took some beautiful shots, and Ylla did also.

The lens artistry of William Gilbert and William Ashbey carry on now in the East. Evelyn Shafer has retired. Missy Yuhl, Bobbi Caminez, Ritter, Toberts, Bennett Associates, Frasie, Graham, Laconte, Norton of Kent, Lloyd Olson, Booth, Petrulis, Schley, Twomey and Sal Miceli have all contributed much beauty to our fancy. Steve Klein, and Frank and Francis have carried on over the years.

All are due a vote of thanks for giving us a lasting record of our great dogs.

THE AFGHAN HOUND ON STAMPS

Many of the foreign nations, especially Eastern Europe and the middle-Eastern countries, derive a great deal of revenue each year by issuing stamps commemorating the culture and industries of their lands. With today's social consciousness so strongly geared to the preservation of wildlife and ecology, we are finding more and more of the issues being concentrated on animals. Realizing how dog-oriented the people of the world have become there has been a great plethora of stamp sets devoted to canines, and many of the dog stamps feature our Afghan Hound.

A magnificent portrait by Marjorie Walker of the late Marion Foster Florsheim's great Int. Ch. Rudiki of Pride's Hill, rendered in 1941.

Created by Richard M. Mauro of Bay Shore, New York, this exquisite statue is from the collection of Werner and Mary Sheldon.

Artist and Afghan Hound owner Richard M. Mauro created this magnificent piece as a Best of Breed trophy for the 1974 Afghan Hound Club of America Specialty Show. Mr. Mauro is from Bay Shore, Long Island, New York.

Kay Finch is out and about at Crown Crest with some of her dogs on the grounds overlooking the canyon and the blue Pacific. This marvelous setting is the home of Afghans, Salukis and Whippets—all winning under the Crown Crest banner!

Chapter XVII

Breeding Your Afghan Hound

Let us assume the time has come for your dog to be bred, and you have decided you are in a position to enjoy producing a litter of puppies that you hope will make a contribution to the breed. The bitch you purchased is sound, her temperament is excellent and she is a most worthy representative of the breed.

You have a calendar and counted off the ten days since the first day of red staining and have determined the tenth to fourteenth day, which will more than likely be the best days for the actual mating. You have additionally counted off 60 to 65 days before the puppies are likely to be born to make sure everything necessary for their arrival will be in good order by that time.

From the moment the idea of having a litter occurred to you, your thoughts should have been given to the correct selection of a proper stud. Here again, the novice would do well to seek advice on analyzing pedigrees and tracing bloodlines for the best breedings. As soon as the bitch is in season and you see color (or staining) and a swelling of the vulva, it is time to notify the owner of the stud you selected and make appointments for the breedings. There are several pertinent questions you will want to ask the stud owners after having decided upon the pedigree. The owners, naturally, will also have a few questions they wish to ask you. These questions will concern your bitch's bloodlines, health, age, how many previous litters she's had, if any, etc.

THE POWER IN PEDIGREES

Someone in the dog fancy once remarked that the definition of a show prospect puppy is one third the pedigree, one third what you see and one third what you *hope* it will be! Well, no matter how you break down your qualifying fractions, we all quite agree that good breeding is essential if you have any plans at all for a show career for your dog! Many breeders will buy on pedigree alone, counting largely on what they themselves can do with the puppy by way of feeding, conditioning and training. Needless to say, that very important piece of paper commonly referred to as the pedigree is mighty reassuring to a breeder or buyer new at the game or to one who has a breeding program in mind and is trying to establish his own bloodline.

One of the most fascinating aspects of tracing pedigrees is the way the names of the really great dogs of the past keep appearing in the pedigrees of the great dogs of today—positive proof of the strong influence of heredity and witness to a great deal of truth in the statement that great dogs frequently reproduce themselves, though not necessarily in appearance only. A pedigree represents something of value when one is dedicated to breeding better dogs.

To the novice buyer or one who is perhaps merely switching to another breed and sees only a frolicking, leggy, squirming bundle of energy in a fur coat, a pedigree can mean everything! To those of us who believe in heredity, a pedigree is more like an insurance policy—so always read them carefully and take heed!

For the even more serious breeder of today who wishes to make a further study of bloodlines in relation to his breeding program, the American Kennel Club library stud books can and should be consulted.

This mother and daughter are such look-alikes that this could almost be a reflection in a mirror! On the left is Khamelot's Portia Panache and Ch. Elmo's Pajourah is on the right. Portia is owned by Gordon McDowell IV and Pajourah is owned by Susan Bahary.

THE HEALTH OF THE BREEDING STOCK

Some of your first questions should concern whether or not the stud has already proved himself by siring a normal healthy litter. Also inquire as to whether or not the owners have had a sperm count made to determine just exactly how fertile or potent the stud is. Determine for yourself whether the dog has two normal testicles.

When considering your bitch for this mating, you must take into consideration a few important points that lead to a successful breeding. You and the owner of the stud will want to recall whether she has had normal heat cycles, whether there were too many runts in the litter and whether a Caesarean section was ever necessary. Has she ever had a vaginal infection? Could she take care of her puppies by herself, or was there a milk shortage? How many surviving puppies were there from the litter, and what did they grow up to be in comparison to the requirements of the breed Standard?

Don't buy a bitch that has problems in heat and has never had a live litter. Don't be afraid, however, to buy a healthy maiden bitch, since chances are, if she is healthy and from good stock, she will be a healthy producer. Don't buy a monorchid male, and certainly not a cryptorchid. If there is any doubt in your mind about his potency, get a sperm count from the veterinarian. Older dogs that have been good producers and are for sale are usually not too hard to find at good established kennels. If they are not too old and have sired quality show puppies, they can give you some excellent show stock from which to establish your own breeding lines.

WHEN TO BREED A GROWN BITCH

The best advice used to be not until her second heat. Today with our new scientific knowledge, we have become acutely aware of such things as hip dysplasia, juvenile cateracts and other congenital diseases. The best advice now seems to be aimed at not breeding your dogs before two years of age when both the bitch and the sire have been examined by qualified veterinarians and declared—in writing—free and clear of these conditions.

THE DAY OF THE MATING

Now that you have decided upon the proper male and female combination to produce what you hope will be—according to the pedigrees—a fine litter of puppies, it is time to set the date. You have selected the two days (with a one day lapse in between) that you feel are best for the breeding, and you call the owner of the stud. The bitch always goes to the stud, unless, of course, there are extenuating circumstances. You set the date and the time and arrive with the bitch *and* the money.

Standard procedure is payment of a stud fee at the time of the first breeding, if there is a tie. For the stud fee, you are entitled to two breedings with ties. Contracts may be written up with specific conditions on breeding terms, of course, but this is general procedure. Often a breeder will take the pick of a litter to protect and maintain his bloodlines; this can be especially desirable if he needs an outcross for his breeding program or if he wishes to continue his own bloodlines if he sold you the bitch to start with, and this mating will continue his line-breeding program. This should all be worked out ahead of time and written and signed before the two dogs are bred. Remember that the payment of the stud fee is for the services of the stud—not for a guarantee of a litter of puppies. This is why it is so important to make sure you are using a proven stud. Bear in mind also that the American Kennel Club will not register a litter of puppies sired by a male that is under eight months of age. In the case of an older dog, they will not register a litter sired by a dog over 12 years of age, unless there is a witness to the breeding in the form of a veterinarian or other responsible person.

Many studs over 12 years of age are still fertile and capable of producing puppies, but if you do not witness the breeding there is always the danger of a "substitute" stud being used to produce a litter. This brings up the subject of sending your bitch away to be bred if you cannot accompany her.

The disadvantages of sending a bitch away to be bred are numerous. First of all, she will not be herself in a strange place, so she'll be difficult to handle. Transportation, if she goes by air (while reasonably safe), is still

Ch. Majara Mahabat, one of the great Afghan Hounds from Marjorie Lathrop's world-famous Majara Kennels. A Best In Show dog and producer of fine show puppies, Mahabat was one of the potent forces in an unbroken line of six generations of Best In Show winners bred at Majara Kennels in Somerville, New Jersey.

383

a traumatic experience. There is always the danger of her being put off at the wrong airport, not being fed or watered properly, etc. Some bitches get so upset that they go out of season and the trip, which may prove expensive, especially on top of a substantial stud fee, will have been for nothing.

If at all possible, accompany your bitch so that the experience is as comfortable for her as it can be. In other words, make sure before setting this kind of schedule for a breeding that there is no stud in the area that might be as good for her as the one that is far away. Don't sacrifice the proper breeding for convenience, since bloodlines are so important, but put the safety of the bitch above all else. There is always a risk in traveling, since dogs are considered cargo on a plane.

The lovely Ch. Hope was the dam of 12 champions as of 1964. A daughter of the fabulous Ch. Taejon of Crown Crest, Hope is the dam of Int. Ch. Crown Crest Mr. Universe, who in turn is the sire of 23 champions as of August, 1964. She was owned by Kay Finch, Crown Crest Kennels, Corona del Mar, California.

Ch. Jester of of Longlesson, sire of 3 champions. Jester was the stud force at the Longlesson's kennel during the late 1950's. He was sired by Ch. Roseclydes Omar Khan *ex* Ch. Turkafa of Grandeur.

HOW MUCH DOES THE STUD FEE COST?

The stud fee will vary considerably—the better the bloodlines, the more winning the dog does at shows, the higher the fee. Stud service from a top winning dog could run up to $500.00. Here again, there may be exceptions. Some breeders will take part cash and then, say, third pick of the litter. The fee can be arranged by a private contract rather than the traditional procedure we have described.

Here again, it is wise to get the details of the payment of the stud fee in writing to avoid trouble.

THE ACTUAL MATING

It is always advisable to muzzle the bitch. A terrified bitch may fear-bite the stud, or even one of the people involved, and the wild or maiden bitch may snap or attack the stud, to the point where he may become discouraged and lose interest in the breeding. Muzzling can be done with a lady's stocking tied around the muzzle with a half knot, crossed under the chin and knotted at the back of the neck. There is enough "give" in the stocking for her to breathe or salivate freely and yet not open her jaws far enough to bite. Place her in front of her owner, who

A mother and daughter siesta at Charles Farley's Kumar Kennels in California. The proud and protective mother is Ami of Kumar and the slightly demure daughter is Kala of Kumar.

holds onto her collar and talks to her and calms her as much as possible.

If the male will not mount on his own initiative, it may be necessary for the owner to assist in lifting him onto the bitch, perhaps even in guiding him to the proper place. Usually, the tie is accomplished once the male gets the idea. The owner should remain close at hand, however, to make sure the tie is not broken before an adequate breeding has been completed. After a while the stud may get bored, and try to break away. This could prove injurious. It may be necessary to hold him in place until the tie is broken.

We must stress at this point that while some bitches carry on physically, and vocally, during the tie, there is no way the bitch can

be hurt. However, a stud can be seriously or even permanently damaged by a bad breeding. Therefore, the owner of the bitch must be reminded that she must not be alarmed by any commotion. All concentration should be devoted to the stud and a successful and properly executed service.

Many people believe that breeding dogs is simply a matter of placing two dogs, a male and a female, in close proximity, and letting nature take its course. While often this is true, you cannot count on it. Sometimes it is hard work, and in the case of valuable stock it is essential to supervise to be sure of the safety factor, especially if one or both of the dogs are inexperienced. If the owners are also inexperienced, it may not take place at all!

ARTIFICIAL INSEMINATION

Breeding by means of artificial insemination is usually unsuccessful, unless under a veterinarian's supervision, and can lead to an infection for the bitch and discomfort for the dog. The American Kennel Club requires a veterinarian's certificate to register puppies from such a breeding. Although the practice has been used for over two decades, it now offers new promise, since research has been conducted to make it a more feasible procedure for the future.

Good morning! Young Master James checks out a litter of Spectrum puppies at the kennels of his parents, Art and Inger James in Vancouver, Canada.

Great dogs may eventually look forward to reproducing themselves years after they have left this earth. There now exists a frozen semen concept that has been tested and found successful. The study, headed by Dr. Stephen W.J. Seager, M.V.B., an instructor at the University of Oregon Medical School, has the financial support of the American Kennel Club, indicating that organization's interest in the work. The study is being monitored by the Morris Animal Foundation of Denver, Colorado.

Dr. Seager announced in 1970 that he had been able to preserve dog semen and to produce litters with the stored semen. The possibilities of selective world-wide breedings by this method are exciting. Imagine simply mailing a vial of semen to the bitch! The perfection of line-breeding by storing semen without the threat of death interrupting the breeding program is exciting also.

As it stands today, the technique for artificial insemination requires the depositing of semen (taken directly from the dog) into the bitch's vagina, past the cervix and into the uterus by syringe. The correct temperature of the semen is vital, and there is no guarantee of success. The storage method, if successfully adopted, will present a new era in the field of purebred dogs.

THE GESTATION PERIOD

Once the breeding has taken place successfully, the seemingly endless waiting period of about 63 days begins. For the first ten days after the breeding, you do absolutely nothing for the bitch—just spin dreams about the delights you will share with the family when the puppies arrive.

Around the tenth day it is time to begin supplementing the diet of the bitch with vitamins and calcium. We strongly recommend that you take her to your veterinarian for a list of the proper or perhaps necessary supplements and the correct amounts of each for your particular bitch. Guesses, which may lead to excesses or insufficiencies, can ruin a litter. For the price of a visit to your veterinarian, you will be confident that you are feeding properly.

The bitch should be free of worms, of course, and if there is any doubt in your mind, she should be wormed now, before the third week of pregnancy. Your veterinarian will advise you on the necessity of this and proper dosage as well.

PROBING FOR PUPPIES

Far too many breeders are overanxious about whether the breeding "took" and are inclined to feel for puppies or persuade a veterinarian to radiograph or X-ray their bitches to confirm it. Unless there is reason to doubt the normalcy of a pregnancy, this is risky. Certainly 63 days are not too long to wait, and why risk endangering the litter by probing with your inexperienced hands? Few bitches give no evidence of being in whelp, and there is no need to prove it for yourself by trying to count puppies.

ALERTING YOUR VETERINARIAN

At least a week before the puppies are due, you should telephone your veterinarian and notify him that you expect the litter and give him the date. This way he can make sure

At the 1972 Afghan Hound Club of California Specialty Show judge Dr. Gerda Kennedy awarded first in the Brood Bitch Class to Ch. Pandora's Xotica of Stormhill, pictured here with her get, Ch. Majestic Knight of Stormhill and Ch. Sno-Foolin' of Stormhill. Breeder-owners are Virginia and Sandy Withington.

that there will be someone available to help, should there by any problems during the whelping. Most veterinarians today have answering services and alternative vets on call when they are not available themselves. Some veterinarians suggest that you call them when the bitch starts labor so that they may further plan their time, should they be needed. Discuss this matter with your veterinarian when you first take the bitch to him for her diet instructions, etc., and establish the method which will best fit in with his schedule.

DO YOU NEED A VETERINARIAN IN ATTENDANCE?

Even if this is your first litter, I would advise that you go through the experience of whelping without panicking and calling desperately for the veterinarian. Most animal births are accomplished without complications, and you should call for assistance only if you run into trouble.

When having her puppies, your bitch will appreciate as little interference and as few strangers around as possible. A quiet place, with her nest, a single familiar face and her own instincts are all that is necessary for nature to take its course. An audience of curious children squealing and questioning,

other family pets nosing around, or strange adults should be avoided. Many a bitch which has been distracted in this way has been known to devour her young. This can be the horrible result of intrusion into the bitch's privacy. There are other ways of teaching children the miracle of birth, and there will be plenty of time later for the whole family to enjoy the puppies. Let them be born under proper and considerate circumstances.

LABOR

Some litters—many first litters—do not run the full term of 63 days. So, at least a week before the puppies are actually due, and at the time you alert your veterinarian as to their arrival, start observing the bitch for signs of the commencement of labor. This will manifest itself in the form of ripples running down the sides of her body, which will come as a revelation to her as well. It is most noticeable when she is lying on her side—and she will be sleeping a great deal as the arrival date comes closer. If she is sitting or walking about, she will perhaps sit down quickly or squat peculiarly. As the ripples become more frequent, birth time is drawing near, you will be wise not to leave her. Usually within 24

Patrician Sharonne appears engulfed by her record litter of 15 surviving puppies which were whelped in 1960 at Elizabeth Harvey Treharne's Robecli Kennels. The sire was Kakasha Larchtree, and this photograph shows the puppies at two weeks of age.

hours before whelping she will stop eating, and as much as a week before she will begin digging a nest. The bitch should be given something resembling a whelping box with layers of newspaper (black and white only) to make her nest. She will dig more and more as birth approaches, and this is the time to begin making your promise to stop interfering unless your help is specifically required. Some bitches whimper and others are silent, but whimpering does not necessarily indicate trouble.

THE ARRIVAL OF THE PUPPIES

The sudden gush of green fluid from the bitch indicates that the water or fluid surrounding the puppies has "broken" and they are about to start down the canal and come into the world. When the water breaks, birth of the first puppy is imminent. The first puppies are usually born within minutes to a half hour of each other, but a couple of hours be-

tween the later ones is not uncommon. If you notice the bitch straining constantly without producing a puppy, or if a puppy remains partially in and partially out for too long, it is cause for concern. Breech births (puppies born feet first instead of head first) can often cause delay or hold things up, and this is often a problem which requires veterinarian assistance.

FEEDING THE BITCH
BETWEEN BIRTHS

Usually the bitch will not be interested in food for about 24 hours before the arrival of the puppies, and perhaps as long as two or three days after their arrival. The placenta which she cleans up after each puppy is high in food value and will be more than ample to sustain her. This is nature's way of allowing the mother to feed herself and her babies without having to leave the nest and hunt for food during the first crucial days. The mother always cleans up all traces of birth in the wilds so as not to attract other animals to her newborn babies.

However, there are those of us who believe in making food available should the mother feel the need to restore her strength during or after delivery—especially if she whelps a large litter. Raw chopmeat, beef boullion and milk are all acceptable and may be placed near the whelping box during the first two or three days. After that, the mother will begin to put the babies on a sort of schedule. She will leave the whelping box at frequent intervals, take longer exercise periods and begin to take interest in other things. This is where the fun begins for you. Now the babies are no longer soggy little pinkish blobs. They begin to crawl around and squeal and hum and grow before your very eyes!

It is at this time, if all has gone normally, that the family can be introduced gradually and great praise and affection given to the mother.

BREECH BIRTHS

Puppies normally are delivered head first. However, some are presented feet first or in other abnormal positions, and this is referred to as a "breech birth." Assistance is often necessary to get the puppy out of the canal, and great care must be taken not to injure the puppy or the dam.

Aid can be given by grasping the puppy with a piece of turkish toweling and pulling gently during the dam's contractions. Be careful not to squeeze the puppy too hard; merely try to ease it out by moving it gently back and forth. Because even this much delay in delivery may mean the puppy is drowning, do not wait for the bitch to remove the sac. Do it yourself by tearing the sac open to expose the face and head. Then cut the cord anywhere from one-half to three-quarters of an inch away from the navel. If the cord bleeds excessively, pinch the end of it with your fingers and count five. Repeat if necessary. Then pry open the mouth with your finger and hold the puppy upside-down for a moment to drain any fluids from the lungs. Next, rub the puppy briskly with turkish or paper toweling. You should get it wriggling and whimpering by this time.

If the litter is large, this assistance will help conserve the strength of the bitch and will probably be welcomed by her. However,

it is best to allow her to take care of at least the first few herself to preserve the natural instinct and to provide the nutritive values obtained by her consumption of the one or more of the afterbirths as nature intended.

DRY BIRTHS

Occasionally the sac will break before the delivery of a puppy and will be expelled while the puppy remains inside, thereby depriving the dam of the necessary lubrication to expel the puppy normally. Inserting vaseline or mineral oil via your finger will help the puppy pass down the birth canal. This is why it is essential that you be present during the whelping—so that you can count puppies and afterbirths and determine when and if assistance is needed.

THE TWENTY-FOUR HOUR CHECKUP

It is smart to have a veterinarian check the mother and her puppies within 24 hours after the last puppy is born. The vet can check

Ch. Balkhwood's Grey Ghost is pictured winning at a show in the 1960's with his handler, Jerry Rigden. The dog was owned by Mr. Anthony Cipolla of Erie, Pennsylvania.

Salem Gunpowder is pictured winning under judge Gordon Carvill at a recent show. Gunpowder is handled by his owner, Joe Inguaggiato, Jebel Musa Afghans, Rochester, New York.

The outstanding quality of the famous Rudiki of Pride's Hill was evident even as a young dog. He is shown here at the beginning of his career when he was owned by Hayes Blake Hoyt.

Winner of the Hound Group at a show a few years back was Ch. El Mari Zhorro. The judge was Kenneth Given and presenting the trophy is Mrs. Shorb Steele. Zhorro is owned by Mary P. Moss.

Ch. Khabira Blue, a breed-winner from the classes over specials. Sired by Ch. Khabiri of Grandeur ex Ch. Khabiri Shady Lady, "The Mouse" is pictured here at 1 year of age with Jennifer Sheldon, daughter of her breeder-owners, Mary and Werner Sheldon, Massapequa, New York.

Ch. Cindy's Brass Replica of Vista is pictured winning under judge William Kendrick. He was handled by Parker Harris for owners Joe and Lill Inguaggiato of Rochester, New York. Unfortunately the dog was stolen from the Inguaggiato's in January, 1972.

Can., Am. and Bda. Ch. Torrent of Rokeish, a lovely black-masked red bitch, was owned by Susan Ball of the Rokeish Kennels in Canada. She was co-bred by Ms. Ball and William Milne. Torrent is the dam of 5 champions, and is a Group and Specialty winner in Canada. She completed her American championship with a Best of Breed from the classes.

Two of June Boone's lovely Afghan Hounds, Bon-Dir and Nina-Nerina, pose especially for the camera. June is the owner of the Kassan Kennels in Kokomo, Indiana.

the puppies for cleft palates or umbilical hernia and may wish to give the dam—particularly if she is a show dog—an injection of Pituitin to make sure of the expulsion of all afterbirths and to tighten up the uterus. This can prevent a sagging belly after the puppies are weaned and the bitch is being readied for the show ring.

FALSE PREGNANCY

The disappointment of a false pregnancy is almost as bad for the owner as it is for the bitch. She goes through the gestation period with all the symptoms—swollen stomach, increased appetite, swollen nipples—even makes a nest when the time comes. You may even take an oath that you noticed the ripples on her body from the labor pains. Then, just as suddenly as you made up your mind that she was definitely going to have puppies, you will know that she definitely is not! She may walk around carrying a toy as if it were a puppy for a few days, but she will soon be back to normal and acting just as if nothing happened—and nothing did!

CAESAREAN SECTION

Should the whelping reach the point where there is complication, such as the bitch's not being capable of whelping the

Ch. Crown Crest Topaz, owned by Gordon and Conni Miller of California. One of the famous Gem Litter bred by Kay Finch, Toby was a top show winner in his own right, and has made his mark as a sire of champions.

One of the truly great Afghan Hounds, Ch. Coastwind Gazebo, was handled for his owners, the Coastwind Kennels in California, by Marvin Gates. This photograph shows the "classic silhouette" of the truly beautiful Afghan Hound.

puppies herself, the "moment of truth" is upon you and a Caesarean section may be necessary. The bitch may be too small or too immature to expel the puppies herself, her cervix may fail to dilate enough to allow the young to come down the birth canal, there may be torsion of the uterus, a dead or monster puppy, a sideways puppy blocking the canal or perhaps toxemia. A Caesarean section will be the only solution. No matter what the cause, get the bitch to the veterinarian immediately to insure your chances of saving the mother and/or the puppies.

The Caesarean section operation (the name derived from the idea that Julius Caesar was delivered by this method) involves the removal of the unborn young from the uterus of the dam by surgical incision into the walls through the abdomen. The operation is performed when it has been determined that for some reason the puppies can not be delivered normally. While modern surgical methods have made the operation itself reasonably safe, with the dam being perfectly capable of nursing the puppies shortly after the completion of the surgery, the chief danger lies in the ability to spark life into the puppies immediately upon their removal from the womb. If the mother dies, the time element is even more important in saving the young, since the oxygen supply ceases upon the death of the dam, and the difference between life and death is measured in seconds.

Khamelot's Portia Panache, one of the top-producing bitches in the country during the 1970's. At this writing Portia has 14 points toward championship, with one of her wins including Best of Winners and Best of Opposite Sex at the Northern California Afghan Hound Club Specialty, which was the largest regional specialty in U.S. history. This win was repeated for another 5-point major under Werner Sheldon at the Afghan Hound Club of Southwest Ohio Specialty. She is owned and shown by Gordon "Rik" McDowell.

After surgery, when the bitch is home in her whelping box with the babies, she will probably nurse the young without distress. You must be sure that the sutures are kept clean and that no redness or swelling or ooze appears in the wound. Healing will take place naturally, and no salves or ointments should be applied unless prescribed by the veterinarian, for fear the puppies will get it into their systems. If there is any doubt, check the bitch for fever, restlessness (other than the natural concern for her young) or a lack of appetite, but do not anticipate trouble.

EPISIOTOMY

Even though most dogs are generally easy whelpers, any number of reasons might occur to cause the bitch to have a difficult birth. Before automatically resorting to Caesarean section, many veterinarians are now trying the technique known as episiotomy.

Used rather frequently in human deliveries, episiotomy (pronounced A-PEASE-E-OTT-O-ME) is the cutting of the membrane between the rear opening of the vagina back almost to the opening of the anus. After delivery it is stitched together, and barring complications, heals easily, presenting no problem in future births.

SOCIALIZING YOUR PUPPY

The need for puppies to get out among other animals and people cannot be stressed enough. Kennel-reared dogs are subject to all sorts of idiosyncrasies and seldom make good house dogs or normal members of the world around them when they grow up.

The crucial age, which determines the personality and general behavior patterns which will predominate during the rest of the dog's life, are formed between the ages of three and ten weeks. This is particularly true during the 21st and 28th day. It is essential that the puppy be socialized during this time by bringing him into family life as much as possible. Walking on floor surfaces, indoor and outdoor, should be experienced; handling by all members of the family and visitors is important; preliminary grooming gets him used to a lifelong necessity; light training, such as setting him up on tables and cleaning teeth and ears and cutting nails, etc., has to be started early if he is to become a show dog. The puppy should be exposed to car riding, shopping tours, a leash around its neck, children—your own and others—and in all possible ways develop relationships with humans.

It is up to the breeder, of course, to protect the puppy from harm or injury during this initiation into the outside world. The benefits reaped from proper attention will pay off in the long run with a well-behaved, well-adjusted grown dog capable of becoming an integral part of a happy family.

REARING THE FAMILY

Needless to say, even with a small litter there will be certain considerations which must be adhered to in order to insure successful rearing of the puppies. For instance, the diet for the mother should be appropriately

Typical inquisitive Afghan Hound... or is he just thirsty? This dog was owned by Mr. and Mrs. R.P. Goodman of Bellaire, Texas, in the mid-1950's.

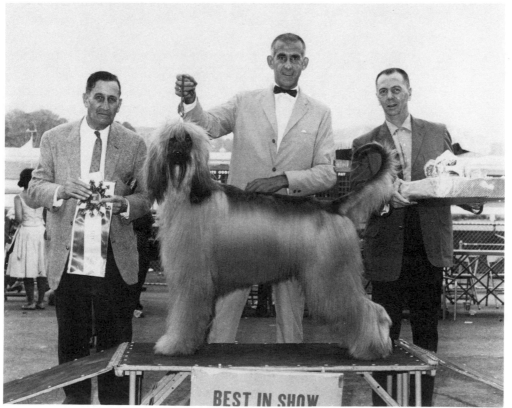

Ch. Holly Hill Draco, bred and owned by Ned and Sue Kauffman of Hubbard, Ohio. This 1961 Best In Show win under the late judge Alva Rosenberg was at the 1961 Chargin Valley Kennel Club Show. Presenting the trophy is Mr. Alan Hauck, Show Chairman. Mr. Kauffman is handling.

increased as the puppies grow and take more and more nourishment from her. During the first few days of rest while the bitch just looks over her puppies and regains her strength, she should be left pretty much alone. It is during these first days that she begins to put the puppies on a feeding schedule and feels safe enough about them to leave the whelping box long enough to take a little extended exercise.

It is cruel, however, to try to keep the mother away from the puppies any longer than she wants to be because you feel she is being too attentive or to give the neighbors a chance to peek in at the puppies. The mother should not have to worry about harm coming to her puppies for the first few weeks. The veterinary checkup will be enough of an experience for her to have to endure until she is more like herself once again.

EVALUATING THE LITTER

A show puppy prospect should be **outgoing**, (probably the first one to fall out of the whelping box!) and all efforts should be made to socialize the puppy which appears to be the most shy. Once the puppies are about three weeks old, they can and should be handled a great deal by friends and members of the family.

During the third week they begin to try to walk instead of crawl, but they are unsteady on their feet. Tails are used for balancing, and they begin to make sounds.

The crucial period in a puppy's life occurs when the puppy is from 21 to 28 days old, so all the time you can devote to them at this time will reap rewards late on in life. This is the age when several other important steps must be taken in a puppy's life. Weaning should start if it hasn't already, and it is the time to check for worms. Do not worm unnecessarily. A veterinarian should advise on worming and appropriate dosage and can also discuss with you at this time the schedule for serum or vaccination, which will depend on the size of the puppies as well as their age.

Exercise and grooming should be started at this time, with special care and consideration given to the diet. You will find that the dam will help you wean the puppies, leaving them alone more and more as she notices that they are eating well on their own. Begin by leaving them with her during the night for comfort and warmth; eventually, when she shows less interest, keep them separated entirely.

"I just washed my hair and can't do a thing with it!" seems to be an appropriate title for this windblown Afghan Hound competing at a recent Bermuda Kennel Club show held at the Botanical Gardens. Bermuda News Bureau photograph.

Ch. Jonathan of Patrician, owned by Joanne D. Gilbert of La Puente, California.

An informal photo of Ali Khyber, owned by Leah P. McConaha.

By the time the fifth week of their lives arrives, you will already be in love with every one of them and desperately searching for reasons to keep them all. They recognize you—which really gets to you!—and they box and chew on each other and try to eat your finger and a million other captivating antics which are special with puppies. Their stomachs seem to be bottomless pits, and their weight will rise. At eight to ten weeks, the puppies will be weaned and ready to go.

SPAYING AND CASTRATING

A wise old philosopher once said, "Timing in life is everything!" No statement could apply more readily to the age-old question which every dog owner is faced with sooner or later. . . to spay or not to spay.

For the one-bitch pet owner, spaying is the most logical answer, for it solves many problems. The pet is usually not of top breeding quality, and therefore there is no great loss to the bloodline; it takes the pressure off the family if the dog runs free with children and certainly eliminates the problem of repeated litters of unwanted puppies or a backyard full of eager males twice a year.

But for the owner or breeder, the extra time and protection which must be afforded a purebred quality bitch can be most worthwhile—even if it is only until a single litter is produced after the first heat. It is then not too late to spay, the progeny can perpetuate the bloodline, the bitch will have been fulfilled—though it is merely an old wives' tale that bitches should have at least one litter to be "normal"—and she may then be retired to her deserved role as family pet once again.

With spaying the problem of staining and unusual behavior around the house is eliminated, as is the necessity of having to keep her in "pants" or administering pills, sprays or shots. . . which most veterinarians do not approve of anyway.

In the case of males, castration is seldom contemplated, which to me is highly regrettable. The owner of the male dog merely overlooks the dog's ability to populate an entire neighborhood, since they do not have the responsibility of rearing and disposing of the puppies. When you take into consideration all the many females the male dog can impregnate, it is almost more essential that the males be taken out of circulation than that the females be. The male dog will still be inclined to roam but will be less frantic about leaving the grounds, and you will find that a lot of the wanderlust has left him.

STERILIZING FOR HEALTH

When considering the problem of spaying or castrating, the first consideration after the population explosion should actually be the health of the dog or bitch. Males are frequently subject to urinary diseases, and sometimes castration is a help. Your veterinarian can best advise you on this problem. Another aspect to consider is the kennel dog which is no longer being used at stud. It is unfair to keep him in a kennel with females in heat when there is no chance for him to be used. There are other more personal considerations for both kennel and one-dog owners, but when making the decision remember that it is final. You can always spay or castrate, but once the deed is done there is no return!

Carol Reisman of Woodmere, New York, poses with Ch. Kai's Turkhan of Grandeur, Ch. Kali of Grandeur and 7 month old Ch. Kai's Kushmir-N-Tuchaas, who relaxes in front.

This Winners Bitch award was enough to finish the championship requirements for Patrician Nighttime. The win was under judge Vincent Perry at the 1966 San Louis Obispo Kennel Club Show. Nighttime was breeder-owner-handled by H.G. Stephenson, Jr., Patrician Afghan Hounds, Topanga, California.

Ch. ben GhaZi's Kaman, winner of the 1958 Tara Afghan Hound Club Specialty Show under judge Alys Carlsen. By the end of 1959 Kaman had won 12 Group Firsts and 23 Group placings. Kaman was bred by Ruth Tongren at her ben ghaZi Kennels in Bloomfield, Connecticut, and is shown here outside her home.

Ch. Kaja's Silky Boy, sired by Ch. Kora's King David. Both of these beautiful dogs were bred and owned by Karen and Julian Armistead of Brooklyn, New York.

Ch. Radizar of Azad, owned by the H. McKee Dorseys of Hollywood, California. In the 1960's King Tut won the *Dog World Award of Canine Distinction* for finishing his championship with three 5-point wins within 5 days. His ring total was 14 Bests of Breed, 3 Group Firsts and 4 other Group placements.

Kharontule Mystique, owned by Mel McCarthy and Nancy McCarthy Slaughter of Teaneck, New Jersey. "Like mother, like daughter," Misty is a replica of her dam, Ch. Sahadi Sequin.

Ch. Tajmir Gunsmoke of Mecca, owned by Dick and Marcia Stoll, is being handled here by Frank Sabella. This Best Hound In Show win under judge Rutledge Gilliland was at the 1965 Texas Kennel Club Show.

Ch. Lipizzan's Big Red Machine was one of the top-winning Afghan Hounds in the breed during the 1970's. This impressive multiple Breed and Group winner is owned by Faye and Howard Ruback of Omaha, Nebraska. His sire was Prince Bearnhart of Lipizzan *ex* Huzzah Rubiyat of Lipizzan.

Chapter XVIII

Feeding and Nutrition

FEEDING PUPPIES

There are many diets today for young puppies, including all sorts of products on the market for feeding the newborn, for supplementing the feeding of the young and for adding this or that to diets, depending on what is lacking in the way of a complete diet.

When weaning puppies, it is necessary to put them on four meals a day, even while you are tapering off with the mother's milk. Feeding at six in the morning, noontime, six in the evening and midnight is about the best schedule, since it fits in with most human eating plans. Meals for the puppies can be prepared immediately before or after your own meals, without too much of a change in your own schedule.

6 A.M.

Two meat and two milk meals serve best and should be served alternately, of course. Assuming the 6 A.M. feeding is a milk meal, the contents should be as follows: goat's milk is the very best milk to feed puppies, but is expensive and usually available only at drug stores, unless you live in farm country where it could be readily available fresh and less expensive. If goat's milk is not available, use evaporated milk (which can be changed to powdered milk later on) diluted two parts evaporated milk and one part water, along with raw egg yolk, honey or Karo syrup, sprinkled with high-protein baby cereal and some wheat germ. As the puppies mature, cottage cheese may be added or, at one of the two milk meals, it can be substituted for the cereal.

NOONTIME

A puppy chow which has been soaked in warm water or beef broth according to the time specified on the wrapper should be mixed with raw or simmered chopped meat in equal proportions with vitamin powder added.

6 P.M.

Repeat the milk meal—perhaps varying the type of cereal from wheat to oats, corn or rice.

"Greater love hath no child. . ." than to share his peanut butter sandwich with his dog! Three-year-old Jon Craig Highfield shares readily with his dog Pinky. This photo also appeared in the *Birmingham News* in Alabama, where Jon and Am. and Can. Ch. Sandina Sparkling Champagne live with Mrs. Vikki Highfield.

MIDNIGHT

Repeat the meat meal. If raw meat was fed at noon, the evening meal might be simmered.

Please note that specific proportions on this suggested diet are not given. However, it's safe to say that the most important ingredients are the milk and cereal, and the meat and puppy chow which forms the basis of the diet. Your veterinarian can advise on the portion sizes if there is any doubt in your mind as to how much to use.

If you notice that the puppies are cleaning their plates, you are perhaps not feeding enough to keep up with their rate of growth. Increase the amount at the next feeding. Observe them closely; puppies should each "have their fill," because growth is very rapid at this age. If they have not satisfied themselves, increase the amount so that they do not have to fight for the last morsel. They will not overeat if they know there is enough food available. Instinct will usually let them eat to suit their normal capacity.

If there is any doubt in your mind as to any ingredient you are feeding, ask yourself, "Would I give it to my own baby?" If the answer is no, then don't give it to your puppies. At this age, the comparison between puppies and human babies can be a good guide.

If there is any doubt in your mind, I repeat: ask your veterinarian to be sure.

Many puppies will regurgitate their food, perhaps a couple of times, before they manage to retain it. If they do bring up their food, allow them to eat it again, rather than

Am. and Can. Ch. Sandina Sparkling Champagne is pictured winning the 1976 Tara Afghan Hound Club Specialty Show under breeder-judge Joe Langford. Pinky is co-owned by breeder-handler Glorvina Schwartz and Vikki Highfield and is one of the top-winning dogs of 1977.

Family portrait! Jo Ann Voss of Longview, Texas, gathers together a group of her Afghan Hounds for this picture of her Ch. Jedashi's Silver Sage and Ch. Ventura's Blue Dacquiri and their four puppies.

clean it away. Sometimes additional saliva is necessary for them to digest it, and you do not want them to skip a meal just because it is an unpleasant sight for you to observe.

This same regurgitation process holds true sometimes with the bitch, who will bring up her own food for her puppies every now and then. This is a natural instinct on her part which stems from the days when dogs were giving birth in the wilds. The only food the mother could provide at weaning time was too rough and indigestible for her puppies. Therefore, she took it upon herself to pre-digest the food until it could be taken and retained by her young. Bitches today will sometimes resort to this, especially bitches which love having litters and have a strong maternal instinct. Some dams will help you wean their litters and even give up feeding entirely once they see you are taking over.

WEANING THE PUPPIES

When weaning the puppies, the mother is kept away from the little ones for longer and longer periods of time. This is done over a period of several days. At first she is separated from the puppies for several hours, then all day, leaving her with them only at night for comfort and warmth. This gradual separation aids in helping the mother's milk to dry up gradually, and she suffers less distress after feeding a litter.

her general condition. If she is being pulled down by feeding a large litter, he may suggest that you start at two weeks. If she is glorying in her motherhood without any apparent taxing of her strength, he may suggest three to four weeks. You and he will be the best judges. But remember, there is no substitute that is as perfect as mother's milk—and the longer the puppies benefit from it, the better. Other food yes, but mother's milk first and foremost for the healthiest puppies!

FEEDING THE ADULT DOG

The puppies' schedule of four meals a day should drop to three by six months and

Waiting at the gate are, left to right, Osah's Su Shan of Summerwine, Osah's Regal Rufus of Summerwine and Osah's Ruly Rhubarb of Summerwine. Bred by Judy and Orvel Sternberg of Dallas, Texas, Rhubarb is co-owned by them with Kathie Ware.

If the mother continues to carry a great deal of milk with no signs of its tapering off, consult your veterinarian before she gets too uncomfortable. She may cut the puppies off from her supply of milk too abruptly if she is uncomfortable, before they should be completely on their own.

There are many opinions on the proper age to start weaning puppies. If you plan to start selling them between six and eight weeks, weaning should begin between two and three weeks of age. Here again, each bitch will pose a different situation. The size and weight of the litter should help determine the time, and your veterinarian will have an opinion, as he determines the burden the bitch is carrying by the size of the litter and

then to two by nine months; by the time the dog reaches one year of age, it is eating one meal a day.

The time when you feed the dog each day can be a matter of the dog's preference or your convenience, so long as once in every 24 hours the dog receives a meal that provides him with a complete, balanced diet. In addition, of course, fresh clean water should be available at all times.

There are many brands of dry food, kibbles and biscuits on the market which are all of good quality. There are also many varieties of canned dog food which are of good quality and provide a balanced diet for your dog. But, for those breeders and exhibitors who show their dogs, additional care is given to

Rhyng Tayl Lnyx, C.D., is shown running free in a park near her home in Chicago, Illinois. The four-year-old bitch holds three speed records for Afghan Hound racing in the Midwest: 110 yards in 8 seconds on an oval track, 10 seconds for 200 yards on a straight track and 18.8 seconds on a 272-yard horseshoe track. She is owned by Joanna Frosch of Chicago.

providing a few "extras" which enhance the good health and good appearance of show dogs.

A good meal or kibble mixed with water or beef broth and raw meat is perhaps the best ration to provide. In cold weather many breeders add suet or corn oil (or even olive or cooking oil) to the mixture and others make use of the bacon fat after breakfast by pouring it over the dog's food.

Salting a dog's food in the summer helps replace the salt he "pants away" in the heat. Many breeders sprinkle the food with garlic powder to sweeten the dog's breath and prevent gas, especially in breeds that gulp or wolf their food and swallow a lot of air. I prefer garlic powder; the salt is too weak and the clove is too strong.

There are those, of course, who cook very elaborately for their dogs, which is not necessary if a good meal and meat mixture is provided. Many prefer to add vegetables,

rice, tomatoes, etc., in with everything else they feed. As long as the extras do not throw the nutritional balance off, there is little harm, but no one thing should be fed to excess. Occasionally liver is given as a treat at home. Fish, which most veterinarians no longer recommend even for cats, is fed to puppies, but should not be given in excess of once a week. Always remember that no one thing should be given as a total diet. Balance is most important; a 100 per cent meat diet can kill a dog.

THE ALL-MEAT DIET CONTROVERSY

In March of 1971 the National Research Council investigated a great stir in the dog fancy about the all-meat dog-feeding controversy. It was established that meat and meat by-products constitute a complete balanced diet for dogs only when it is further fortified.

Therefore, a good dog chow or meal mixed with meat provides the perfect combination for a dog's diet. While the dry food is a complete diet in itself, the fresh meat additionally satisfies the dog's anatomically and physiologically meat-oriented appetite. While dogs are actually carnivores, it must be remembered that when they were feeding themselves in the wild they ate almost the entire animal they captured, including its stomach contents. This provided some of the vitamins and minerals we must now add to the diet.

In the United States the standard for diets which claim to be "complete and balanced" is set by the Subcommittee on Canine Nutrition of the National Research Council (NRC) of the National Academy of Sciences. This is the official agency for establishing the nutritional requirements of dog foods. Most foods sold for dogs and cats meet these requirements and manufacturers are proud to say so on their labels, so look for this when you buy. Pet food labels must be approved by the Association of American Feed Control Officials (AAFCO) Pet Foods Committee. Both the Food and Drug Administration and the Federal Trade Commission of the AAFCO define the word "balanced" when referring to dog food as:

"Balanced is a term which may be applied to pet food having all known required nutrients in a proper amount and proportion based upon the recommendations of a recognized authority (The National Research Council is one) in the field of animal nutrition, for a given set of physiological animal requirements."

With this much care given to your dog's diet, there can be little reason for not having happy well-fed dogs in proper weight and proportions for the show ring.

OBESITY

As we mentioned before, there are many "perfect" diets for your dogs on the market today. When fed in proper proportions, they should keep your dogs in "full bloom." However, there are those owners who, more often than not, indulge their own appetites and are inclined to overfeed their dogs as well. A study in Great Britain in the early 1970's found that a major percentage of obese people also had obese dogs. The entire family was overfed and all suffered from the same condition.

Obesity in dogs is a direct result of the animal's being fed more food that he can pro-

perly "burn up" over a period of time, so it is stored as fat or fatty tissue in the body. Pet dogs are more inclined to become obese than show dogs or working dogs, but obesity also is a factor to be considered with the older dog, since his exercise is curtailed.

A lack of "tuck up" on a dog, or not being able to feel the ribs, or great folds of fat which hang from the underside of the dog can all be considered as obesity. Genetic factors may enter into the picture, but usually the owner is at fault.

The life span of the obese dog is decreased on several counts. Excess weight puts undue stress on the heart as well as the joints. The dog becomes a poor anesthetic risk and

Huzzah Ozymandias, owned by Linda Morrison of Torr, California. The sire was Ch. Coastwind Gazebo ex Red Rock.

Ready to eat! Three Spectrum Afghan Hounds, their protective snoods in place, stand waiting for their dinner. Iceblue Tiffany, Pewter Viking and Touch of Velvet all belong to Art and Inger James of the Spectrum Kennels, Vancouver, Canada. Snoods are great deterents for sloppy eaters!

has less resistance to viral or bacterial infections. Treatment is seldom easy or completely effective, so emphasis should be placed on not letting your dog get FAT in the first place!

ORPHANED PUPPIES

The ideal solution to feeding orphaned puppies is to be able to put them with another nursing dam who will take them on as her own. If this is not possible within your own kennel, or a kennel that you know of, it is up to you to care for and feed the puppies. Survival is possible but requires a great deal of time and effort on your part.

Your substitute formula must be precisely prepared, always served heated to body temperature and refrigerated when not being fed. Esbilac, a vacuum-packed powder, with complete feeding instructions on the can, is excellent and about as close to mother's milk as you can get. If you can't get Esbilac, or until you do get Esbilac, there are two alternative formulas that you might use.

Mix one part boiled water with five parts of evaporated milk and add one teaspoonful of di-calcium phosphate per quart of formula. Dicalcium phosphate can be secured at any drug store. If they have it in tablet form only, you can powder the tablets with the back part of a tablespoon. The other formula for newborn puppies is a combination of eight ounces of homogenized milk mixed well with two egg yolks.

Warren Bobrow of Madison, New Jersey, takes his Sahadi Fire for a run! The sire was Ch. Sahadi Sinbad *ex* Ch. Crown Crest Khalifah.

408

Two-week-old Balto of Robecli gets a good bottle-feeding from his owner, Elizabeth Harvey Treharne. Whelped in 1960, he was just one of a litter of 15 surviving puppies—a record at that time and quite a load for a bitch to feed on her own! Balto was bred at the Robecli Kennels with Kakashah Larchtree as sire and Patrician Sharonne as dam.

You will need baby bottles with three-hole nipples. Sometimes doll bottles can be used for the newborn puppies, which should be fed at six-hour intervals. If they are consuming sufficient amounts, their stomachs should look full, or slightly enlarged, though never distended. The amount of formula to be fed is proportionate to the size, age, growth and weight of the puppy, and is indicated on the can of Esbilac or on the advice of your veterinarian. Many breeders like to keep a baby scale nearby to check the weight of the puppies to be sure they are thriving on the formula.

At two to three weeks you can start adding Pablum or some other high protein baby cereal to the formula. Also, baby beef can be licked from your finger at this age, or added to the formula. At four weeks the surviving puppies should be taken off the diet of Esbilac and put on a more substantial diet, such as wet puppy meal or chopped beef. However, Esbilac powder can still be mixed in with the food for additional nutrition. The jarred baby foods of pureed meats make for a smooth changeover also, and can be blended into the diet.

HOW TO FEED THE NEWBORN PUPPIES

When the puppy is a newborn, remember that it is vitally important to keep the feeding procedure as close to the natural mother's routine as possible. The newborn puppy should be held in your lap in your hand in an almost upright position with the bottle at an angle to allow the entire nipple area to be full of the formula. Do not hold the bottle upright so the puppy's head has to reach straight up toward the ceiling. Do not let the puppy nurse too quickly or take in too much air and possibly get the colic. Once in a while, take the bottle away and let him rest a while and swallow several times. Before feeding, test the nipple to see that the fluid does not come out too quickly, or by the same token, too slowly so that the puppy gets tired of feeding before he has had enough to eat.

When the puppy is a little older, you can place him on his stomach on a towel to eat, and even allow him to hold on to the bottle or to "come and get it" on his own. Most puppies enjoy eating and this will be a good indication of how strong an appetite he has and his ability to consume the contents of the bottle.

It will be necessary to "burp" the puppy. Place a towel on your shoulder and hold the puppy on your shoulder as if it were a human baby, patting and rubbing it gently. This will also encourage the puppy to defecate. At this time, you should observe for diarrhea or other intestinal disorders. The puppy should eliminate after each feeding with occasional eliminations between times as well. If the puppies do not eliminate on their own after each meal, massage their stomachs and under their tails gently until they do.

You must keep the puppies clean. Under no circumstances should fecal matter be al-

409

M.J. and Edward Odron's favorite photo of their Afghan Hound puppy, Sesame's Kasim Baba of Majeod. Photographer C. Merrill captured this typical puppy expression on film when Kasim was 8 months old, at his owner's home in Springfield, Virginia.

Ch. Maharanee Kohibaba, a lovely daughter of Int. Ch. Rudiki of Pride's Hill, is pictured winning the Hound Group at the Albany, New York, Kennel Club Show many years ago.

An impressive win and a beautiful sight to see. . . John Buchanan and his magnficent team of Afghan Hounds that captured so many wins at the California shows pose proudly for the camera. This win was under judge Carley Harriman, with David Upright presenting the trophy. A Joan Ludwig photograph.

lowed to collect on their skin or fur.

All this—plus your determination and perseverance—might save an entire litter of puppies that would otherwise have died without their real mother.

GASTRIC TORSION

Gastric torsion, or bloat, sometimes referred to as "twisted stomach," has become more and more prevalent. Many dogs that in the past had been thought to die of blockage of the stomach or intestines because they had swallowed toys or other foreign objects are now suspected of having been the victims of gastric torsion and the bloat that followed.

Though life can be saved by immediate surgery to untwist the organ, the rate of fatality is high. Symptoms of gastric torsion are unusual restlessness, excessive salivation, attempts to vomit, rapid respiration, pain and the eventual bloating of the abdominal region.

The cause of gastric torsion can be attributed to overeating, excess gas formation in the stomach, poor function of the stomach or intestine, or general lack of exercise. As the food ferments in the stomach, gases form which may twist the stomach in a clockwise direction so that the gas is unable to escape. Surgery, where the stomach is untwisted counter-clockwise, is the safest and most successful way to correct the situation.

To avoid the threat of gastric torsion, it is wise to keep your dog well exercised to be sure the body is functioning normally. Make sure that food and water are available for the dog at all times, thereby reducing the tendency to overeat. With self-service dry feeding, where the dog is able to eat intermittently during the day, there is not the urge to "stuff" at one time.

If you notice any of the symptoms of gastric torsion, call your veterinarian immediately! Death can result within a matter of hours!

Betty Leap, of the Caravan Kennels, sits quietly with her beautiful brood bitch Akaba's Moonlight Sonata.

Beautiful headstudy of Ch. Zaamarakuri of Ghazni, Best In Show winner and sire of a Best In Show winning son, Ch. Hassan Ben of Moornistan, owned by Dr. William Moore. Kuri was owned by Mary Kenney of Dayton, Ohio, and was shown in the 1950's.

This beautiful photograph is of a Xanadu Afghan Hound owned by Johanna Tanner of Friendswood, Texas. The photograph was taken in Palo Duro Canyon in September, 1976.

In 1956 Kay Finch created this fabric design in her California studio. It was a popular fashion item with Afghan enthusiasts who had it made up into skirts, drapery and scarf items that were often used as bench decorations at the dog shows. Perhaps no other artist in America has done more to popularize the Afghan Hound in ceramic statuary and pottery than Kay Finch. Her Corona del Mar studio features hundreds of animals, and Afghan Hounds in particular.

Ch. Pele of Stormhill takes a moment out to pose for this lovely photograph. He is owned by Jim and Joyce Saarinen, Afghans Al Rashid, Astatula, Florida.

Sultan of Ekselo is pictured taking Best of Winners honors at the 1969 Wallkill Kennel Club Show under judge Isador Shoenberg. Sultan is owned by Blossom and Norman Shuman, Man Shu Kennels, Brooklyn, New York. Mr. Shuman handling.

Koh-I-Baba, C.D.X., seems to be enjoying a bicycle ride and can't wait to get those training wheels off! He was trained and owned by Virginia Withington, Stormhill Kennels.

No bicycle riding at the Beyer's house. Their "working hound," Ch. Gunga Din el Encino, rides a tractor for owners Bob and Tillie Beyer.

Ch. Irisarbor Karah Kul-Darya, a lovely bitch owned by Kay Morochko of Levittown, Long Island, New York, was shown during the 1960's.

Chapter XIX

The Blight of Parasites

Anyone who has ever spent hours peering intently at their dog's warm, pink stomach waiting for a flea to appear will readily understand why I call this chapter the "blight of parasites." It is that dreaded onslaught of the pesky flea that heralds the subsequent arrival of worms.

It you have seen even one flea scoot across that vulnerable expanse of skin, you can be sure there are more lurking on other areas of your dog. They seldom travel alone. So, it is now an established fact that *la puce*, as the French refer to the flea, has set up housekeeping on your dog! It is going to demand a great deal of your time before you manage to evict them—probably just temporarily at that—no matter which species your dog is harboring.

Fleas are not always choosy about their host, but chances are your dog has what is commonly known as *Ctenocephalides canis*, the dog flea. If you are a lover of cats also, your dog might even be playing host to a few *Ctenocephalides felis*, the cat flea, or vice versa! The only thing you can be really sure of is that your dog is supporting an entire community of them, all hungry and sexually oriented, and you are going to have to be persistent in your campaign to get rid of them.

One of the chief reasons fleas are so difficult to catch is that what they lack in beauty and eyesight (they are blind at birth, throughout infancy, and see very poorly if at all during adulthood), they make up for in their fantastic ability to jump and scurry about.

While this remarkable ability to jump—some claim 150 times the length of their bodies—stands them in good stead with circus entrepreneurs and has given them claim to fame as chariot pullers and acrobats in side show attractions, the dog owner can be reduced to tears at the very thought of the onset of fleas.

Modern research has provided a panacea in the form of flea sprays, dips, collars and tags which can be successful to varying degrees. However, there are those who still swear by the good old-fashioned methods of removing them by hand, which can be a challenge to your sanity as well as your dexterity.

Since the fleas' conformation (they are built like envelopes, long and flat), with their spiny skeletal system on the outside of their bodies, is specifically provided for slithering through forests of hair, they are given a distinct advantage to start with. Two antennae on the head select the best spot for digging and then two mandibles penetrate the skin and hit a blood vessel. It is also at this moment that the flea brings into play his spiny contours to prop himself against surrounding hairs to avoid being scratched off as he puts the bite on your dog. A small projecting tube is then lowered into the hole to draw out blood and another tube pumps saliva into the wound; this prevents the blood from clotting and allows the flea to drink freely. Simultaneously, your dog jumps into the air and gets one of those back legs into action, scratching endlessly and in vain, and ruining some coat at the same time!

If you should be so lucky as to catch an itinerant flea as it mistakenly shortcuts across your dog's stomach, the best hunting grounds in the world are actually in the deep fur all along the dog's back from neck to tail. However, the flea, like every other creature on earth, must have water, so several times during its residency it will make its way to the moister areas of your dog's anatomy such as

Crown Crest Behapi Goluki was one of the first and fastest racing Afghan Hounds in California in the 1950's. This picture shows Luki, with his #4 silks and muzzle, taking off down the track during a race. Luki, the sire of 2 champions, was referred to as "the father of Afghan racing in the United States." He was trained for racing and hunting with Wendy Howell's Whippets, and during the first annual Hound races at Santa Barbara, California, he raced in every race and trained many of the other early racing Afghans in that area. His owners were Betty and Earl Stites, Hullabaloo Afghans, now of Arlington, Texas. Photo by J. Barry O'Rourke.

the corners of the mouth, the eyes or the genital parts. This is when the flea collars and tags are useful. Their fumes prevent fleas from passing the neck to get to the head of your dog.

Your dog can usually support several generations of fleas, if it doesn't scratch itself to death or go out of its mind with the itching in the interim. The propagation of the flea is insured by the strong mating instinct and the well-judged decision of the female flea as to the best time to deposit her eggs. She has the rare capacity to store semen until the time is right to lay the eggs after some previous brief encounter with a passing member of the opposite sex.

When that time comes for her to lay, she does so without so much as a backward glance and moves on. The dog shakes the eggs off during a normal day's wandering, and they remain on the ground until hatched and the

Yurki, a Best In Show winner at Puebla, Mexico, on January 20, 1952.

The beautiful Ayesha's Midnight Masquerade was photographed at 16 months of age. Masquerade was bred and owned by Carol Ann Callahan, Afghans of Ayesha, Belvedere, South Carolina. The sire was Dynasty's Midnight Sun *ex* Dynasty's My Funny Valentine.

Sweet Pea and Bumper caught during a relaxed moment at the home of their owner, Johanna Tanner of Texas.

baby fleas are ready to jump back onto a passing dog. If any of the eggs have remained on the original dog, chances are that in scratching an adult flea, he will help the baby fleas emerge from their shells.

Larval fleas are small and resemble slender maggots; they begin their lives eating their own egg shells until the dog comes along and offers them a return to the world of adult fleas, whose excrement provides the predigested blood pellets they must have to thrive. They cannot survive on fresh blood, nor are they capable at this tender age of digging for it themselves.

After a couple of weeks of this freeloading, the baby flea makes his own cocoon and becomes a pupa. This stage lasts long enough for the larval flea to grow legs, mandibles, and sharp spines and to flatten out and in general become identifiable as the commonly known and obnoxious *Ctenocephalides canis*. The process can take several weeks or several months, depending on weather conditions, heat, moisture, etc., but generally three weeks is all that is required to enable the flea to start gnawing your dog in its own right.

And so the life-cycle of the flea is renewed and begun again. If you don't have plans to stem the tide, you will certainly see a population explosion that will make the human one resemble an endangered species. Getting rid of fleas can be accomplished by the aforementioned spraying of the dog, or the flea collars and tags, but air, sunshine and a good shaking out of beds, bedding, carpets, cushions, etc., certainly must be undertaken to get rid of the eggs or larvae lying around the premises.

However, if you love the thrill of the chase, and have the stomach for it, you can still try to catch them on safari across your dog's stomach. Your dog will love the attention, that is if you don't keep pinching a bit of skin instead of that little blackish critter. Chances are great you will come up with skin rather than the flea and your dog will lose interest and patience.

Should you be lucky enough to get hold of one, you must either squeeze it to death (which isn't likely) or break it in two with a sharp, strong fingernail (which also isn't likely) or you must release it *underwater* in the toilet bowl and flush immediately. This prospect is only slightly more likely.

417

The winner of the 1973 First Regional Specialty Show of the Afghan Hound Club of America was Ch. Panjhet of Stormhill. This beautiful brindle captured here on canvas is also a multiple breed and Group winner. The sire was Ch. Holly Hill Black Magic *ex* and Mex. Ch. Pandora of Stormhill. Bred and owned by Virginia and Sandy Withington.

There are those dog owners, however, who are much more philosophical about the flea, since, like the cockroach, it has been around since the beginning of the world. For instance, that old-time philosopher, David Harum, has been much quoted with his remark, "A reasonable amount of fleas is good for a dog. They keep him from broodin' on bein' a dog." We would rather agree with John Donne who in his *Devotions* reveals that, "The flea, though he kill none, he does all the harm he can." This is especially true if your dog is a show dog! If the scratching doesn't ruin the coat, the inevitable infestation of parasites left by the fleas will!

We readily see that dogs can be afflicted by both internal and external parasites. The external parasites are known as the aforementioned fleas, plus ticks and lice; while all of these are bothersome, they can be treated. However, the internal parasites, or worms of various kinds, are usually well-infested before discovery and require more substantial means of ridding the dog of them completely.

INTERNAL PARASITES

The most common worms are the round worms. These, like many other worms, are carried and spread by the flea and go through a cycle within the dog host. They are excreted in egg or larval form and passed on to other dogs in this manner.

Worm medicine should be prescribed by a veterinarian, and dogs should be checked for worms at least twice a year, or every three months if there is a known epidemic in your area, and during the sumer months when fleas are plentiful.

Major types of worms are hookworms, whipworms, tapeworms (the only non-round worms in this list), ascarids (the "typical" round worms), heartworms, kidney and lung worms. Each can be peculiar to a part of the country or may be carried by a dog from one area to another. Kidney and lung worms are fortunately quite rare; the others are not. Some symptoms for worms are vomiting intermittently, eating grass, lack of pep, bloated stomach, rubbing the tail along the ground, loss of weight, dull coat, anemia and pale gums, eye discharge, or unexplained nervousness and irritability. A dog with worms will usually eat twice as much as he normally would.

Never worm a sick dog, or a pregnant bitch after the first two weeks she has been bred, and never worm a constipated dog. . . it will retain the strong medicine within the body for too long a time.

HOW TO TEST FOR WORMS

Worms can kill your dog if the infestation is severe enough. Even light infestations of worms can debilitate a dog to the point where he is more susceptible to other serious diseases that can kill, if the worms do not.

Today's medication for worming is relatively safe and mild, and worming is no longer the traumatic experience for either the dog or owner that it used to be. Great care must be given, however, to the proper administration of the drugs. Correct dosage is a "must" and clean quarters are essential to rid your

Ch. Charaj Summer Storm, owned by Robert Stein. Storm is one of the 14 champions finished by this kennel since its establishment in 1955. The sire was Ch. Akaba's Royal Flush *ex* Ch. Charaj El Samantha.

The Afghan Hound in action and at its best with coat flying in the wind! Pictured is the magnificent Ch. Summerwine's Pisco Punch, owned by the Monroe Jacksons of Texas.

Left:
The exotic Okura's Yonde Coude, photographed at 10 months of age, was bred by Rhonda Yeates and co-owned by her and James and Kathy Dickerson. The sire was Ch. Bishr's Amon-Re *ex* Sukkera's Daiquiri DeLuxe.

Right:
Okura's Pistol Pack 'n Mama, photographed at 10 months of age. Her breeder was Rhonda M. Yeates, Okura Kennels, and the owners are Joyce and Michow Huston of Kansas City, Missouri.

A beautiful silver-blue bitch named Sadi. She was bred by the Hewitts many years ago.

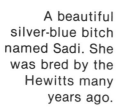

Dragonwyck Toddy of Jamaden, owned by Joy Madden of Bradenton, Florida. The sire was Ch. Altai Ataturk *ex* Ch. Cinnamon Sinner of Shalam.

Left:
Zafara Captain Sunshine, photographed at 4 months of age. His owners are Pam and Al McQueen and Bob and Bobbi Keller of Rantoul, Illinois. The sire was Ch. Coastwind Abraxas *ex* Ch. Jublian's Second Spring. Photo by Peggy McHenry.

Right:
Ch. Jedashi's Blu-Barry was sired by Apache's Ichiban of Jedashi *ex* Shireff. Bred and owned by Shirle Maines of Burleson, Texas, he is co-owned by Don Davidson.

kennel of these parasites. It is almost impossible to find an animal that is completely free of parasites, so we must consider worming as a necessary evil.

However mild today's medicines may be, it is inadvisable to worm a dog unnecessarily. There are simple tests to determine the presence of worms and this chapter is designed to help you learn how to make these tests yourself. Veterinarians charge a nominal fee for this service, if it is not part of their regular office visit examination. It is a simple matter to prepare fecal slides that you can read yourself on a periodic basis. Over the years it will save you much time and money, especially if you have more than one dog or a large kennel.

All that is needed by way of equipment is a microscope with 100X power. These can be purchased in the toy department of a department or regular toy store for a few dollars. The basic, least expensive sets come with the necessary glass slides and attachments.

After the dog has defecated, take an applicator stick, a toothpick with a flat end or even an old-fashioned wooden matchstick and gouge off a piece of the stool about the size of a small pea. Have one of the glass slides ready with a large drop of water on it. Mix the two together until you have a cloudy film over a large area of the slide. This smear should be covered with another slide or a cover slip—though it is possible to obtain readings with just the one open slide. Place your slide under the microscope and prepare to focus in on it. To read the slide you will find that your eye should follow a certain pattern. Start at the top and read from left to right, then right back to the left and then left over to the right side once again until you have looked at every portion of the slide from the top left to the bottom right side.

Make sure that your smear is not too thick or watery or the reading will be too dark and confused to make proper identification. If you decide you would rather not make your own fecal examinations, but would prefer to have the veterinarian do it, the proper way to present a segment of the stool for him to examine is as follows:

After the dog has defecated, a portion of the stool, say a square inch from different sections of it, should be placed in a glass jar or plastic container and labeled with the dog's name and address of the owner. If the sample cannot be examined within three or four

Ch. Andramai Cheyenne Evil Eye, bred and owned by John and Audrone Vikta, Andrami Afghans, Park Forest, Illinois. The sire was Ch. Mecca's Zeus *ex* Ch. Scharlau Anisette.

hours after passage, it should be refrigerated. Your opinions as to what variety of worms you suspect is sometimes helpful to the veterinarian and may be noted on the label of the jar you submit to him for the examination.

Checking for worms on a regular basis is advisable not only for the welfare of the dog but for the protection of your family, since most worms are transmissible, under certain circumstances, to humans.

421

Fifteen-year-old Ch. Shirkhan of Grandeur, one of the greatest Afghans that ever lived, shows both his age and his magnificence in this cherished photograph. He was bred and owned by Sunny Shay of Hicksville, New York. This memorable photograph courtesy of Joseph Kluchinsky.

Chapter XX

Your Dog, Your Veterinarian and You

The purpose of this chapter is to explain why you should never attempt to be your own veterinarian. Quite the contrary, we urge emphatically that you establish good liaison with a reputable veterinarian who will help you maintain happy, healthy dogs. Our purpose is to bring you up to date on the discoveries made in modern canine medicine and to help you work with your veterinarian by applying these new developments to your own animals.

We have provided here "thumbnail" histories of many of the most common types of diseases your dog is apt to come in contact with during his lifetime. We feel that if you know a little something about the diseases and how to recognize their symptoms, your chances of catching them in the preliminary stages will help you and your veterinarian effect a cure before a serious condition develops.

Today's dog owner is a realistic, intelligent person who learns more and more about his dog—inside and out—so that he can care for and enjoy the animal to the fullest. He uses technical terms for parts of the anatomy, has a fleeting knowledge of the miracles of surgery and is fully prepared to administer clinical care for his animals at home. This chapter is designed for study and/or reference and we hope you will use it to full advantage.

We repeat, we do *not* advocate your playing "doctor." This includes administering medication without veterinary supervision, or even doing your own inoculations. General knowledge of diseases, their symptoms and side effects will assist you in diagnosing diseases for your veterinarian. He does not ex-pect you to be an expert, but will appreciate your efforts in getting a sick dog to him before it is too late and he cannot save its life.

ASPIRIN: A DANGER

There is a common joke about doctors telling their patients, when they telephone with a complaint, to take an aspirin, go to bed and let him know how things are in the morning. Unfortunately, that is exactly the way it turns out with a lot of dog owners who think aspirins are cure-alls and give them to their dogs indiscriminately. They finally call the veterinarian when the dog has an unfavorable reaction!

Aspirins are not panaceas for everything —certainly not for every dog. In an experiment, fatalities in cats treated with aspirin in one laboratory alone numbered ten out of 13 within a two-week period. Dogs' tolerance was somewhat better, as far as actual fatalities, but there was considerable evidence of ulceration in varying degrees on the stomach linings when necropsy was performed.

Aspirin has been held in the past to be almost as effective for dogs as for people when given for many of the everyday aches and pains. The fact remains, however, that medication of any kind should be administered only after veterinary consultation and a specific dosage suitable to the condition is recommended.

While aspirin is chiefly effective in reducing fever, relieving minor pains and cutting down on inflammation, the acid has been proven harmful to the stomach when given in strong doses. Only your veterinarian is qualified to determine what the dosage is or whether it should be administered to your particular dog at all.

WHAT THE THERMOMETER CAN TELL YOU

You will notice in reading this chapter dealing with the diseases of dogs that practically everything a dog might contract in the way of sickness has basically the same set of symptoms: loss of appetite, diarrhea, dull eyes, dull coat, warm and/or runny nose and FEVER!

Therefore, it is most advisable to have a thermometer on hand for checking temperature. There are several inexpensive metal rectal-type thermometers that are accurate and safer than the glass variety which can be broken. This may happen either by dropping or perhaps even breaking off in the dog because of improper insertion or an aggravated condition with the dog that makes him violently resist the injection of the thermometer.

A famous headstudy of the foundation bitch of the Devi-Baba Kennels in Hanson, Massachusetts. Her name is Ch. Crown Crest Babaloo, trained and shown by Gertrude Curnyn.

Ch. Faith, C.D., a beautiful black-masked red bitch who not only excelled in the obedience ring, but her show ring wins made her the top-winning bitch on the West Coast in 1955. Faith was co-owned by J.E. Robiette and Virginia S. Mika of California.

Whichever type you use, it should be first sterilized with alcohol and then lubricated with Vaseline to make the insertion as easy as possible.

The normal temperature for a dog is 101.5 degrees Fahrenheit, as compared to the human 98.6 degrees. Excitement as well as illness can cause this to vary a degree or two, but any sudden or extensive rise in body temperature must be considered as cause for alarm. Your first indication will be that your dog feels unduly "warm" and this is the time to take the temperature, not when the dog becomes very ill or manifests additional serious symptoms. With a thermometer on hand, you can check temperatures quickly and perhaps prevent some illnesses from becoming serious.

COPROPHAGY

Perhaps the most unpleasant of all phases of dog breeding is to come up with a dog that takes to eating stool. This practice, which is referred to politely as coprophagy, is one of the unsolved mysteries in the dog world. There simply is no confirmed explanation as to why some dogs do it.

Aisu Kuriimu of Grandeur was a foundation bitch at the kennels of Dale and Beverly Henry of Oklahoma. Bred by Sunny Shay, Aisu is one of the rare pure white Afghan Hounds.

However, there are several logical theories, all or any of which may be the cause. Some people cite nutritional deficiencies; others say that dogs that are inclined to gulp their food (which passes through them not entirely digested) find it still partially palatable. There is another theory that the preservatives used in some meat are responsible for an appealing odor that remains through the digestive process. Then again, poor quality meat can be so tough and unchewable that dogs swallow it whole and it passes through them in large undigested chunks.

There are others who believe the habit is strictly psychological, the result of a nervous condition or insecurity. Others believe the dog cleans up after itself because it is afraid of being punished as it was when it made a mistake on the carpet as a puppy. Some people claim boredom is the reason, or even spite. Others will tell you a dog does not want its personal odor on the premises for fear of attracting other hostile animals to itself or its home.

The most logical of all explanations and the one veterinarians are inclined to accept is that it is a deficiency of dietary enzymes. Too much dry food can be bad and many vet-erinarians suggest trying meat tenderizers, monosodium glutamate or garlic powder, which gives the stool a bad odor and discourages the dog. Yeast or certain vitamins or a complete change of diet are even more often suggested. By the time you try each of the above you will probably discover that the dog has outgrown the habit anyway. However, the condition cannot be ignored if you are to enjoy your dog to the fullest.

There is no set length of time that the problem persists, and the only real cure is to walk the dog on leash, morning and night and after every meal. In other words, set up a definite eating and exercising schedule before coprophagy is an established pattern.

MASTURBATION

A source of embarrassment to many dogs owners, masturbation can be eliminated with a minimum of training.

The dog which is constantly breeding anything and everything, including the leg of the piano or perhaps the leg of your favorite

Am., Bda. and Can. Ch. Varuna of Ekselo was the winner of the 1969 Colonial Afghan Hound Club Specialty Show under judge Wally Pede. Jaz is co-owned by Sally B. Frank and Ellen O'Leske of Brookline, Massachusetts.

Dragonwyck Tiaga Owl is pictured after winning Best of Breed under judge Judith Fellton at the 1973 Ft. Meyers Kennel Club Show. This Horningsea Tiger's Eye granddaughter is owned and shown by Mrs. Joy Madden, Jamaden Afghan Hounds, Bradenton, Florida.

Ch. Yev'Rah Yady, owned and bred by Mark and Geniel Harvey of Watsonville, California, is pictured winning at a Simi Valley Kennel Club Show and finishing for championship. Yady is handled by Mark Harvey.

Kaihorn Calliope of Bokhara is pictured winning under the late well-known breeder-judge Eunice Clark at a 1971 show. Sired by Ch. Mecca Tajma Khan of Tajmir *ex* Poona Ho of Stormhill, Calliope is shown and owned by Joseph Kluchinsky of Spotswood, New Jersey.

The marvelous aloof look of the Afghan Hound! Jubilan's Silver Shotgun is co-owned by L. Garrett Lambert and Joe and Lill Inguaggiato of Rochester, New York.

Ch. Ninth Turn Argus, an all-breed Best In Show winner and a multiple specialty winner, is pictured winning under breeder-judge Werner Sheldon. Argus was handled here by Rosemarie Crandahl for owners Frank and Diane LaGreca of West Hempstead, New York. Diane LaGreca is president of the Afghan Hound Club of America, and because of this Argus was retired from active showing as of 1976. During his 3 years in the show ring his record was 1 all-breed Best In Show, 3 specialty show titles, 13 Group Firsts, 37 Group placements and 71 Bests of Breed. In 1974 he was #4 Afghan Hound in the country and was never less than #8 in the ratings of all the systems.

Am. and Can. Ch. Rustic's Peach-N-Cream was sired by Ch. Dureigh's Baku *ex* Joleen J. Juliet. Peach finished her U.S. championship and went Best of Breed her first time out as a special. She is owned by the M. Wolfes of Huron, Ohio.

427

guest, can be broken of the habit by stopping its cause.

The over-sexed dog—if truly that is what he is—which will never be used for breeding can be castrated. The kennel stud dog can be broken of the habit by removing any furniture from his quarters or keeping him on leash and on verbal command when he is around people or in the house where he might be tempted to breed pillows, people, etc.

Hormone imbalance may be another cause and your veterinarian may advise injections. Exercise can be of tremendous help. Keeping the dog's mind occupied by physical play when he is around people will also help relieve the situation.

Females might indulge in sexual abnormalities like masturbation during their heat cycle, or again, because of a hormone imbalance. But if they behave this way because of a more serious problem, a hysterectomy may be indicated.

A sharp "no!" command when you can anticipate the act, or a sharp "no!" when caught in the act will deter most dogs if you are consistent in your correction. Hitting or other physical abuse will only confuse a dog.

RABIES

The greatest fear in the dog fancy today is still the great fear it has always been—rabies!

What has always held true about this dreadful disease still holds true today. The only way rabies can be contracted is through the saliva of a rabid dog entering the bloodstream of another animal or person. There is, of course, the Pasteur treatment for rabies which is very effective. There was of late the incident of a little boy bitten by a rabid bat having survived the disease. However, the Pasteur treatment is administered immediately if there is any question of exposure. Even more than dogs being found to be rabid, we now know that the biggest carriers are bats, skunks, foxes, rabbits and other warmblooded animals, which pass it from one to another since they do not have the benefit of inoculation. Dogs that run free should be inoculated for protection against these animals. For city or house dogs that never leave their owner's side, it may not be as necessary.

For many years, Great Britain, because it is an island and because of the country's strictly enforced six-month quarantine, was entirely free of rabies. But in 1969 a British

Winning the Hound Group at a California show under judge Fred Hunt is Ch. Sandhihi Joh-Cyn Tana Baba, co-owned by Brandt and Dorothy Houtsma. Handled by Mr. Houtsma.

Group and Specialty winner, Ch. Gandhi of Lakoya, owned by Mrs. John Jeffrey. This exotic pure white Afghan Hound carries a gold saddle and the desired dark pigmentation.

Ch. Seria of Scheherezade and her kennel mate, Ch. Alibaba of Scheherezade, owned by Lt. Col. Wallace Pede (retired) of Virginia.

officer brought back his dog from foreign duty and the dog was found to have the disease soon after being released from quarantine. There was a great uproar about it, with Britain killing off wild and domestic animals in a great scare campaign, but the quarantine is once again down to six months and things seem to have returned to a normal, sensible attitude.

Health departments in rural towns usually provide rabies inoculations free of charge. If your dog is outdoors a great deal, or exposed to other animals that are, you might wish to call the town hall and get information on the program in your area. One

cannot be too cautious about this dread disease. While the number of cases diminishes each year, there are still thousands being reported and there is still the constant threat of an outbreak where animals roam free. Never forget, there is no cure.

Rabies is caused by a neurotropic virus which can be found in the saliva, brain and sometimes the blood of the afflicted warm-blooded animal. The incubation period is usually two weeks or as long as six months, which means you can be exposed to it without any visible symptoms. As we have said, while there is still no known cure, it can be controlled.

Mike Bagley poses with Ch. Sandina Susquehanna, the #1 bitch in the country for 1975. Mike and Sue Bagley are owners of the Top Flite Kennels in Kokomo, Indiana.

Ch. Crown Crest Mr. Vanguard, owned by Dr. and Mrs. E.F. Winter of Oshkosh, Wisconsin, is pictured winning Best In Show at a Mid-Kentucky Kennel Club show several years ago. The judge was Charles Krebs and Jack Funk handled for the owners. Alexander photo.

You can help effect this control by reporting animal bites, educating the public to the dangers and symptoms and prevention of it, so that we may reduce the fatalities.

There are two kinds of rabies; one form is called "furious" and the other is referred to as "dumb." The mad dog goes through several stages of the disease. His disposition and behavior change radically and suddenly; he becomes irritable and vicious. The eating habits alter, and he rejects food for things like stones and sticks; he becomes exhausted and drools saliva out of his mouth almost constantly. He may hide in corners, look glassy eyed and suspicious, bite at the air as he races around snarling and attacking with his tongue hanging out. At this point paralysis sets in, starting at the throat so that he can no longer drink water though he desires it desperately; hence, the term hydrophobia is given. He begins to stagger and eventually convulse and death is imminent.

In "dumb" rabies paralysis is swift; the dog seeks dark, sheltered places and is abnormally quiet. Paralysis starts with the jaws, spreads down the body and death is quick.

Ch. Siah Nayd of Shahi-Taj, many times a Group winner for owner William Walsh of Harrisonburg, Virginia.

430

Contact by humans or other animals with the drool from either of these types of rabies on open skin can produce the fatal disease, so extreme haste and proper diagnosis is essential. In other words, you do not have to be bitten by a rabid dog to have the virus enter your system. An open wound or cut that comes in touch with the saliva is all that is needed.

The incubation and degree of infection can vary. You usually contract the disease faster if the wound is near the head, since the virus travels to the brain through the spinal cord. The deeper the wound, the more saliva is injected into the body, the more serious the infection. So, if bitten by a dog under any circumstances—or any warmblooded animal for that matter—immediately wash out the wound with soap and water, bleed it profusely, and see your doctor as soon as possible.

Also, be sure to keep track of the animal that bit, if at all possible. When rabies is suspected the public health officer will need to send the animal's head away to be analyzed.

Lugins First Kaotic Moment, a black-masked red bitch puppy, is owned by Janet and David Brown of Tenafly, New Jersey. Bred by Lee and Paul Gindlesberger, this Ch. Sahadi Sessu grand-daughter has 14 points, including both majors.

This litter of 4 month old puppies was sired by Continental Maajah Mazara *ex* Ch. Hullabaloo's Jalal Dixieland. They were bred by Betty and Earl Stites of Arlington, Texas.

431

If it is found to be rabies free, you will not need to undergo treatment. Otherwise, your doctor may advise that you have the Pasteur treatment, which is extremely painful. It is rather simple, however, to have the veterinarian examine a dog for rabies without having the dog sent away for positive diagnosis of the disease. A ten-day quarantine is usually all that is necessary for everyone's peace of mind.

Rabies is no respector of age, sex or geographical location. It is found all over the

Toddy and his master Mike Madden are thoroughly absorbed in a coloring book. Mrs. Joy Madden of Bradenton, Florida, says Toddy can hardly wait for Mike to finish so he can eat the crayons.

Ch. Dic Mar Shaja's Cha Cha, the foundation bitch for the Dallas, Texas, kennel of Sharon and Monroe Jackson. Cha Cha was a top-producing bitch for 1972 and 1973, the dam of 4 champions, and in remarkable condition, as is evidenced by this picture taken at 10½ years of age.

realistic and strict schedule of vaccination. Many puppyhood diseases can be fatal—all of them are debilitating. According to the latest statistics, 98 per cent of all puppies are being inoculated after 12 weeks of age against the dread distemper, hepatitis and leptospirosis and manage to escape these horrible infections. Orphaned puppies should be vaccinated every two weeks until the age of 12 weeks. Distemper and hepatitis live-virus vaccines should be used, since they are not protected with the colostrum normally supplied to them through the mother's milk. Puppies weaned at six to seven weeks should also be inoculated repeatedly because they will no longer be receiving mother's milk. While not all will receive protection from the serum at this early age, it should be given and they should be vaccinated once again at both nine and 12 weeks of age.

Ch. Kings Royal Ra-Bul, owned by Richard Wurtz, wins Best In Show at the 1971 Kankakee Kennel Club Show under judge Robert Wills. Handling for the owner is Betty Orseno. Mrs. J. Carter, presenting the trophy, completes the picture.

world from North Pole to South Pole, and has nothing to do with the old wives' tale of dogs going mad in the hot summer months. True, there is an increase in reported cases during summer, but only because that is the time of the year for animals to roam free in good weather and during the mating season when the battle of the sexes is taking place. Inoculation and a keen eye for symptoms and bites on our dogs and other pets will help control the disease until the cure is found.

VACCINATIONS

If you are to raise a puppy, or a litter of puppies, successfully, you must adhere to a

Leptospirosis vaccination should be given at four months of age with thought given to booster shots if the disease is known in the area, or in the case of show dogs which are exposed on a regular basis to many dogs from far and wide. While animal boosters are in order for distemper and hepatitis, every two or three years if sufficient for leptospirosis, unless there is an outbreak in your immediate area. The one exception should be the pregnant bitch since there is reason to believe that inoculation might cause damage to the fetus.

Strict observance of such a vaccination schedule will not only keep your dog free of these debilitating diseases, but will prevent an epidemic in your kennel, or in your locality, or to the dogs which are competing at the shows.

SNAKEBITE

As field trials and hunts and the like become more and more popular with dog enthusiasts, the incident of snakebite becomes more of a likelihood. Dogs that are kept outdoors in runs or dogs that work the fields and roam on large estates are also likely victims.

Most veterinarians carry snakebite serum, and snakebite kits are sold to dog owners for just such purpose. To catch a snakebite in time might mean the difference between life and death, and whether your area is populated with snakes or not, it behooves you to know what to do in case it happens to you or your dog.

Your primary concern should be to get to a doctor or veterinarian immediately. The victim should be kept as quiet as possible (excitement or activity spreads the venom through the body more quickly) and if possible the wound should be bled enough to clean it out before applying a tourniquet, if the bite is severe.

First of all, it must be determined if the bite is from a poisonous or non-poisonous snake. If the bite carries two horseshoe shaped

Ch. Crown Crest Bongo Bongo, a multiple Group winner during the 1960's. The sire was Ch. Crown Crest Kabul *ex* Ch. Crown Crest Taejblu Minx. Bongo was co-owned by breeder Kay Finch and Betty Stites of Arlington, Texas.

On top of the prey! Reddy To Love Thru Kindness, F. Ch., is poised and ready to pounce on her catch. Reddy, whelped in 1971, is a keen competitor in Open Field courses and winner of a Courser of Merit award. He was the first Afghan Hound to place at a mixed lure course, and was the first Afghan Hound field champion.

On top of the prey! Reddy To Love Thru Kindness, F. Ch., is poised and ready to pounce on her catch. Reddy, whelped in 1971, is a keen competitor in Open Field courses and winner of a Courser of Merit award. He was the first Afghan Hound to place at a mixed lure course, and was the first Afghan Hound field champion. He was the top-ranked Afghan Hound courser for 1972, 1973 and second for 1974. In 1973 he was ranked sixth among all sighthounds. Reddy is owned by Mark and Geaniel Harvey of Watsonville, California.

A trio of American, Bermudian and Canadian champions. . . left is Cyndar of Ekselo with Sally B. Frank, center is Ellen O'Leske with Can. Ch. Thaon's Kashta of Ekselo, and on the right is Varuna of Ekselo with Carol O'Leske. This photograph was taken in October, 1976.

pinpoints of double row of teeth, the bite can be assumed to be non-poisonous. If the bite leaves two punctures or holes—the result of the two fangs carrying venom—the bite is very definitely poisonous and time is of the essence.

Recently, physicians have come up with an added help in the case of snakebite. A first aid treatment referred to as hypothermia which is the application of ice to the wound to lower body temperature to a point where the venom spreads less quickly minimizes swelling, helps prevent infection and has some influence on numbing the pain. If ice is not readily available, the bite may be soaked in ice-cold water. But even more urgent is the need to get the victim to a hospital or a veterinarian for additional treatment.

EMERGENCIES

No matter how well you run your kennel or keep an eye on an individual dog, there will almost invariably be some emergency at some time that will require quick treatment until you get the animal to the veterinarian. The first and most important thing to remember is to keep calm! You will think more clearly and your animal will need to know he can depend on you to take care of him. However, he will be frightened and you must beware of fear biting. Therefore, do not shower him with kisses and endearments at this time, no matter how sympathetic you feel. Comfort him reassuringly, but keep your wits about you. Before getting him to the veterinarian try to alleviate the pain and the shock.

If you can take even a minor step in this

434

The magnificent Ch. Crown Crest Rubi, bred by Kay Finch and owned by the Robert Tongrens, ben ghaZi Kennels, Bloomfield, Connecticut.

An informal photograph of specialty show winner Ch. Karan of Khanhasset, owned in the 1940's by Leah P. McConaha.

Am., Mex. and Can. Ch. Crown Crest Mr. Jhan Jhan, bred and owned by Kay Finch and Eleanor Clark. Jhan Jhan was a world traveler, accompanying Eleanor on her trips all over the world. Whelped in April, 1961, Mr. Jhan Jhan died in December, 1971.

Ch. Gandhi of Lakoya is pictured winning Group Second at the 1962 Del Monte Kennel Club Show with his handler Frank Sabella. Lakoya was owned by Mr. and Mrs. John Jeffrey of Orinda, California.

direction it will be a help toward the final cure. Listed here are a few of the emergencies which might occur and what you can do AFTER you have called the vet and told him you are coming.

BURNS

If you have been so foolish as not to turn your pot handles toward the back of the stove —for your children's sake as well as your dog's—and the dog is burned, apply ice or ice cold water and treat for shock. Electrical or chemical burns are treated the same, but with an acid or alkali burn, use, respectively, a bicarbonate of soda and a vinegar solution. Check the advisability of covering the burn when you call the veterinarian.

DROWNING

Most animals love the water, but sometimes get in "over their heads." Should your dog take in too much water, hold him upside down and open his mouth so that water can empty from the lungs, then apply artificial respiration or mouth-to-mouth resuscitation. With a large dog, hang the head over a step or off the end of a table while you hoist the rear end in the air by the back feet. Then treat for shock by covering him with a blanket, administering a stimulant such as coffee with sugar, and soothing him with your voice and hands.

FITS AND CONVULSIONS

Prevent the dog from thrashing about and injuring himself, cover with a blanket and hold down until you can get him to the veterinarian.

FROSTBITE

There is no excuse for an animal getting frostbite if you are on your toes and care for the animal. However, should frostbite set in, thaw out the affected area slowly with a circulatory motion and stimulation. Use vaseline to help keep the skin from peeling off and/or drying out.

HEART ATTACK

Be sure the animal keeps breathing by applying artificial respiration. A mild stimulant may be used and give him plenty of air. Treat for shock as well, and get to the veterinarian quickly.

SHOCK

Shock is a state of circulatory collapse that can be induced by a severe accident, loss of blood, heart failure or any injury to the

Sikula of Stardust, C.D., is owned by Tom and Cheta Dickson, Bar Crescent Afghans, Euless, Texas. The photo is by Jack Gerrits, owner of the Rudan Afghans. Sikula was one of the top twenty obedience Afghan Hounds in 1975 according to the *Afghan Hound Review* magazine system. Trained by Cheta Dickson, Hassan began his training at 4½ months and finished his C.D. title within 9 months in three shows.

Ch. Thunder Bay's Roo of Eastwinds, owned by Jif Kennels in Westwood, Massachusetts, and photographed here in 1962.

Moornistan's Moonraker, winner of the 1968 Afghan Hound Club of California Specialty Show under judge Herman Fellton. Moonraker was bred, owned and handled by Dr. William Moore, III, of Pennsylvania.

Ouijah of Al'yram, photographed in 1967. Bred by Roberta Breath, the sire was Ch. Sahadi Sinbad ex Sahadi White Cloud. Owned by Peter Belmont.

nervous system. Until you can get the dog to the veterinarian, keep him warm by covering with a blanket and administer a mild stimulant such as coffee or tea with sugar. Try to keep the dog quiet until the appropriate medication can be prescribed. Relapse is not uncommon, so the dog must be observed carefully for several days after initial shock.

SUFFOCATION

Administer artificial respiration and treat for shock with plenty of air.

SUN STROKE

Cooling the dog off immediately is essential. Ice packs, submersion in ice water, and plenty of cool air are needed.

WOUNDS

Open wounds or cuts which produce bleeding must be treated with hydrogen peroxide and tourniquets should be used if bleeding is excessive. Also, shock treatment must be given, and the animal must be kept warm.

THE FIRST AID KIT

It would be sheer folly to try to operate a kennel or to keep a dog without providing for certain emergencies that are bound to crop up when there are active dogs around. Just as you would provide a first aid kit for people, you should also provide a first aid kit for the animals on the premises.

The first aid kit should contain the following items:

BFI or other medicated powder
jar of Vaseline
Q-tips
bandage—1" gauze
adhesive tape
Band-Aids
cotton
boric acid powder

A trip to your veterinarian is always safest, but there are certain preliminaries for cuts and bruises of a minor nature that you can care for yourself.

Cuts, for instance, should be washed out and medicated powder or Vaseline applied with a bandage. The lighter the bandage the better so that the most air possible can reach the wound. Q-tips can be used for removing debris from the eyes, after which a mild solution of boric acid wash can be applied. As for sores, use dry powder on wet sores, and Vaseline on dry sores. Use cotton for washing out wounds and drying them.

Brazilian Ch. Bedowin of Gran Salaam, owned by Ronaldo Orselli of Rio de Janeiro, attained his championship in four straight shows. His wins included an all-breed Best In Show and two Specialty Bests In Show. Bred by Diane LaGreca, Bedowin is two points away from his Brazilian Grand Championship.

Hajji Baba of Grandeur, bred and owned by Sunny Shay of Hicksville, New York. The sire was Ch. Turkuman Nissim's Laurel, and the dam Ch. Zala of Grandeur.

Crown Crest Mr. California was the winner of the Grand Prize Futurity at the 1962 Afghan Hound Club of California Specialty Show from the 19 litters nominated. Handled by his breeder, Kay Finch, Mr. "C" was owned by Forrest H. Hansen and Donald D. McIlvain of the Dahnwood Kennels, Seattle, Washington.

The impressive Ch. Hedlund's Atlas, the black and tan show winner owned by Mrs. Arthur Hedlund of Downers Grove, Illinois. Photo by Ritter.

Nickoles Ego of Lifestyle, owned by Mr. and Mrs. Ronald Nosek. The sire was Ch. Mecca's Zeus *ex* Mecca's Renaissance Rhapsody.

Bucky, Tina and Chris round the bend in a practice heat during their training at the Devi Baba Kennels in Massachusetts.

Ch. Akaba's Glacier Blue, pictured winning at a show in the 1960's. Trudi, a silver-blue bitch, was sired by Ch. Shirkhan of Grandeur *ex* Akaba's Gi Gi in White and was bred and owned by Lois Boardman of California.

Ch. Kleopatra of Scheherezade, C.D., pictured at 8 years of age. She is owned by Kathleen O'Brien of Willingboro, New Jersey.

A particular caution must be given here on bandaging. Make sure that the bandage is not too tight to hamper the dog's circulation. Also, make sure the bandage is made correctly so that the dog does not bite at it trying to get it off. A great deal of damage can be done to a wound by a dog tearing at a bandage to get it off. If you notice the dog is starting to bite at it, do it over or put something on the bandage that smells and tastes bad to him. Make sure, however, that the solution does not soak through the bandage and enter the wound. Sometimes, if it is a leg wound, a sock or stocking slipped on the dog's leg will cover the bandage edges and will also keep it clean.

HOW NOT TO POISON YOUR DOG

Ever since the appearance of Rachel Carson's book *Silent Spring*, people have been

An informal photograph of Int. Ch. Rudika of Blakeen, taken following one of her Best In Show wins. She was owned by the late Marion Foster Florsheim of Darien, Connecticut, many years ago.

asking, "Just how dangerous are chemicals?" In the animal fancy where disinfectants, room deodorants, parasitic sprays, solutions and aerosols are so widely used, the question has taken on even more meaning. Veterinarians are beginning to ask, "What kind of disinfectant do you use?" or "Have you any fruit trees that have been sprayed recently?" When animals are brought in to their offices in a toxic condition, or for unexplained death, or when entire litters of puppies die mysteriously, there is good reason to ask such questions.

The popular practice of protecting animals against parasites has given way to their being exposed to an alarming number of commercial products, some of which are dangerous to their very lives. Even flea collars can be dangerous, especially if they get wet or somehow touch the genital regions or eyes. While some products are a great deal more poisonous than others, great care must be taken that they be applied in proportion to the size of the dog and the area to be covered. Many a dog has been taken to the vet with an unusual skin problem that was a direct result of having been bathed with a detergent rather than a proper shampoo. Certain products that are safe for dogs can be fatal for cats. Extreme care must be taken to read all ingredients and instructions carefully before use on any animal.

The same caution must be given to outdoor chemicals. Dog owners must question the use of fertilizers on their lawns. Lime, for instance, can be harmful to a dog's feet. The unleashed dog that covers the neighborhood on his daily rounds is open to all sorts of tree and lawn sprays and insecticides that may prove harmful to him, if not as a poison, then as a producer of an allergy.

There are numerous products found around the house which can be lethal, such as rat poison, boric acid, hand soap, detergents, car anti-freeze and insecticides. These are all available in the house or garage and can be tipped over easily and consumed. Many puppy fatalities are reported from consuming mothballs. All poisons should be placed on high shelves out of the reach of both children and animals.

Perhaps the most readily available of all household poisons are plants. Household plants are almost all poisonous, even if taken in small quantities. Some of the most dangerous are the elephant ear, the narcissus bulb,

Ch. Gitana Del Desierto, known as Gypsy, is from the show and racing kennels of Pearson Crosby of Albuquerque, New Mexico. Gypsy also hunts jack rabbits on the New Mexico desert, leaping from the roof of Mr. Crosby's truck as they cross the open sands. Gitana is a perfect example of an Afghan Hound that is a true dual purpose hound.

any kind of ivy leaves, burning bush leaves, the jimson weed, the dumb cane weed, mock orange fruit, castor beans, Scottish broom seeds, the root or seed of the plant called four o'clock, cyclamen, pimpernel, lily of the valley, the stem of the sweet pea, rhododendrons of any kind, spider lily bulbs, bayonet root, foxglove leaves, tulip bulbs, monkshood roots, azalea, wisteria, poinsettia leaves, mistletoe, hemlock, locoweed and arrowglove. In all, there are over 500 poisonous plants in the United States. Peach, elderberry and cherry trees can cause cyanide poisoning if the bark is consumed. Rhubarb leaves either raw or cooked can cause death or violent convulsions. Check out your closets, fields and grounds around your home, and especially the dog runs, to see what should be eliminated to remove the danger to your dogs.

Khabira White Cloud tries to entice his kennel mate, Tina's Drummer Boy, into some play! These pals were photographed in January, 1975 in the back yard of the home of their owners, Jennifer and Mary Sheldon of Massapequa, New York. White Cloud was sired by Ch. Sarkhan of Kharysthan *ex* Khabira Angora.

SYMPTOMS OF POISONING

Be on the lookout for vomiting, hard or labored breathing, whimpering, stomach cramps, and trembling as a prelude to the convulsions. Any delay in a visit to your veterinarian can mean death. Take along the bottle or package or a sample of the plant you suspect to be the cause to help the veterinarian determine the correct antidote.

The most common type of poisoning, which accounts for nearly one-fourth of all animal victims, is staphylococcic—infected food. Salmonella ranks third. These can be avoided by serving fresh food and not letting it lie around in hot weather.

There are also many insect poisonings caused by animals eating cockroaches, spiders, flies, butterflies, etc. Toads and some frogs give off a fluid which can make a dog foam at the mouth—and even kill him—if he bites just a little too hard!

Some misguided dog owners think it is "cute" to let their dogs enjoy a cocktail with them before dinner. There can be serious effects resulting from encouraging a dog to drink—sneezing fits, injuries as a result of intoxication and heart stoppage are just a few. Whiskey for medicinal purposes, or beer for brood bitches should be administered only on the advice of your veterinarian.

There have been cases of severe damage and death when dogs have emptied ash trays and consumed cigarettes, resulting in nicotine poisoning. Leaving a dog alone all day in a house where there are cigarettes available on a coffee table is asking for trouble. Needless to say, the same applies to marijuana. The narcotic addict who takes his dog along with him on "a trip" does not deserve to have a dog. All

Ch. Elmo's Pajourah, the first Afghan Hound in U.S. history to win championship points at three specialties and finish at a fourth. P.J. was sired by Ch. Coastwind Graffiti *ex* Khamelot's Portia Panache, and bred by Peter Belmont and Gordon B.F. McDowell. She is owned by Susan Bahary of Huntington Bay, Long Island. P.J. finished her championship as Best of Winners under judge Gerda Kennedy at the 1976 Afghan Hound Club of Long Island Specialty Show.

Opposite:
Kabik's Tammarra of Sadak and her blue brindle son are captured on film while lure coursing in this photo by Cal Fanders. Both dogs are owned by Bonita Rabell, Makosa Afghans, Bothell, Washington.

Ch. Crown Crest Khittiku, C.D., owned by Patricia Sinden, Tajmir Kennels, Chicago, Illinois. This black-masked silver bitch finished her championship with five major wins. Handled by Jack Funk, Khittiku has been an important breeding force at Mrs. Sinden's kennel.

Jonathan of Patrician wins Best of Winners under the respected judge Marion Foster Florsheim at the 1956 Del Monte Kennel Club Show. Breeder-owner H.G. Stephenson, Jr., is handling.

Mex., Can. and Am. Ch. Riptide Vodka of Holly Hill, owned by the Maja Kennels of Norma L. Schmalhausen and N. Sherri Newkirk of Indianapolis, Indiana. Vodka was Best In Show at the 1975 San Miguel Kennel Club Show in Mexico.

the ghastly side effects are as possible for the dog as for the addict, and for a person to submit an animal to this indignity is indeed despicable. Don't think it doesn't happen. Unfortunately, in all our major cities the practice is becoming more and more a problem for the veterinarian.

Be on the alert and remember that in the case of any type of poisoning, the best treatment is prevention.

THE CURSE OF ALLERGY

The heartbreak of a child being forced to give up a beloved pet because he is suddenly found to be allergic to it is a sad but true story. Many families claim to be unable to have dogs at all; others seem to be able only to enjoy them on a restricted basis. Many children know animals only through occasional visits to a friend's house or the zoo.

While modern veterinary science has produced some brilliant allergists, the field is still working on a solution for those who suffer from exposure to their pets. There is no permanent cure as yet.

Over the last quarter of a century there have been many attempts at a permanent cure, but none has proven successful because the treatment was needed too frequently, or was too expensive to maintain over extended periods of time.

However, we find that most people who are allergic to their animals are also allergic to a variety of other things as well. By eliminating the other irritants, and by taking medication given for the control of allergies in general, many are able to keep pets on a restricted basis. This may necessitate the dog's living outside the house, being groomed at a professional grooming parlor instead of by the owner, or merely being kept out of the bedroom at night. A discussion of this "balance" factor with your medical and veterinary doctors may give new hope to those willing to try.

A paper presented by Mathilde M. Gould, M.D., a New York allergist, before the American Academy of Allergists in the 1960's and reported in the September-October 1964 issue of the *National Humane Review* magazine, offered new hope to those who are allergic by a method referred to as hyposensitization. You may wish to write to the magazine and request the article for discussion with your medical and veterinary doctors on your individual problem.

Surely, since the sixties there have been

Am. and Can. Ch. Coastwind Graffiti was captured on canvas in oils by Elizabeth H. Treharne. This exquisite 26" x 30" oil is in the art collection of Peter Belmont. Commissioned by him, Mrs. Treharne painted this remarkably life-like portrait in 1972 from a "live" sitting in front of a class of over 100 art students.

additional advances in the field of allergy since so many people—and animals—are affected in so many ways.

ALLERGIES IN DOGS

It used to be that you recognized an allergy in your dog when he scratched out his coat and developed a large patch of raw skin or sneezed himself almost to death on certain occasions. A trip to the veterinarian involved endless discussion as to why it might be and an almost equally endless "hit and miss" cure of various salves and lotions with the hope that one of them would work. Many times the condition would correct itself before a definite cure was affected.

However, during the 1970's preliminary findings at the University of Pennsylvania veterinary school evolved a diagnosis for allergies that eliminated the need for skin sensitivity tests. It is called RAST, and is a radioallergosobant test performed with a blood serum sample. It is not even necessary in all cases for the veterinarian to even see the dog.

A cellulose disc laced with a suspected allergen is placed in the serum, and if the dog is allergic to that particular allergen the serum will contain a specific antibody that adheres to the allergen on the disc. The disc is placed in a radioactively "labeled" antiserum that is attracted to that particular antibody. The antiserum binds with the antibody and can be detected with a radiation counter.

445

A darling Afghan puppy bitch is "up to mischief" at the Crown Crest Kennels. This Ch. Crown Crest Opal puppy, 3 months old in this photo taken in 1955, was sold to the Little Oak Kennels in Chanute, Kansas.

Furthermore, the scientists at the University of Pennsylvania also found that the RAST test has shown to be a more accurate diagnostic tool than skin testing because it measures the degree, and not merely the presence, of allergic reactions.

DO ALL DOGS CHEW?

Chewing is the best possible method of cutting teeth and exercising gums. Every puppy goes through this teething process, and it can be destructive if the puppy uses shoes or table corners or rugs instead of the proper item for the best possible results. All dogs should have a Nylabone available for chewing, not only to teethe on but also for inducing growth of the permanent teeth, to assure normal jaw development and to settle the permanent teeth solidly in the jaws. Chewing on a Nylabone also has a cleaning effect and serves as a "massage" for the gums, keeping down the formation of the tartar that erodes tooth enamel.

When you see a puppy pick up an object to chew, immediately remove it from his mouth with a sharp "No!" and replace the object with a Nylabone. Puppies take anything and everything into their mouths so they should be provided with several Nylabones to prevent damage to the household. This same Nylabone eliminates the need for the kind of "bone" which may chip your dog's mouth or stomach or intestinal walls. Cooked bones, soft enough to be powdered and added to the food, are also permissible if you have the patience to prepare them, but Nylabone serves

446

all the purposes of bones for chewing that your dog may require, so why take a chance on meat bones?

Electrical cords and wires of any kind present a special danger which must be eliminated during puppyhood and glass dishes which can be broken and played with are also hazardous.

The answer to the question about whether all dogs chew is an emphatic yes—and the answer is even more emphatic in the case of puppies.

SOME REASONS FOR CHEWING

Chewing can also be a form of frustration or nervousness. Dogs sometimes chew for spite, if owners leave them alone too long or too often. Bitches will sometimes chew if their puppies are taken away from them too soon; insecure puppies often chew thinking they're nursing. Puppies which chew wool, blankets, carpet corners or certain other types of materials may have a nutritional deficiency or something lacking in their diet, such as cra-

This glamorous headstudy is of the show and obedience ring winner, Ch. Crown Crest Khittiku, C.D. Retired shortly after her second birthday for breeding purposes, Khittiku has several champion offspring to her credit.

Ch. Crown Crest Taejhanne, dam of four champions in her first litter. A daughter of the famous Ch. Taejon of Crown Crest, Taejahnne is owned by H.G. Stephenson of the Patrician Kennels in Topango, California.

Ch. Swedika Joh-Cyn is pictured winning Best of Breed over champions at the 1960 Santa Cruz, California, Show under judge Helen Walsh. Swedika was bred and is owned by Mrs. Cynthia Guzevich of New Mexico. She is a daughter of the famous Int. Ch. Tanjores Domino and the equally famous bitch, Int. Ch. Tajmahal Kenya. Handler for Mrs. Guzevich was the late Roland Muller.

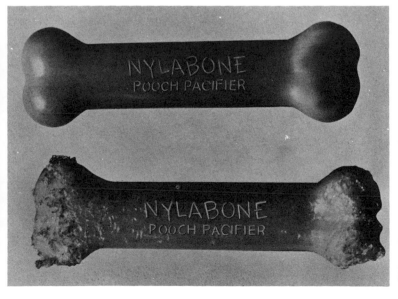

NYLABONE © is a necessity that is available at your local petshop (not in supermarkets). The puppy or grown dog chews the hambone flavored nylon into a frilly dog toothbrush, massaging his gums and cleaning his teeth as he plays. Veterinarians highly recommend this product. . . but beware of cheap imitations which might splinter or break.

The cover of a 1944 issue of the *Saturday Evening Post* featured the famous Afghan Hounds of Marion Florsheim. This cover was a gift to the author from Mrs. Florsheim many years ago and is a treasured piece in her collection of Afghan art and memorabilia.

ving the starch that might be left in material after washing. Perhaps the articles have been near something that tastes good and it has retained the odor of food.

The act of chewing has no connection with particular breeds or ages, any more than there is a logical reason for dogs to dig holes outdoors or dig on wooden floors indoors.

So we repeat, it is up to you to be on guard at all times until the need—or habit—passes.

HIP DYSPLASIA

Hip dysplasia, or HD, is one of the most widely discussed of all animal afflictions, since it has appeared in varying degrees in just about every breed of dog. True, the larger breeds seem most susceptible, but it has hit the small breeds and is beginning to be recognized in cats as well.

While HD in man has been recorded as far back as 370 B.C., HD in dogs was more than likely referred to as rheumatism until veterinary research came into the picture. In 1935 Dr. Otto Schales, at Angell Memorial Hospital in Boston, wrote a paper on hip dysplasia and classified the four degrees of dysplasia of the hip joints as follows:

Grade 1—slight (poor fit between ball socket)

Grade 2—moderate (moderate but obvious shallowness of the socket)

Grade 3—severe (socket quite flat)

Grade 4—very severe (complete displacement of head of femur at early age)

Ch. Fantasi's Get It While You Can, owned by Shirle Maines of Burleson, Texas. The sire was Ch. Akaba's Speak of the Devil ex Fantasi's Mood Indigo.

HD is an incurable, hereditary, though not congenital disease of the hip sockets. It is transmitted as a dominant trait with irregular manifestations. Puppies appear normal at birth but the constant wearing away of the socket means the animal moves more and more on muscle, thereby presenting a lameness, a difficulty in getting up and severe pain in advanced cases.

The degree of severity can be determined around six months of age, but its presence can be noticed from two months of age. The problem is determined by X-ray, and if pain is present it can be relieved temporarily by medication. Exercise should be avoided since motion encourages the wearing away of the bone surfaces.

Dogs with HD should not be shown or bred, if quality in the breed is to be maintained. It is essential to check a pedigree for dogs known to be dysplastic before breeding, since this disease can be dormant for many generations.

ELBOW DYSPLASIA

The same condition can also affect the elbow joints and is known as elbow dysplasia. This also causes lameness, and dogs so affected should not be used for breeding.

PATELLAR DYSPLASIA

Some of the smaller breeds of dogs suffer from patella dysplasia, or dislocation of the knee. This can be treated surgically, but the surgery by no means abolishes the hereditary

Okura's Red Rocket, photographed at 1½ years of age. Bred by Rhonda Yeates, the sire was Ch. Bishr's Amon-Re ex Sukkera's Daiquiri Deluxe. Red Rocket is co-owned by Rhonda and Effie Yeates, Okura Kennels, Lee's Summit, Missouri.

Best In Show at the 1974 Afghan Hound Club of Dallas Specialty Show was Ch. Summerwine's Cuba Libra, shown by Monroe Jackson, and co-owned by him and Sharon Jackson. The judge is Joan Brearley.

Am. and Can. Ch. Dynasty's The Devil With You, a Group winner and multiple Best In Show winner in Canada, is pictured winning the breed at the 1976 McKinley Kennel Club Show under judge Robert Stein. Sired by Ch. Akaba's Blue Devil *ex* Ch. Dynasty's Lady Dealer, Devil also won the specialty show held by the Afghan Hound Club of Canada in 1975. Devil is owned by Gail Bassick, Yankeerun Afghans, Masury, Ohio.

Piper Sanzin of Rani, a lovely black daughter of Ch. Sahadi Sinbad, is owned by Carol Reisman of Woodmere, New York and photographed in June, 1976 at 9 years of age.

Left:
Kharontule Kaptin Tom was the winner of Best Puppy In Match at the Afghan Hound Club of America Match Show in 1962. Handled by owner-breeder Nancy McCarthy Slaughter of Teaneck, New Jersey, Tom was also Reserve Dog and best in the Bred by Exhibitor class at the Afghan Hound Club of America Specialty Show under judge Kay Finch.

factor. Therefore, these dogs should not be used for breeding.

All dogs—in any breed—should be X-rayed before being used for breeding. The X-ray should be read by a competent veterinarian, and the dog declared free and clear.

THE UNITED STATES REGISTRY

In the United States we have a central Hip Dysplasia Foundation, known as the OFA (Orthopedic Foundation for Animals). This HD control registry was formed in 1966. X-rays are sent for expert evaluation by qualified radiologists.

All you need do for complete information on getting an X-ray for your dog is to write to the Orthopedic Foundation for Animals at 817 Virginia Ave., Columbia, Mo. 65201, and request their dysplasia packet. There is no charge for this kit. It contains an envelope large enough to hold your X-ray film (which you will have taken by your own veterinarian), and a drawing showing how to position the dog properly for X-ray. There is also an application card for proper identification of the dog. Then, hopefully, your dog will be certified "normal." You will be given a registry number which you can put on his pedigree, use in your advertising, and rest assured your breeding program is in good order.

All X-rays should be sent to the address above. Any other information you might wish to have may be requested from Mrs. Robert Bower, OFA, Route 1, Constantine, Mo. 49042.

We cannot urge strongly enough the importance of doing this. While it involves time and effort, the reward in the long run will more than pay for your trouble. To see the heartbreak of parents and children when their beloved dog has to be put to sleep because of severe hip dysplasia as the result of bad breeding is a sad experience. Don't let this happen to you or to those who will purchase your puppies!

Additionally, we should mention that there is a method of palpation to determine the extent of affliction. This can be painful if the animal is not properly prepared for the examination. There have also been attempts to replace the animal's femur and socket. This is not only expensive, but the percentage of success is small.

For those who refuse to put their dog down, there is a new surgical technique which can relieve pain, but in no way constitutes a cure. This technique involves the severing of the pectinius muscle which for some unknown reason brings relief from pain over a period of many months—even up to two years. Two veterinary colleges in the United States are performing this operation at the present time. However, the owner must also give permission to "de-sex" the dogs at the time of the muscle severance. This is a safety measure to help stamp out hip dysplasia, since obviously the condition itself remains and can be passed on.

Ch. Javelin of Camri, owner-handled by Betty Richards to this 1960's show win. Photo by January.

Mr. and Mrs. Waldron S. Macdonald's Zingiber meets a young friend in the Boston Public Garden.

This typical 4-month-old puppy, Odyssey's Tia Maria of Okura, was bred by Celeste Masson and owned by Rhonda and Effie Yeates, Okura Kennels.

HD PROGRAM IN GREAT BRITAIN

The British Veterinary Association (BVA) has made an attempt to control the spread of HD by appointing a panel of members of their profession who have made a special study of the disease to read X-rays. Dogs over one year of age may be X-rayed and certified as free. Forms are completed in triplicate to verify the tests. One copy remains with the panel, one copy is for the owner's veterinarian, and one for the owner. A record is also sent to the British Kennel Club for those wishing to check on a particular dog for breeding purposes.

JUVENILE CATARACTS

During the sixties there was a great deal of discussion in the breed about the alarming number of incidents of juvenile cataracts. By 1968 the parent club recognized the need to be kept abreast of *all* serious conditions which afflict the Afghan Hound, and at the May, 1968 meeting of the Board of Directors a Committee for Biological Defects was established. The committee's purpose was to inform the club on their recommendations for control and possible prevention.

Constance Miller, who had been very active in revealing the condition on the West Coast, has actually done test breedings and has written extensively on the subject. She was appointed Chairman of the committee, with Dr. William Wasko and Donald A. Smith as members. Later, Dr. J.R. Assenzo and Sue Kauffman were added to their ranks.

While the committee was to investigate all congenital diseases, such as hip dysplasia, defective dentition, progressive retinal atrophy, familial spinal deterioration, and mismarks, their immediate attention was focused on juvenile cataracts.

Eye clinics were already operating in California by the time this committee went into action, of course. The first All-Afghan Hound eye clinic was held in April, 1968. Sixty-two Afghan Hounds were examined and the session was declared a success. There were follow-up clinics as well.

Shahara Friendly Persuasion, pictured at 4 months of age, is owned by Danny Dunlap of Hixson, Tennessee. Bred by Martha Cain of the Shahara Kennels, the sire was Best In Show Ch. Pamir Sweet William *ex* Ch. Shahara Majorca Daktari.

The Afghan Hound Club of Northern New Jersey was the first club on the East Coast to sponsor an all-Afghan Hound juvenile cataract clinic and it also was an obvious success. At the first meeting there were 98 Afghan Hounds on hand for examination. The clinic was open to all, non-members being as enthusiastic as the club members. The Kennel Club of Northern New Jersey was also the first club to eastablish a fund to financially aid owners who could not afford the complete cost of necessary corrective surgery in the event that juvenile cataracts were found upon examination. One of the qualifications for this financial assistance was that the pedigree and complete information concerning the afflicted dog be submitted to the Afghan Hound Club of America Committee on Biological Defects.

It is not at all unusual these days for breeders who are advertising stud service to include in their ads "X-rayed clear of Juvenile Cataracts." If they have puppies for sale the statement "Parents X-rayed Clear of J.C. and H.D." is apt to appear in the ad. It is wise for anyone inquiring about stud service or puppies for sale to ask for proof of whether or not any congenital diseases are in the bloodlines if this information has not been offered in the advertising or during preliminary conversations.

Your veterinarian is the best person to describe the symptoms and the cure for juvenile cataracts, and whether operation and/or medication is necessary. Any indication of a blank, milky surface on the eyes is cause for an immediate examination, since the sooner the condition is diagnosed and repaired the better it is for your dog.

GERIATRICS

If you originally purchased good healthy stock and cared for your dog throughout his life, there is no reason why you cannot expect your dog to live to a ripe old age. With research and the remarkable foods produced for dogs, especially in this past decade or so, his chances of longevity have increased considerably. If you have cared for him well, your dog will be a sheer delight in his old age, just as he was while in his prime.

We can assume you have fed him properly if he is not too fat. Have you ever noticed how fat people usually have fat dogs because they indulge their dogs' appetite as they do their own? If there has been no great illness, then you will find that very little additional care and attention are needed to keep him well. Exercise is still essential, as is proper food, booster shots and tender loving care.

Even if a heart condition develops, there

Amber, owned by Mike and Pat Lobenberg of Oxnard, California, is pictured here coursing along the beach at 9 months of age.

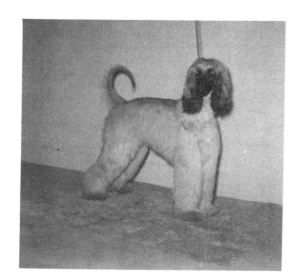

Above:
Bokhara's Satan, sired by Dureigh's Spirit of the Dragon *ex* Kaihorn Calliope of Bokhara. He is owned by Joseph Kluchinsky of Spotswood, New Jersey.

Left, top photo:
Ch. Khayam's Last Tango, owned by Marjy Chadwick, Mirriah Hounds, Cincinnati, Ohio, is pictured here at 3 years of age. Tango is a full brother to Ch. Khayams Ares.

Left, bottom photo:
Ch. Crown Crest Zarzanya, bred by Kay Finch and owned by Jack Houston, Kalamazoo, Michigan. The sire was Ch. Crown Crest Zardonx *ex* Ch. Crown Crest Tae-Joan.

Ch. Longlesson Electra is pictured here at 4 years of age. Electra was a Group winner and the daughter of Ch. Jestor of Longlesson *ex* Ch. Turkafa of Grandeur. Electra is owned by Mr. and Mrs. L. Swayze, III, of Atlanta, Georgia.

Above:
Ch. X'Actly Xanadu, Reserve Winners Dog at the Austin and Houston Afghan Hound Specialty Shows in 1975. Xanadu is owned by Johanna Tanner of Friendswood, Texas.

Right, top photo:
The Group-winning Ch. Rubyyat's Blu Terres is owned by Guy and Sue Bagley, Top Flite Kennels, Kokomo, Indiana. Among his other important wins on the way to championship was a Winners Dog title at the 1973 Greater Detroit Afghan Hound Club. Portrait by Pozen.

Right, bottom photo:
Sasha of Soolia Tu, 11 months of age, poses with the black and silver Kashmiri's Rhataan, 20 months old. This beautiful Glen Mills portrait was taken in March, 1976 for owner Ylla C. Kontos of Arvada, Colorado.

Pictured winning at a 1969 dog show under judge Henry Stoecker is Jane Howey's Step's Mountain Climber. Gilbert photograph.

is still no reason to believe your dog cannot live to an old age. A diet may be necessary, along with medication and limited exercise, to keep the condition under control. In the case of deafness, or partial blindness, additional care must be taken to protect the dog, but neither infirmity will in any way shorten his life. Prolonged exposure to temperature variances, overeating, excessive exercise, lack of sleep or being housed with younger, more active dogs may take an unnecessary toll on the dog's energies and introduce serious trouble. Good judgment, periodic veterinary checkups and individual attention will keep your dog with you for many added years.

When discussing geriatrics, the question of when a dog becomes old or aged usually is asked. We have all heard the old saying that one year of a dog's life is equal to seven years in a human. This theory is strictly a matter of opinion, and must remain so, since so many outside factors enter into how quickly each individual dog "ages." Recently, a new chart was devised which is more realistically equivalent:

DOG	MAN
6 months	10 years
1 year	15 years
2 years	24 years
3 years	28 years
4 years	32 years
5 years	36 years
6 years	40 years
7 years	44 years
8 years	48 years
9 years	52 years
10 years	56 years
15 years	76 years
21 years	100 years

It must be remembered that such things as serious illnesses, poor food and housing, general neglect and poor beginnings as puppies will take their toll on a dog's general health and age him more quickly than a dog that has led a normal, healthy life. Let your veterinarian help you determine an age bracket for your dog in his later years.

While good care should prolong your dog's life, there are several "old age" disorders to be on the lookout for no matter how well he may be doing. The tendency toward obesity is the most common, but constipation is another. Aging teeth and a slowing down of the digestive processes may hinder digestion and cause constipation, just as any major change in diet can bring on diarrhea. There is

Ch. Jorogz' Domino Dolly was owner-handled to championship in 11 shows and finished with four majors. She was bred, owned and handled by John Roger Morton.

Am. and Can. Ch. Dhon Dhis Faker Phipps is pictured winning on the way to his championship at the 1975 Santa Barbara Kennel Club Show. The win was under English judge Mrs. David Patton. Mike Hansen is handling Phipps for owners Lewis and Rayellen Goldstein of Phoeniz, Arizona.

also the possibility of loss or impairment of hearing or eyesight which will also tend to make the dog wary and distrustful. Other behavioral changes may result as well, such as crankiness, loss of patience and lack of interest; these are the most obvious changes. Other ailments may manifest themselves in the form of rheumatism, arthritis, tumors and warts, heart disease, kidney infections, male prostatism and female disorders. Of course, all these require a veterinarian's checking the degree of seriousness and proper treatment.

Bokhara's The Grey Ghost, bred by Joseph Kluchinsky.

DOG INSURANCE

Much has been said for and against canine insurance, and much more will be said before this kind of protection for a dog becomes universal and/or practical. There has been talk of establishing a Blue Cross-type plan similar to the one now existing for humans. However, the best insurance for your dog is YOU! Nothing compensates for tender, loving care. Like the insurance policies for humans, there will be a lot of fine print in the contracts revealing that the dog is not covered after all. These limited conditions usually make the acquisition of dog insurance expensive and virtually worthless.

Blanket coverage policies for kennels or establishments which board or groom dogs can be an advantage, especially in transporting dogs to and from their premises. For the one-dog owner, however, whose dog is a constant companion, the cost for limited coverage is not necessary.

THE HIGH COST OF BURIAL

Pet cemetaries are mushrooming across the nation. Here, as with humans, the sky can be the limit for those who wish to bury their pets ceremoniously. The costs of plots and satin-lined caskets, grave stones, flowers, etc., run the gamut of prices to match the emotions and means of the owner.

IN THE EVENT OF YOUR DEATH

This is a morbid thought perhaps, but ask yourself the question, "If death were to strike at this moment, what would become of my dogs?"

Perhaps you are fortunate enough to have a relative, children, spouse or friend who would take over immediately, if only on a temporary basis. Perhaps you have already left instructions in your last will and testament for your pet's dispensation, as well as a stipend for their perpetual care.

Provide definite instructions before a disaster occurs and your dogs are carted off to the pound to be destroyed, or stolen by commercially minded neighbors with "resale" in mind. It is a simple thing to instruct your lawyer about your wishes in the event of sickness or death. Leave instructions as to feeding, etc., posted on your kennel room or kitchen bulletin board, or wherever your kennel records are kept. Also, tell several people what you are doing and why. If you prefer to keep such instructions private, merely place them in sealed envelopes in a known place with directions that they are to be opened only in the event of your death. Eliminate the danger of your animals suffering in the event of an emergency that prevents your personal care of them.

KEEPING RECORDS

Whether or not you have one dog, or a kennel full of them, it is wise to keep written records. It takes only a few moments to record dates of inoculations, trips to the vet, tests for worms, etc. It can avoid confusion or mistakes, or having your dog not covered with immunization if too much time elapses between shots because you have to guess at the last shot.

Make the effort to keep all dates in writing rather than trying to commit them to memory. A rabies injection date can be a problem if you have to recall that "Fido had the shot the day Aunt Mary got back from her trip abroad, and, let's see, I guess that was around the end of June."

In an emergency, these records may prove their value if your veterinarian cannot be reached and you have to use another, or if you move and have no case history on your dog for the new veterinarian. In emergencies you do not always think clearly or accurately, and if dates and types of serums used, etc., are a matter of record, the veterinarian can act more quickly and with more confidence.

Handler and dog at their best! Mr. John H. Hill is pictured here after guiding the beautiful Ch. Ali Khyber to another Best In Show title. This pair was a dominant force in the 1940's show scene, garnering numerous Best In Show titles. This win was at the 1945 Saw Mill River Kennel Club Show under judge Edward H. Goodwin. Ali Khyber was owned by Leah P. McConaha. Percy Jones photo.

Ch. Crown Crest Devikkarokit, owned by Gertrude Curnyn, is pictured here winning Best of Breed at the 1957 Troy Kennel Club Show under judge Louis Murr. He was handled to the win by Robert Forsyth. Devi was also a top racing Afghan and ran on his owner's private track, along with other Afghan Hounds in the Massachusetts area where racing is a popular sport in the breed.

Chapter XXI

Pursuing a Career in Dogs

One of the biggest joys for those of us who love dogs is to see someone we know or someone in our family grow up in the fancy and go on to enjoy the sport of dogs in later life. Many dog lovers, in addition to leaving codicils in their wills, are providing in other ways for veterinary scholarships for deserving youngsters who wish to make their association with dogs their profession.

Unfortunately, many children who have this earnest desire are not always able to afford the expense of an education that will take them through veterinary school, and they are not eligible for scholarships. In the 1960's during my tenure as editor of *Popular Dogs* magazine, I am happy to say I had something to do with the publicizing of college courses whereby those who could not go all the way to a veterinary degree could earn an Animal Science degree and thereby still serve the fancy in a significant way. The Animal Science courses cost less than half of what it would take to become a veterinarian, and those achieving these titles have become a tremendous assistance to the veterinarian.

We all have experienced the more and more crowded waiting rooms at the veterinary offices, and are aware of the demands on the doctor's time, not just for office hours but for his research, consultation, surgery, etc. The temendous increase in the number of dogs and cats and other domestic animals, both in cities and the suburbs, has resulted in an almost overwhelming consumption of veterinarians' time.

Until recently most veterinary assistance consisted of kennel men or women who were restricted to services more properly classified as office maintenance rather than actual veterinary aid. Needless to say, their part in the operation of a veterinary office is both essential and appreciated, as are the endless details and volumes of paperwork capably handled by office secretaries and receptionists. However, still more of a veterinarian's duties could be handled by properly trained semi-professionals.

With exactly this additional service in mind, many colleges are now conducting two-year courses in animal science for the training of such semi-professionals, thereby opening a new field for animal technologists. The time saved by the assistance of these trained technicians, who now relieve the veterinarians of the more mechanical chores and allow them additional time for diagnosing and general servicing of their clients, will be beneficial to all involved.

"Delhi Tech," the State University Agricultural and Technical College at Delhi, New York, was one of the first to offer the required courses for this degree. Now, many other institutions of learning are offering comparable courses at the college level. Entry requirements are usually that each applicant must be a graduate of an approved high school or have taken the State University admissions examination. In addition, each applicant for the Animal Science Technology program must have some previous credits in mathematics and science, with chemistry an important part of the science background.

The program at Delhi was a new educational venture dedicated to the training of competent technicians for employment in the biochemical field and has been generously

Gran Salaam Lorelei, whelped in 1973, was sired by Ch. Ninth Turn Argus *ex* Gran Salaam Carte Blanche. Bred by Diane La Greca and Kathleen V. Murray of Malverne, New York, she will be handled by Richard Mauro for her owner, Kathleen Murray. Photo by Werner Sheldon.

supported by a five-year grant, designated as a "Pilot Development Program in Animal Science." This grant provided both personal and scientific equipment with obvious good results when it was done originally pursuant to a contract with the United States Department of Health, Education and Welfare. Delhi is a unit of the State University of New York and is accredited by the Middle States Association of Colleges and Secondary Schools. The campus provides offices, laboratories and animal quarters and is equipped with modern instruments to train technicians in laboratory animal care, physiology, pathology, microbiology, anesthesia, X-ray and germ-free techniques. Sizable animal colonies are maintained in air-conditioned quarters: animals housed include mice, rats, hamsters, guinea-pigs, gerbils and rabbits, as well as dogs and cats.

First-year students are given such courses as livestock production, dairy food science, general, organic and biological chemistry, mammalian anatomy, histology and physiology, pathogenic microbiology and quantitative and instrumental analysis, to name a few. Second year students matriculate in general pathology, animal parasitology, animal care and anesthesia, introductory psychology, animal breeding, animal nutrition, hematology and urinalysis, radiology, genetics, food sanitation and meat inspection, histological techniques, animal laboratory practices and axenic techniques. These, of course, may be supplemented by electives that prepare the student for contact with the public in the administration of these duties. Such recommended electives include public speaking, botany, animal reproduction and other related subjects.

In addition to Delhi, one of the first to offer this program was the State University of Maine. Part of their program offered some practical training for the students at the Animal Medical Center in New York City. Often after this initial "in the field" experience, the students could perform professionally immediately upon entering a veterinarian's employ as personnel to do laboratory tests, X-rays, blood work, fecal examinations and general animal care. After the courses at college, they were equipped to perform all of

Can. Ch. Sodal's Gabriella of Makosa is pictured winning at the Victoria City Kennel Club Show in Canada. Owned and shown by Bonita Rabell, Makosa Afghans, Bothell, Washington.

460

the following procedures as semi-professionals:

* Recording of vital information relative to a case. This would include such information as the client's name, address, telephone number and other facts pertinent to the visit. The case history would include the breed, age of animal, its sex, temperature, etc.
* Preparation of the animal for surgery.
* Preparation of equipment and medicaments to be used in surgery.
* Preparation of medicaments for dispensing to clients on prescription of the attending veterinarian.
* Administration and application of certain medicines.
* Administration of colonic irrigations.
* Application or changing of wound dressings.
* Cleaning of kennels, exercise runs and kitchen utensils.
* Preparation of food and the feeding of patients.
* Explanation to clients on the handling and restraint of their pets, including needs for exercise, house training and elementary obedience training.
* First-aid treatment for hemorrhage, including the proper use of tourniquets.

Ch. Dynasty's Superstarter is owned by Mr. and Mrs. Thomas Daley of Wauwatosa, Wisconsin, and co-owned by his breeder-handler, Fredric M. Alderman.

Bermudian Ch. Sandina Sun Bonnet of Ariston, pictured after winning her Bermuda title in May, 1976 with her owner, Lee Abraham of Ariston Kennels, New Milford, New Jersey.

* Preservation of blood, urine and pathologic material for the purpose of laboratory examination.
* General care and supervision of the hospital or clinic patients to insure their comfort. Nail trimming and grooming of patients.

Credits are necessary, of course, to qualify for this program. Many course of studies include biology, zoology, anatomy, genetics and animal diseases, and along with the above mentioned courses the fields of client and public relations are touched upon as well as a general study of the veterinary medical profession.

By the mid-1970's there were a reported 30,000 veterinarians practicing in the United States. It is estimated that within the following decade more than twice that number will be needed to take proper care of the domestic animal population in this country. While veterinarians are graduated from 22 accredited veterinary colleges in this country and Canada, recent figures released by the veterinary medical society inform us that only one out of

461

One of the greatest Afghan Hounds of all time! The illustrious Ch. Shirkhan of Grandeur was painted from life in 1960 by the well-known artist, Elizabeth Harvey Treharne.

Caravan's Solid Blue is pictured winning at a recent show with handler Vinny Leap, the co-owner and co-breeder with Betty Leap of Hicksville, New York. The sire was Ch. Akaba's Blue Banner *ex* Akaba's Moonlight Sonata.

Two Afghan "greats" at rest. Ch. Dureigh's Golden Harvest and Ch. Eljac's Dragon Lady of Dureigh are owned by Dewey and Reigh Abrams, Dureigh Afghan Hounds, Wellington, Ohio.

The young Jawahars Fabiola, sired in Sweden by the American import Fantasis' Sport In Life *ex* the Swedish bitch Silverlidens Beauty Prinsa.

Ch. Majara Munshi and her owner, Mrs. Moore, were photographed by C. Hadley Smith several years ago.

Ali Yram Tahmboka, a beautiful black dog owned by Kurt Kroll of Hawthorne, New Jersey. Tambo was bred by Roberta Breath of Long Island, sired by Ch. Sahadi Sinbad *ex* Sahadi Aztec Silver Arrow.

Mecca's Love Story of Shamar, owned by Bruce and Mary Dee Huntsman, Afghans of Shamar, Salem, Oregon. The sire was Blue Silks Karu *ex* Melancholy Baby.

Left:
Top-winning Afghan Hound in Spain for 1976 was Norman Huiolobro's multiple Best In Show winner Int. Ch. Antar Tizoc of Crown Crest. This American-bred dog was a champion in four countries before his arrival in Spain at the Huilaco Kennels, where he is a major stud force. His sire was Crown Crest Citation of Devi-Baba *ex* Mex. Ch. Antar Af-Zar Xochiquetzal.

every seven applicants is admitted to these colleges. It becomes more and more obvious that the semi-professional person will be needed to back up the doctor.

Students having the desire and qualifications to become veterinarians, however, may suffer financial restrictions that preclude their education and licensing as full-fledged veterinarians. The Animal Science Technologist with an Associate degree in Applied Science may very well become the answer as a profession in an area close to their actual desire.

Their assistance in the pharmaceutical field, where drug concerns deal with laboratory animals, covers another wide area for trained assistance. The career opportunities are varied and reach into job opportunities in medical centers, research instituitions and government health agencies; at present, the demand for graduates far exceeds the current supply of trained personnel.

As far as the financial remunerations, yearly salaries are estimated at an average of $5,000.00 for a starting point. As for the estimate of basic college education expenses, they

Ch. Shaadar's Blajnhe of Karlyle, foundation bitch for the Coastwind Kennels. She is the dam of 7 champions, including two Best In Show winners.

Jude's Nissim of Grandeur is pictured winning at a 1974 show with his handler-owner Sunny Shay of Hicksville, New York. Nissim is co-owned by Loraine P. Munter of Rye, New York.

range from $1,800.00 to $2,200.00 per year for out-of-state residents, and include tuition, room and board, college fees, essential textbooks and limited personal expenses. These personal expenses, of course, will vary with individual students, as well as the other expenses, but we present an average. It is obvious that the costs are about half of the costs involved in becoming a full-fledged veterinarian, however.

High school graduates with a sincere affection and regard for animals and a desire to work with veterinarians and perform such clinical duties as mentioned above will find they fit in especially well. Women may be particularly useful since, over and beyond the strong maternal instinct that goes so far in the care and the recovery phase when dealing with animals, women will find the majority of their duties well within their physical capabilities. Since a majority of the positions will be in the small animal field, their dexterity will also fit in well.

Those interested in pursuing a career of this nature might obtain the most current list of accredited colleges and universities offering these programs by consulting the American Veterinary Medical College, 600 S. Michigan Avenue, Chicago, Illinois 60605.

Ch. Rana's Kamseen of Five Mile is shown winning the Hound Group under judge Rees Davies at a Sahuaro State Kennel Club Show in Phoeniz, Arizona, many years ago. Kamseen also had several other Hound Group wins to his credit. Handling is Porter Washington for owners Mr. and Mrs. R. Herbert Price, Paganwood Kennels, Los Angeles, California.

As the popularity of this profession increased, additional attention was given to the list of services and the degrees to which one could aspire was increased. We are beginning to learn that there are semi-professionals with Associate of Science degrees, and some colleges and universities have extended the courses to four years duration which lead to Bachelor of Science degrees.

At the University of Minnesota Technical College, a two year course offers a degree of Associate in Applied Science after the successful completion of 108 credit hours. This Animal Health Technology course prepares the students for future careers in the following fields:

* Laboratory Animal Technician (Junior)
* Experimental Animal Technician
* Clinical Laboratory Animal Assistant
* Laboratory Animal Assistant in Radiology
* Laboratory Animal Research Assistant
* Small Animal Technician (General)
* Small Animal Veterinarian's Assistant
* Small Animal Veterinarian's Receptionist
* Animal Hospital Technician
* Zoo Technician
* Large Animal Technician (General)
* Large Animal Veterinarian's Receptionist
* Large Animal Clinic Assistant
* Meat Animal Inspection Technician

Kadallah's War Paint is pictured at three months of age and as a grown dog of 15 months. Ashah won his first points toward championship from the puppy classes. He is owned by Mike Cooper, Auburn, Maine.

PART TIME KENNEL WORK

Youngsters who do not wish to go on to become veterinarians or animal technicians can get valuable experience and extra money by working part-time after school and weekends, or full-time during summer vacations, in a veterinarian's office. The exposure to animals and office procedure will be time well spent.

Kennel help is also an area that is wide open for retired men. They are able to help out in many areas where they can learn and stay active, and most of the work allows them to set their own pace. The gentility that age and experience brings is also beneficial to the animals they will deal with; for their part, the men find great reward in their contribution to animals and will be keeping their hand in the business world as well.

PROFESSIONAL HANDLING

For those who wish to participate in the sport of dogs and whose interests or abilities do not center around the clinical aspects of the fancy, there is yet another avenue of involvement.

For those who excel in the show ring, who enjoy being in the limelight and putting their dogs through their paces, a career in professional handling may be the answer. Handling may include a weekend of showing a few dogs for special clients, or it may be a full-time career which can also include boarding, training, conditioning, breeding and showing of dogs for several clients.

Depending on how deeply your interest runs, the issue can be solved by a lot of preliminary consideration before it becomes nec-

essary to make a decision. The first move would be to have a long, serious talk with a successful professional handler to learn the pros and cons of such a profession. Watching handlers in action from ringside as they perform their duties can be revealing. A visit to their kennels for an on-the-spot revelation of the behind-the-scenes responsibilities is essential! Working for them full or part time would be the best way of all to resolve any doubt you might have!

Ch. Mahabii's Continental Sytar, owned by Jonna Frosch and Robert Izenstark and handled for them by Stanley Flowers, is pictured winning Best In Show at the 1968 Crab Apple Kennel Club Show in Illinois. The judge was the late Alva Rosenberg. Presenting the trophy is club president T. Glenn Schuetz. Earl Graham photograph.

466

Three-month-old Spectrums Dreamspeaker gets some early show practice from owner Inger James of Vancouver, British Columbia, Canada.

Ch. Tarawazir of Carloway Crown Crest is pictured with co-owner Kay Finch and judge Hollis Wilson at the Beverly Riviera Kennel Club Show in California. Wazir was bred at Sheila Devitt's Caroloway Kennels in England and was later co-owned and campaigned by Alma L. Wells of Dover, New Jersey.

Ch. Azari's Snow Owl of Shandi-Ghar, photographed with his handler Gene Blake, at 14 months of age. Hoot is owned by Selene Serio of Hannibal, Missouri, and went Best of Breed and Group Second from the classes while finishing his championship.

Am. and Mex. Ch. Crown Crest Great Mogul, owned by Dr. A.L. Jenkins of Weslaco, Texas. Mogul is pictured here taking Best of Breed at the San Antonio Kennel Club Show. Maxine Beam handled for the owner.

Professional handling is not all glamour in the show ring. There is plenty of "dirty work" behind the scenes 24 hours of every day. You must have the necessary ability and patience for this work, as well as the ability and patience to deal with the CLIENTS—the dog owners who value their animals above almost anything else and would expect a great deal from you in the way of care and handling. The big question you must ask yourself first of all is: do you *really* love dogs enough to handle it. . .

DOG TRAINING

Like the professional handler, the professional dog trainer has a most responsible job! You not only need to be thoroughly familiar with the correct and successful methods

Chanhu Sleaze With Ease, pictured at 1 year of age. Sleaze is owned by Nora Dodson of Tucson, Arizona.

Still winning at 10 years of age! The magnificent Ch. Sarkhan of Kharysthan wins under judge Cynthia Guzevich. Her owner-handler is Jennifer Sheldon of Massapequa, New York. Khan's sire was Ch. Sahadi Shikari *ex* Ch. Naftali's Dina.

of training a dog but also must have the ability to communicate with dogs. True, it is very rewarding work, but training for the show ring, obedience or guard dog work must be done exactly right for successful results to maintain a business reputation.

Training schools are quite the vogue nowadays, with all of them claiming success. Careful investigation should be made before enrolling a dog, and even more careful investigation should be made of their methods and of their actual successes before becoming associated with them.

GROOMING PARLORS

If you do not wish the 24-hour a day job which is required by a professional handler or professional trainer, but still love working with and caring for dogs, there is always the very profitable grooming business. Poodles started the ball rolling for the swanky, plush grooming establishments which sprang up like mushrooms all over the major cities, many of which seem to be doing very well. Here again, handling dogs and the public is necessary for a successful operation, as well as skill in the actual grooming of the dogs, and of all breeds.

While shops flourish in the cities, some of the suburban areas are now featuring mobile units which by appointment will visit your home with a completely equipped shop on wheels and will groom your dog right in your own driveway!

THE PET SHOP

Part-time or full-time work in a pet shop can help you make up your mind rather quickly as to whether or not you would like to have a shop of your own. For those who love animals and are concerned with their care and feeding, the pet shop can be a profitable and satisfying association. Supplies which are available for sale in these shops are almost limitless, and a nice living can be garnered from pet supplies if the location and population of the city you choose warrant it.

DOG JUDGING

There are also those whose professions, age or health prevent them from owning, breeding or showing dogs, and who turn to judging at dog shows after their active years in the show ring are no longer possible. Breeder-judges make a valuable contribution to the fancy by judging in accordance with their years of experience in the fancy, and the

Ch. Jorogz' Indigo Illusia, pictured here winning Best of Breed at a 1976 show, is the most recent champion daughter of the late Ch. Akaba's Indigo Blue. Luzy, an exquisite black, has the distinction of being one of the few multiple breed winning bitches against Best In Show competition. Owned by John Roger Morton, Kansas City, Missouri. The judge is Peter Belmont, Jr.

assignments are enjoyable. Judging requires experience, a good eye for dogs and an appreciation of a good animal.

MISCELLANEOUS

If you find all of the aforementioned too demanding or not within your abilities, there are other aspects of the sport for you to enjoy and participate in at will. Writing for the various dog magazines, books or club newsletters, dog photography, portrait painting, club activities, making dog coats, or needlework featuring dogs, typing pedigrees or perhaps dog walking. All, in their own way, contribute to the sport of dogs and give great satisfaction.

Ch. Mecca's Falstaff, owned by the Guidebecks of Marietta, Georgia.

Ch. Crown Crest Vegas Ghamblr of Belden, shown to this Hound Group win by his owner Leo Goodman. Judge at this 1961 Hoosier Kennel Club Show was Mr. Jack Spear, of Irish Setter fame.

Srinagar Sura Salim and Suzanne Neill were photographed on the windy coast of California in 1970.

Ch. Elmo's Pajourah made breed history when she became the first Afghan in the history of the breed to gain championship points toward her title in three specialties. She broke her own record by finishing her title owner-handled by Susan Bahary at the Afghan Hound Association of Long Island Specialty thus winning her fourth specialty as Best of Winners and Best Opposite Sex under breeder-judge Dr. Gerda Kennedy. Bred by Gordon McDowell and Peter Belmont, she is pictured here with owner Susan Bahary.

Gran Salaam Blackglama, a 7-month-old black bitch owned by Frank and Diane La-Greca of West Hempstead, New York. Her sire was Ch. Ninth Turn Argus ex Ch. Gran Salaam Echo of Holly Hill.

Ch. Tamerlane II was chosen Best In Show at the March, 1950 National Capital Kennel Club Show. Mary Young handled Tammy for owner Dr. William Ivens, Jr., of Ardmore, Pennsylvania. Tammy was later owned by the George Wheelers of Connecticut. Shafer photograph.

Int. Ch. Crown Crest Mex-I-Kan, owned by Antonio Kyriac of Mexico City, wins Best In Show while on the Pan American dog show circuit sponsored by the Kennel Club of Cuba in November, 1959. The Best In Show judge was American Edwin Pickhardt. Jose Rojo de la Vega, Jr., is the handler; Mr. Jose Loredo, president of the Kennel Club of Cuba, presents the trophy.

A lovely informal photograph of Ch. The Gay Kaptivator of Ariston, taken in 1964 by his owners, Mr. and Mrs. Kurt Abraham of New Milford, New Jersey. Bred by Nancy McCarthy, he is sired by Ch. Sahadi Sessu *ex* Sahadi Shawnee Pocahantus.

POSTSCRIPT

One of my favorite authors over the years has been Robert Louis Stevenson. As a child his "The world is so full of a number of things, I'm sure we should all be as happy as kings," perfectly expressed my philosophy of life. In fact, it still does. So many of his writings are about animals, cats and dogs in particular. Another of his touching verses is the one entitled, "To One Who Has Lost His Dog." It goes like this:

"He has but turned a corner
He is not dead, this friend
But in the path we mortals tread,
Got some few trifling steps ahead,
And nearer to the end,
So that you, too, once past the bend,
Shall meet again.
He loiters with a backward smile,
till you can overtake—"

A PRAYER FOR ANIMALS
by
Albert Schweitzer

Hear our humble prayer, O God, for our friends the animals, especially for animals who are suffering; for any that are hunted or lost or deserted or frightened or hungry; for all that must be put to death. We entreat for them all Thy mercy and pity, and for those who deal with them we ask a heart of compassion and gentle hands and kindly words. Make us, ourselves to be true friends to animals and so to share the blessings of the merciful.

Index